Politics and Divinization in
Augustan Poetry

Politics and Divinization in Augustan Poetry

BOBBY XINYUE

Great Clarendon Street, Oxford, OX2 6DP,
United Kingdom

Oxford University Press is a department of the University of Oxford.
It furthers the University's objective of excellence in research, scholarship,
and education by publishing worldwide. Oxford is a registered trade mark of
Oxford University Press in the UK and in certain other countries

© Bobby Xinyue 2022

The moral rights of the author have been asserted

First Edition published in 2022

Impression: 1

All rights reserved. No part of this publication may be reproduced, stored in
a retrieval system, or transmitted, in any form or by any means, without the
prior permission in writing of Oxford University Press, or as expressly permitted
by law, by licence or under terms agreed with the appropriate reprographics
rights organization. Enquiries concerning reproduction outside the scope of the
above should be sent to the Rights Department, Oxford University Press, at the
address above

You must not circulate this work in any other form
and you must impose this same condition on any acquirer

Published in the United States of America by Oxford University Press
198 Madison Avenue, New York, NY 10016, United States of America

British Library Cataloguing in Publication Data
Data available

Library of Congress Control Number: 2021951883

ISBN 978–0–19–285597–8

DOI: 10.1093/oso/9780192855978.001.0001

Printed and bound by
CPI Group (UK) Ltd, Croydon, CR0 4YY

Links to third party websites are provided by Oxford in good faith and
for information only. Oxford disclaims any responsibility for the materials
contained in any third party website referenced in this work.

For my grandmother,
my mothers,
and my wife
mulieribus optimis

Acknowledgements

I spent the best part of twelve years writing this book—the final stretch overlapped with a global pandemic. During this long (and occasionally dark) gestation period, I was lucky to have the company and advice of some of the most extraordinary people I have ever encountered.

My work benefitted at an early stage from the guidance of Fiachra Mac Góráin and Maria Wyke, under whose excellent supervision this book began life as a doctoral thesis at UCL. Part of my doctoral research was conducted at the University of Virginia: there, I was fortunate to have the input of John Miller. In the last few years, a number of friends, colleagues, and former teachers offered comments on drafts of various kinds, and to this day I am still amazed by their kindness and intellectual generosity. I thank especially Nick Freer, Ian Goh, Nandini Pandey, Mira Seo, Stephen Harrison, Jennifer Ingleheart, Steve Heyworth, Matthew Robinson, Alison Cooley, Elena Giusti, Tom Geue, Jinyu Liu, and Ingrid De Smet. Conversations with former students also helped me to clarify my thoughts and expressions.

I also thank the Classics Commissioning Editor at OUP, Charlotte Loveridge, for taking a punt on this book and for supporting me every step of the way. Of course, I also owe much to the press's anonymous readers, whose incisive comments helped me to improve the quality of my ideas. Of a different nature of 'help' was the sixteen-page report produced by another anonymous reader who saw an earlier draft of this book (which was sent to a different press). It is fair to say that I did not appreciate the report at the time, but I have since come to the view that it was by far the most beneficial critique I have ever received on my book.

The research I have undertaken for this book was generously supported by a number of British and European institutions. I am grateful to the Department of Greek and Latin at UCL for offering me a doctoral scholarship. I am deeply indebted to the British Academy for the award of a postdoctoral fellowship, which gave me much appreciated time to complete this book. The Fondation Hardt and the Ludwig Boltzmann Institute provided me with idyllic settings to refine the arguments I present here, while the NHS came to my aid when things did not go according to plan.

viii ACKNOWLEDGEMENTS

The time I spent writing this book would have been much less enjoyable had I not been able to call on friends to complain about it. Among those who offered unfailing companionship and delightful distraction, I thank especially Luke Richardson, Luke Gillin, Melanie McGovern, and a swarm of ex-colleagues at the University of Exeter.

Finally, I thank my daughter, Tamara, for enforcing me to take a break every so often, and my family for not once asking me 'When is your book coming out?'. Above all, I thank my wife, Naomi, for her wisdom, patience, and unwavering belief in me.

Contents

Texts, Translations, Abbreviations	xi
Introduction	1
1. *Libertas*, Peace, and Divine Dependence	35
2. Divinization and the Transformation of Rome from Republic to Principate	67
3. Conquest and Immortality in Horace's *Odes*	113
4. Divinization and the Inevitability of Augustan Rome	155
Epilogue: To Divinity and Beyond	187
References	203
Index Locorum	229
General Index	236

Texts, Translations, Abbreviations

This book uses the *Oxford Classical Texts* as the default editions of Greek and Latin texts, unless otherwise indicated. Translations of ancient passages are my own. Abbreviations of Greek and Latin authors and works follow the conventions of the *Oxford Classical Dictionary* (ed. S. Hornblower, A. Spawforth, and E. Eidinow, 4th edn, Oxford, 2012). In addition, the following abbreviations are used throughout:

Austin–Bastianini	C. Austin and G. Bastianini (eds), *Posidippi Pallaei quae supersunt omnia*. Milan, 2002.
Banti–Simonetti	A. Banti and L. Simonetti, *Corpus Nummorum Romanorum*, 18 vols. Florence, 1972–9.
BMCRE	H. Mattingly and R. A. G. Carson, *Coins of the Roman Empire in the British Museum*, 6 vols. London, 1923–62.
BMCRR	H. Grueber, *Coins of the Roman Republic in the British Museum*, 3 vols. London, 1910.
CAH X	A. K. Bowman, E. Champlin, and A. Lintott (eds), *The Cambridge Ancient History*, Vol. X: *The Augustan Empire, 43 B.C.–A.D. 69*. 2nd edn. Cambridge, 1996.
Campbell	D. A. Campbell, ed. and trans., *Greek Lyric*, Vol. II: *Anacreon, Anacreontea, Choral Lyric from Olympus to Alcman*. Cambridge, MA, 1988.
CIL	*Corpus Inscriptionum Latinarum*. Berlin, 1862– .
EJ²	V. Ehrenberg and A. H. M. Jones, *Documents Illustrating the Reigns of Augustus and Tiberius*. 2nd edn. Oxford, 1979.
FGrH	F. Jacoby et al., *Die Fragmente der griechischen Historiker*. Leiden, 1923– .
Funaioli	H. Funaioli (ed.), *Grammaticae Romanae Fragmenta*. Leipzig, 1907.
Goetz–Schoell	G. Goetz and F. Schoell (eds), *M. Terenti Varronis De Lingua Latina quae supersunt*. Leipzig, 1910.
Harder	A. Harder (ed.), *Callimachus: Aetia*, 2 vols. Oxford, 2012.
Lobel–Page	E. Lobel and D. L. Page (eds), *Poetarum Lesbiorum fragmenta*. Oxford, 1966.
Mass.	G. Massimilla (ed.), *Callimaco: Aitia, libri primo e secondo*. Pisa, 1996; *Callimaco: Aitia, libri terzo e quarto*. Pisa and Rome, 2010.
MRR	T. R. S. Broughton, *The Magistrates of the Roman Republic*. New York, 1951–2; supplement, 1986.
OCT	*Oxford Classical Texts*.

xii TEXTS, TRANSLATIONS, ABBREVIATIONS

OLD	*Oxford Latin Dictionary*, ed. P. G. W. Glare. 2nd edn. Oxford, 2012.
Pf.	R. Pfeiffer (ed.), *Callimachus*, Vol. I: *Fragmenta*. Oxford, 1949; *Callimachus*, Vol. II: *Hymni et Epigrammata*. Oxford, 1953.
RIC I^2	C. H. V. Sutherland, *Roman Imperial Coinage*, Vol. I: *From 31 BC to AD 69*. Rev. edn. London, 1984.
RRC	M. H. Crawford, *Roman Republican Coinage*, 2 vols. Cambridge, 1974.
Sk.	O. Skutsch (ed.), *The Annals of Q. Ennius*. Oxford, 1985.
TLL	*Thesaurus linguae Latinae*. Leipzig, 1990– .
Voigt	E. M. Voigt (ed.), *Sappho et Alcaeus*. Amsterdam, 1971.
West	M. L. West (ed.), *Iambi et elegi Graeci ante Alexandrum cantati*, 2 vols. 2nd edn. Oxford, 1989–92.

Introduction

templa, quamvis sciret etiam proconsulibus decerni solere, in nulla tamen provincia nisi communi suo Romaeque nomine recepit. nam in urbe quidem pertinacissime abstinuit hoc honore; atque etiam argenteas statuas olim sibi positas conflavit omnis exque iis aureas cortinas Apollini Palatino dedicavit. dictaturam magna vi offerente populo genu nixus deiecta ab umeris toga nudo pectore deprecatus est.

(Suet. *Aug.* 52)

Although [Augustus] knew that temples were usually voted even to proconsuls, he did not accept them in any province unless jointly in his own name and that of Roma. In the city [of Rome] itself, he refused this honour with utmost determination; and he even melted down the silver statues that had been set up for him earlier, and from the proceeds of this he dedicated gold tripods to Palatine Apollo. When the people forcefully offered him the dictatorship, he went down on his knee, threw off his toga from his shoulders, and with a bare breast begged them not to.

The Politics of Divinization

In his biography of Augustus, Suetonius presents this episode as an example of the restraint displayed by Rome's first emperor in the early years of his reign.[1] According to this picture, Augustus scrupulously made sure that he did not overstep the mark when it came to his personal veneration in the provinces; meanwhile in the political centre, where there was greater scrutiny,

---

[1] The joint cult of Augustus and Roma was set up in Asia and Bithynia as early as 29 BC (Cass. Dio 51.20.6–8); Augustus' dedication of tripods took place in 28 BC (*R.G.* 24.2; Cass. Dio 53.22.3); his refusal of dictatorship happened in 22 BC (*R.G.* 5.1, where Augustus says that he refused the offer of dictatorship first when he was absent and then in person after returning to Rome in summer 22 BC; this second occasion is what Suetonius focuses on). For further discussion of this passage of Suetonius, see Louis (2010) ad loc.; Wardle (2014) 371–4.

Politics and Divinization in Augustan Poetry. Bobby Xinyue, Oxford University Press. © Bobby Xinyue 2022.
DOI: 10.1093/oso/9780192855978.003.0001

2 POLITICS AND DIVINIZATION IN AUGUSTAN POETRY

he flat out refused to be honoured as a god and repelled any suggestion of harbouring autocratic ambitions. Yet, there is reason to suspect that Augustus' actions reflected more than his restraint. The emperor took different approaches to accepting divine honours in the provinces and in Rome, suggesting that he made some use of personal worship when it suited him.[2] By melting down his statues and using the proceeds to fund dedications to Apollo, Augustus commodified the veneration shown to him by his subjects, and reinvested it to cultivate further his affiliation with his patron god—a form of divine self-imaging that sat better with his domestic audience.[3] And if we can trust Suetonius' portrayal of Augustus as a great actor on the political stage (cf. *Aug.* 99.1),[4] then it is hard to see the emperor's dramatic rejection of the offer of dictatorship as anything but spectacular showmanship.[5]

The difficulty of working out whether Augustus' refusals were an elaborate act is hinted at by Suetonius himself, as the biographer uses the word *civilitas*, instead of the more common *moderatio*, to characterize Augustus' actions (cf. *clementiae civilitatisque eius multa et magna documenta sunt*, 'the proofs of his clemency and *civilitas* are numerous and strong', *Aug.* 51). *Civilitas* in Suetonius clearly means something like 'behaviour of ordinary person' or 'civilian-ness';[6] and the display of genuine *civilitas* by the subjects of Suetonius' *Lives* is a reliable litmus test that separates good emperors from bad ones.[7] However, *civilitas* has another meaning, one that is equally relevant to an emperor's public image. In his discussion of the role of oratory in public life, Quintilian uses *civilitas* as the Latin equivalent of πολιτική (*Inst.* 2.15.25; 2.15.33). Later on, citing the example of Aristotle's *Rhetoric*, Quintilian argues that oratory is not merely the art of speech, but an aspect of *civilitas*, in other

---

[2] On Augustus' worship in the eastern provinces, see Bowersock (1965); Price (1984a) 58; Burrell (2004) 275–6; Kropp (2009) 100. On the religious development in the Latin West, see Fishwick (1987) I, 90–1; (2002) III pt 1, 213–19, 229–30. On the public art and architecture associated with the imperial cult in the provinces, see Zanker (1988) 297–333.

[3] See also Whittaker (2000) 105; Stewart (2003) 173. Some of these statues probably came from Greece, but were unlikely to be cult statues; see Wardle (2014) 373.

[4] On his deathbed, Augustus apparently asked friends gathered around him 'whether it seemed to them that he had played the mime of life fittingly' (*admissos amicos percontatus, ecquid iis videretur mimum vitae commode transegisse*). For further discussion of Suet. *Aug.* 99.1, see Wardle (2007) 449–52; Louis (2010) 567; Pandey (2018) 1–2.

[5] Critics are divided on the connotations of Augustus' gesture of baring his chest (*nudo pectore*, Suet. *Aug.* 52): see Alföldy (1972) 9–10; Hallett (2005) 100; Wardle (2014) 374. For further discussion of Augustus' refusal of exceptional powers as political theatre, see Freudenburg (2014), esp. 105–13.

[6] *OLD civilitas* s.v. 2. See also Wallace-Hadrill (1982) 42: '*Civilitas* aptly evokes the behaviour of a ruler who is still a citizen in a society of citizens'; Hurley (2001) 63.

[7] Claudius, for example, is accused of being an *iactator civilitatis* (Suet. *Claud.* 35.1)—that is, one who makes an ostentatious display of their 'civilian-ness'. Hurley (2001) ad loc.: 'C's [i.e. Claudius'] gracious behaviour...was a sham.'

INTRODUCTION 3

words, of 'politics' or 'governing' (*Inst.* 2.17.14).[8] Whether Augustus' emphatic, dramatic rejections of state cult and dictatorship were a true reflection of his exemplary ordinariness or a resounding performance in the art of politics, only Augustus knows. Nevertheless, these anecdotes suggest that Augustus was aware of not only the implications of these honours but also the political advantages of rejecting them. For the man who insisted that he had liberated the Republic from oppression (*R.G.* 1) and relinquished personal power at the first opportunity (*R.G.* 34), the acceptance of state cult and dictatorship would have done irreparable damage to his statecraft. Filing Augustus' refusals of divine honours and dictatorship under the same rubric, Suetonius subtly underlines the semantic contiguity between divinization and autocracy in the early Principate, drawing attention to what an emperor's divine status might imply and how his careful management of it matters to his public image, his 'politics'.

Indeed, the way Augustus handled divine imagery in his self-representation during the early years of his rule was certainly careful. In the triumviral period the new Caesar, like his rivals, made frequent use of divine imagery to compete for political legitimacy. After the civil war, however, explicit assimilations of the new Caesar to divinities quickly disappeared.[9] In their place, implicit suggestions or indirect evocations of godlike attributes and divine destiny became part of a totalizing discourse of Augustan power. For example, official coinage from the mint of Rome stopped showing Augustus in the guise of Apollo, Jupiter or Neptune after 27 BC[10]—the year in which Augustus by his own account had completed the handover of the state from his power to the control of the Roman Senate and people (Aug. *R.G.* 34).[11] Yet the iconography of the Julian Star (*sidus Iulium*), which originated in the comet that appeared during Julius Caesar's funeral games (44 BC) and initially symbolized Caesar's apotheosis,[12] continued to appear in different forms alongside

---

[8] *sed idem et de arte rhetorica tris libros scripsit, et in eorum primo non artem solum eam fatetur, sed ei particulam civilitatis sicut dialectices adsignat* ('Yet he [i.e. Aristotle] also wrote three books on the art of rhetoric, in the first of which he not only admits that rhetoric is an art, but assigns it as an aspect of politics and also of logic'). See Reinhardt and Winterbottom (2006) 269–70 on Quintilian's usage of *civilitas* and further examples of *civilitas* meaning 'politics'. Note also *TLL* s.v. *civilitas* I, *de regendis civibus*.

[9] Wissowa (1912) 73; Taylor (1931) 162–7; Weinstock (1971) 305, 408; Fishwick (1987) I, 72, 83–4; Gradel (2002) 109, 265.

[10] Pollini (1990) 350, 356. In the period from 31 to 27 BC, however, association with the divine was expressed more or less directly in Octavian's official coinage; see Pollini (1990) 336, 346–50.

[11] On the much debated handover of power, see Millar (1973); Judge (1974); Galinsky (1996) 42–79; Lange (2009); Le Doze (2015).

[12] Plin. *HN* 2.93–4; Suet. *Iul.* 88; Cass. Dio 45.7.1; *Serv. Dan.* ad *Ecl.* 9.46.

4 POLITICS AND DIVINIZATION IN AUGUSTAN POETRY

portraits of the *princeps* on Augustan coinage, and gradually evolved to convey the divine favour of the *gens Iulia* and Augustus' own greatness.[13]

The architectural complex on the Palatine Hill was another example.[14] Upon its opening in 28 BC, the close integration of Augustus' house with the Temple of Apollo—a design reminiscent of the royal complexes of Hellenistic monarchs—underlined the firm association between Rome's first man and his patron deity without identifying them as one.[15] The cult statue of Apollo (cf. Prop. 2.31.15–16) and the famous painting of Apollo found in the house of Augustus depicted the god holding a cithara instead of his customary bow: this change in Apollo's representation no doubt added force to the transition of Augustus' own image from that of a wartime general to peacetime restorer of Rome and patron of the arts.[16] Visitors to the complex would also have found resonances of Augustus' victory over Antony and Cleopatra in the artistic themes throughout the compound, especially in the sculptural depiction of the punishment of the Niobids on one of the temple-doors (cf. Prop. 2.31.12–14): the artwork's underlying messages of justice and divine retribution provided the interpretive framework for the viewer's interaction with the new imperial centre.[17] Without explicitly assimilating Augustus to Apollo, the Palatine complex emphatically underscored the godlike supremacy of the *princeps* in Rome, and showed that subtle intimations of Augustus' divinity were to become an important constituent of the new regime's language of power.

Of course, there is reliable archaeological and epigraphic evidence to suggest that Augustus did receive personal worship in private homes and in temples at municipal level (even in Italy).[18] There may even have been unauthorized spontaneous cultic observances of the *princeps* amongst certain social groups

---

[13] See esp. *RIC* I² 415 = *BMCRE* I (Rome), 124–5, the *denarius* of Augustus showing on the reverse Augustus placing a star on the head of a statue of Divus Julius (12 BC). Major discussions of the development of the iconography of the *sidus Iulium* include: Weinstock (1971) 371–84, 399–401; White (1988); Gurval (1997) 45–60; Williams (2003); Osgood (2006) 40–1; Pandey (2018) 35–81, esp. 37–50, 64–8. Pandey's study of the Augustan poets' reading of this iconography challenges the traditional idea that Octavian 'spun' the comet into a politically advantageous symbol for himself (cf. White 1988: 335; Gurval 1997: 40–1; Ramsey and Licht 1997: 65) and emphasizes instead that there was no consensus on the interpretation of the image, and that the poets—through their constant critique of it—contributed to the evolving symbolic meaning of the *sidus Iulium*. I discuss Pandey's work in detail below.

[14] For an overview, see Zanker (1988) 65–70, 84–9; Galinsky (1996) 213–24; Gurval (1995) 111–31; Miller (2009) 185–252; Pandey (2018) 8–11, 83–92.

[15] See Iacopi and Tedone (2005–6) for a new plan of the Palatine complex based on their excavations.

[16] Pandey (2018) 84. See Roccos (1989) on the design of the cult statue.

[17] Zanker (1988) 49–50.

[18] Augustus' worship in Italy is comprehensively documented by Gradel (2002) 73–108.

and classes.[19] Artefacts such as the *Gemma Augustea* (AD 12–14), which circulated within an extremely narrow, refined, and ultra-elite circle, continued to depict Augustus and members of his family explicitly as members of a kind of Olympian pantheon.[20] But on the state level, Augustus' approach consisted of categorical rejection of formal cult and careful orchestration of divine imagery in public art. The refusal of state cult allowed Augustus to communicate that the procedures and frameworks (or, as Le Doze puts it, 'les manières de faire') of the Republic were being restored under the current regime.[21] At the same time, the controlled and selective usage of divinizing language played a crucial role in shaping the supremacy of the *princeps*, framing the current regime and its leader in terms that legitimized their authority and unprecedented status. The interplay between these two modes of self-representation was characteristic of the ambiguity and polysemy of the Augustan Principate, and it encapsulated the way that Augustus pointedly never defined his exact position within the Roman power structure.

While Augustus made a point of refusing his divinization (especially during the early years of his rule), the poets of the Augustan period hardly refrained from deifying their *princeps*. In the works of Virgil, Horace, and Propertius, who lived through the civil war to see the establishment of the Principate, explicit images and discussions of Augustus' divinization are commonplace. In the prologue to the *Georgics*, Virgil prays to the new Caesar and openly proclaims his apotheosis as a certainty (*G.* 1.24–5); later, at the beginning of Book 3, the poet pointedly offers his forthcoming epic as a 'temple' to the new ruler of Rome (*G.* 3.12–16). In the *Odes*, Horace variously presents Augustus as a god incarnate (*Carm.* 1.2.41–52), a deified hero in the making (3.3.9–12), a 'god manifest' to Romans and conquered nations (3.5.1–4; *praesens divus*, 3.5.2), or a divinity worshipped by farmers in their homes (4.5.29–40). Even more emphatically, and without any qualifying conditions at all, Propertius twice in his elegies presents Augustus simply as *deus* (Prop. 3.4.1; 4.11.60). With the notable exception of Tibullus, the first generation of Augustan poets made the divinization of Augustus a thematic staple in their poetry. To put it another way, there appears to be a divergence between

---

[19] On the spontaneous offering of divine honours, see Gradel (2002) 44–9; Tarpin (2002) 153; Koortbojian (2013) 158–70. A new cult of the *lares Augusti* spread rapidly throughout the crossroads shrines (*compita*) of Rome in and soon after 7 BC: see Flower (2017) 255–90. However, there is no sufficient evidence to suggest that a cult of Augustus' *genius* was found at the crossroads in Rome or in the home during his lifetime: see Mouritsen (2011) 249 and Flower (2017) 266, 299–310. I discuss the private worship of Augustus with reference to Horace's *Ode* 4.5 in the Epilogue.

[20] Zanker (1988) 230–2; Pollini (1993); Galinsky (1996) 120–1; Smith (2021).

[21] Le Doze (2015) 88.

6 POLITICS AND DIVINIZATION IN AUGUSTAN POETRY

Augustus' approach to the issue of his divinization, an approach that is carefully choreographed to convey both the republicanism and the extraordinariness of the new political order, and the poets' approach to the question, one that is characterized by subtle but insistent questioning of the status of the *princeps*, Rome's first 'man'.

This book concentrates on what we can make of this tension between official language and poetic language. In the following chapters, I will argue that poetry's frequent discussions of Augustus' divinity functioned as a medium of political thought for the early Augustan poets as they tried to come to terms with Rome's transformation from Republic to Principate. As witnesses to a unique political process during which the constitutional identity of Rome became increasingly difficult to pin down, the poets focused on the subject of divinization, and, through their creative dialogue with official language and with each other, turned discussions on this subject into a form of figured speech that enabled them to convey the disorienting experience of not knowing how the future would turn out and where they stood in relation to Augustus.[22] In particular, this book will suggest that the poetic discourse on Augustus' divinity articulates the irreducible paradox of Augustan power as both salvific and disempowering, indispensable and autocratic; and that as time goes on, considering Augustus as a god becomes a means for the poets to reflect on the frictions and complicities between literature and ideology in a rapidly changing political system. Re-examining familiar texts through this new lens, the present study is very much intended as an attempt to reopen debate on questions which some consider to be settled. By offering the argument outlined above, I hope to offer a new way of interpreting one of the most prominent themes in Latin poetry, which goes to the heart of how we understand the relationship between art and power in ancient Rome.

What's in a Topos?

The traditional understanding of the poets' thinking on Augustus' divinity, especially amongst scholars of Roman religion, is that it need not be taken seriously, because it is not an expression of religious belief, but the 'charismatic' language of court literature—a sign of 'poetic licence' that was condoned by

---

[22] On 'figured speech' in Graeco-Roman literature, see Ahl (1984). Ahl's key insight, which I draw on throughout this book, is that ancient orators and poets crafted (or, in Ahl's terminology, 'figured') their language in order to embed meanings and criticisms which may be unsafe to be expressed directly, but are important for the audience/reader to discover.

INTRODUCTION   7

Augustus.[23] Moreover, since the motif of the ruler's divine status is by all appearances a poetic topos inherited from Hellenistic models, it is said that the purpose of using this language is to express gratitude to Augustus,[24] or to show respect to the *princeps*,[25] or to flatter him in a way that could not be accommodated in official communications.[26] The poetic language of divinization, according to these studies, is no more than an inconsequential expression of praise, and its excessiveness is something which Augustus is only too happy to overlook.

Recent analytical efforts are more attuned to the full semantic possibilities of this poetic language.[27] Consequently, these studies are more willing to prise open the political implications of this motif and the potential ambiguities of assimilating Augustus to a divine figure of authority. One common approach is to treat this language as more or less a sociological metaphor for the unequal social relation between poet and *princeps*.[28] This mode of reading tends to focus on the poets' emphatic claims of the immortalizing power of their art: by insinuating that the immortality of Augustus ultimately depends on their poetry (as Horace does in *Odes* 4.8.22–34 and 4.9.25–8), or by presenting themselves as equal partners in Augustus' journey towards immortality (as Virgil implies at *Georgics* 3.9–10), the poets—so the argument generally goes—redress the imbalance of power, albeit only symbolically and to a limited extent.[29] More recently, scholarly appreciation of this poetic motif as a form of political commentary on the power of Augustus manifests itself most strikingly in studies which highlight the subversive quality of poetry's divinizing images.[30] Concentrating on the fact that this poetic motif is closely associated with the monarchies of the Hellenistic world, critics have argued that its cultured reappearance in Augustan poetry subtly, and apprehensively, draws attention to the rise of singular authority and the infiltration of monarchic practices in Augustan Rome.[31]

---

[23] Fishwick (1987) I, 90–1.   [24] This view has been espoused since Taylor (1931) 111–12, 162.
[25] Veyne (1976) 501, 508.   [26] Gradel (2002) 110.
[27] Ahl's study led the way by showing that broaching the subject of the emperor's divinity was always more complex than it appeared: even the most egregiously panegyrical treatment was concerned with gaining control over or manipulating the lauded subject/victim; see Ahl (1984) 197–200.
[28] See e.g. Williams (1978) 159–60; Nappa (2005) 2–8; Le Doze (2014a) 598–600.
[29] See most recently Hejduk (2020) 142–5, 152–3 on Horace's claim to divinity; see Lowrie (2009) 150, 155–6 and Miller (2009) 3–6, 140, 147–8 on the opening to *Georgics* 3.
[30] See e.g. Gale (2000) 26–31, 35–6, 194 and (2003) 325–32, 348–9 on the *Georgics*; Gale (2013) 288–90 on the *Eclogues*. Others see this motif as a means by which the poets help to propagate Augustan power; see e.g. Grebe (2004) on the *Aeneid*; Powell (2010) on *Odes* 3.
[31] See e.g. Cole (2001) 68–75, 90 on *Odes* 1–3.

8 POLITICS AND DIVINIZATION IN AUGUSTAN POETRY

Although these interpretations diverge significantly, there is something common to all of them: they all implicitly maintain that the poetic discourse on Augustus' divinization can only be representations of *attitude* towards Augustus. Whether one sees this discourse as praise, or dissent, or a metaphor for deeply unequal social status, or a symbolic reassertion of authority, the unspoken assumption of all these approaches is that poetic representations of Augustus as divine are merely—and can only be—ineffectual sentiments of (dis)allegiance. This view, I would suggest, requires revisiting. An attitude-oriented interpretation of Augustan poetry generally leads us down the path of the 'pro- versus anti-Augustan' debate, which is surely too schematic to accommodate linguistic complexity and thus reality.[32] Yet there is still a tendency to treat poetry's discourse on Augustus' divine status as sentiment-driven rhetorical performances or imitative tropes. I want to challenge that idea below by demonstrating that the motif in question can operate in a more discursive manner, as a means to critique Rome's complex relationship with autocratic power; I suggest further that this function of literary discussions of divinization was already well embedded in the political writing of the late Republic.

Divinization in Roman Literary Culture

Stories of apotheosis encapsulated the lively debate among Roman intellectuals in their evaluation of a statesman's power and achievement. On the one hand, these narratives played a central role in the republican discourse on meritocratic authority, and often formed the basis of discussions on how to reward outstanding public service. In Cicero's *De re publica*, for example, apotheosis was an important tenet of an emerging political philosophy on the ideal statesman. Throughout the text, the divine afterlives of Romulus and Scipio were used as examples to substantiate the belief that those now worshipped as gods were originally men of great achievement (cf. Cic. *Rep.* 2.4; 2.17; 6.13; fr. inc. 5–6 = Lactant. *Div. inst.* 1.18.11).[33] Both this line of thinking, and the paradigmatic status of the apotheoses of Romulus and Scipio, remained prevalent in the works of the Augustan poets (cf. *bonis...ducibus*,

---

[32] This is the crux of Kennedy's (1992) incisive critique of the 'pro- vs anti-Augustan' debate. See also Sharrock (1994) and Davis (1999). The word 'reductive' makes several appearances in relation to the 'pro- vs anti-Augustan' debate in a recent volume of the *Classical World* (vol. 111.1 [2017]) exploring the impact of the 'Harvard School' reading of the *Aeneid*.

[33] Cole (2006) and (2013) 85–102; Myers (2009) 201.

INTRODUCTION 9

Hor. *Carm.* 4.8.14–15; *Epist.* 2.1.5–6). In addition, Roman writers adopted the canon of deified heroes found in Greek praise poetry and Hellenistic encomia,[34] and placed special emphasis—as Cicero did in the *De natura deorum* (2.62)—on the presence of Hercules among them.[35] The incorporation of this catalogue into Roman political literature showed that apotheosis was a focal point of the conversation surrounding the relationship between achievement on earth and reward in the afterlife. Indeed, the admission of a new, contemporary figure into this canon of deified men—as in the case of Augustus in Horace's *Ode* 3.3 (9–16)—became a way of suggesting that this figure was already perceived to be an extraordinary benefactor of mankind.

On the other hand, the contested nature of the (apparent) apotheosis of Romulus underlined the divergence among Roman intellectuals in their appraisal of the relationship between the state and its leader. Ancient sources gave two completely different accounts of what happened to Romulus. One tradition explained his sudden vanishing from the city as a well-earned apotheosis, which in some versions was enacted by his father Mars (cf. Enn. *Ann.* 1.54–5 Sk.; Livy 1.16.1–3; Ov. *Met.* 14.805–28). But a competing tradition explained his abrupt disappearance as fatal dismemberment by those who could no longer tolerate his despotism (cf. Livy 1.16.4; Dion. Hal. *Ant. Rom.* 2.56.3).[36] The 'apotheosis tradition' clearly took a generous view of Romulus' rule, and the story was meant as a seal of approval to his reign. By contrast, the 'dismemberment tradition' soberly rationalized Romulus' disappearance, and imagined a starker, more plausible outcome for the man who accumulated excessive power during his lifetime. Importantly, the 'apotheosis tradition' appeared to have originated in Ennius' historical epic, the *Annales,*

---

[34] Meister (2020) 78–80 offers an overview of narratives of heroic immortalization in archaic and Classical Greek poetry. Doblhofer (1966) 134–8 discusses the use of catalogues of deified heroes in Hellenistic encomia. Griffiths (1979) 51–106 explicates the crucial role Theocritus played in the development of immortalizing panegyric. On the importance of the 'pantheon' of deified heroes in Hellenistic ruler cult, see Chaniotis (2003) 432–7.

[35] See Pease (1958) on Cic. *Nat. D.* 2.62. Hercules' status in Rome as the deified hero par excellence has been well discussed by Galinsky (1972) 136–49 and Feeney (1991) 155–2 amongst others. On the importance of Herakles to Greek political thought on kingship, see Huttner (1997a). On Herakles as a paradigm of immortalization in Pindar's victory odes, see Meister (2020) 99–107, 114–17. For an overview of Greek sources on the death and apotheosis of Herakles, see Shapiro (1983). On the 'Herculean' republican statesman in Cicero's speeches, see Cole (2013) 80–5. Augustus sought to cultivate a connection with Hercules by staging his triple triumph (29 BC) on the day after the annual festival of Hercules at the Ara Maxima: Grimal (1951) 51–5; Binder (1971) 42–3; Huttner (1997b); Feeney (2007) 161–3. The poets' varied treatments of this connection have attracted much scholarly attention: see Galinsky (1972) 153–66, Morgan (1998), and Loar (2017) on *Aen.* 8; Morgan (2005a) on Hor. *Carm.* 3.14; Janan (2001) 128–45 and Welch (2005) 112–32 on Prop. 4.9.

[36] See further discussion by Bremmer and Horsfall (1987) 457 and Myers (2009) 201–2.

10 POLITICS AND DIVINIZATION IN AUGUSTAN POETRY

which ensured that the story would go on to have an elevated cultural status.[37] However, even after the 'apotheosis tradition' had become the orthodox version of events, aspects of this story were still questioned by writers in Augustus' day. Livy (1.16.5–8), for instance, was surprised that the testimony of Romulus' apotheosis provided by a certain Julius Proculus proved so persuasive to its original audience.

In the end, the question of whether Romulus had undergone apotheosis was not as revealing as what the story of apotheosis symbolized. The invention and propagation of Romulus' apotheosis reflected an attempt to transfigurate historical uncertainty as political myth, and it pointed to a willingness to validate autocratic leadership as political achievement. It was this ideological inclination—and its expression in divinizing imagery—that was challenged by the rationalizing tradition of Romulus' disappearance. The fact that this critique of Romulus' apotheosis took place throughout Roman history and across different literary genres strongly indicates that the divinization of a statesman was far from a run-of-the-mill practice or merely a poetic topos, but rather a constantly renewed point of cultural contention that encapsulated the Roman intellectual elites' sustained interest in the political symbolism of this custom.

Divinization as a Language of Political Negotiation

In the late Republic, as one military general after another obtained extraordinary powers (and some, namely Sulla and Julius Caesar, were even granted dictatorships), concepts such as divine salvation, divine favour, and immanent divine quality fully entered into Roman political debate. As a result, discussions of a statesman's 'divinity' cut to the core of how the ruling aristocracy negotiated the idea of one-man rule. To appreciate the extent to which this body of divinizing language became part of the contemporary political discourse, we might look to Cicero's *Pro lege Manilia* (66 BC) and *Pro Marcello* (46 BC). Produced twenty years apart, Cicero's discussion of the 'divinity' of Pompey and Caesar in these speeches shines a harsh light on the propensity

---

[37] Skutsch (1985) 205 and Cole (2006) argue the apotheosis of Romulus was the invention of Ennius; see now also Farrell (2020) 82 and his argument (pp. 80–2) that Romulus' deification in the *Annales* conforms closely to Ennius' interest in Euhemerism (as shown by his translation of Euhemerus' *Sacred History*). On the other hand, Elliott (2013) 178–9 suggests that the extent to which Ennius' epic embraced Romulus' apotheosis has been exaggerated by Cicero, and that this Ciceronian distortion has shaped subsequent readings of the *Annales*.

of the Roman political institution to lean on the executive power of an individual in times of crisis and to use the notion of divine leadership to justify it.[38]

In the *Pro lege Manilia*, Cicero speaks in support of Gaius Manilius' bill granting Pompey sole command in the Third Mithridatic War, including the power to assume full control of Asia Minor and the authority to wage war and conclude treaties on his own discretion.[39] In order to make the case that Pompey is uniquely suited to taking up these ostensibly dictatorial powers with the best intentions,[40] Cicero makes full use of divinizing language to present Pompey as a god-sent saviour upon whom the authority of Rome depended (*Leg. Man.* 41–2):[41]

> itaque omnes nunc in eis locis Cn. Pompeium sicut aliquem non ex hac urbe missum sed de caelo delapsum intuentur;[42] nunc denique incipiunt credere fuisse homines Romanos hac quondam continentia...; nunc imperi vestri splendor illis gentibus lucem adferre coepit .... et quisquam dubitabit quin huic hoc tantum bellum permittendum sit qui ad omnia nostrae memoriae bella conficienda divino quodam consilio natus esse videatur?

> Therefore all those now in those places look upon Gnaeus Pompeius not as one sent from this city but fallen from heaven. Now, at last, they begin to believe that there were once Roman men with this level of self-control...; now the splendour of your rule begins to bring light to the eyes of those nations .... And will anyone doubt that this war, which is so great, should be handed over to him, who seems to have been born by some divine counsel in order to complete all the wars in our memory?

Cicero here shifts from discussing the reverence Pompey received 'in those places' (*in eis locis*)—that is, in the Greek East—to asking his audience to show similar veneration and obedience in Rome by handing over extraordinary

---

[38] Lowrie's forthcoming studies on *securitas* in Roman culture is expected to examine similar issues. See also Lowrie (2015) and (2016) 76–80.

[39] On the *lex Manilia*, its relation to the *lex Gabinia*, and the apparent opposition to the *lex Manilia*, see Steel (2001) 113–23. In addition to Steel's study, Classen (1985) 268–303 and Fantham (1997) offer extended analyses of the speech.

[40] Steel (2001) 130–5 demonstrates that Cicero identifies four qualities of Pompey's character (*virtus*, 'courage'; *temperantia*, 'self-control'; *auctoritas*, 'influence'; and *felicitas*, 'luck') that make him the ideal candidate (cf. *summus...imperator*, *Leg. Man.* 36) to lead Rome's war against Mithridates.

[41] Gildenhard (2011) 255–72 and Cole (2013) 34–48 examine in detail Cicero's elevation of Pompey to divine status and the orator's handling of the language of divine favouritism.

[42] Gildenhard (2011) 264 rightly notes the connotation of epiphany in the expression *de caelo delapsum*.

12 POLITICS AND DIVINIZATION IN AUGUSTAN POETRY

power to the Roman general.[43] Cicero in effect proposes that Romans should adopt the non-Roman notion of the divine saviour in their decision-making process in order to give the state the best possible chance of defending its interests.[44] Later in the speech, Cicero escalates the force of this idea by recommending that the Roman people should unhesitatingly embrace the divine assistance embodied by Pompey and, more importantly, seek to secure his powerful, salvific presence in Rome for as long as possible (*Leg. Man.* 48):

> hoc brevissime dicam, neminem umquam tam impudentem fuisse qui ab dis immortalibus tot et tantas res tacitus auderet optare quot et quantas di immortales ad Cn. Pompeium detulerunt. quod ut illi proprium ac perpetuum sit, Quirites, cum communis salutis atque imperii tum ipsius hominis causa, sicuti facitis, et velle et optare debetis.

> Let me say this as briefly as possible: no one was ever so impudent that he should dare silently to desire so many and such great things from the immortal gods as the immortal gods have conferred upon Gnaeus Pompeius. In order that this favour may continue to be his and be perpetual, you, Romans, ought to wish and pray—as indeed you do—both for the sake of the common safety and sovereignty, and for the sake of the man himself.

Spencer Cole points out that the presentation of Pompey as Rome's new saviour mirrors the general's image as a σωτήρ in the Greek East where he received divinizing honours.[45] But there is more. Here Cicero uses the notions of divine favour and god-sent salvation to sanctify a proposal that is fundamentally antithetical to republicanism. By entwining the *salus* and *imperium* of Rome with Pompey's apparently immanent divine qualities and his all-surpassing status, Cicero's divinizing language reframes a highly controversial bill designed to grant Pompey extraordinary powers as an unmissable opportunity to ensure long-term political stability and Roman prosperity. The concept of a god-sent saviour is thus used to naturalize a potentially problematic handover of power to one man, embellishing or even helping to usher in Rome's lurch towards a Pompeian military dictatorship.[46]

---

[43] Cole (2013) 43.

[44] It has been suggested that Hellenistic encomia and Hellenistic manuals on kingship influenced Cicero's praise of Pompey; see Fears (1981) 797 and Steel (2001) 132–3.

[45] Cole (2013) 47. See Fishwick (1987) I, 47 on the divinizing honours offered to Pompey in the Greek East.

[46] It should be noted that throughout the speech Cicero seeks to distinguish Pompey from Sulla, presenting Pompey's authority as more appealing and less threatening than Sulla's. See Gildenhard (2011) 268–70.

INTRODUCTION   13

The ways in which the *Pro lege Manilia* mobilizes a discourse of divinity to justify Pompey's singularity and accommodate autocratic power within a republican structure find further expressions in the *Pro Marcello*.[47] Delivered in September 46 BC, this speech was Cicero's response to Caesar's (somewhat unexpected) agreement to pardon one of his most committed political enemies, a former supporter of Pompey, Marcus Claudius Marcellus.[48] By this point Caesar was effectively the sole ruler of Rome, having recently secured for himself the office of dictator for ten years.[49] In his speech, Cicero praises Caesar's many virtues as a statesman, but in particular his *clementia* (*Marcell.* 8):

> animum vincere, iracundiam cohibere, victo temperare, adversarium nobilitate, ingenio, virtute praestantem non modo extollere iacentem sed etiam amplificare eius pristinam dignitatem, haec qui faciat, non ego eum cum summis viris comparo, sed simillimum deo iudico.

> But to conquer one's own temper, to check one's anger, to show moderation towards the conquered, to take a fallen enemy pre-eminent in birth, character, and virtue, and not merely raise him up, but actually enhance his former standing—*that* is the act of someone whom I would not rank with the greatest of men, but would judge most like a god.

Cicero's use of divinizing language here is reminiscent of his praise of Pompey's outstanding virtues in the *Pro lege Manilia*. Just as he presents Pompey's effective and yet restrained leadership as a divine property that distinguishes him from the rest (cf. *Leg. Man.* 41), here the leniency, self-control, and magnanimity of Caesar are framed by Cicero as qualities that almost make him a god amongst men.[50] A further similarity between the *Pro lege Manilia* and the *Pro Marcello* can be observed in Cicero's assertion in both speeches that the welfare of the Republic depends singularly on its divinely

---

[47] Major studies of Cicero's use of divine language in the *Pro Marcello* include Levene (1997) 68–77, Gildenhard (2011) 361–4, and Cole (2013) 111–26.

[48] For an overview of the historical context of the speech and the occasion of its first delivery, see Tempest (2013) 298–301. The panegyrical character and epideictic elements of the *Pro Marcello* have been well observed: see Levene (1997) 68–77; Krostenko (2005); Manuwald (2011) 89–92.

[49] Cf. Cass. Dio 43.14. For further discussion of Cicero's relationship with Caesar during this period, see Hall (2009). Later in February 44, Caesar was given the title *dictator perpetuo* (cf. *MRR* 2. 317–18; Cic. *Phil.* 2.87; Weinstock 1971: 281 n. 5); for the implications of this title, see Yavets (1983) 38–45.

[50] Cole (2013) 124 points out that the loaded expression, *simillimum deo* ('most *like* a god'), captures Caesar's all-surpassing status without actually imputing divinity to the dictator outright. See further discussion below. Tempest (2013) 308–9 traces the influences of Hellenistic encomia and Philodemus' *On the Good King According to Homer* in this passage.

14   POLITICS AND DIVINIZATION IN AUGUSTAN POETRY

favoured leader.[51] In the *Pro lege Manilia*, as we have just seen, Cicero implies that the *salus* and *imperium* of Rome are intertwined with the divine qualities of Pompey (cf. *Leg. Man.* 48). In the *Pro Marcello*, we find an even stronger expression of this idea (*Marcell.* 18):

> ut mihi quidem videantur di immortales, etiam si poenas a populo Romano ob aliquod delictum expetiverunt, qui civile bellum tantum et tam luctuosum excitaverunt, vel placati iam vel satiati aliquando omnem spem salutis ad clementiam victoris et sapientiam contulisse.

> So it seems to me, then, that even if it was in order to punish the Roman people for some offence or other that the immortal gods provoked so terrible and tragic a civil war, they have now at any rate been appeased or sated, and have at long last transferred all hope of safety to the clemency and wisdom of the victor.

By asserting that the gods have put the *salus* of the state in Caesar's *clementia* and *sapientia*, Cicero suggests that the political stability of the Republic can only be mediated by Caesar's crafted statesmanship. This is an extraordinary claim, especially as the passage is inundated with references to Caesar's recent victory (cf. *victoris*) in the 'terrible and tragic civil war' (*civile bellum tantum et tam luctuosum*). To rely on a conqueror's politics of mercy implies not only willing subjection to one's former enemy but also the acceptance of a dangerously lopsided power dynamic as the only solution to long-term political stability.[52] However, by framing Caesar's *clementia* as a quality of divine proportions, and by presenting him as a divinely appointed saviour of Roman interests, Cicero's divinizing language achieves more than just the transformation of Caesar's image from that of a conqueror in Rome's civil war to a presiding god administering justice and protection: it makes the dependence on the unpredictable politics of a dictator more palatable to his Roman audience.

Despite Cicero's ostensible attempt to reconcile autocratic power with republican ideals, the *Pro Marcello* is by no means a thoroughgoing panegyric of Caesar's dictatorship.[53] The thrust of the speech is to challenge the most

---

[51] Lowrie (2015) 329–30 argues that the link between the safety of the leader and that of the group became more prominent after Caesar defeated Pompey and took over as Rome's new ruler.

[52] See also Connolly (2015) 198: 'This is a eulogy that attempts to come to terms with the loss of the republic.'

[53] Dyer (1990) argues that the *Pro Marcello* is far from a genuine eulogy, but an ironic oration that covertly criticizes Caesar and warns him of the consequences of his despotism. This view has been accepted by some and developed further; see e.g. Gagliardi (1997) 143–77. However, there are good grounds for believing that Cicero's praise was sincere (Winterbottom 2002), whilst also acknowledging

INTRODUCTION 15

powerful man of Cicero's day and goad him into doing what *Cicero* thinks is best for the Republic;[54] as we shall see, the concept of divinization is centrally involved in this process of negotiation. Throughout the speech, Cicero explicitly identifies *clementia* as the utmost political virtue that would enable the healing of the Republic after Pharsalus.[55] By emphasizing that Caesar's display of *clementia* in his pardoning of Marcellus puts him *almost* on par with the gods (cf. *simillimum deo iudico*, 'I would judge *most like* a god', *Marcell.* 8), Cicero sets the task of restoring the Republic for Caesar as if it were a personal assignment to achieve indisputable divine status.[56] In subtly implying that true immortality lies in rebuilding the Republic, Cicero turns divine aspiration into a straitjacket on Caesar's personal ambitions, steering the dictator onto a political path defined by him as being in the interest of the Republic rather than that of the dictator.[57] This attempt to regain control of Rome's political future through a debate on how to achieve divinity intensifies later in the speech, where Cicero again challenges Caesar to restore the Republic (*Marcell.* 27),[58] and then openly claims that Caesar's desire for immortality is misguided unless he understands immortality simply as perpetual *memoria* (*Marcell.* 27–8):

> quamquam iste tuus animus numquam his angustiis quas natura nobis ad vivendum dedit contentus fuit, semper immortalitatis amore flagravit. nec vero haec tua vita ducenda est quae corpore et spiritu continetur: illa, inquam, illa vita est tua quae vigebit memoria saeculorum omnium, quam posteritas alet, quam ipsa aeternitas semper tuebitur.

> And yet that spirit of yours has never been content to stay within the confines that nature has given us to live in: it has always burned with the desire for immortality. But your life should not be thought of as what is confined to

---

that the speech can be ambivalent (Dugan 2013) and contains seeds of 'constructive criticism' (Tempest 2013: 315). Connolly (2015) 172–202 links the hyperbolic language of the *Pro Marcello* to Cicero's attempt to inform his audience that Rome is entering into an era that is 'impossible to believe': the rule of one man, a 'state of emergency exceeding natural limits' (p. 183).

[54] Gildenhard (2011) 365 speaks of Cicero's 'exhortation of Caesar to restore the republican institutions'.

[55] Weinstock (1971) 235–43 argues that Cicero's *Caesarian Orations* played a major role in the increased prominence of *clementia* as a political virtue during the late Republic.

[56] Clark (2007) 248 notes that throughout the *Caesarian Orations* Cicero presents *clementia* as an extraordinary quality with which a man of Caesar's status ought to wish to be associated.

[57] Cole (2013) 115 observes that Cicero uses *clementia* 'adroitly to define Caesar in ways that could ultimately constrain him'.

[58] Cf. *haec igitur tibi reliqua pars est: hic restat actus, in hoc elaborandum est, ut rem publicam constituas* ('this part therefore still awaits you, this act remains, this is what you must work at: to place the Republic on a sound footing').

16   POLITICS AND DIVINIZATION IN AUGUSTAN POETRY

the body and breath: your life, I say, is what will flourish in the memory of every age, what posterity will nurture, and what eternity itself will always preserve.

Cicero configures Caesar's divine aspiration as an excess of political ambition, but he does concede that he cannot persuade Caesar from wishing otherwise. Instead, the orator proposes a different form of immortality that hinges on returning peace to Rome and will only be possible after death.[59] In doing so, Cicero dangles the possibility of his version of posthumous divinity to Caesar, challenging Caesar to live up to his personal aspiration while at the same time subjecting the dictator to continuous service to the Republic.

In his discussion of this passage, Cole argues that Cicero's redefinition of immortality as perpetual *memoria* 'cuts against the notion of Caesar as a newly arrived *praesens deus*', since the dictator was voted a number of extra-ordinary honours after his victory at Thapsus (April 46 BC), which signalled the distinct possibility of deification during his lifetime.[60] These honours included a forty-day *supplicatio*,[61] and a statuary group on the Capitol con-sisting of a chariot, a bronze statue of Caesar originally inscribed with the words *Deo Caesari* or similar,[62] and a globe placed either alongside or under the foot of the statue of Caesar—imagery that was thought to evoke a famous painting of Demetrius Poliorcetes, the archetypal deified Hellenistic mon-arch, sitting atop a globe.[63] Since Caesar was awarded these honours only a few months before the *Pro Marcello* was delivered, Cicero's attempt at redefin-ing immortality as posthumous *memoria* does appear to be aimed at putting the brakes on Caesar's momentum towards obtaining lifetime deification. But there is more at stake than just Caesar's divine honours. On a fundamental level, simply by initiating a debate on the topic of divinization, Cicero per-forms the important political act of contesting the discursive authority of

---

[59] See also Cole (2013) 125; he offers a detailed analysis (on pp. 124–6) of how the *Pro Marcello* strategically defers Caesar's immortality.

[60] Cole (2013) 125–6. For further discussions, see Weinstock (1971) 40–59, 62–4; North (1975) 173–4; Wardle (2009) 105–7; Koortbojian (2013) 95–6.

[61] Traditionally, *supplicationes* were reserved for the gods and usually lasted only a few days; but in the late Republic, more and more humans were given this honour; on this shift, see Wallace-Hadrill (1990) 160; Hickson-Hahn (2000) 245–46; Cole (2013) 74. On the voting of the *supplicatio*, see Beard (2007) 191–201.

[62] The inscription was eventually removed on Caesar's orders (Cass. Dio 43.21.2); therefore, schol-arly reconstructions were made based on Dio's report of the artefact, ὅτι ἡμίθεός ἐστι ('that he is a demigod', 43.14.6). Weinstock (1971) 53 recommends *Deo Caesari*; Fishwick (1987) I, 57 opts for *Caesari Romulo*; Wardle (2009) 106 thinks it possible that the original inscription was in Greek.

[63] As suggested by Weinstock (1971) 155–8 and Fishwick (1987) I, 57.

INTRODUCTION   17

Caesar, through which Cicero regains a measure of *libertas* and revives the possibility of demarcating limits on an increasingly autocratic system.[64] In fact, as Cicero reinterprets immortality as how one's life is to be remembered by others, the orator de-centres achievement from the concept of divinization and re-centres in its place the divinizing role of the people, the critic, and the political subject. The debate surrounding divinization, therefore, functions as a discursive proxy for negotiating, and preserving, a limited ideological independence and critical authority for the disempowered subject during Rome's shift towards one-man rule.

The immortalizing imagery and the discussion of deification in Cicero's *Pro lege Manilia* and *Pro Marcello* thus show that the concept of divinization and divinizing language were far from an inconsequential trope. The political instability of the late Republic, combined with the rising influence of military dictators and the increasing prominence of ideas and practices associated with Hellenistic ruler cult, created an environment wherein discussions of divinization and depictions of one's 'divinity' operated as a means to reinforce, figure out, or negotiate relationships between those who had raw political power and those who did not. While there may have been an element of brinksmanship in Cicero's use of divinizing concepts in these speeches,[65] it is nevertheless clear that his discussions of the divinity of these charismatic leaders were no mere sociological metaphor or conventional flattery. Rather, divinizing rhetoric constituted a key part of Cicero's overall strategies to accommodate autocratic forms of power within a nominally republican system (as in the *Pro lege Manilia*), or to mediate reconciliation between dictator and ex-republicans (as in the *Pro Marcello*). In other words, the discussion of divinization began to function as a figurative language of political negotiation during a time of constitutional uncertainty. Moreover, it encapsulated and communicated both the hope and the anxiety, tension as well as complicity, within the social elite at the point of political transition. This kind of experimental yet consequential play with divinizing discourse, as I shall demonstrate throughout this book, permeates the Augustan poets' discussions of the divinity of their *princeps*.

---

[64] Connolly (2015) 198 notes that the speech is 'an attempt to remind Caesar of what Cicero is, and what the other senators are, in an effort to define his responsibilities and to demarcate limits to Caesar's potentially tyrannical freedom of action'.

[65] Cole (2013) 113 suggests that Cicero's thinking on divinization may not be representative of the majority view on the subject.

Poetry under the Augustan Principate

But of course there are fundamental differences between poetry and oratory. For a start, whereas Cicero was often part of a decision-making body that could initiate or stall measures that heralded constitutional change, the poets who lived through the triumviral period and the early Principate had no such constitutional influence. The Augustan poets were simply unable to intervene in the day-to-day business of political administration with their verses in the way that Cicero could with his speeches. However, while the poets had little say in the formation of the Principate following Octavian's victory in the civil war, their art had political agency and was sought after by the new regime. The clearest indication of an attempt to cultivate a literary network around the *princeps* is the notable presence of Maecenas in the works of Virgil, Horace, and Propertius. The exact nature of the relationship between Maecenas and the poets is far from clear; but the socio-economic interactions between them certainly give the impression that Maecenas' status was akin to that of a patron.[66] Whether one treats Virgil's curious expression *tua, Maecenas, haud mollia iussa* ('at your order, Maecenas, and a rather tough one at that', *G.* 3.41) as an unusually candid reference to Maecenas' direct interference in poetic composition,[67] or (more likely) an admission from Virgil about the difficulty of the present task,[68] there is no doubt that the poets were fully aware that their art was a prominent aspect of the new cultural landscape. Over the course of time, Augustus himself even appeared to supersede Maecenas as 'patron', and certainly as addressee, of the poetry of Horace and, to a lesser extent, Propertius (cf. *tua, Caesar, aetas*, Hor. *Carm.* 4.15.4; *tua tempora, Caesar*, Hor. *Epist.* 2.1.4).[69] Even in the case of Tibullus, who does not mention Augustus in his work and addresses his poetry to M. Valerius Messalla (rather than Maecenas),[70] the poet appears to be conversant with the regime's sloganeering, as he adopts the universalizing formula *terra marique*

---

[66] Major discussions of the relationship between Maecenas and the poets include: White (1993); Freudenburg (2001) 19–23, 60–71; Gowers (2012) 2–20; Le Doze (2014a) 161–266; (2014b); (2019); Chillet (2016). See Graverini (1997) for a full report of studies on Maecenas in the twentieth century.

[67] Stahl (2015) 450–1. White (1993) 136 and 266–8 shows that *iussa* is the conventional term for literary requests, but does not think that Virgil's phrase here is a complaint; see note below.

[68] The majority view: see e.g. Thomas (1988) ad loc.; Mynors (1990) ad loc.; White (1993) 135–6; Volk (2002) 135; Erren (2003) 585–6. A variation is provided by Nappa (2005) 123: he too argues against the idea of literary request, but adds that the phrase may imply that Maecenas is having a hard time maintaining his readerly interest in Virgil's didactic.

[69] Maecenas disappears from view in Book 4 of Propertius and the final book of the *Odes*. It is suspected that Maecenas suffered a fall from favour at some point in the early 10s BC; but critics are divided. See key discussions by Williams (1990); White (1991); Le Doze (2009).

[70] On the literary patronage of Messalla, see esp. Fantham (1996) 92–5.

in reference to Messalla's military activities and, in so doing, inscribes his 'patron' into the discourse of self-aggrandizing Augustan propaganda (*te bellare decet terra, Messalla, marique*, 'it is a fine thing, Messalla, for you to wage war on land and sea', Tib. 1.1.50).[71] Therefore, while the poetic word could not materially affect the political situation during Rome's transition from Republic to Principate, the poets signalled their involvement in the shaping of the dominant political discourse under Augustus.

This then brings us to the question: what kind of role did poetry have in the production of consensus or resistance? This is a problem that closely mirrors the one addressed in various ways by Marxist and neo-Marxist cultural critique, which argues that the dominant force in any given society channels the intellectual and social energies of the governed in such a way as to maintain existing structures of control, or to manage their evolution in ways that are advantageous to those in power.[72] Notably, this involves the management of dissent, such that oppositional forces are recruited in support of the status quo. I would say that at this point in time, some sixty years after the advent of the 'Harvard School' reading of Virgil's *Aeneid*,[73] most studies of Augustan literature take the view that Augustus successfully channelled virtually all forms of socio-cultural production, especially those of an oppositional nature, in such a way as to strengthen the position of the regime and the larger social structures on which the power of the regime rested.[74] Subsequently, and especially after the publication of Duncan Kennedy's essay '"Augustan" and "Anti-Augustan": Reflections on Terms of Reference',[75] it has become very difficult to maintain that there was genuine resistance coming from the poets, as opposed to 'resistance' that is defined and limited by mainly generic conventions (such as the *recusatio*) which ultimately strengthens Augustus' hand and the socio-political orthodoxy.[76]

Under such circumstances, the entire poetic discourse of Augustus' divinity becomes both more limited and more open in what it can actually convey. It can no longer speak 'for' or 'against' the regime any more than one might speak 'for' or 'against' gravity. Instead of eliciting support or resistance, this

---

[71] The phrase *terra marique* bears a heavy freight of ideological significance, as evidenced by its recurrent appearance on the coinage of the Augustan age. See Momigliano (1942a); Cornwell (2017) 81–120, esp. 97–107.

[72] See esp. Althusser (1970); Jameson (1971); Eagleton (2002).

[73] Parry (1963); Clausen (1964); Putnam (1965). See also *Classical World* 111.1 (2017).

[74] For a recent exposition of this view, see Giusti (2016a).   [75] Kennedy (1992).

[76] See similar views by Roman (2014) 166–9. Freudenburg (2014) points out further that the poets' *recusationes* are to a large extent informed by, and replicate the theatrics of, Augustus' persistent refusal of power.

20 POLITICS AND DIVINIZATION IN AUGUSTAN POETRY

discourse, as I would suggest, is concerned with trying to make sense of the regime as a new and ineluctable political reality.

Take for example Propertius 3.11.[77] I choose this poem—a Latin love elegy to be sure—partly because Roman elegy is often thought of as a genre of political resistance; and partly because the study of poetic representations of divinization tends to focus on 'higher' genres (especially epic). In addition, some critics take the view that divinizing language is used frivolously in elegy, as any *puella* or indeed *amator* can be depicted as divine or becoming divine in a love poem;[78] and therefore, an elegist's play with this motif—unlike an epic poet's engagement with it—has no true political significance.[79] These assumptions will be challenged in my reading of Propertius' poem below.

Published sometime between 23 and to 20 BC,[80] elegy 3.11, in its round-about way, commemorates the battle of Actium (31 BC) as a turning-point for Rome. The poem begins by discussing the power women have over men, and evolves into a celebration of Augustus' victory against Cleopatra, who is presented as the ultimate *femme fatale*.[81] In his panegyric, Propertius paints Augustus as Rome's saviour who liberated the city from foreign tyranny (*Romana poposcit | moenia et addictos in sua regna patres*, 'she demanded Roman walls and the Senate bound to her rule', 3.11.31-2; *Roma...longum Augusto salva precare diem*, 'Rome, saved, pray for a long life for Augustus', 3.11.49-50);[82] and claims that Augustus' achievement is such that he outranks republican heroes of the past (3.11.59-64) and is virtually superior to Jupiter (*vix timeat salvo Caesare Roma Iovem*, 'while Caesar is safe and sound Rome should scarcely fear Jupiter', 3.11.66).[83] The poet's implicit suggestion that Augustus could challenge Jupiter emphasizes the extraordinary status of the *princeps*;[84] but by qualifying this hubristic assertion with *vix* ('scarcely'), the

---

[77] This poem has attracted a great deal of scholarship; see esp. Nethercut (1971); Putnam (1980a); Stahl (1985) 234-47; Gurval (1995) 189-208; Wyke (2002) 205-16; Wallis (2018) 83-92.

[78] Catullus (68.70) describes his lover as *mea...candida diva* ('my shining goddess'). Propertius depicts himself as becoming divine in moments of sexual gratification (cf. 2.14.9-10; 2.15.39-40). The elegist also envisages his poetic immortality (cf. Prop. 3.2.17-26) in a manner similar to Horace's *Ode* 3.30.

[79] See e.g. Boucher (1974) 83-4; Fedeli (1985) on 3.4.1.

[80] There is scholarly consensus on the date-range for the publication of Propertius Book 3: after the appearance of Horace's *Odes* 1-3 (23 BC), but prior to the Parthian settlement (20 BC).

[81] On the poem's misleading, misogynistic, and Orientalist portrayal of Cleopatra as a dominating *meretrix*, see esp. Nethercut (1971) 421-3; Mader (1989); Wyke (2002) 195-243.

[82] I use Heyworth's *OCT* edition of Propertius throughout.

[83] The order of the transmitted verses 57-68 is debatable; moreover, Heyworth marks a lacuna after verse 57. However, critics agree that the meaning of verse 66 is not obscured by the textual problems surrounding it.

[84] Note the contrast between this Propertian passage and Hor. *Carm.* 1.12.49-60: in the latter, Augustus is the junior partner and earthly representative of Jupiter (cf. *te minor*, 1.12.57). Pitting Augustus against Jupiter is evidently meant to be provocative: see Miller (2004) 148 and now Hejduk (2020) 198. But Fedeli (1985) ad loc. thinks that the sequence of *Caesare Roma Iovem* builds up to the

exact limit of what Augustus is capable of becomes something of a grey area. One thing is certain, however: as the sole liberator and protector of Rome who eclipses all previous republican heroes, Augustus 'undermines the republican tradition of power-sharing and non-monopolistic apportioning of glory'.[85] Propertius' divinizing rhetoric thus brings out the sense that the poet does not quite know how powerful Augustus is, but is fully aware of his extraordinary authority and status.

Secondly, Propertius' divinizing rhetoric crystallizes the irresolvable paradox of Augustus and his rule. It has been noted that the momentum of the poem suggests a path of domination leading from elegiac women to Augustus, from *servitium amoris* to imperial power, which in turn lends force to the idea that 'the liberator [Augustus] is at the same time the conqueror'.[86] Building on this observation, we might note a further movement embedded in the shift from *Roma... salva* (3.11.49–50) to *salvo Caesare* (3.11.66), which underlines the extent to which the 'saved' city has become dependent on, even shackled to, its saviour. Through this subtle play with salvific imagery, Propertius foregrounds the ironic indispensability of absolute power to the freedom and security of Rome, while drawing attention to the blurred lines between the concept of salvation and the advent of autocracy. Propertius' poem 'resists' Augustan power only to the extent that the *amator*, who revels in his submission to the dominance of his *puella*, identifies with those who fell prey to Cleopatra, and not with Augustus who proved himself unsusceptible to her seductive power.[87] The poem's depiction of the *princeps* as an all-surpassing figure of divine proportions—a completely different kind of creature to the submissive *amator*—further reinforces the irreconcilability between elegiac and Augustan ideals.[88] But the elegiac lover's opposition to sociopolitical norms is a generic pose, with little real-life significance. In contrast, the poem's divinizing depiction of Augustan power as almost limitless, as both reassuring and yet unprecedented, salvific but also overwhelming, underlines the poet's realization of the irreducible contradictions of the new Augustan regime.

The reading offered above represents the kind of new insight I wish to offer throughout this book. My key claim is that the poetic discourse on the divinity

---

supremacy of Jupiter; while Wallis (2018) 87 argues that this verbal cluster restores traditional order and hierarchy, rectifying the inversion of male–female authority paradigm with which the poem begins. Propertius' hyperbolical evaluation of Augustus' status, as Hejduk (2020) 198 rightly points out, anticipates the kind of ironic praise to be found later in Ovid.

[85] Roman (2014) 189.   [86] Putnam (1980a) 101.

[87] Griffin (1977) 24; Stahl (1985) 239–43 argues that at Prop. 3.11.33–8 alludes to not only Antony's but also Julius Caesar's liaison with Cleopatra.

[88] See also Wallis (2018) 83.

22   POLITICS AND DIVINIZATION IN AUGUSTAN POETRY

of Augustus conveys the experience of trying to learn more about a new political order and of having to come to terms with it. Through invoking it as Propertius did, the poets are able to articulate how things are simultaneously stabilizing and destabilized as Rome reconstitutes itself under Augustus after the civil war. By using this discourse to gesture at the adjustments, concessions, or commitments they must make in order to thrive (or simply survive) in the new Augustan age, the poets subtly foreground the extent to which the political situation now moves beyond their control. From Augustus' perspective, the poets' dramatized realization and eventual acceptance of the (divine) status quo make for a compelling endorsement of the regime, for it gives the impression that the process of conforming to hegemonic power is an organic, polyphonic, and voluntary activity.

Learned Tongues: Intertexts, Identities, Discourses

While the poetic motif of Augustus' divinity on the whole conveys the idea of encountering and adjusting to a new political reality, it is by no means lacking critical agency. Through allusions and intertexts, juxtapositions and interpolations, silences and absences, and pointed choices of form and diction literature can 'contradict, reveal, or even resist the ideological distortions supporting the social formations of a particular period'.[89] The legitimacy of the Augustan Principate was partly built on a distorted version of the civil war. The new regime sought to retell Augustus' victory over Antony and Cleopatra as a civilizational clash between Rome and Egypt, culminating in the triumph of Roman ideals over foreign aggression. This warped version of events was a staple in the works of the Augustan poets, as they variously assimilated Augustus' victory to the Gigantomachy or Jupiter's victory against the Titans, which in turn reinforced the status of Augustus and his regime as the forces of order (cf. Hor. *Carm.* 3.4; Prop. 2.1.17–42; Tib. 2.5.5–10; Verg. *Aen.* 8. 671–713; Ov. *Tr.* 2.61–76).[90] On the other hand, the poets did not exclusively use this theme to mirror and extend the regime's distortion: they

---

[89] Bowditch (2001) 141.

[90] See esp. Hardie (1986) 85–9. He argues compellingly that the Gigantomachy–Titanomachy theme embeds into the *Aeneid* (and elsewhere) the idea of order overcoming chaos, which in turn frames the Augustan regime as order-restoring Olympians. More recently, Chaudhuri (2014) traces the development of the theme of 'war on god' in Latin literature, arguing that the Gigantomachy–Titanomachy may be seen as part of a broader discourse of theomachy, which at its core is concerned with the (shifting) distinctions between human and divine.

INTRODUCTION   23

also exploited its potential as a symbolism of the chaos of *civil* conflict.[91] For instance, in an elegy addressed to Maecenas, Propertius conspicuously juxtaposes the Giants' attack on Olympus with Remus' doomed assault on his brother's settlement on the Palatine, presenting both as possible topics for a future patriotic poem (3.9.47–50).[92] This kind of disruptive intervention in the regime's self-fashioning can also be observed in poetic discussions of Augustus' divinity. Aesthetic play with the discourse of divinization, as I shall suggest below, enables the Augustan poets to critique or refuse the ways in which divinizing rhetoric has been used by the regime to reinvent Rome's recent history.

A core aspect of the aesthetic play of Latin poetry lies in its dialogue with Greek literary forerunners. Throughout their works, the Augustan poets underline the influence of Greek predecessors while highlighting their own desire and ability to tendentiously play with, innovate upon, or outdo their literary models. The poetic discourse on Augustus' divinity encapsulates this creative tension, and as a result, it enables the poets to speak to larger questions about cultural interactions between Augustan Rome and the Greek world, the effects of conquest and empire, and Roman identity. The final four verses of Propertius' panegyric of Augustus in elegy 3.11 are a good example of this (69–72):

> Leucadius versas acies memorabit Apollo:
>   tantum operis belli sustulit una dies.[93]   70
> at tu, sive petes portus seu, navita, linques,
>   Caesaris in toto sis memor Ionio.

Leucadian Apollo will record the turning of the battle lines: a single day of war took away so much labour. But you, sailor, whether making for port or leaving it, be mindful of Caesar through all the Ionian Sea.

---

[91] O'Hara (2007) 98–103 warns against reducing the Gigantomachy–Titanomachy motif to a narrow 'order versus chaos' binary, and argues that its inconsistent application by Virgil in the *Aeneid*—where both Aeneas and Turnus are compared to Giants—should draw our attention to not only the contradictions within the poem but also the ambivalent nature of Rome and the historical process that has led to the politics of Virgil's day (p. 102). See also Connors (1998) 117; Stover (2014) 80–1, 114–15; Wright (2018) 123–53.

[92] These lines suffer from textual problems. Heyworth's *OCT* keeps 47–50 intact; but Fedeli's Teubner edition suggests the following sequence: 47–8, 51, 50, 49. The proposed transpositions do not seriously alter the meaning of this section of the poem.

[93] Housman's conjecture, *tanti...bellum*, does not make material difference to the meaning of verse 70.

24 POLITICS AND DIVINIZATION IN AUGUSTAN POETRY

The first thing we might say is that the juxtaposition of Apollo and Caesar, set against geographical references to the area around Actium (cf. *Leucadius*, 69; *Ionio*, 72), evokes the close association between the *princeps* and his patron god in the commemorative projects set up in response to the naval victory, especially those in the newly founded Greek settlement Nicopolis.[94] So the poem's interest in Augustus' divine self-imaging extends beyond the regime's visual programme in Rome as the elegist looks towards the Greek East. But there is more. Commentators have noted that the phrase *tantum operis* in verse 70 is used earlier by Propertius in elegy 3.3 to refer to the composition of Roman historical epic (*Visus eram*... | *reges, Alba, tuos et regum facta tuorum,* | *tantum operis, nervis hiscere posse meis*, 'I had dreamt that... I had the power in my sinews to gape at your kings, Alba, and the deeds of your kings, so great a work', 3.3.1–4); and that the entire verse in fact recalls a similar expression from Ennius' *Annales: multa dies in bello conficit unus* ('one day accomplishes much in war', fr. 258 Sk.). The victory at Actium, so Propertius implies, has put an end to traditional martial epic as much as to Rome's protracted warfare.[95] However, by emphasizing the idea that a *single* battle changed the outcome of history, the elegist suggests at the same time that Augustus' supremacy was built on and could be destroyed in a day.

The elegy's final couplet (71–2), addressed to an anonymous sailor, then brings to mind an epigram of Posidippus, who worked in the Alexandrian court of Ptolemy I and II (Posid. 39 Austin–Bastianini):[96]

> καὶ μέλλων ἅλα νηὶ περᾶν καὶ πεῖσμα καθάπτειν
> χερσόθεν, Εὐπλοίαι 'χαῖρε' δὸς Ἀρσινόηι,
> πότνιαν ἐκ νηοῦ καλέων θεόν, ἣν ὁ Βοΐσκου
> ναυαρχῶν Σάμιος θήκατο Καλλικράτης
> ναυτίλε, σοὶ τὰ μάλιστα· κατ᾽ εὔπλοιαν δὲ διώκει   5
> τῆσδε θεοῦ χρήιζων πολλὰ καὶ ἄλλος ἀνήρ·
> εἵνεκα καὶ χερσαῖα καὶ εἰς ἅλα δῖαν ἀφιεὶς
> εὐχὰς εὑρήσεις τὴν ἐπακουσομένην.

---

[94] After his victory, Octavian enlarged the Temple of Apollo at Actium; instituted the Actian games (Cass. Dio 51.1.2; Strabo 7.7.6); and set up a victory monument on the location of his campsite, which became part of a new sanctuary of Apollo in the newly founded city of Nicopolis (Strabo 7.7.6; Suet. *Aug.* 18.2; Cass. Dio 51.1.2–3). On these developments, see Murray and Petsas (1989); Zachos (2003); Lange (2009) 95–124. On Apollo's presence in the Nicopolis site, see esp. Zachos (2003) 823 and (2007) 413–14; Lange (2009) 104–5; Miller (2009) 56 n. 6. In addition, *Leucadius...Apollo* (3.11.69) may also evoke the Temple of Apollo above the cliffs of Leucas; see Camps (1966) ad loc.

[95] Heyworth and Morwood (2011) on 3.11.69–70.

[96] This intertext is also discussed by Heyworth and Morwood (2011) in their commentary.

Both when you are about to cross the sea by ship and fasten the cable from the land, give a greeting to Arsinoe Euploia, invoking the revered goddess from her temple, which the son of Boescus, the Samian admiral Callicrates, built especially for you, o sailor. Another man, wishing good passage, also invokes this goddess, because whether heading for dry land or the divine sea, you will find her attentive to your prayers.

The displacement of a deified Hellenistic monarch by Augustus in Propertius' poem suggests on the one hand that the *princeps* now presides over the Roman world like a living god-king, a notion that is both flattering and problematic.[97] On the other hand, by subsuming this panegyrical Greek epigram into a Latin poem about Roman conquest, Propertius plays up the idea that the Greek world and their symbolic discourses, which the Roman aristocracy appreciated and inherited over long expanses of time, are now defined by their contribution to the *translatio imperii et studiorum* ('transfer of power and learning') taking place under Augustus. By hinting at the termination of Roman historical epic while adopting the formula of Hellenistic encomiastic epigram, Propertius' cross-cultural allusions bring out the idea that, as Augustus subjugates and annexes what was once a centre of Greek-Hellenistic culture, one has to find new ways—non-Roman ways—of conceptualizing Augustan power. In this way, elegy 3.11 ends on a note that calls into question the demarcated categories of Roman and Other.

Set within this framework, the poem's implicit comparison of Augustus to a deified Hellenistic monarch is more than just a tongue-in-cheek comment on the nature of his rule, but adverts the reader's attention to the extent to which non-Roman concepts, discourses, and power structures have been cultivated to sustain and reproduce Roman *imperium*.[98] The repurposing of Posidippus' eulogy of Arsinoe for a Latin panegyric about Augustus underscores the difficulty of maintaining any strict cultural distinction between Augustan Rome and Ptolemaic Alexandria, Roman and Other, 'us' and 'them'.[99] It is through this kind of learned reflection on Roman identity that Propertius disrupts the regime's characterization of the civil war as a conflict between Rome and a

---

[97] As Barchiesi (2005) 285 well sums up, allusion and intertextuality are 'processes of literary signification [that] cut both ways'.

[98] It should not surprise us that the poem ends on a contemplative note. As I mentioned above, 3.11 was published approximately ten years after the victory at Actium: Propertius has had some time to reflect on Augustus' rule.

[99] Furthermore, the anonymity of the *navita* (Prop. 3.11.71)—a Roman sailor? a Greek seafarer? a survivor at Actium?—only reinforces the ambiguity of identity in the poem's closure.

26 POLITICS AND DIVINIZATION IN AUGUSTAN POETRY

foreign aggressor, and Augustus' image as a salvific defender of Roman values and authority.

In using Propertius 3.11 as a case study, I hope to have shown that poetry's discourse on Augustus' divinity does not interact directly or confrontationally with some apparent monolithic 'ideology'.[100] Rather, it exercises its critical agency by engaging (tendentiously) with the Augustan retelling of Rome's political transformation, and by artistically challenging the use of divinizing discourse in the regime's self-fashioning. Through these activities, as I shall demonstrate throughout this book, the poets go some way to interrogate the Augustan narrative of the past, treating the Augustan mythologization of recent history as if it were a 'text' to be critiqued and rewritten.[101] In this sense, poetry's relationship to official discourse may be seen as analogous to its intertextual engagement with literary forms; and this in turn enables the poets to exercise their creative authority to appraise, contest, or even pull at the seams of the Augustan construction of power through divinizing expressions.[102]

Indeed, in his influential book *The Power of Images in the Age of Augustus* (originally *Augustus und die Macht der Bilder*), Paul Zanker shows that themes such as the apotheosis of the ancestors of the *gens Iulia*, which can be observed throughout the regime's visual programme, are curated in such a way that they become instrumental in conveying the message of Augustan supremacy and control.[103] Building on this, we might say that an important aspect of the poets' play with Augustus' divinity is to highlight a core element of the regime's production of political consensus, and to position their own art in relation to this process. To speak effusively or elusively about Augustus' divinity is therefore not simply a matter of flattery or resistance: it is an attempt to understand and communicate the ongoing evolutions of Augustan power,

---

[100] That is not to say that the Principate lacked ideological underpinning. As Le Doze (2010) argues, under the Principate, republican concepts of the right to intervene in politics were gradually displaced by new notions that linked Rome' future to the *gens Augusta* alone—a sure sign of an ideological shift in the ways of governing. The evolutions of Augustus' powers, on which see Ferrary (2001), further indicated that new concepts of political authority were conceived and implemented under Augustus. The attribution of *maiestas* ('greatness') to the *princeps*, which allowed him to dominate at the highest levels of Roman aristocracy, was likewise an ideologically driven move that granted more power to Augustus; see Ando (2011) 99–107. For a recent and succinct account of how the Augustan Principate differed ideologically from the Republic, see Hammer (2014) 19–25; for further discussion, see esp. Lacey (1996).

[101] In taking this view, I follow the lead set by Hinds (1998) and others, which analyse deliberate literary allusions within a broader understanding of all discourse as being fundamentally 'intertextual'— that is, constituted by negotiations between texts or between cultural expressions analysable as 'texts'.

[102] This view of the relationship between poetic and official discourses also underpins the recent study of Pandey (2018); see further discussion below.

[103] Zanker (1988) 192–215.

INTRODUCTION 27

the workings of the Principate, and the cultural impact of a new political system.[104] To this extent, I would contend that the poets are akin to political theorists, trying to comprehend and develop a way of analysing political change. This book, in short, strives to demonstrate the new interpretive scope and fresh understandings that come with taking this view of the poets' discussions of Augustus' divinity.

Studies on Cognate Topics (and 'The Tibullus Question')

In recent years, there has been a surge of interest in Roman political thought among scholars of Classics and other disciplines. While much of the scholarship has focused on Roman historians (especially Sallust, Livy, and Tacitus),[105] a number of studies have shown that Latin poetry too developed theories of governing,[106] addressed political-theoretical issues such as the limit of individual sovereignty,[107] and provided linguistic and conceptual frameworks for documenting the constitutional history of Rome.[108] The present study capitalizes on this renewed appreciation of poetry's intellectual range and political reach. In its attempt to cast new light on divinizing language by construing it as a means to grapple with and communicate political change, this book can be seen to stand adjacent to the growing body of scholarship on Roman political thought.

By focusing on poetry's interaction with the figurative language of Augustan power, my methodology aligns with that of a number of recent studies that address aspects of Augustus' self-representation as divine, particularly John Miller's *Apollo, Augustus, and the Poets* and Nandini Pandey's *The Poetics of Power in Augustan Rome*.[109] In the course of an extended examination of the figure of Apollo in Augustan poetry, Miller demonstrates that the poets variously took part in or subtly resisted Augustus' appropriation of Apollo and the ideological project arising from it. The present study extends

[104] West (1995) 15 has spoken of how Horace was feeling his way to 'a grammar of panegyric' in *Ode* 1.2 when the poet depicted the new Caesar as a god incarnate. Here I expand on West's idea by suggesting that poetry's divinizing language is not merely testing rhetorical waters, but probing into broader ideological and discursive shifts.

[105] See e.g. Hammer (2008) and (2014); Kapust (2011); Connolly (2015); Vasaly (2015); Atkins (2018).

[106] See e.g. Hammer (2014) 93–144 on Lucretius.

[107] See e.g. Connolly (2015) 115–54 on Horace's *Satires*.

[108] See e.g. Lushkov (2020) 211–27 on the relationship between Ennius and Livy.

[109] Miller (2009); Pandey (2018). A number of shorter but equally informative studies on cognate issues have also influenced my thinking: Schiesaro (2009); Cucchiarelli (2011a) and (2011b); Geue (2013); Lowrie (2015). In addition, Lowrie (2009), esp. pp. 83–97, 123–57, 349–59, has left an indelible mark on the way I understand the performative aspect of a poetic proclamation of divine status.

28 POLITICS AND DIVINIZATION IN AUGUSTAN POETRY

the critical perspective of Miller's book by treating the poets' exploration of the different guises of Apollo as one aspect of poetry's attempt to unpick the regime's self-representational strategies (see Chapter 4). The poets' sustained interest in the correspondence between Augustus and Jupiter also brings me into contact with Julia Hejduk's recent monograph, *The God of Rome: Jupiter in Augustan Poetry*.[110] In the following chapters, I develop her general observation that the changing presentation of Jupiter in Augustan poetry correlates with the metamorphosis of Rome's political and moral climate under its first *princeps*.[111] On the whole, however, Hejduk's book is dedicated to showing the complexity of the Augustan poets' portrayal of Jupiter (as father, king, lover, rapist, etc.)—a complexity which may 'illuminate their inevitably complex feelings about the man who came increasingly to be seen as the chief god's earthly avatar'.[112] While I identify with her attentiveness to Jovian representational complexity, the present study approaches poetry's interest in the Jupiter–Augustus equivalence not as *the* defining expression of the poets' feelings towards their *princeps*, but rather as one of a number of ways in which poetry tries to apprehend and come to terms with a new form of extraordinary power.

Pandey's book takes as its starting point that Augustus relied on innovative uses of symbolic images of power to maintain authority among his subjects and investigates how the poets treated the central motifs of the regime's visual programme, such as the *sidus Iulium*, the *triumphus*, and the Forum Augustum. In her work, Pandey compares the dynamic between image-maker and viewer to that between poet and reader; identifies ways in which the poets grant authority to their readers (or themselves) over the interpretation of symbolic images of Augustan power; and argues, very compellingly, that the process of 'reading' functions as a political metaphor whereby the reader-viewer and the poet can critique, resist, and refuse giving their consent to Augustus' construction of political power.[113] The present study does not follow Pandey in framing the author–reader relationship as a hermeneutic model for the negotiation of political consent. However, by approaching

---

[110] Hejduk (2020).
[111] Hejduk (2020) 32; see especially her reading of Horace's *Odes* (pp. 111–29, 150–5), Propertius (pp. 173–5, 195–8, 202–11), and Ovid's *Fasti* and exilic poetry (245–89). Though in her conclusion (pp. 294–6), Hejduk suggests that Jupiter is too multifaceted a character to be seen simply as the celestial counterpart of Augustus.
[112] Hejduk (2020) 2.
[113] Pandey (2018) 6: 'the poets reclaim for themselves and their audience intellectual authority over the symbols and ideas that underpinned the principate, imaginatively transforming Rome's empire into a *res publica* of readers.'

INTRODUCTION 29

poetry's discourse on divinity as a medium through which the poets explore their (limited) agency and train their critical gaze at an Augustan discourse of power, this book parallels and further develops the interpretive angle of Pandey's monograph.

Finally, I want to mention a much earlier, but nevertheless still relevant, discussion by Peter White, in his book *Promised Verse: Poets in the Society of Augustan Rome*.[114] The primary interest of White's book is literary patronage and the degree of independence possessed by the poets. In this vein, White takes the divine transfiguration of Augustus as a case study that could potentially shed light on how much creative freedom the poets had. The conclusion reached by White is that the literary representation of Augustus' divinity testifies to poetry's considerable independence from political constraints, because the poets either do not follow the leads that were laid down in the public discourse (such as the divine honours given to Augustus by the Senate) or adopt very different positions to that of the regime.[115] In any case, White adds, after the mid-20s the poets 'simply lose interest in the theme'.[116]

Although a number of White's conclusions will be challenged by the present study (especially his claim regarding the loss of interest),[117] they are extremely useful in some ways. White is most persuasive when he suggests that the poets did not speak about Augustus in divine terms under compulsion or because of direct pressure from above.[118] He also raises the interesting idea that the poets had the freedom to *not* engage with whatever divinizing imagery was exhibited in official media. And this brings me to Tibullus. The complete absence of the theme of Augustus' divinization in the poetry of Tibullus—if we go along with White's idea—could be seen as the most extreme manifestation of the poet exercising his artistic freedom. We may infer two points from this situation. First, the absence of this theme in Tibullus *could* be a striking political statement conveying the elegist's disregard for Augustus' worldly powers. However, countercultural gestures in Latin love elegy are rarely unmediated, authentic expressions of resistance. Moreover, Tibullus in elegy 1.7 does employ divinizing language to reflect and foreshadow the achievements of his well-travelled patron Messalla, who was an important ally of Octavian/Augustus.[119] The poem's encomium of

---

[114] White (1993).   [115] White (1993) 169–82.

[116] White (1993) 170–1; quotation from p. 170.

[117] Chapter 4 will show that the poets' interest in Augustus' divinity not only lasted beyond the mid-20s but even intensified.

[118] Though it would be naïve to assume that Maecenas had no influence whatsoever.

[119] For further discussion of Tib. 1.7, see Gaisser (1971); Bright (1975); Konstan (1978); Moore (1989); Knox (2005); Bowditch (2011).

30 POLITICS AND DIVINIZATION IN AUGUSTAN POETRY

Osiris/Bacchus as a culture hero (1.7.29–48), as one recent study suggests, 'may play into Messalla's own contributions to civilization as a road-builder' (cf. 1.7.57–64),[120] which in turn reflects positively on the Augustan expansionist project. Thus, the absence of Augustus' divinization as a literary theme in Tibullus' poetry is more likely to be muted acceptance than silent protest.

The second, and critical, point is that the absence of this theme in Tibullus' work indicates that its *presence* in the poetry of Virgil, Horace, and Propertius is the product of conscious *choice*. The contemporaries of Tibullus evidently took it upon themselves to discuss this issue when (as his work shows) they could have avoided it altogether. And this is where my work fundamentally differs from those of White and others. I understand the prominence of this theme in the works of Virgil, Horace, and Propertius not (or at least not only) as an extension or reflection of something external; but as a crucial communicative tool to which the poets frequently turn in their own negotiation of Rome's political change. By examining the texts of Virgil, Horace, and Propertius from this new perspective, I intend the following chapters to demonstrate that the motif of Augustus' divinization functioned a lot like a language of political science for these poets.

Outline of Contents

Chapter 1 ('*Libertas*, Peace, and Divine Dependence') examines how the motif of divinization is centrally involved in the poets' attempts to understand and reconcile with the changing parameters of *libertas* as Rome gradually falls under the control of Augustus. I argue that, in the *Eclogues*, *libertas* is already being characterized as something that can only be mediated by the acceptance of a more authoritarian regime. The First *Eclogue* especially disembeds *libertas* from its political context, conflates it with *otium*, and reimagines it as a condition which only an exceptionally powerful benefactor can guarantee. In this way, the pastoral drama centred around Tityrus' worship of his *iuvenis* encapsulates a discourse whereby *libertas* and dependence on extraordinary political power, freedom and subjection, are notionally compatible, thereby foreshadowing the defining ideological character of the Augustan Principate. As the new regime takes shape, however, the poets' depiction of Augustus as a divine guarantor of peace becomes a way of reflecting on the limits of *libertas* under the Principate. Here I lay the groundwork through a reading of Livy's

---

[120] Roman (2014) 159.

Preface. Then, shifting my focus onto the *sphragis* of Virgil's *Georgics* and Propertius' elegy 3.4, I suggest that the poets frame the return of peace to Rome under Augustus as a form of civic security underpinned by political subordination and that the divine portraits of Augustus in these poems highlight the simultaneously overwhelming and indispensable nature of his power.

Chapter 2 ('Divinization and the Transformation of Rome from Republic to Principate') is chiefly concerned with the poetry produced around the time of the battle of Actium. Here I argue that the poets' deployment of divinizing imagery is synchronized with the dawning realization that a new political order is about to emerge in Rome. My reading of Horace's *Epode* 9 and *Satire* 2.1 demonstrates that the language of 'aboveness', singular prominence, and divine status in these poems is not simply a trope expressing a power gap, but also reflects an attempt by the poet to work out and reconcile with the new regime. Following on from this, the chapter presents a reading of the shifting relationship between poet and Caesar in Virgil's *Georgics*. I argue that the interactions between these two figures in the course of the poem dramatize Rome unstoppable drift towards autocracy. The poem begins with Virgil attempting to direct the career of Octavian through his poetry, but ends with the poet accepting that he is unable to alter the heaven-reaching path which Octavian has created for himself. By conflating his diminishing poetic efficacy with the emergence of Octavian as a self-determining authority, Virgil underscores (and prepares himself for) the changing relationship between creative power and Augustan power in the aftermath of Actium. The final part of Chapter 2 picks up on, and fleshes out, a recurrent theme in Horace's and Virgil's divinizing representations of Octavian around the time of Actium, namely Octavian's growing stature as a legal authority (cf. Hor. *Sat.* 2.1; Verg. *G.* 4.561–2). Through a discussion of Prop. 2.7 and the elegist's much later elegy 4.11—both of which deal with Augustan marital *leges* and depict Augustus' legal authority in divine terms—I argue that Propertius' divinizing language underlines the extent to which personal speech and individual action are increasingly coming under state control as Rome steps out of the shadows of the civil war and looks ahead to the formation of the Principate.

Chapter 3 ('Conquest and Immortality in Horace's *Odes*') focuses on Horace's lyrically inflected discussions of Augustus' divinization in the first three books of the *Odes*, a work of 23 BC. I interpret them within the broader context of Roman imperialism and the regime's attempt to control the political narrative of post-civil war Rome. The chapter offers a two-pronged argument. Firstly, I argue that Horace's presentation of Augustus' divinization draws attention to the extent to which the discourse of Rome's remarkable transformation—from being mired in civil strife to pacifying the world again—has contributed to Augustan power. While the *Odes* on the whole frame Augustus' mission to be a deified *Weltherrscher* as mirroring the expansion of Roman imperial authority, the ways in which Horace renders ambiguous the distinctions between triumph and defeat, Roman and foreign, and self and other in many of the poems (most notably in *Carm.* 1.37) obliquely contest the idea of *pax parta victoriis* ('peace acquired by victories'; cf. Aug. *R.G.* 13) and the regime's reinvention of civil war as foreign conflict. Building on this, the second prong of my argument is that the issue of Augustus' divinization is used by Horace as a proxy to discuss the incompatibility between Horatian lyric and Augustan panegyric—between creative authority and political allegiance. I emphasize how Horace—especially in the 'Bacchic Odes' (e.g. *Carm.* 2.7, 2.19, 3.25) and the 'Roman Odes' (*Carm.* 3.1–6)—presents the motif of Augustus' divinization as something that tests both the limits of his lyric poetry and his credentials as a nationalistic *vates*. By framing the topic of Augustus' apotheosis in this way, Horace implicitly conveys that even his most panegyrical poems are underpinned by a tension between accepting the regime's self-mythologizing discourse and holding onto his artistic and ideological autonomy.

Chapter 4 ('Divinization and the Inevitability of Augustan Rome') further develops the argument that poetry's presentation of Augustus' divinization is deeply concerned with the Augustan rewriting of history. Focusing on Virgil's *Aeneid*, but also bringing into discussion Horace's *Carmen Saeculare* and Propertius 4.6, I argue that the poets' formulation of Augustus' divinization as the predestined culmination of Roman history both reflects and interrogates the teleological thinking and ideological distortion that underpin the regime's claim to supremacy. Primarily, this chapter aims to demonstrate that prophecies of Augustus' divinization in the *Aeneid* may be read as the poem's critique of its own involvement in the Augustan reinvention of history. I suggest firstly that the tension between inevitability and contingency in the poem's prophetic scenes may be interpreted as Virgil's way of showing to the reader that there are different ways of viewing Augustus' rise to power—different ways of thinking about the past and the future of Rome: as predestined, or as a process that is unknowable and rarely straightforward. I argue further that, in these prophetic scenes, Virgil emphasizes that the perception of history as 'fate' relies heavily upon representation; and I show that in doing so the poet foregrounds the role his epic plays in the rewriting of the past. Thus highlighting reinvention's dependence on representation, Virgil gestures at how his poetry inculcates the regime's retelling of the past, renders Augustan supremacy 'inevitable', and reframes ideological construct as imperial fact.

The *Aeneid*'s interrogation of its own role in the retelling of history as destiny not only serves to draw the reader's attention to the slippage between reality and representation in contemporary political discourse but also encapsulates the frictions and complicities between art and power in the 'post-truth' age of Augustus.

The Epilogue ('To Divinity and Beyond') firstly summarizes the core arguments of the previous chapters. Then, in the second part, I focus on a few passages from Horace's *Odes* 4, and explore how the main points of this study could be extended. Alternating between backward glances to Augustus' achievements and proleptic visions of the future of the Principate, Horace's final collection of lyric poetry is an apt place on which to end. In my reading of *Odes* 4, I draw attention to the idea that on the one hand this poetic collection makes frequent references to the ageing of Augustus (a biological process from which the gods are immune), while on the other hand it constantly emphasizes that the 'golden age-esque' stability of Roman society is entirely tied up with the presence of the *princeps* and the perpetuation of his authority. Thus *Odes* 4 is underpinned by tensions between the unstoppable passage of time and the desire for timelessness, absence and presence, finality and perpetuity. I suggest that Horace's presentation of the divinization of Augustus in *Ode* 4.5 encapsulates these tensions; and that as such, this motif presents a way for the poet to diplomatically raise the issue that the *aetas* of Augustus (cf. *tua, Caesar, aetas*, 4.15.4) will have to come to an end at some point. As Horace frames the divinization of Augustus as the symbolic culmination of a glorious historical process on the one hand, and the transitional point to a future without Augustus on the other, *Odes* 4 powerfully renders apparent the (now insoluble) problem of identifying the peace and stability of Rome with the life of Augustus—the problem of putting the hopes and fears of the state in one *man*.

The decision to focus on the above topics is not intended to suggest that these are the most important aspects of poetry's discourse on Augustus' divinity. Nor, in dividing them into self-contained chapters, do I wish to imply that they are unrelated categories: in fact, I would emphasize that much of the force of this poetic discourse derives from the close connection, or even overlapping, of ideas. The selection of these topics, and their sequence in this book, rather reflect my desire to offer a series of distinctive case studies that capture both the breadth of this theme and the basic chronology of the early years of Augustus' reign.

The poetic texts discussed in this book represent only a small portion of the literary material we have on Augustus' divinity: Ovid's treatment of

34 POLITICS AND DIVINIZATION IN AUGUSTAN POETRY

this topic—especially in his exilic corpus where the poet approaches Augustus as a divine figure from a unique geographical and political perspective—demonstrates other important expressive possibilities of this literary theme.[121] However, there is advantage in focusing closely on Virgil, Horace, and Propertius—the generation that witnessed the transformation from Republic to Principate. By examining how the 'first-generation' Augustan poets used divinizing language in their discussions of Augustus, this book will provide a fresh account of the process by which Roman intellectual elites encountered and came to terms with radical ideological shift, and the extent to which poetry embodied and evolved with political change.

---

[121] See e.g. Lowrie (2009) 259–75; McGowan (2009) 63–92.

1

Libertas, Peace, and Divine Dependence

When Virgil published his First *Eclogue* in 35 BC,[1] in which a young man (*iuvenis*, 1.42) is deified for having restored freedom (*libertas*, 1.27) to Tityrus and released him from enslavement (*servitio*, 1.40), the poet could not have foreseen that some fifty years later Augustus, on the verge of divinization, would open his *Res Gestae* with the sentence:

> annos undeviginti natus exercitum privato consilio et privata impensa comparavi, per quem rem publicam a dominatione factionis oppressam in libertatem vindicavi.

> Aged nineteen years old I mustered an army at my personal decision and at my personal expense, and with it I liberated the state, which had been oppressed by a despotic faction.

It is striking that in both texts the liberation from slavery is tied up to the intervention of a single individual as liberator. While there is no compelling reason to think that Augustus had in mind Virgil's poem when he looked back on the achievements of his life,[2] the thematic correspondence between the opening of the *Res Gestae* and the First *Eclogue* underlines how the official history of a regime can cast a retroactive pall over earlier literary representations,[3] and, conversely, how poetry can express what would eventually become the central tenet of a master narrative. The ways in which the Augustan poets interacted with 'official history', particularly the regime's sanctioned account of the civil war and its attempt to mythologize the supremacy of Augustus, are

---

[1] The composition of individual poems of the *Eclogues* may have started as early as 42 BC: see Coleman (1977) 14–21, though his attempt to ascertain the date of each poem proves inconclusive. The *Eclogues* probably underwent continuous modification until the moment of their publication as a single volume in 35 BC; see Clausen (1994) 125–6 on the revision process, and Bowersock (1971) on the date of publication. Cucchiarelli (2012) 15–16 proposes an earlier publication date of *c.*37 BC.

[2] The opening passage of the *R.G.* does, however, appear to echo the *Philippics*, where Cicero frequently turned to the theme of the young Caesar's liberation of Rome (cf. Cic. *Phil.* 3.3, 3.5, 4.2, 4.4); see Cooley (2009) 109 for further discussion. The notion of political liberation is a prevalent motif in the political writing of the late Republic: see also Lepidus' speech in Sall. *Hist.* 1.

[3] See esp. Galinsky (2006) 6–8, who argues that the Virgilian *libertas* in *Ecl.* 1 correlates precisely with the later Augustan concept of *libertas* as *securitas*.

Politics and Divinization in Augustan Poetry. Bobby Xinyue, Oxford University Press. © Bobby Xinyue 2022.
DOI: 10.1093/oso/9780192855978.003.0002

36 POLITICS AND DIVINIZATION IN AUGUSTAN POETRY

the subjects of two later chapters (Chapter 3 and Chapter 4). In this first chapter, I want to focus on how poetic discourse can be moulded in such a way so as to naturalize or embed the power of the dominant political force.

My principal aim is to show that poetry's naturalizing tendencies can be observed most clearly in the representations of Augustus' restoration of *libertas* in divine terms, which often come hand in hand with the poets' idealization of their inferior status. Virgil, Horace, and Propertius not only depict Augustus as a peace-restoring benefactor who is treated as a god by his beneficiaries but even frame his elevated status and their dependence on his authority as crucial to maintaining civic harmony. I will focus especially on Virgil's First *Eclogue* and argue that this poem plays a significant role in naturalizing the power discourse of the future Principate.[4] By entwining depictions of Augustus as a divine figure with expressions of being content with a life of peaceful pleasure, the poets flatten the difference between subjection and *otium*, thereby embedding voluntary subservience into contemporary political discourse.

As the Principate takes shape, however, poetic depictions of Augustus as a divine bringer of peace begin to operate as a means to critique the nature of *libertas* under Augustan rule. The second half of this chapter will focus on the way in which Virgil and Propertius juxtapose the divinity of Caesar with their otiose self-fashioning. Reading the *sphragis* of the *Georgics* and elegy 3.4 comparatively, I will suggest that the poets situate their *otium* ambiguously between the security of life and the deprivation of individual agency; and that in doing so, Virgil and Propertius draw out the paradox of Augustan power as being both liberating and constraining, indispensable and autocratic.

Divine Self-Imaging and the Battle for *Libertas*

Recent scholarship on the cultivation of divine associations by prominent figures of the late Republic—commonly referred to as 'divine self-imaging'—has drawn attention to how this practice constituted and shaped the political discourse of that time.[5] As Cucchiarelli puts it succinctly, 'the confrontation between the various political leaders took shape in part as a confrontation between different models of divinity.'[6] In fact, all the evidence we have of

---

[4] The present chapter's argument on the *Eclogues* is mostly based on Xinyue (2021).

[5] The most informative recent works on the interaction between 'divine self-imaging' and contemporary poetry are those of Miller (2009) 15–53; Cucchiarelli (2011a) 155–60; Pandey (2018) 36–50. Earlier studies, such as Weinstock (1971), Pelling (1988), and Gurval (1995), remain important. Cole (2013) has shown that divinization and divine impersonation were already an important element of elite discourse by 44 BC.

[6] Cucchiarelli (2011a) 157.

LIBERTAS, PEACE, AND DIVINE DEPENDENCE   37

divine self-imaging in this period points to it being used as a way of articulating political scenarios—tensions, rivalries, allegiances—in suggestive and animated terms.[7] For example, Octavian's self-presentation as the *Divi filius* was a way for him to stake his claim to Caesar's legacy and announce his arrival as a genuine political force.[8] The mutual distrust between Octavian and Antony in the early years of the triumvirate was reflected in the infamous story of Octavian masquerading as Apollo at an 'Olympian' banquet (Suet. *Aug.* 70)— an event that was probably exaggerated (or invented) and circulated by Antony's faction.[9] By the mid-30s, divine impersonation as political discourse appears to have gathered pace. Soon after Sextus Pompey's defeat at Naulochus in 36 BC, Octavian and Antony separately adopted Sextus' Neptunian designs on their own numismatic issues as a means of asserting their maritime supremacy.[10] The appropriative and dialogic character of their practice strongly indicates that divine self-representation was no mere 'role play'. Rather, the image of a 'god-man' captures how different factions of the triumviral period competed for legitimacy and sought to identify themselves with useful political values.

Chief among these contested political values was *libertas*. While 'liberty' for Romans could be broadly defined as a condition of non-domination,[11] in the

[7] There is evidence to suggest that some Italian communities in the mid-30s included Octavian among their own tutelary deities (App. *B Civ.* 5.132, with Marcone 2010: 208–10). But these isolated instances of local worship do not coalesce into a coherent picture of the politicians themselves fostering religious activity through their divine impersonation.

[8] It is tempting to think that Octavian's choice to portray himself as a 'son' may have something to do with the fact that he was once disparagingly referred to as a mere *puer* by some in the Senate (Cic. *Phil.* 13.24; App. *B Civ.* 3.43.176; Suet. *Aug.* 12; Cass. Dio 46.30.1); see Manuwald (2007) I, 94–5. Octavian also appropriated the sidereal iconography following the confirmation of Caesar's deification (1 January 42). See e.g. *RRC* 535/2 (possibly 38 BC): the obverse shows Octavian's head with the legend DIVI·F and a star. The reverse of some earlier issues (*RRC* 525/1–2; 526/1–3) shows Octavian's head with the legend DIVI IULI·F; see further Weinstock (1971) 399–401. In addition, the design of the gilded equestrian monument voted to Octavian in January 43 BC is said to have undergone modification to make its subject resemble a divinity more closely (Cic. *Ad Brut.* 1.15.7; Vell. Pat. 2.61.3; App. *B Civ.* 3.51; Cass. Dio 46.29.2). The change of design can be seen by comparing the images on *RRC* 490/1 and 3 (marked S·C) with those on a later coin, *RRC* 518/2 (marked POPVL·IVSSV); see Zanker (1988) 37–9; Osgood (2006) 117.

[9] On the interpretation of the 'Olympian' banquet, see Charlesworth (1933) 175; Scott (1933) 30; Gagé (1955) 487; Weinstock (1971) 15; Gurval (1995) 96–8; Miller (2009) 16–18. There is sufficient evidence to suggest that prior to Philippi (42 BC) it was Brutus, and not Octavian, who had the strongest public Apolline profile; see Miller (2009) 24–6.

[10] Miller (2009) 24. See Pollini (1990) 344–5 on Antony's naval iconography (*c.*36–35 BC) on *BMCRR* II (East), 149–53. See Zanker (1988) 97 on the cameo of 35–30 BC, which depicts a nude Octavian standing in a chariot holding a trident. Note also that both Horace in *Epode* 4 and, later, Augustus in *R.G.* 25 portray Sextus' faction as slaves-turned-pirates (cf. *latrones atque servilem manum*, Hor. *Epod.* 4.19; *mare pacavi a praedonibus. eo bello servorum* . . . , Aug. *R.G.* 25).

[11] Arena (2012) 8 defines *libertas* as a status of 'non-subjection to the arbitrary will of either a foreign power or a domestic group or individual'. Arena's thinking is critically informed by among others the works of Skinner (1998); Ando (2011); Pettit (2012). See also earlier studies by Wirszubski (1950); Klein (1969) 1–22; Hellegouarc'h (1972) 542–59; Brunt (1988).

38 POLITICS AND DIVINIZATION IN AUGUSTAN POETRY

late Republic *libertas* became an extremely polysemous notion that 'meant different things to different people' as various political factions competed to be associated with it.[12] Following the assassination of Julius Caesar, Brutus and Cassius naturally identified themselves as the *liberatores*, thus giving the term *libertas* an anti-Caesarian dimension. But after their defeat at Philippi, Octavian and Antony each claimed to be protecting the *libertas* of the state.[13] Later, when the relationship between these two men broke down, the new Caesar, as we saw above (cf. *R.G.* 1), asserted that he protected *libertas* by keeping Antony—the unnamed *factio* in the opening of the *Res Gestae*—away from Rome. The Dionysiac identity cultivated by Antony in the Greek East was weaponized against him by Octavian, who portrayed his rival as a morally bankrupt, disorderly, and foreign force that threatened Roman *libertas*.[14]

The poetry of the triumviral period was particularly alive to the political struggle for *libertas*. The studies of Du Quesnay, Kennedy, and Henderson, among others, have shown that in *Satires* 1 (a near-contemporary of the *Eclogues*), Horace repeatedly sought to suggest that Maecenas and Octavian—and not the defeated enemy of Octavian—were the true protectors of *libertas*.[15] In the case of Virgil's First *Eclogue*, critics have long thought that Tityrus' attainment of *libertas* indirectly casts a positive light on Octavian. For example, Clausen has argued that the poem 'deliberately confuses the private with the public sense of *libertas*' in order to produce a coded praise of Octavian.[16] In a similar vein, but more teleological in his presentation, Galinsky has suggested that the Virgilian notion of *libertas* as 'freedom *from* interference and oppression' was precisely the concept of liberty that was later operative under Augustus.[17]

---

[12] Brunt (1988) 283. Arena (2012) 244–57 shows that, in the lead-up to the battle of Mutina (43 BC), claiming to support *libertas* became a convenient way of gaining political legitimacy for opposing sides.

[13] See Tatum (2020a) 208–9 on Antony's attempt to associate himself with *libertas* in the immediate aftermath of Philippi. Prior to that, in 44–43 BC Antony positioned himself as the true *libertatis vindex* in response to Cicero's allegation that he threatened republican freedom; see Tatum (2020a) 189–207. Welch (2020) makes a strong case for seeing Antony as an innovative and effective image-maker, whose self-representation on coinage and in speeches made him a difficult opponent for Cicero and Octavian.

[14] On Antony's self-identification with Dionysus, see esp. Brenk (1995); also Pollini (1990); La Rocca (1992); Tatum (2020b) 452–5. It is worth noting that Antony's Dionysian impersonation may have had a mixed reception even in Greece and the East: see Plut. *Ant.* 24.4–5, with a recent discussion by Mac Góráin (2020) 21.

[15] Du Quesnay (1984) 27–32; Kennedy (1992) 29–33; Henderson (1994) 81. Later in *Epode* 9, Horace implicitly assimilated Octavian's victories at Naulochus and Actium, and strongly implied that they were wars of 'liberation' and not civil wars (*Neptunius | dux ... | minatus Vrbi vincla*', 'the Neptunian leader threatened to put the City in chains', 7–9; '*Romanus ... | emancipatus feminae | ... miles et spadonibus | servire rugosis potest*', 'a Roman, enslaved to a woman ... and, a soldier no less, is capable of serving wrinkled eunuchs', 11–14).

[16] Clausen (1994) 31–2.   [17] Galinsky (2006) 6, original emphasis.

The present study takes the position that something more—and far more insidious—is at play in the First *Eclogue*. In an illuminating study of the poetic language of patronage, Bowditch has argued that, by assimilating the social discourse of benefaction to the conventions of bucolic voluntarism, Virgil's *Eclogues* naturalize the triumviral political structure in which power lies in the hands of the oligarchic few.[18] In this chapter, I take a similarly suspicious view of the First *Eclogue*'s apparently sanguine attempt at fostering a connection between the unnamed benefactor and *libertas*.[19] Whereas Bowditch's study ultimately finds that the First *Eclogue* reproduces and reinforces the framework of the triumvirate, I argue that the poem's portrayal of the relationship between Tityrus and the *iuvenis* implicitly endorses the idea that *libertas* cannot be achieved without accepting a *new* system of power. I will show firstly that *Eclogue* 1 from its outset attempts to associate the benefactor's power with pastoral stability, and that, as the poem proceeds, *otium* is conflated with *libertas*. This conflation of *otium* and *libertas* serves to disembed *libertas* from its contemporary political context, reframing it evasively as a condition which only an extraordinary benefactor can guarantee, thus sanctifying the concentration of power in one man's hands.

Next, I will expand on this reading and tackle head-on the question of who the poem's *iuvenis* is. I wish to make the case that the anonymity of the *iuvenis* should not be treated as a riddle to which Octavian (or anyone else) is the answer.[20] Virgil does not so much invite the reader to identify the deified *iuvenis* with Octavian as create an image of a political system with a single powerful 'liberator' at its centre—an image that comes remarkably close to the Augustan

---

[18] Bowditch (2001) 121–3.

[19] As with Bowditch, my 'suspicious' approach is informed by the notion of 'negative hermeneutics', which was first discussed by Paul Ricoeur (1965: 33–44) and developed further by Fredric Jameson (1971). As Jameson (1971: 119–20) explains: 'We must ... distinguish between what Paul Ricoeur has called negative and positive hermeneutics, between the hermeneutics of suspicion and the hermeneutics of a restoration of some original, forgotten meaning .... For Ricoeur, of course, the latter cannot be imagined as anything other than the sacred .... Negative hermeneutic, on the other hand, is at one with modern philosophy itself, with those critiques of ideology and illusory consciousness which we find in Nietzsche and in Marx.'

[20] Scholars generally identify this *iuvenis* as Octavian, or at least as an allusion to him. Even among those who do not, the approach is generally one of candidate-searching. Liegle (1943) 219–26 argues that the *iuvenis* is L. Antonius, brother of the triumvir and leader of one side in the Perusine War. Grisart (1966) thinks that the *iuvenis* is Virgil himself. Berkowitz (1972) 26 n. 26 makes the case for Varus, or Gallus, or Pollio, with the latter gaining further support from Cairns (2008) 70–4. Wright (1983) suggests that the *iuvenis* resembles Apollo. Critics interested in the Epicurean tenets of *Eclogue* 1 argue that the poem's image of the deified benefactor brings to mind Epicurus: see esp. Bing (2016); but also Rundin (2003); Hardie (2006a) 290–1; Papanghelis (2006) 376–7; Karakasis (2011) 176–7; Davis (2012) 79–98; Scholl (2014) 493–4. Relatedly, Kronenberg (2016) draws attention to the presence of Lucretius in Virgil's depiction of the *iuvenis* and Daphnis in *Eclogues* 1 and 5, respectively. One exception is Mayer (1983) 20–6, who treats the *iuvenis* as a symbol of Rome's power for the good.

40 POLITICS AND DIVINIZATION IN AUGUSTAN POETRY

Principate. It is this prefigurative instantiation of the Augustan regime that has played a large part in persuading readers to see the *iuvenis* as Octavian.

I will then contextualize my reading of the First *Eclogue* more broadly within the collection, and offer new reflections on Virgil's depiction of the saviour-figure in *Eclogues* 9 and 4. It will be argued that Virgil's poetic anonymization throughout the *Eclogues* is no simple pastoral obfuscation, but rather does the hard graft of soft launching a new political system.

Eclogue 1: A Sign of Things to Come

Benefaction, *otium*, and *libertas*

Both the volatility of the triumviral period and the disruption to rural life caused by Octavian's settlement of veterans after Philippi (Suet. *Aug.* 13) can be detected in the opening exchange of the First *Eclogue*.[21] Meliboeus' song (*Ecl.* 1.1–5), which discloses that he is about to face exile (1.3–4) while his companion Tityrus somehow manages to hold on to pastoral security (1.1–2, 4–5), already hints at the idea that the shepherds themselves are not in control of their lives.[22] Tityrus' reply, while confirming that he is indeed more fortunate, highlights further the shepherds' lack of agency (1.6–10):

> *T:*   O Meliboee, deus nobis haec otia fecit.
>   namque erit ille mihi semper deus, illius aram
>   saepe tener nostris ab ovilibus imbuet agnus.
>   ille meas errare boves, ut cernis, et ipsum
>   ludere quae vellem calamo permisit agresti.   10

Tityrus: O Meliboeus, it is a god who gave us this peace—for a god he shall ever be to me; often shall a tender lamb from our folds stain his altar. He allowed my oxen to roam, as you see, and I myself to play what I wish on my rustic pipe.

---

[21] On the dissatisfaction of both the veterans and the threatened landowners, see App. *B Civ.* 5.12–13; Cass. Dio 48.6–12. While ancient biographies of Virgil claim that the poet's farm was confiscated and returned to him (cf. Donat. *Vit. Verg.* 19), it is patently clear that this story was extrapolated from the poem itself. See esp. Farrell (2002) 24–6; Korenjak (2003); Laird (2009).

[22] On the exilic connotation of *patriam fugio*, cf. *OLD* s.v. *fugio* and Coleman (1977) on *patriae* at 1.3. See also Ov. *Tr.* 1.5.65–6 (clearly reacting to the opening lines of *Eclogue* 1): *ille suam laetus patriam victorque petebat:* | *a patria fugi victus et exul ego* ('He was seeking his native land in joy and as a victor; I have fled mine, defeated and an exile').

The verbs *fecit* (1.6) and *permisit* (1.10) make clear that the pleasures of pastoral life, namely singing and herding (1.1–2, 4–5, 9–10), which Tityrus generalizes as *otia* (1.6), are possible only because a 'god' had granted them.[23] The shepherd himself had no hand in procuring his present condition. Since Tityrus' explanation rests firmly on his conviction that this good fortune has been mediated exclusively through divine agency, it follows that he implicitly recognizes its inherently contingent nature.[24] By expressing his gratitude in this way, Tityrus' words underscore the extent to which the livelihood of these shepherds is dependent on the whim of a single benefactor.

What also stands out from this opening exchange is the way Tityrus engages with Meliboeus' language of contrasting experience (cf. *tu* and *nos*, 1.1–4), appropriating it to insinuate that his benefactor can transform not only his own fortune but the lives of many. In his response to Meliboeus, Tityrus quickly asserts that he is one of a number of shepherds who have benefitted from the god (*nobis*, 1.6), even though the shift from *nobis* to *mihi* in the next line (1.7) indicates that the decision to treat this benefactor as a god is Tityrus' own.[25] In the next two lines, Tityrus repeats the same trick: *nostris . . . ovilibus* (1.8) creates the impression that a community of shepherds is making sacrifice to this provider of *otium*, but *meas . . . boves* (1.9) makes one wonder who else other than Tityrus has seen such a good turn of fortune. Thus in his response to Meliboeus' suggestion that the shepherds are suddenly divided into those who have and those who have not, Tityrus repeatedly tries to pass his individual blessing off as a shared positive experience, thereby countering any claim that this benefactor could have sown division in the pastoral community. Combined with his usage of the time-defying adverbs *semper* (1.7) and *saepe* (1.8), Tityrus conjures up an idealized image of a patron–beneficiary relation, whereby an act of benefaction will restore long-lasting peace and common satisfaction. For Tityrus, the honouring of his benefactor as a divinity is no mere personal expression of gratitude, but a unifying societal ritual.

---

[23] Note the contrast between efficacy (*fecit*, 1.6) and the frivolousness of Tityrus' action (*ludere*, 1.10). *Ludere*, of course, can also be read metapoetically as the production of Callimachean poetry.

[24] Davis (2012) 20.

[25] See Coleman (1977) on 1.7; Du Quesnay (1981) 104; Clausen (1994) on 1.7. The plural *nobis* (1.6) also disputes Meliboeus' suggestion that Tityrus' good fortune is a case of individual blessing (cf. the repetition of *tu* at verses 1 and 4). Of course, plural pronouns can equally well refer to an individual as to a collective; cf. Lucr. 5.19 (Lucretius on Epicurus), *quo magis hic merito nobis deus esse videtur* ('for which reason he more rightly seems to be a god to us'), where *nobis* could refer to the poet himself or both Lucretius and Memmius, the latter mentioned a little earlier in the text (Lucr. 5.11); for further discussion, see Bing (2016) 175.

42 POLITICS AND DIVINIZATION IN AUGUSTAN POETRY

Perplexed by Tityrus' good fortune, Meliboeus then asks him about his 'god' (*sed tamen iste deus qui sit, da, Tityre, nobis,* 'But still, tell me, Tityrus, who is that god?', 1.18). At first, Tityrus avoids answering the question by telling Meliboeus that he went to Rome (1.19–20).[26] However, when Meliboeus presses him on why he had visited the city, Tityrus finally offers a proper reply, but still keeps the nature of his *deus* elusive (1.26–35):

> *M:* Et quae tanta fuit Romam tibi causa videndi?
> *T:* Libertas, quae sera tamen respexit inertem,
> candidior postquam tondenti barba cadebat,
> respexit tamen et longo post tempore venit,
> postquam nos Amaryllis habet, Galatea reliquit.   30
> namque (fatebor enim) dum me Galatea tenebat,
> nec spes libertatis erat nec cura peculi.
> quamvis multa meis exiret victima saeptis,
> pinguis et ingratae premeretur caseus urbi,
> non umquam gravis aere domum mihi dextra redibat.   35

Meliboeus: And what was the great occasion of your seeing Rome?
Tityrus: Freedom, who, though late, yet cast her eyes upon me in my sloth, when my beard began to whiten as it fell beneath the scissors. Yet she did cast her eyes on me, and came after a long time—after Amaryllis began her sway and Galatea left me. For—yes, I must confess—while Galatea ruled me, I had neither hope of freedom nor thought of savings. Though many a victim left my stalls, and many a rich cheese was pressed for the thankless city, never would my hand come home money-laden.

It appears that Tityrus went to Rome in order to free himself from the psychological and emotional captivity caused by his amatory encounters (1.30–2), as well as to procure some kind of alleviation from unrewarding labour (1.33–5). The terms *libertas* (1.27; *spes libertatis*, 1.32) and *cura peculi* (1.32), both set within the context of economic exchange and poverty (1.33–5), have generally encouraged scholars to view Tityrus as a literal slave and interpret his quest for 'freedom' as manumission.[27] At the same time, since amatory themes are frequent in Theocritus' *Idylls* and here Virgil's shepherd is recounting his love life, the language of entrapment in Tityrus' speech (*me Galatea*

---

[26] This conceit recalls the convention of naming the *sedes* of the *laudandus* in a hymn for a deity; see Du Quesnay (1981) 113; Davis (2012) 23.

[27] See e.g. Coleman (1977) 89–91; Du Quesnay (1981); Clausen (1994) 30–1; Wimmel (1998) Galinsky (2006).

tenebat, 1.31) may suggest that his slavery is also to some extent metaphorical, and that *libertas* for him is not just manumission, but also the freedom from *servitium amoris* (specifically from Galatea).[28]

The ambiguity of *libertas* cannot be solved by the poem's opening image of Tityrus' pastoral security either. There, he may be construed as both a freedman who has managed to retain his possessions and a lover who is untroubled by his amatory life (*formosam resonare doces Amaryllida silvas*, 'you teach the woods to resound "fair Amaryllis"', 1.5). In fact, Tityrus' earlier designation of these delights in his life as *otia* (1.6) blurs the distinction between economic and political stability and the contented ease of an individual, thereby conflating 'freedom' with 'pleasure'. *Libertas* understood as manumission or the status of non-subjection implies the attainment or reassertion of agency, control and self-governing authority. However, by conflating *libertas* with the return of pleasant pastoral life, the term is stripped of its acute political meaning and anti-authoritarian resonance. Instead, as we approach the midpoint of Virgil's poem and with the presence of the benefactor looming, *libertas* appears to be framed as something akin to an untroubled life, but which can only be mediated through external intervention. Set against a contemporary political climate where the meaning and ownership of *libertas* were fluid and constantly appropriated, the poem's dissociation of *libertas* from its immediate Roman context is no accident. I would suggest that Tityrus' evasive aestheticization of his 'liberty', along with the shepherd's enthusiastic worship of his *iuvenis*, translate the factional political competition for *libertas* into a quest to find the benefactor who could bring about a better way of life. In doing so, the First *Eclogue* creates a new discourse of *libertas* that not only presumes the subject's lack of agency but even idealizes external intervention as salvific power.

Who (or What) Is the *Iuvenis*?

This particular discourse of *libertas* is exactly what we find when Tityrus finally reveals how he met his benefactor (1.40–5):

> *T*: Quid facerem? neque servitio me exire licebat   40
>   nec tam praesentis alibi cognoscere divos.

---

[28] Eckerman (2016) 262–3; anticipated by Clausen (1994) 44–5. Eckerman convincingly identifies an allusion to Theoc. *Id.* 14.52–5 in Tityrus' account of how he found emotional alleviation by leaving home and his mistress. Note later at 1.40 (*servitio . . . exire*), it is still not clear whether Tityrus' servitude is literal or metaphorical.

44 POLITICS AND DIVINIZATION IN AUGUSTAN POETRY

> hic illum vidi iuvenem, Meliboee, quotannis
> bis senos cui nostra dies altaria fumant.
> hic mihi responsum primus dedit ille petenti:
> 'pascite ut ante boves, pueri; summittite tauros.'   45

Tityrus: What was I to do? I could not quit slavery nor elsewhere find gods so ready to aid. Here, Meliboeus, I saw that youth for whom our altars smoke twelve times a year. Here he was the first to give my plea an answer: 'Feed your oxen as before, boys; rear your bulls.'

In this account, Tityrus emphasizes again his inability to take action for himself through the impersonal construction *me . . . licebat* (1.40).[29] His instinct, as the next verse shows, is to find help from greater authorities (*divos*, 1.41).[30] However, the most remarkable aspect of this report is that, instead of elucidating what happened during his encounter with the *iuvenis*, Tityrus rather obfuscates what his benefactor actually did. While it is clear that Tityrus' condition has been transformed from a state of *servitium* to *libertas*, the quoted injunction of the *iuvenis* (1.45) suggests not so much a liberation, but rather a restoration (*ut ante*, 'as before', 1.45). To be sure, the attainment of new liberty and the return to pastoral vocation are not necessarily mutually exclusive; but Tityrus ostensibly conflates *libertas* with *otium* again, or at least fails to make any meaningful distinction between the two. For this grateful devotee of the *iuvenis*, freedom, peace, and pleasure mean much the same thing.

Even though both the identity of the *iuvenis* and the precise nature of his intervention are concealed by Virgil's poem, critics have not stopped trying to ascertain who the *iuvenis* is.[31] As mentioned above, ancient commentators and modern scholars have frequently suggested Octavian as the candidate, since he carried out the land confiscations and claimed the title *Divi filius*

---

[29] Eckerman (2016) 262.

[30] Modern scholars generally agree that *divus* (1.41) here is just a variation of *deus*. Note also its appearance in Hor. *Carm.* 3.5.2–4 in connection with Augustus: *praesens divus habebitur | Augustus adiectis Britannis | imperio gravibusque Persis* ('Augustus will be held a god in our midst when Britons and dread Persians are added to the empire'). Outside the poetic context, however, there is a significant distinction between *divus* and *deus*. As Price (1984b: 83) points out, from the cult of the deceased Julius Caesar onwards, *divus* in official terminology referred exclusively to former emperors and members of their family. But whether some kind of distinction had already existed when the deceased Julius Caesar was given the title *divus* remains unclear. Varro's attempts to define these two terms (Serv. ad *Aen.* 12.139 = Varro *Ling.* fr. 2 Goetz–Schoell; Serv. ad *Aen.* 5.34 = Varro fr. 424 Funaioli) are considered unsatisfactory by modern critics; see Weinstock (1971) 29; Gradel (2002) 63–6; Koortbojian (2013) 7–8.

[31] There is, I think, a subtle but important difference between active concealment (what Virgil does here) and leaving the details of a high-stakes situation vague (e.g. what Horace does in *Sat.* 1.5 with regard to the purpose of his trip and the whereabouts of Octavian).

during this period. Moreover, given that he was the only triumvir in Rome at the time of the *Eclogues'* composition (whereas Antony was in the East and Lepidus was exiled to Circeii after the battle of Naulochus), and Virgil's poem underscores Rome as the site of the perceived divine intervention (cf. *hic*, 1.42 and 44), Octavian's presence in the city makes him even more likely to be the historical person behind Virgil's *iuvenis*.[32] Indeed, the depiction of Octavian as a salvific, divine young man has a precedent in Cicero's Fifth *Philippic* (delivered on 1 January 43 BC). The orator paints a bleak image of life starved of hope and freedom under Antony (*nondum ullos duces habebamus, non copias; nullum erat consilium publicum, nulla libertas*, 'we did not yet have any leaders, nor forces; there was no public council, no freedom', *Phil.* 5.42), and he welcomes the arrival of Octavian (5.43):

> quis tum nobis, quis populo Romano obtulit hunc divinum adulescentem deus? qui, cum omnia ad perniciem nostram pestifero illi civi paterent, subito praeter spem omnium exortus prius confecit exercitum quem furori M. Antoni opponeret quam quisquam hoc eum cogitare suspicaretur.

> What god then presented to us and to the Roman people this godlike young man? When every road to our destruction lay open to that baneful citizen, suddenly, to the surprise of all, *he* arose: he got together an army to oppose Marcus Antonius' madness before anyone suspected him of such a thought.

Cicero's young Octavian is a *divinus* liberator, whose appearance is sudden, whose help unexpected and whose action emphatically effective.[33] This depiction of the *Divi filius* is similar to that of the *iuvenis* in the First *Eclogue*. Tityrus' suggestion that the Roman youth was more *praesens* (1.41) than divinities from elsewhere,[34] and the shepherd's claim that he had 'seen' (*vidi*, 1.42) his saviour,[35] whose oracular injunction (*responsum*, 1.44) he could vividly

---

[32] See also Cucchiarelli (2011a) 159–60.

[33] In Cicero's speech, the overlapping of political and religious discourses is encapsulated in the word *exortus*, which elevates Octavian's status and evokes the emergence of a celestial divinity (further connecting Octavian to the apotheosis of Julius Caesar).

[34] *Praesens* evokes the Hellenistic concept of a sovereign as θεὸς ἐπιφανής: see Cucchiarelli (2012) on 1.41. On divine rulers as 'present' deities in the Hellenistic world, see Koenen (1993) 65; Clauss (1996), esp. 406–7; Chaniotis (2011) 174–6. Note also that Cicero records Hercules as a benefactor of mankind with the description *tantus et tam praesens* (Cic. *Tusc.* 1.28), which further suggests that *praesens* is used of those who are semi-divine or deified for their earthly acts of salvation.

[35] Note also Tityrus' promise later in the poem, that he would never forget the 'face' of his saviour (*illius ... vultus*, 1.63).

46 POLITICS AND DIVINIZATION IN AUGUSTAN POETRY

report,[36] combine to create the impression that Tityrus' encounter with the *iuvenis* was surprising, timely, and close to the experience of a divine epiphany.

However, this correspondence between the Ciceronian Octavian and the Virgilian *iuvenis* should not necessarily be adduced as further evidence for Octavian being the candidate. Elsewhere in the *Eclogues*, Virgil mentions contemporary Roman political figures without any ambiguity: the names of Pollio, Varus, Julius Caesar, and Gallus appear explicitly in *Eclogues* 4, 6, 9, and 10.[37] Therefore we must infer that the undisclosed identity of the divine benefactor in *Eclogue* 1 is a salient artistic choice, and that this choice is not an obstacle to interpretation, but has a bearing on it.[38]

The point of this act of anonymization, I would suggest, is twofold. Firstly, the anonymity of the deified *iuvenis* helps to distance the image of the 'god-man'—perhaps especially Octavian's image as the *Divi filius*—from the suffering and strife described in the poem, and to re-connect it with positive change. The poem's decidedly vague conceptualization of *libertas* as a condition which only the 'god-man' can provide not only turns the triumviral contest for political legitimacy into an apparently noble process of civic emancipation but also reframes divine impersonation as a practice rooted in securing peace and stability. At the same time, as Tityrus insinuates that even the worship of an unidentifiable benefactor could have a unifying effect on a community (cf. 1.6–8), the First *Eclogue* transforms the 'god-man' into a personification of political cohesion, which in turn rehabilitates the image of the *Divi filius* among the poem's contemporary audience.

Secondly, with this act of anonymization Virgil makes it difficult for the reader to identify the *iuvenis* with any one particular figure or tradition of divinization. This pointed avoidance of specificity, I argue, foreshadows Augustus' self-representation and the political language of the Augustan Principate. As critics have noted, Virgil's depiction of the worship of the *iuvenis* is informed not only by contemporary political usages of divinizing imagery but also by several other traditions including Hellenistic ruler cult, Epicurean philosophy, Roman republican hero worship, as well as the poetry of Theocritus, Hesiod, and Callimachus. To be precise, the appearance and reported speech of the *iuvenis* recall the Hesiodic Muses in the *Theogony* (Hes. *Theog.* 24–6) and Callimachus' Apollo in the *Aetia* (Callim. *Aet.*

---

[36] *OLD* s.v. *responsum* 1b, 2a; Du Quesnay (1981) 134; Davis (2012) 27.

[37] Pollio: 4.12. Varus: 6.7–12 and 9.26–7. Julius Caesar: 9.47. Gallus: 6.64 and 10 passim. In addition, the names of the poets Varius and Cinna appear in 9.35.

[38] For a recent critical reconsideration of the significance of anonymity in Latin literature, see Geue (2019), esp. 1–20.

LIBERTAS, PEACE, AND DIVINE DEPENDENCE   47

fr.1.21–4 Harder [= 1.21–4 Pf. = 1.21–4 Mass.]), thereby suggesting that Virgil's *iuvenis* is likewise an initiator of poetry.[39] Meanwhile, the idea of a 'present' god-man (*praesentis*, 1.41) suggests the possible influence of the language and practice of Hellenistic ruler-cult on Virgil's poetry (see n. 34). In terms of the ritual details of Tityrus' worship, they appear to be modelled on the sacrifices which Ptolemy II Philadelphus and Arsinoe are said to have offered to Ptolemy I Soter and Berenice in Theocritus' *Idyll* 17 (especially verses 124–30),[40] as well as the monthly celebrations of Epicurus held by his followers.[41] Furthermore, it is also possible that the offerings given to the *iuvenis* are drawn from the practice of republican hero cult, such as the ones offered to Gaius Marius and Marius Gratidianus.[42] This amalgamation of different traditions attests to the First *Eclogue's* varied dialogues with its poetic predecessors and the lively debate surrounding divinization during the late Republic.[43] On the other hand, by combining a number of figures and traditions in his depiction, Virgil avoids making his *iuvenis* look too much like one thing or the other, thus implying that the *iuvenis* is both the θεὸς ἐπιφανής of Greek ruler cult and the Muse-like figure of Greek poetry (and a whole bunch of other things). In other words, the indecipherability of the status of the *iuvenis* is part of the point. That the exact nature of this revered *iuvenis* is not clearly recognizable, but also not entirely unfamiliar, suggestively epitomizes the ambiguous position Augustus will come to occupy in the Principate. What is more, the conflation of *libertas* and *otium* in Tityrus' speeches culminates in the dissolution of difference between emancipation (from *servitium*) and restoration (cf. *ut ante*); and this discursive evasiveness of Virgil's poem bears

[39] This Hesiodic-Callimachean double-allusion lies in the combination of *primus* (1.44) and *ut ante* (1.45); see Wright (1983) 118–20 and Cucchiarelli (2012) on 1.44–5. The instruction of the *iuvenis* about dealing with animals also contains etymological plays that connote bucolic composition (cf. βουκολέω, Theoc. *Id.* 7.92; βουκολιάζομαι, 7.36, 9.1); see Wright (1983) 114–17.

[40] Hunter (2001) 160. The fact that the *iuvenis* is placed in the exact centre of Virgil's poem is similarly reminiscent of a well-known Theocritean encomiastic motif from the same idyll: ἀνδρῶν δ' αὖ Πτολεμαῖος ἐνὶ πρώτοισι λεγέσθω | καὶ πύματος καὶ μέσσος (*Id.* 17.3–4). See Wright (1983) 119; and also Octavian's appearance at the halfway point of the prologue to the *Georgics* and in the so-called 'proem in the middle' of *Georgics* 3.

[41] Diog. Laert. 10.16–22, with further discussion by Davis (2012) 28. Bing (2016: 176) also points out that the Varronian etymology of *iuvenis* from *iuvare* brings to mind Epicurus, whose name means the one who 'comes to aid' of another (ἐπίκουρος).

[42] Marius received offerings of food and libations along with the gods for his victories over Jugurtha and the Germans: Plut. *Mar.* 27.9; Val. Max. 8.15.7. Lesser offerings of incense and candles were awarded to Marius Gratidianus in 85 BC: Cic. *Off.* 3.80; Sen. *De ira* 3.18.1; Plin. *HN* 33.132. While republican hero worship did not always involve animal sacrifice in the manner of the cult of Tityrus' benefactor, the kind of outburst of popular support for a political leader resulting in the institution of his cult is ostensibly reflected in Tityrus' fervent devotion to his Roman *iuvenis*. See Beard et al. (1998) I, 143–4 for further discussion of the cult of republican politicians.

[43] On the Romans' interest in and scepticism surrounding divinization, see Beard et al. (1998) I, 140–9.

48   POLITICS AND DIVINIZATION IN AUGUSTAN POETRY

the hallmark of the language of the later Augustan Principate, which pointedly refuses to define whether Rome has been transformed or restored by the new Caesar.[44] In short, the divine young man of the First *Eclogue* most probably 'is' Octavian; but when this poetic portrait is consumed within a cultural milieu shaped by and responding to the politics of *libertas* and divine self-imaging, the *iuvenis* is certainly more than *just* Octavian. Reading deep into this image of a deified Roman benefactor who (somehow) heralds both transformation and restoration, it might just be possible to see the silhouettes of the discursive operation of the Augustan Principate.

Poetry and Freedom in a New Age

In this section, I would like to return to the idea that the *iuvenis* of the First *Eclogue*, like the Hesiodic Muses and the Callimachean Apollo, is a kind of poetic initiator. Given that Virgil's poem opens with an image of Tityrus singing freely and without worry (1.1–4), the implication that the *iuvenis* can influence the production of poetry demands further attention. By assimilating the intervention of the *iuvenis* to the inspiration provided by poetic divinities, Virgil may well be drawing on the literary tradition of depicting one's patron as a god.[45] However, the *iuvenis* of the First *Eclogue* appears to have more control over the shepherds' artistic output than an ordinary patron: as Tityrus implied, this young man exclusively granted him the permission to sing (*permisit*, 1.10). If creative productivity and artistic *libertas* are subject not only to divine inspiration and patronal support but also to obtaining permission from a figure of authority, it then raises questions about how free Tityrus' poetic speech really is.[46] Notably, Meliboeus, who has not encountered a powerful benefactor, announces later in the poem that there would be no more songs from him (*carmina nulla canam*, 1.77). Pastoral poetry, and the fictional world it generates, is conventionally built on the premise of an organic exchange of songs between shepherds. However, by subjecting this

---

[44] Geue (2013) 56 also points out that the expression *ut ante* (1.45) functions as a means of naturalizing change via a discourse of continuity; and so the *iuvenis* appears simultaneously as the guarantor *and* inventor of tradition, much like Augustus himself. On interactions between oppositional ideological constructs (such as tradition and innovation) in the Augustan age, see esp. Galinsky (1996).

[45] This motif in Roman literature appears to have its origin in comedy, where parasites refer to their benefactors as divinities or *genii* (see e.g. Plaut. *Mer.* 138).

[46] Roman poets were particularly alive to the idea that certain genres enjoyed more 'freedom' than others, cf. Hor. *Epist.* 2.1.145–55, *Ars P.* 281–4; and Gowers (2012) 148–51, 154–5 on Hor. *Sat.* 1.4. On the poets' sensitivity to the issue of 'free speech' under the Principate, see Feeney (1992).

LIBERTAS, PEACE, AND DIVINE DEPENDENCE   49

creative process to the whim of a benefactor, through which the framework of exchange is replaced by an economy of permission-and-obligation, the First *Eclogue* hints at the poetry's transition into an aesthetic product of a new ideological system.

Indeed, the final scene of *Eclogue* 1 goes even further by suggesting that social cohesion too relies on this new system of benefaction (1.79–83):

> *T:* Hic tamen hanc mecum poteras requiescere noctem
> fronde super viridi: sunt nobis mitia poma,   80
> castaneae molles et pressi copia lactis,
> et iam summa procul villarum culmina fumant
> maioresque cadunt altis de montibus umbrae.

Tityrus: Yet this night you could rest here with me on the green leafage. We have ripe apples, soft chestnuts, and a wealth of pressed cheeses. Even now the housetops afar are smoking and longer shadows fall from the mountain heights.

A lot hangs on how one construes the verb *poteras* (1.79). The form of the imperfect can be hypothetical (i.e. 'you might have/could have rested here with me'), in which case Tityrus is not really offering hospitality, but rather gesturing towards the end of the old dispensation under which it would have been normal for Meliboeus to spend the night at his.[47] But if the *poteras* is supposed to introduce a genuine invitation, then Tityrus' offer of temporary accommodation (1.79) and personal produce (1.80–1) puts *him* in the role of the benefactor. Through this promise of aid, which is delivered in the form of a song-reply (just like the richly poetic speech-act of the *iuvenis*), security and community spirit are thus restored, albeit for one night only (*hanc . . . noctem*, 1.79). Bowditch has argued that here pastoral song succeeds in 'assimilating the social and historical discourse of benefaction to the conventions of bucolic generosity and community', which in turn 'dramatizes the ideological potential of pastoral song . . . to overcome historical division and provide a shared set of values'.[48] By closing his poem with an idealized image of pastoral song mediating social cohesion, Virgil leaves the door open for readers to construe the First *Eclogue* as a text that is complicit in implementing a sociopolitical system that relies on and privileges the agency of an empowered individual. It is in this respect that the First *Eclogue* appears to produce the grammar of

---

[47] I thank Tom Geue for bringing this important point to my attention.
[48] Bowditch (2001) 129.

50 POLITICS AND DIVINIZATION IN AUGUSTAN POETRY

authoritarianism, articulating what will eventually become the central ideological tenets of the Augustan Principate.

Of course, the *Eclogues* are not short of moments where Virgil displays profound sympathy for those who have become victims of the triumvirs' struggle for power. The voice and suffering of Meliboeus in *Eclogue* 1 counteract the poem's discourse of idealized authoritarianism. In *Eclogue* 9, which is widely considered a companion-piece to *Eclogue* 1 (and possibly the earlier of the two), we find another example of this dynamic.[49] Here the shepherd Moeris is forced off his land, just as Meliboeus is in the opening poem; and Moeris' account of the new landowner's tyrannical brutality paints a stark picture of authoritarian power (*haec mea sunt; veteres migrate coloni*, 'these are mine; move on, old tenants', 9.4). In the ensuing exchange between Moeris and Lycidas, we learn that the shepherds had hoped that their song-master Menalcas would come to their rescue in the land dispute, like the *iuvenis* of the First *Eclogue* (*audieram . . . | omnia carminibus vestrum servasse Menalcan*, 'I had heard that your Menalcas had saved everything with his songs', 9.7–10). But this turns out to be false (*audieras, et fama fuit*, 'you had heard it, and that was the story', 9.11), and the failure of Menalcas makes clear that he is no *iuvenis*.

Indeed, *Eclogue* 9 appears to undercut the notion that a powerful figure of authority could make things better. In parallel to the anonymous *iuvenis* who comes to the aid of Tityrus in a moment of crisis, *Eclogue* 9 ends with Moeris appealing for help from a figure of authority identified only as *ipse* (9.66–7):

> *M*: Desine plura, puer, et quod nunc instat agamus;
> carmina tum melius, cum venerit ipse, canemus.

> *Moeris*: Say no more, boy, and let us get on with what is pressing now. We shall sing our songs better, when he himself has come.

Commentators are surely right to identify *ipse* (9.67) as Menalcas, but the vagueness of the final line is troubling. *Venerit* anticipates the arrival of the song-master, but we are not told when that will be. *Melius . . . canemus* looks ahead to the resumption of pastoral singing,[50] but that seems unlikely when

---

[49] *Eclogue* 9 depicts a pastoral world in the aftermath of the post-Philippi land confiscations; but this does not necessarily mean that it was composed in late 42 BC. However, the tone and political outlook of *Eclogue* 9 do seem to point to an earlier date than *Eclogue* 1, which, as some have argued (e.g. Clausen 1972; Coleman 1977: 17–18; Perutelli 1995: 30–1), may well be one of the latest in the collection.

[50] Cucchiarelli (2012) 478 reads this line as the final 'rilancio' of pastoral poetry in the book, before Virgil announces his intention to 'go up' a genre in the final poem (cf. *surgamus*, 10.75).

Menalcas has already failed to save the shepherds with song (9.7–11, above). Indeed, Virgil's poem appears to cast doubt on both the efficacy of song and the prospect of pastoral recovery. Earlier in the poem, Lycidas tries to console Moeris by reciting a song he had once heard from his friend—a song about a blessed age heralded by the star of Caesar (9.44–50; especially, *ecce Dionaei processit Caesaris astrum,* | *astrum quo segetes gauderent frugibus,* 'see the star of Caesar, born of Dione, has risen—the star by which the fields rejoice with corn', 9.47–8).[51] However, Moeris immediately says that he cannot remember singing it (9.51–5). By distancing himself from a song about peace under the deified Caesar, Moeris' reaction not only underlines the fragmentation of shared cultural memory and the breakdown social cohesion in contemporary Rome[52] but also punctures the idealism that the pastoral world can depend on the power of a benefactor for stability. Set against this backdrop where the power of song is repeatedly dismissed in the face of crisis, any optimism in the poem's final line is undercut.

Furthermore, the absence of Menalcas' name in final line of *Eclogue* 9 contrasts sharply with the ending of *Eclogue* 5, which has *Menalca* as its last word (5.90). In that poem, Menalcas not only knew songs like those of *Eclogues* 2 and 3 (5.86–7) but was even able to divinize Daphnis and reinvigorate the pastoral community with song (5.56–80).[53] The absence of Menalcas' name at the end of *Eclogue* 9 therefore hints at the elusiveness of pastoral recovery. If the unknown identity of the salvific *iuvenis* of *Eclogue* 1 adds to his powerful mystique, then the absence of Menalcas' name here does precisely the opposite. Far from signalling that change is under way, the anonymity of *ipse* gestures at the unlikelihood of the shepherds' salvation and the intangibility of hope. As the poem ends, we are left with no secure idea of what help this vaguely identified *ipse* will bring, or when, or how. The poetics of anonymity cuts both ways: it may be used either to open up salvific possibility (all the more potent and appealing for being undefined), or to undermine this potential altogether.

---

[51] Following most modern scholars, I attribute lines 46–50 to Lycidas (rather than Moeris) and identify Moeris as the 'original singer' of this recited song. For further discussion of these textual issues, see Perkell (2001) 73–4.

[52] Meban (2009) 112–15; see also Davis (2012) 42 on the poem's performance of 'consolation of poetic memory'.

[53] Cucchiarelli (2012) 478. On the efficacy of Menalcas' poetic performance, see Lowrie (2009) 145–6. Already by the time of Servius, Virgil's Daphnis was seen as an allegory for Julius Caesar (Serv. ad *Ecl.* 5.20, *alii dicunt significari per allegoriam C. Iulium Caesarem*). Modern scholarship has expanded on the Daphnis-Caesar correspondence: Leach (1974) 182–6; Coleman (1977) 173–4; Dobbin (1995) 32–3; Lowrie (2009) 145 n. 9; Meban (2009) 118–24; Cucchiarelli (2011a) 164; Gale (2013) 280.

52 POLITICS AND DIVINIZATION IN AUGUSTAN POETRY

The tension between the *Eclogues'* naturalization of authoritarian ideology and the poems' sympathy and despair for the victims of despotic forces cannot be resolved. Nor does it need to be. This irresolvability is what makes the pastoral world of the *Eclogues* so pertinent to its contemporary readers: it is through this tension that these poems speak to reality. In other words, to get a better sense of the *Eclogues'* political inclinations, we need to find moments where Virgil lets go of tension and enters instead the realm of idealism. Luckily, there is one such instance: *Eclogue* 4.

In this poem, Virgil envisages the return of the Golden Age inaugurated by the birth of a miraculous *puer*. The poem's unhindered optimism was probably generated by the temporary reconciliation between Octavian and Antony following the Treaty of Brundisium (40 BC), brokered by G. Asinius Pollio.[54] If so, the *puer* at the time of the poem's composition most likely represented an anticipated offspring of Antony and Octavia (whose marriage sealed the alliance), or a symbol of hope for peace in the Roman world.[55]

In its sketch of Rome's Golden Age, *Eclogue* 4 strikes a parallel with *Eclogue* 1 by integrating the idea of willing subjection into its discourse on *libertas*. The poem imagines the forthcoming glorious age first and foremost as a time in which the Roman world will be freed from fear and ancestral sin (*si qua manent sceleris vestigia nostri, | inrita perpetua solvent formidine terras*, 'if some traces of our sin remain, they will be nullified and free the lands from lasting fear', 4.13–14); and we know from the later works of Virgil and Horace that the imagery of the Romans' past sins often operates as a metaphor for the civil war.[56] However, as soon as Virgil proclaims this forthcoming liberation and age of peace for his fellow Romans, the poet makes the anonymous *puer* their ruler (4.15–17):

---

[54] Pollio's consulship is portrayed in *Eclogue* 4 as the incubating period for the Golden Age: 4.11–12.

[55] Coleman (1977) 150–2 offers a summary of the *puer*-identity hypotheses proposed by ancient and modern commentators. Broadly speaking, the *puer* has been variously thought to represent an anticipated offspring of Antony and Octavia (e.g. Du Quesnay 1976: 31–8), or of Pollio (e.g. Cairns 2008: 54–63), or of Octavian (e.g. Harrison 2007a: 39–44). A number of scholars insist on identifying the *puer* with Octavian himself (e.g. Leclercq 1996: 198–206 and Snijder 2010) despite the obvious representational awkwardness. More plausibly, some have suggested that the *puer* could represent Virgil's hope for Octavian (e.g. Cucchiarelli 2012: 240), or the poet's hope for a global transformation from bad fortune to universal peace and prosperity (e.g. Davis 2012: 65). On the cultural origins of the poem's idea of a temporal mega-cycle synced to the birth of a child, see Norden (1924); Rose (1942); and Nisbet (1978), amongst others.

[56] Cf. Verg. *G.* 1.501–2; Hor. *Epod.* 7, *Carm.* 1.2, 1.12. See further discussion in Chapter 3.

LIBERTAS, PEACE, AND DIVINE DEPENDENCE 53

> ille deum vitam accipiet divisque videbit   15
> permixtos heroas et ipse videbitur illis,
> pacatumque reget patriis virtutibus orbem.

He shall receive the gift of divine life, shall see heroes mingled with gods, and shall himself be seen by them, and shall rule the world to which his father's prowess brought peace.

The expression *reget . . . orbem* (4.17) unmistakably carries the connotation of the authoritarian rule of a single man;[57] but in Virgil's formulation of Rome's Golden Age, this form of domination happily coexists with the return of *libertas*. In addition, as Hunter has noted, these lines of *Eclogue* 4 allude to the divinization of the Ptolemies in Theocritus' *Idyll* 17.13–22.[58] By assimilating the *puer* to Hellenistic monarchs, Virgil conflates the beginning of Rome's journey towards a Golden Age of liberty with the introduction of a new, unrepublican, system of power.

Furthermore, just as the First *Eclogue* relies on the conventions of bucolic generosity to naturalize a system of benefaction and inequality, here in *Eclogue* 4 the idea of Golden Age voluntarism is used by Virgil to romanticize consent to autocratic rule. In this passage, the *puer* is depicted as eventually 'accepting' (*accipiet*, 4.15) a life amongst the gods as if he were receiving a gift. The implicit characterization of his divinization as an honour conferred upon a benefactor implies that the reign of the *puer* was something that people gratefully consented to and celebrated. Later in the poem, even the natural world appears to be responding enthusiastically to the boy's reign, as the earth happily produces 'little gifts' for him (*nullo munuscula cultu . . . tellus . . . fundet*, 4.18–20). By the end, socioeconomic exchange ceases to exist and is replaced by agricultural voluntarism (*nec nautica pinus | mutabit merces; omnes feret omnia tellus*, 'nor will the pine ship trade goods; every land will produce everything', 4.38–9).[59] This shift from reciprocity to unidirectional and spontaneous production, glossed here as utopian fecundity, aestheticizes the onset of a hierarchy based on willing submission. By imagining Rome's

---

[57] Bowditch (2001) 135.

[58] Hunter (2001) 160; also Heyworth (2016) 241–2. Verse 16 in particular evokes the Theocritean image of Alexander and Herakles (to whom the Ptolemies traced their ancestry) joining the company of the Olympian gods (Theoc. *Id.* 17.20–2).

[59] Bowditch (2001) 135–7, who offers an excellent discussion of the theme of voluntarism in the poem, reads the *munuscula* as symbol for poetry. See also Stöckinger (2016) 9–10, 30.

54 POLITICS AND DIVINIZATION IN AUGUSTAN POETRY

future in this way, *Eclogue* 4—much like *Eclogue* 1—creates a conceptual framework wherein the advent of autocratic power would be embraced.

However, in not giving this authoritarian system a 'recognizable face', Virgil makes an important point about contemporary Roman politics and the nature of power. Both *Eclogue* 4 and *Eclogue* 1 present an unidentified individual as being more significant than other established forms of power; yet in both instances, Virgil pointedly refuses to identify this one entity that matters. In *Eclogue* 4, the entire Roman world pins its hope on the *puer*, while traditional deities barely feature: they show up when the boy is born (*iam redit et Virgo*, 'now too the Virgin returns', 4.6), politely give their support (*tu modo nascenti puero . . . | casta fave Lucina*, 'only do you, chaste Lucina, smile on the birth of the child', 4.8–10), and wait for him in heaven (4.15–16, above). The *puer* clearly overshadows the importance of the Olympian pantheon. In *Eclogue* 1, Tityrus draws a sharp contrast between the absence and insufficiency of traditional *divi* (1.41) and the presence and power of the singular *iuvenis*. Indeed, one gets the impression that the pastoral world simply would not function without him. Virgil's emphasis on the efficacy of one-ness, I would suggest, mirrors the way that the triumvirate (three men competing for power) is moving towards the Principate (one man in power). In fact, the way in which all the wannabe one-man rulers of the triumviral period identify themselves with *one* particular divinity—and wear these identities as masks that conceal their own—further underscores this movement towards a new, depersonalized one-ness. Against this background, Virgil's strategy of not identifying the actual figure of authority subtly constructs one-man rule as a deeply anonymized form of government, wherein the one person who matters the most is so removed from ordinary mortal men that the locus of power is ultimately unknowable.

To sum up thus far, I have argued that Virgil's First *Eclogue* translates the harsh reality of citizens' disempowerment amid the triumviral contest for political legitimacy into a narrative of liberation, whereby the powerful few, and Octavian in particular, are framed as the only party capable of restoring 'liberty' and bringing positive change. In so doing, the poem not only redefines *libertas* as a condition of security and peacetime pleasure which can only be activated by those who already have political agency but also naturalizes the idea of political benefaction, which necessarily entails subjection and dependence. Combining this particular interpretation of 'liberation' with a story of a benefactor's divinization, Virgil's poem sanctifies a political structure headed by an overwhelmingly influential individual. It hardly matters who this individual is, because Virgil's poem manages to naturalize a *system* of power. The anonymity of the poem's *iuvenis* is part of this naturalizing strategy, as it allows anyone—Octavian or some other charismatic leader—to be placed in the role of society's saviour. And the same anonymizing act is deployed again to a similar effect in *Eclogue* 4. Seen in this light, the divinizing discourse of the *Eclogues* is far more than an expression of gratitude for the benefactor. Rather, by glorifying the idea that beneficent power rests with a singular charismatic man, and by idealizing one's total dependence on an influential benefactor, the *Eclogues* give expression to what will become the central ideological tenets of the Augustan Principate.

Divine Honours and the Problem of Dependence

Following Octavian's victory in the civil war, divine self-imaging qua political discourse did not cease to function, but even intensified. Scholars have identified a number of ways in which Octavian and the Senate deployed divine imagery to present the victor as a god-equalling protector of Rome, elevating the new Caesar to the status of a saviour of the state. Firstly, after the battle of Actium, Octavian's on-site commemoration of his patron god Apollo sealed the affiliation between these two figures that stretched back to at least 36 BC (when Octavian vowed a temple to the god on his Palatine property).[60] Apollo's traditional associations with light and rationality, combined with his opposition to Dionysus (which had been established in Rome as well as in Greece),[61] enabled the victor at Actium to paint himself firmly as the restorer of peace and order. Secondly, Octavian's claim to being the force behind Rome's return to peace was reinforced by a flurry of honours conferred on him by the Senate. As Lange points out, in the period between the news of the victory at Actium announced in Rome and the eventual triumphal return of Octavian almost two years later, the Senate lavished him with numerous honours—some of which placed him on par with the gods of the conventional

---

[60] On the commemorative site in Nicopolis, see Introduction n. 94. Back in Rome, the Palatine temple was still under construction, but it no doubt became quickly associated with the Actian victory, see Miller (2009) 191–3. The eccentric view of Gurval (1995) 118–27, namely that the temple had little association with Actium, should be jettisoned. The current scholarly debate on the circumstances behind Octavian's decision to build the Palatine temple remains polarized: see the differing views of Zanker (1988) 50; Gurval (1995) 115; Galinsky (1996) 213; Hekster and Rich (2006); Miller (2009) 20–3.

[61] On the prevalence of the Apolline–Dionysiac opposition in Roman thought, see esp. Miller (2009) 26–8.

56   POLITICS AND DIVINIZATION IN AUGUSTAN POETRY

Graeco-Roman pantheon.[62] There was the decree that priests and priestesses were to pray for Octavian (as well as the Senate and people), and that a libation was to be poured to him at all public and private banquets (Cass. Dio 51.19.7; cf. Hor. *Carm.* 4.5.31–6; Ov. *Fast.* 2.635–8; Petron. *Sat.* 60).[63] Dio also reports that the Senate arranged for the name of Octavian to be included in public hymns equally with gods (51.20.1; cf. *R.G.* 10.2). These god-equalling honours, or ἰσόθεοι τιμαί,[64] helped to create the impression that the new Caesar was not just any triumphal general, but a larger-than-life guardian of Rome, upon whom the security of the state and the livelihood of citizens were dependent. Indeed, a silver cistophorus minted in Ephesus in 28 BC showed Octavian's head with the title *Libertatis Vindex* on the obverse, and the goddess Pax on the reverse.[65] The iconographical dialogue between the two sides of the coin, which flattens difference between *libertas* and *pax*, emphatically attributes both the non-subjection of the state and the stability of life under the Roman empire to Octavian. By integrating the new Caesar into prayers, libations, and hymns, these honours not only formally enshrined the relationship between Octavian and the Roman citizens as one between divine benefactor and grateful beneficiaries, but also associated the peace and stability of the state—embodied and experienced in the performance of public and private ceremonies—firmly with his exceptional status.

The poets' depiction of Octavian/Augustus in the years soon after the civil war ostensibly intersects with the divinizing measures taken by the Senate to establish Caesar as the unparalleled guardian of Rome. In their works, Virgil and Horace present the relationship between Octavian and the Roman citizens explicitly as one between indispensable saviour and helpless dependents; and through this language of dependence, the poets imply that the fate of Rome now hinges as much on Octavian's power as any traditional divinities. In the final scene of Book 1 of the *Georgics*, which appeared in 29 BC,[66] Virgil casts the reader's mind back to the civil war and invokes the native gods of Rome to allow a certain *iuvenis*—later identified as *Caesar* (1.503)—to come to the Romans' rescue (1.498–501):

---

[62] These honours are recorded mainly in Cass. Dio 51.19.1–20.5. Lange (2009) 125–58 offers a meticulous study of all the honours. He concludes that the accumulated honours point to 'the hope that Octavian would help the *res publica* back to normality and peace (absence from civil war, not war in general)', p. 156.

[63] Lange (2009) 129.   [64] Gradel (2002) 25–9.

[65] See further Galinsky (1996) 53–4; Cooley (2009) 109–11.

[66] There is widespread agreement among scholars that the *Georgics* was published in 29 BC. However, it has been argued that Virgil originally composed a 'Hesiodic song' consisting of the current Books 1 and 2 only, which he read to Octavian in 29 BC, and subsequently composed Books 3 and 4 between 29 and 27 BC. See Martin in Della Corte (1984–91) 666–8.

LIBERTAS, PEACE, AND DIVINE DEPENDENCE   57

> di patrii Indigetes et Romule Vestaque mater,
> quae Tuscum Tiberim et Romana Palatia servas,
> hunc saltem everso iuvenem succurrere saeclo   500
> ne prohibete.

Gods and heroes of my country, Romulus, and Mother Vesta, who guard the Tuscan Tiber and Roman Palatine, do not prevent this young man at least from rescuing a world turned upside down!

Virgil's presentation of Octavian as a *iuvenis* who can 'come to the aid' (*succurrere*, 1.500) of those in need and restore order to an *eversum saeclum* (1.500), recalls simultaneously the intervention of the *iuvenis* in *Eclogue* 1 and the divine *puer* of *Eclogue* 4.[67] This twofold evocation of anonymous salvific figures from the triumviral-era *Eclogues* impresses upon readers the idea that Rome has *always* depended on Caesar—even if it was not clear at the time. Furthermore, there is a striking parallel between the way in which Virgil uses a prayer to retrospectively identify Octavian as the hope for Rome's survival, and the way in which the Senate's divine honours for Octavian—particularly the one stipulating that his name be included in prayers (Cass. Dio 51.19.7)—retrospectively cast him in a salvific light. This similarity between poetic prayer and senatorial decree can also be observed in *Ode* 1.2.[68] Here Horace imaginatively reworks Octavian's appearance at the end of *Georgics* 1 by depicting him as a god (Mercury) who once disguised himself as a young man (*sive mutata iuvenem figura | ales in terris imitaris almae | filius Maiae*, 'O winged son of kindly Maia, if you imitate a young man on earth by transforming your own appearance', *Carm.* 1.2.41–3).[69] Then, in a manner similar to Virgil, Horace offers a prayer asking Octavian to not abandon his people, but stay and safeguard Rome (*serus in caelum redeas diuque | laetus intersis populo Quirini . . . | neu sinas Medos equitare inultos | te duce, Caesar*, 'may you delay your return to heaven and dwell happily among the people of Romulus for a long time . . . and may you not allow the Parthians to ride unpunished while you are our leader, Caesar', 1.2.45–6, 51–2).[70] The correspondence between these poetic prayers and the divinizing expression adopted

---

[67] Note also the echoes of *priscae vestigia fraudis* (*Ecl.* 4.31) in *Laomedonteae . . . periuria Troiae* (*G.* 1.502).

[68] The date of composition for *Carm.* 1.2 is commonly given as *c*.29–27, but it is by no means certain; see further discussion in Chapter 3.

[69] See Chapter 3 for extensive discussion of the Mercury–Caesar conceit.

[70] The dialogue between *Ode* 1.2 and the finale of *Georgics* 1 has been well noted; see Commager (1959); Nisbet and Hubbard (1970) 16–21; Lyne (1995) 43–6.

58 POLITICS AND DIVINIZATION IN AUGUSTAN POETRY

by the Senate in its honouring of Caesar indicates that poetry is very much implicated in the process of reinventing Octavian as a *servator* of the state. Moreover, by praying for the Romans to be saved and looked after by Caesar alone, Virgil and Horace co-opt the language of dependence to reframe singular political power as indispensable to the stability of the state.

However, the danger of linking the peace of Rome to Caesar's singular power is of course that it paves the path for autocratic rule. Livy gestures at this idea in the *Preface* to his *Ab urbe condita*, where he asks readers to trace how Rome's collapse gathered pace 'until it has reached this age, in which we can endure neither our vices nor their remedies' (*donec ad haec tempora quibus nec vitia nostra nec remedia pati possumus perventum est*, *Praef.* 9). Livy's use of *remedia*, as various critics have argued, is a code for one-man rule; and this sense is further reinforced by Tacitus' use of the same word to characterize Augustus' reign (*non aliud discordantis patriae remedium fuisse quam <ut> ab uno regeretur*, 'there was no other remedy for a country in conflict than the rule of one man', Tac. *Ann.* 1.9).[71] If Livy's *Preface* is to be allowed a pre-Actium date,[72] then what we have here is the historian thinking hard about whether one-man rule is a price worth paying for Rome's rehabilitation. Judging by the way that Livy depicts Augustus' restoration of peace later in Book 1 (*post bellum Actiacum ab imperatore Caesare Augusto pace terra marique parta*, 'after the Actian war, when peace on land and sea was secured by the ruler Caesar Augustus' 1.19.3), a passage that is almost certainly a later insertion (*c*.25 BC),[73] it would appear that Livy gradually came around to the view that giving power to one man was in the end the only (bearable?) *remedium* for Rome's ills. Nonetheless, the fact that Livy found himself in a state of aporia when he confronted the political realities of his age should lead us to consider whether Livy's contemporaries shared his concerns.

The final scene of the *Georgics* indicates that Virgil too was uneasy about what it would mean for Rome to be reliant on Caesar as the answer to the country's crisis, even though the poet portrays himself as a content observer of Caesar's rise to power. The poem concludes with a *sphragis* ('seal' or

---

[71] Woodman (1988) 132–4; von Haehling (1989) 213–15; Moles (1993) 151–2. The latter suggests further that Livy's *remedia* is a true plural, 'alluding to both one-man rule and to the moral value of AUC history' (Moles 1993: 153). Similarly, Vasaly (2015) 22–4 argues that Livy's *Preface* sets up his composition of the *Ab urbe condita* as a service to the state, thus presenting the work (as Vasaly sees it) as having a didactic value.

[72] Woodman (1988) 132–4. Conventionally, a *terminus post quem* of 27 BC is posited for Livy's first pentad.

[73] Luce (1965) 218.

LIBERTAS, PEACE, AND DIVINE DEPENDENCE 59

'signature') in which Virgil compares Caesar's career with his own.[74] Caesar 'thunders' (*fulminat*, 4.561) in the Euphrates, restores order to a subjugated world (*victorque volentis | per populos dat iura*, 4.561–2), and 'seeks a path to Olympus' (*viamque adfectat Olympo*, 4.562). His guise here—reminiscent of both the king of the gods, Jupiter, and the power-usurping Giants—encapsulates how the new Caesar is establishing himself at the top of the political order while also overthrowing it.[75] By contrast, the poet emphasizes his marginality to the centre of power by presenting himself in the act of pursing the 'lowly pleasure' of composing poetry (4.563–6):

> illo Vergilium me tempore dulcis alebat
> Parthenope studiis florentem ignobilis oti,
> carmina qui lusi pastorum audaxque iuventa,   565
> Tityre, te patulae cecini sub tegmine fagi.

At that time sweet Parthenope was nourishing me, Virgil, joyous in the pursuits of lowly leisure, I who toyed with shepherds' songs, and, in youth's boldness, sang of you, Tityrus, in the spreading beech-tree's shade.

The next chapter will examine in detail what the divergent pursuits and statuses of Caesar and poet can tell us about the shifting relationship between art and power in Rome's transition from Republic to Principate. Here I want to focus on the way in which Virgil frames his *otium* (4.564). Through the citation of the opening line of the First *Eclogue* (4.566),[76] the Georgic-*sphragis* establishes a parallel between Virgil and Tityrus, and assimilates the *otium* that was provided for each of them by a powerful man.[77] Whereas in *Eclogue* 1 Tityrus zealously takes on the task of deifying his benefactor and seeks to establish communal life around the power and the worship of the *iuvenis*, here in the *Georgics* Virgil retreats into the background and idealizes his inferiority (*ignobili*, 4.564) and distance from political life (*dulcis...*

---

[74] The *sphragis* is a common vehicle for reflexive discussions of poetry and the poet's literary achievement; see Thomas (1988) ad 4.559–66.

[75] Hollis (1996) and Gale (2003) 327–8 suggest that the expression *viamque adfectat Olympo*, set against the backdrop of warfare (*bello*, 4.561), aligns Octavian's mission with the Gigantomachy.

[76] The syntactical ambiguity of the final line of the *Georgics* even allows readers to see Tityrus as a Virgilian persona. As Nauta (2006) 308 notes, line 566 could be translated as either 'I sang you, Tityrus, [you who were] in the shade of the spreading beech'; or 'I sang you, Tityrus, [while I was] in the shade of the spreading beech'. The identification of Tityrus with Virgil is also encouraged in *Eclogue* 6 of course.

[77] The kind of unitary rereading of both poems which I attempt here takes its cue from Fowler's theorization of the 'supertextual closure' (Fowler 1989: 82).

60 POLITICS AND DIVINIZATION IN AUGUSTAN POETRY

Parthenope, 4.563–4).[78] By blurring the line between political marginalization and peaceful ease in his presentation of *otium*, Virgil implicitly underlines the cost of Caesar's rehabilitation of Rome. As much as Virgil here appears to be content with his own triviality, this pose freezes the poet in a state of powerlessness. The *otium* which Virgil has at his disposal to pursue 'ignoble' interests is far from a state of true *libertas*, but a symptom of political disempowerment. In this way, the *sphragis* of the *Georgics* intimates that the flipside of allowing Caesar to take control of the Roman world is that it consigns the former ruling class to the role of powerless spectators. Put another way, the *remedium* creates new problems. Set against a confounding image of Octavian as both Jovian ruler and Gigantic disruptor, Virgil's self-portrait conveys how the Roman political subject—caught up in a moment of constitutional uncertainty—finds himself dependent on and marginalized by a new form of political power.

The Elegist's *Libertas*

I want to conclude this chapter by shifting our focus onto Propertius 3.4, and use the elegist's depiction of Augustus as a godlike ruler of Rome to demonstrate further how poetry insinuates a crucial paradox of Augustan power. As will be seen, the way in which Propertius uses divine imagery in his eulogy of the *princeps* dramatizes the idea that the unrivalled authority of Caesar both engenders and circumscribes an individual's *libertas*.

Since much of the discussion below concerns the interpretation of Propertius' praise of Augustus and the poet's view of the regime more broadly, I will outline my position on these issues in advance. The elegist's praise of Augustus is often thought of as 'lip service' by scholars who detect varying degrees of resistance, opposition, or irony in the poet's eulogy.[79] However, both the countercultural thesis, and the attitude-analysis approach which forms its premise, have been challenged by Keith, who traced a complex interdependence between imperial conquest and the poet's life of leisure.[80]

---

[78] *Parthenope, studia,* and *ignobile otium* appearing in succession also evokes the Epicurean pursuit of the quietist and contemplative life, λάθε βιώσας; see also Gale (2003) 326–7.

[79] For the term 'lip service', see Stahl (1985) 190, 194–5, 204; also, Heyworth (2007a) 114: 'regularly there is an underlying tone of cynicism and disdain'. However, Cairns (2006) 325–6 finds Propertius' attitude towards the regime to be so 'deliberately anti-social' that he argues that it had the reverse effect of negatively reinforcing the political orthodoxy.

[80] Keith (2008) 139–65 focuses especially on Propertius' often irreverent juxtaposition of his enjoyment of non-military pursuits with Augustan militarism.

LIBERTAS, PEACE, AND DIVINE DEPENDENCE 61

For Keith, Propertian elegy's 'countercultural' lionization of the lover's *otium* and *nequitiae* constituted an indirect acknowledgement of Roman power, subtly gesturing at the embeddedness of Augustan *imperium* in elite culture.[81] This sense that Propertian elegy could implicitly reinforce the authority of the state, or even collude with the regime, was thrown into sharp relief by Bowditch in her reading of elegies 2.31–2—a poetic sequence dealing firstly with the opening of the Palatine Temple of Apollo and then the sexual profligacy of Cynthia.[82] Focusing on the way in which this poetic sequence constructs the reader as both viewer and subject of a nascent surveillance state, Bowditch noted a striking correspondence between the regime and the poet in their respective circumscribing of the *libertas* of the viewed subjects.[83] By foregrounding Propertian elegy's propagandistic sleight of hand, studies such as those of Keith and Bowditch have shown that even the most apparent expressions of opposition in Propertius may not be what they seem; indeed, more recent Propertian scholarship has further developed the view that 'the very premise of resistance confers prestige on the one thus resisted.'[84]

Yet critics have not banished the possibility that Propertian elegy is capable of reasserting its political autonomy, if not authority. Luke Roman has shown that Propertius in Book 3 carefully re-defines his poetic domain as a grander, but visibly demarcated, space at a time when poetry's restrictive enclosures began to take on greater public significance.[85] In a similar vein, Heslin has argued that Propertius' aesthetic polemics with Virgil worked to delineate the artistic independence of his love elegy (as opposed to Virgil's Augustan epic).[86] In another recent study, Pandey has suggested that Propertius underlines his poetry's capacity to aid, or even rival, the regime's symbolic language of power by turning the Augustan *triumphus* into an object for aesthetic consumption and emphasizing the viewers' role in constructing meaning.[87] In short, the thrust of Propertian scholarship over the last decade or so has

---

[81] See esp. Keith (2008) 165: 'The pleasures of Propertian elegy—both licit and illicit—lie precisely in this heady combination of imperial leisure, love, and luxury, anchored as they are in the knowledge of Roman power and legitimacy.'

[82] There is good reason to treat 2.31–2 as one continuous sequence, see Luck (1979) 85–8; but Heyworth (2007b) 246 has doubts.

[83] Bowditch (2009). See also Keith (2008) 149, who argues that elegy 2.31 'invites the collusion of reader (and critic) in the aesthetic "mystification" of Roman militarism.'

[84] Roman (2014) 166, and 168–9 for detailed explication.

[85] Roman (2014) 169–201, esp. 183–94. See also Rimell (2015) 82–112 on the breaching of poetic enclosures in Horace.

[86] Heslin (2018) 5, 17–20. Further, in his discussion of Prop. 2.34, Heslin (2018) 214–22 well observes that Propertius combatively (mis)represents the forthcoming *Aeneid* as an annalistic and nationalistic tome.

[87] Pandey (2018) 201–9 on Prop. 3.4.

62 POLITICS AND DIVINIZATION IN AUGUSTAN POETRY

shown that, far from (and far more complex than) resisting or dissenting against Augustus, the poet in various ways re-centres his freedom as lover, citizen, and artist; and that in doing so, Propertian elegy encapsulates the tension, as well as the complicity, between political and creative authorities.

Approaching Propertius' poetry from this angle, depictions of Augustus as the godlike ruler of Rome become more than eulogistic or subversive distillations of Augustan power. This mode of representation constitutes rather a site of confrontation in which Propertius draws out the complex interrelatedness of Augustan power and the poet's *libertas*. The poem that best demonstrates this is elegy 3.4. It opens with the dramatic statement that 'Divine Caesar is planning war against rich India' (*Arma deus Caesar dites meditatur ad Indos*, 3.4.1);[88] following which Propertius envisages himself 'singing favourable omens' (*omina fausta cano*, 3.4.8). The significance of this opening movement is twofold. Firstly, Propertius' *deus Caesar*—in sharp contrast to the anonymity of Virgil's *iuvenis*—is the first time in extant Latin poetry where Augustus is named and openly referred to as *deus* without any qualification. Secondly, the opening of Propertius 3.4 plays on the opening words of Virgil's *Aeneid* (*Arma virumque cano*, 1.1),[89] as well as Horace's sacerdotal self-representation in the 'Roman Odes'—a poetic sequence that repeatedly urges Augustus to pacify the East.[90] By substituting the 'man' (*vir*) of Virgil's epic with Augustus the 'god' (*deus*), Propertius outperforms the poet of the *Aeneid* in praising Caesar; and as if this was not enough, the elegist then slips into the role of an Augustan *vates*, eclipsing Horace in his fervent cry for Roman glory.[91] Propertius' emulative stunt implicitly presents the still-in-progress *Aeneid* and the near-contemporary 'Roman Odes' as expressions of artistic commitment par excellence. By competing with and appropriating the authorial voices of Virgil and Horace, Propertius attributes to his poem a degree of political urgency and creative conformity not usually associated with love elegy.

In the second half of the poem, however, the elegist dramatically scales back his involvement in the Augustan conquest and imagines himself only as

---

[88] War on India is clearly fanciful, but it recalls the region's previous conquerors, Bacchus and Alexander, both of whom were eventually worshipped as gods.

[89] The *Aeneid* was published after Propertius 3, but elegy 2.34, which appeared in *c.*25 BC, showed that Propertius was acutely aware of Virgil's ongoing composition of the *Aeneid* and its subject matter. See Camps (1967); Cairns (2006) 295–319; Heslin (2018) 219–21.

[90] Cf. Hor. *Carm.* 3.1.1–4 (the lyric poet as *sacerdos*); 3.2.1–6, 3.3.42–4, 3.5.1–4 (Augustan conquest of the East); all of which are discussed in detail in Chapter 3. For further discussion of the correspondence between Prop. 3.1–5 and the 'Roman Odes', see Nethercut (1970) 386–7.

[91] Miller (2004) 150, on the other hand, thinks that the evocation of the Virgilian *vir* demythologizes the Propertian *deus*, thus hinting at the fact that both Aeneas and Augustus were really only *viri*.

LIBERTAS, PEACE, AND DIVINE DEPENDENCE   63

a bystander in Caesar's triumph.[92] Treating the day of the triumphal procession as an erotic excursion (*inque sinu carae nixus spectare puellae | incipiam*, 'and leaning on the bosom of my sweetheart I begin to watch', 3.4.15–16), Propertius is content with private *otium* on an occasion that encourages public display of political engagement. The sharp contrast between Propertius' image as an Augustan *vates* earlier in the elegy, and his self-fashioning here as a mere spectator and diffident lover, is usually interpreted by scholars as a reassertion of the demarcation of political and elegiac domains.[93] Indeed, the opening verse of elegy 3.5 reinforces the opposition between Augustan militarism and elegiac pleasure by positioning *Pax* as a rival divinity to *Caesar* (*Pacis Amor deus est; pacem veneramur amantes*, 'Love is the god of peace: we lovers worship peace', 3.5.1).[94] However, Propertius' suspension of involvement is more than just a reassertion of opposition. I suggest that this poetic pose epitomizes the Roman citizen's experience of not being able to truly intervene in the political process, which in turn interrogates whether the citizen still has a say in the constitution of state power. Propertius' visualization of the triumphal procession (3.4.11–13, *lac.*, 17–18, *lac.*, 14–6)[95] culminates with the poet contentedly declaring that he shall 'read' the names of captured cities: *titulis oppida capta legam* (3.4.16). On the one hand, this act of reading is a subtle allusion to the Roman triumph's increasing reliance on symbolic representation and abstraction;[96] on the other hand, it evokes an earlier poem by the Roman elegist Gallus, in which the poet–narrator also presents himself as a 'reader' of a triumphal ceremony.[97] The double reference to reading underscores Propertius' transformation from singer (cf. *omina fausta cano*, 3.4.9) to reader (*legam*), from active participant to passive audience in the state's cultural activities. But more than that, it also draws attention to the shift of narrative authority from the poet, who fantasizes about Roman con-

---

[92] On the fictionality of this *triumphus*, see Pandey (2018) 185–6, 207–8; though the poem's call for the retrieval of Roman standards lost at Carrhae (cf. *Crassos clademque piate*, 3.4.9) suggests that the imagined triumph is probably conceived in response to Augustus' proposed Parthian campaign.

[93] Hubbard (1974) 104–5; Roman (2014) 186–7; Pandey (2018) 208–9. Contra Keith (2008) 149, who argues that the poet's enjoyment of *otium* on the day of Augustus' triumph hints at 'the intimate commerce of elegy with empire'.

[94] Cairns (2006) 345, rather eccentrically, interprets the *pax* of Prop. 3.5 as a shorthand for *pax parta victoriis*.

[95] The *lacunae* and transpositions suggested by modern editors of Propertius (here I follow the text of Heyworth) make no material difference to my discussion of the poem.

[96] Beard (2007) 143–86; Östenberg (2009) 189–261; Pandey (2018) 186–90.

[97] Cf. Gallus, fr. 2.4 *fixa legam spoliis divitiora tuis*. The Gallus fragment from Qaṣr Ibrîm was first published by Anderson et al. (1979). We still do not know for sure whether the 'Caesar' in the Gallus fragment is Julius or Augustus: most critics opt for Julius, but Hutchinson (1981) argues for Augustus. For further discussions of the relationship between Gall. fr. 2.2–5 and Prop. 3.4, see Putnam (1980b); Miller (1981).

64 POLITICS AND DIVINIZATION IN AUGUSTAN POETRY

quest, to Augustus, who will eventually curate the account of his triumph. As a 'reader', Propertius can subject Augustus' triumphal 'text' to his critique and reclaim some authority in this way;[98] but ultimately the poet plays no part in the crafting of Augustan power.[99] The procession of subjugated armies and defeated nations in captivity (*captos . . . duces*, 3.4.18; *oppida capta*, 3.4.16) holds up a mirror to the *libertas* which Roman citizens like Propertius still possess.[100] But Propertius' role as a passive reader and backseat observer of Augustus' spectacle of power conveys at the same time a stark absence of political agency amongst the citizen body. The elegist performs his *libertas* by choosing to distance himself from the celebration of Caesar, giving the impression that there is still 'free' speech under the Principate; however, it is far from clear whether the poet's marginal self-positioning conveys jocular indifference or awareness of one's disempowerment.

At this point, we should recall that a principal function of the Roman *triumphus* was to mediate the relations between the emperor, Senate, and citizen body.[101] Traditionally, the ceremony began by exalting a general to divine status, which Propertius' poem alludes to in the most striking manner (*deus Caesar*). But the ceremony usually ends with the reaffirmation of the *triumphator*'s mortality and the reassertion of the Senate and people's balancing authority. By imagining the Augustan triumph as the setting for an erotic excursion, and by 'reading' (*legam*) its fictive content as if a text awaiting readerly critique, Propertius' elegy does to an extent redress the balance the power.[102] However, in suspending his act as the politically engaged *vates* and choosing to be a mere spectator of Augustus' triumph, Propertius ultimately renounces his role in the power mediation process.

In the elegy's penultimate couplet, Propertius simply asks Venus to guarantee Caesar's immortality, thereby virtually accepting the longevity of Augustus' authority (*ipsa tuam serva prolem, Venus: hoc sit in aevum | cernis ab Aenea quod superesse caput*, 'Protect your offspring, Venus: may he, in whom you see the succession of Aeneas, live on forever!', 3.4.19–20). The final verse of the poem, *mi sat erit Sacra plaudere posse Via* ('enough will be for me to cheer them on the Sacred Way', 3.4.22), drives home both the poet's contented

---

[98] Pandey (2018) 208.

[99] See esp. Brilliant (1999) 222: 'Thus, as both a unifying structure and one dominated by a resplendent protagonist, the triumphal procession established an ideologically significant distinction between a single, hegemonic presence and his many spectating subjects.'

[100] Most scholars would accept that the Roman triumphal procession helped to crystallize what is meant to be Roman and non-Roman; see esp. Östenberg (1999) 261–72.

[101] See esp. Beard et al. (1998) 142–3; also Favro (1994) 153–6; Beard (2007) 199–218, esp. 218.

[102] This is in essence the argument of Pandey (2018) 208–9.

self-marginalization and playful disavowal of political agency. The contrast between the elegist's eventual embrace of his marginality and the poem's opening portrait of Augustus as *deus* also recalls the comparison between poet and Caesar in the *sphragis* of Virgil's *Georgics*.[103] By reprising the final image of Virgil's poem in which the poet reflects on his *ignobile otium* (Verg. *G.* 4.564), Propertius indirectly draws attention to how *otium* is framed in his own poem. As *amator*, citizen, and imperial subject, Propertius situates his *otium* somewhere between elegiac self-distancing from Augustan cultural orthodoxy, the security of empire, and an acceptance of powerlessness. Occupying an ambiguous position that straddles creative irreverence and political marginalization, Propertius' *otium* underlines how Augustan power both provides and prescribes *libertas*. Thus encompassing autonomy and disempowerment at once, the ambiguity of Propertius' *otium* gives expression to the difficulty of disentangling the gains and losses of Roman citizens under the Augustan Principate.

Conclusions

This chapter set out to examine the ways in which the motif of divinization in Augustan poetry helped to produce, and later critiqued, the notion of the restoration of *libertas*, which evolved to become a central tenet of the ideological construct of the Augustan Principate. As I have shown, this discursive interaction was underpinned by the poets' presentation of *otium* as on the one hand a benefaction rendered by a social superior to those below, and on the other hand a state of political marginalization and disempowerment. Through the conflation or juxtaposition of these two conceptualizations of *otium*, the poets variously interrogated the extent to which *libertas* was predicated on accepting the overwhelming authority of a singular leader, whom the poets eventually identified with Octavian/Augustus.

In Virgil's First *Eclogue*, the contemporary Roman practice of divine self-imaging and the triumviral competition for *libertas* inform the poem's depiction of its *iuvenis*—a salvific benefactor worshipped for his restoration of *libertas/otium*. In the course of the poem, *libertas* is conflated with *otium*, disembedded from its immediate political context, and re-imagined as

---

[103] The evocation of Virgil's *sphragis* is strengthened by the presence of two Virgilian motifs here at the end of Propertius' poem: (1) the succession of the *gens Iulia* in the prayer to Venus, cf. 3.4.19–20; (2) the description of imperial conquest as *labores* (3.4.21), a term closely associated with the *Georgics*. On the topos of comparing oneself to a powerful acquaintance, see Fedeli (1985) on 3.4.21–2.

something that can only come about through the intervention of an exceptionally powerful benefactor. In this way, the pastoral fiction of the *Eclogues* ushers in a discourse wherein *libertas* and autocratic power are not merely compatible but even symbiotic.

After the civil war, poetic depictions of Octavian as the divine saviour of the state engage in a dialogue with the divinizing honours awarded to the victor by the Roman Senate. By co-opting the language of dependence, Virgil and Horace further naturalize the unparalleled status of Octavian, sanctifying the authority of Rome's new ruler. However, by highlighting their status as powerless beneficiaries of Caesar's godlike protection, the poets also draw attention to the increasingly blurred line between the security of life and the deprivation of individual agency. In the *sphragis* of the *Georgics*, Virgil's ambiguous characterization of his *otium* sensitizes readers to the idea that the discourse surrounding Caesar's godlike protection of Rome allows autocratic power to become indispensable. Later, Propertius in elegy 3.4 extends this line of critique by dramatizing both his 'freedom' as an Augustan citizen-artist and his self-conscious withdrawal from the state's political process. Propertius' conflicted conception is underpinned by the elegist's double self-construction as an apparently 'countercultural' citizen on the one hand, and a passive subject who consents to Caesar's superiority on the other. Straddling these two positions at once, the elegist's juxtaposition of his eulogy to 'Divine Caesar' with his marginal self-positioning captures the way in which Augustan poetry attempts to work out the meaning and scope of *libertas* in an age when *libertas* is increasingly defined by Augustus.

2

Divinization and the Transformation of Rome from Republic to Principate

There is a moment in the final poem of Horace's first book of *Satires* (36/35 BC),[1] where Octavian almost makes an appearance (Hor. *Sat.* 1.10.72–7, 81–8):

> saepe stilum vertas, iterum quae digna legi sint
> scripturus, neque te ut miretur turba labores,
> contentus paucis lectoribus an tua demens
> vilibus in ludis dictari carmina malis?   75
> non ego; nam satis est equitem mihi plaudere, ut audax,
> contemptis aliis, explosa Arbuscula dixit.
>
> ...
>
> Plotius et Varius, Maecenas Vergiliusque,   81
> Valgius et probet haec Octavius optimus atque
> Fuscus et haec utinam Viscorum laudet uterque.
> ambitione relegata te dicere possum,
> Pollio, te, Messalla, tuo cum fratre, simulque   85
> vos, Bibule et Servi, simul his te, candide Furni,
> conpluris alios, doctos ego quos et amicos
> prudens praetereo....

You should often turn your stylus back, if you are to write something worthy of being read repeatedly; and you should not strive to impress the crowd, but be content with the few as your readers. Are you so foolish as to want your poems dictated in schools? Not I. 'It is enough for me if the knights applaud me'—as the proud Arbuscula said when she hissed at those who made light of her.... Let only Plotius and Varius approve of these verses, and Maecenas, Virgil, and Valgius, and Octavius, and the most excellent Fuscus; and let only the two Visci praise my work. Without the desire to flatter, I can name you,

---

[1] On the date of *Satires* 1, see Du Quesnay (1984) 20–1 and Gowers (2012) 1–5.

Politics and Divinization in Augustan Poetry. Bobby Xinyue, Oxford University Press. © Bobby Xinyue 2022.
DOI: 10.1093/oso/9780192855978.003.0003

68 POLITICS AND DIVINIZATION IN AUGUSTAN POETRY

Pollio; you, Messalla, and your brother; also you, Bibulus and Servius; and you as well, honest Furnius, and a good number of others, learned men and friends, whom I discreetly pass over.

Octavius Musa, a poet and friend of Horace, is the *Octavius* in this catalogue of 'future practitioners and enablers of Augustan poetry' (81–6).[2] But this passage certainly teases us with the presence of the triumvir, Gaius Caesar Octavianus. In the build-up to the catalogue, Horace twice emphasizes his desire to please only the few (*paucis* 74; *equitem*, 76) whose opinions mattered.[3] And the way in which Horace confidently assembles an 'influential gang'[4] of supporters to pre-empt his critics hints at the absent presence of Octavian among those whom the poet knowingly passes over (*prudens praetereo*, 88).[5]

If Octavian only figures in the background of the cultural landscape of *Satire* 1.10, then his irrepressible presence in the minds of Horace and his contemporaries is very much foregrounded in the opening poem of the second book of *Satires*, which appeared some five years later (30 BC).[6] Here, the *princeps*-to-be, now hailed as *Caesar invictus* (*Sat.* 2.1.11), is being talked about by Horace and Trebatius as a literary critic (2.1.82–6):

> 'si mala condiderit in quem quis carmina, ius est
> iudiciumque.' 'esto, siquis mala; sed bona siquis
> iudice condiderit laudatus Caesare? siquis
> opprobriis dignum latraverit, integer ipse?'   85
> 'solventur risu tabulae, tu missus abibis.'

Trebatius: 'If someone shall have composed harmful verses against anyone, there are the law and the courts.'
Horace: 'So be it, if the verses are bad. But what if he composes good verses and earns the praise of Caesar as judge? What if he barks at someone deserving reproof, while free from blame himself?'
Trebatius: 'The tablets will be cancelled amid laughter, and you will go away let off.'

Caesar's judgement clearly carries weight. In fact, Caesar appears to be more than just a literary critic. The expression *iudice...Caesare* ('Caesar as judge', 84),

---

[2] Gowers (2012) 308.   [3] Freudenburg (2021) 53.   [4] Freudenburg (2021) 53–4.
[5] Feeney (2002) 174.
[6] There are good reasons to believe that *Satires* 2 and Horace's *Epodes* are roughly of the same date, published sometime around 30 BC; see Muecke (1993) 1 and Gowers (2012) 3.

DIVINIZATION AND THE TRANSFORMATION OF ROME   69

set alongside the insinuation that the Roman legal system (cf. *tabulae*, 86, which may refer to law tablets) could be rendered obsolete (*solventur*, 86) in the presence of a delighted Caesar (*risu*, 86), implies that Octavian's authority is such that he may even transcend the power of the law.[7] A year or so later (29 BC), we find that Virgil too appeals to Octavian as a decisive reader and extraordinary authority in the prologue and the *sphragis* to the *Georgics* (Verg. *G.* 1.24–42; *volentis | per populos dat iura viamque adfectat Olympo*, 'he sets laws on willing peoples and strives for a path to Olympus', *G.* 4.561–2).

Placing these poems side by side, the contrast between Octavian's portrayal in *Satires* 1, which was composed at the height of the triumviral period, and his images later in *Satires* 2 and the *Georgics*, which were published soon after the battle of Actium, highlights the extent to which power has gravitated towards the new Caesar as he rose to the top of the Roman political world. The prominence of Octavian's authority in Horace and Virgil's post-Actian poetry, and the imagery used by the poets to articulate it, have caught the attention of a number of scholars, who have argued that in the approximate five-year interval between Horace's two books of *Satires* (36/35–30 BC), but especially after the victory at Actium, there appeared to a palpable totalitarian turn in Rome.[8] The purpose of this chapter is to examine how this change of constitutional course is reflected in the poets' language of divinization. By focusing on the poetry produced in the period leading up to and immediately after the battle of Actium, it will be argued that the poets' deployment of divinizing imagery at this time is synchronized with a dawning realization that a new political order is about to take hold in Rome. It will be suggested further that these divine portraits of the man who will soon become Augustus not only reflect an anxiety about the growing power of the new Caesar but also underscore the uncertainties in the poets' minds about the future direction of their art under the nascent regime.

This chapter is not devoted to the analysis of a particular aspect of divine imagery (though there will be further discussion of the poets' depiction of Caesar as *liberator*); but instead treats the discourse of divinization as a broad category comprising ideas such as elevation in status, change of identity, and transgression of hierarchical order. By framing divinity in this way as an enacted state (rather than a curated identity), I wish to highlight that divinization embodies a process of transition with all its possibilities and

---

[7] See esp. Freudenburg (2001) 106 and (2021) on *Sat.* 2.1.84 and 86; Lowrie (2009) 345–8; also Muecke (1993) 114; Tatum (1998) 694.

[8] Freudenburg (2001) 71–82. See also Lowrie (2009) 311–48 and, in milder terms, Gowers (2005) 57.

70   POLITICS AND DIVINIZATION IN AUGUSTAN POETRY

uncertainties, and that, as a highly metaphorical discourse, divinization is at its core concerned with sociopolitical change. Taking this approach throughout this chapter, the first part argues that, across Horace's two books of *Satires* and the *Epodes*, images of Octavian's hierarchical aboveness, singular prominence, and unprecedented status gradually cement the relationship between the new Caesar and those around him—including and especially the poet—into one between divine and human. In doing so, Horace draws attention to a widening, and eventually unbridgeable, disparity in power between Octavian and those who will soon become his subjects, through which the poet hints at Rome's shift from republicanism to authoritarian rule. In the case of *Epode* 9 and *Satire* 2.1, both of which are set dramatically in the aftermath of Actium, I argue that the divinizing imagery in these poems also encapsulate the process of the poet trying to work out, and eventually accepting, the power structures of the nascent regime and his new place within it. Although my position on Horace's triumviral poetry falls broadly in line with the current scholarly view that the two books of *Satires* attest to an increasing restriction on social mobility and the freedom of speech (especially after the battle of Actium),[9] the present study casts into fresh light the ways in which Horace's poetry articulated this uncertain period of political change through the discourse of divinization, and highlights how this discourse operated as both a metaphor for Rome's constitutional transformation and a figurative language for the poet's ideological reckoning.

Building on this line of argument, the second part of this chapter examines Virgil's repeated reflections on the apparently certain prospect of Octavian's divinization in the *Georgics*, and draws out the significance of the poet's depiction of his diminishing control on this issue.[10] In the course of the poem, Octavian is seen gradually veering away from the celestial course set by Virgil. By the time we reach the *sphragis*, the *princeps*-to-be is already embarking on his own path to divinity, while the poet appears to play no further part in this process. Through this shifting relationship between poet and Caesar, the *Georgics* not only dramatizes its failure to intervene in Rome's march toward Augustan autocracy but also gestures to an imminent change in the relationship between art and authority. My reading will emphasize in particular the ways in which Virgil swerves from attempting to direct Octavian with his poetry, to accepting the heaven-reaching path that Octavian has set for himself. In doing so, Virgil conflates the loss of poetic efficacy with his acquiescence to a political future over which he has little control; and it is through

---

[9] Freudenburg (2001) 71–82 and (2021) 51; Lowrie (2009) 311–48.
[10] My argument on the *Georgics* represents a revised version of Xinyue (2019).

DIVINIZATION AND THE TRANSFORMATION OF ROME   71

this conflation, I argue, that Virgil underlines the extent to which poetry must reconcile with the incipient regime.

The final part of this chapter rounds up the discussion by examining the significance of Octavian's image as an embodiment of extraordinary legal authority, which not only recurs in the poetry of Horace and Virgil but also characterizes Propertius' depiction of the *princeps*. Through a discussion of Propertius 2.7 and the poet's much later elegy 4.11—both of which deal with the Augustan marital *leges* and speak of Augustus' authority in divine terms— I argue that these Propertian elegies, like the post-Actian poetry of Horace and Virgil, pointedly highlight how individual action and poetic autonomy increasingly came under state control as Rome stepped out of the shadows of the civil war and reconstituted itself under Augustus.

Horace's *Satires* and *Epodes*: Finding Caesar

Octavian before Actium

Even though Octavian barely features in Horace's earliest poetry, it is still clear to see that he occupies a position above and beyond the ordinary. In *Satire* 1.3, the poet takes aim at the singer Tigellius, accusing him of refusing to perform upon request: not even Caesar could get a tune out of him (1.3.4–6):

> Caesar, qui cogere posset,
> si peteret per amicitiam patris atque suam, non   5
> quicquam proficeret;....

If Caesar, who could just compel him, asked in the name of his own friendship and his father's, he would not get anything....

This is the sole mention of Octavian in *Satires* 1: a brief cameo and he's gone.[11] Yet, as Gowers's commentary points out, his appearance is a rather ominous one.[12] The conspicuously positioned phrase, *qui cogere posset* (1.3.4), implies that if Octavian fails to achieve what he wished through conventional means

---

[11] Horace hints at Octavian's presence on a couple of occasions. The oblique focus on the expulsion of kings from Rome at *Sat.* 1.7.33–5 (and particularly the words, *per magnos...deos*, 1.7.33) brings to mind the assassination and deification of Octavian's father by posthumous adoption, Julius Caesar; see further Dufallo (2015) 328–9. There is also the passing reference to the *horti Caesaris* at *Sat.* 1.9.18. But only in *Sat.* 1.3 is Octavian mentioned by name.

[12] Gowers (2012) ad loc.

72 POLITICS AND DIVINIZATION IN AUGUSTAN POETRY

(cf. *per amicitiam*, 1.3.5), he can get it done by less charming methods. The force that the triumvir has at his disposal clearly suggests that a request from Octavian is a different proposition compared to a request from anybody else.[13] Moreover, the even briefer cameo of Julius Caesar (cf. *patris*, 1.3.5) conjures up the image of Octavian (not so subtly?) reminding Tigellius of the influence he wields in the name of his deified father.[14] Unfazed by the stature of the Caesars, Tigellius' refusal to sing indicates that he still has some agency in his dealings with the de facto ruler of Rome; and the power of Octavian is thus 'demystified', as Dufallo puts it.[15] Yet, despite Tigellius gaining the upper hand on this (entirely imaginary) occasion (cf. *si peteret*, 1.3.5), it would seem that Octavian is no ordinary *amicus* within Tigellius' social circle.[16] The decisive authority that the new Caesar has over his 'friends', set alongside his political pedigree as the adoptive son of a former dictator, rather makes him a powerful outsider.

This idea that Octavian is far from being immersed in the ordinary political ecosystem comes into view again in *Satire* 1.5, which offers the briefest of glimpses into the simmering tension between Octavian and Antony.[17] This poem recounts Horace's journey from Rome to Brundisium, during which he joins Maecenas, Cocceius, and Fonteius Capito, who are travelling on a diplomatic mission to negotiate what appears to be a peace treaty, most likely the Treaty of Tarentum (37 BC).[18] Octavian never actually appears in the poem, but the way in which Horace pointedly denies his readers of Octavian's presence only adds to the sense that the triumvir is far beyond normal people's reach (1.5.27–33):

> huc venturus erat Maecenas optimus atque
> Cocceius, missi magnis de rebus uterque
> legati, aversos soliti componere amicos.

---

[13] Griffin (1984) 191.   [14] Dufallo (2015) 318.

[15] Dufallo (2015) 318. His main argument (pp. 313–16) is that *Satires* 1 tries to strike a balance between sacralizing and demystifying Octavian and his inner circle, through which Horace sends out the reassuring message that Octavian's circle understood what kind of relationship the people wanted to have with political power.

[16] On the concealment of inequality in the notion of *amicitia*, see White (1993), esp. p. 29. Hunter (1985) 486–90 and Kennedy (1992) 31–4 note that the political dimension of terms such as *amicitia* and *libertas* is often 'domesticated' in *Satires* 1.

[17] Scholars have long emphasized that the partisan politics of the triumviral era are instrumental to understanding the social reality of *Satires* 1, even if readers only get the merest signs of the dominant political subjects of the time. See e.g. Du Quesnay (1984); Kennedy (1992); Henderson (1993) and (1994); Oliensis (1997); Cucchiarelli (2001) 84–118; Miller (2009) 40–4.

[18] For further discussion and bibliography on the plausibility of the Treaty of Tarentum, see Gowers (2012) 183; also Brown (1993) 139.

DIVINIZATION AND THE TRANSFORMATION OF ROME   73

> hic oculis ego nigra meis collyria lippus   30
> illinere. interea Maecenas advenit atque
> Cocceius Capitoque simul Fonteius, ad unguem
> factus homo, Antoni, non ut magis alter, amicus.

Here Maecenas—most excellent man—and Cocceius were to come, each of them despatched as ambassadors on some big business, well accustomed as they are to reconciling estranged friends. Here I smear some black ointment on my eyes for my conjunctivitis. In the meantime, Maecenas arrived, and so did Cocceius, together with Fonteius Capito, a character of tailored perfection, second to none in his friendship to Antony.

A tense political standoff between two major rivals is conceived of as a dispute among friends (*aversos... amicos*, 1.5.29).[19] Yet Horace still refuses our access—and even claims his own lack of access—to what goes on beyond the scenes.[20] Only the *optimus* (1.5.27) can possibly effect a change in the current situation,[21] while the poet—applying ointment on his infected eyes just as the delegation is about to arrive (1.5.30–1)—literally cannot see or do anything.[22] The eventual appearance of Antony's name (1.5.32) provides the identity of only one of the *amici*, but Octavian remains anonymous throughout, kept invisible in the world of 'big business' (*magnis... rebus*, 1.5.28). Horace twice teases the reader with the seemingly imminent arrival of Octavian with enjambments at lines 27–8 and 31–2 (*Maecenas optimus atque | Cocceius... Maecenas advenit atque | Cocceius*), but the comically deflating appearance of Cocceius is only half of the story. As these lines build up to the dramatic epiphany of the only person who might trump 'the best' (*optimus*, 1.5.27), Octavian's no-show underscores just how far he lies beyond the likes of Horace.[23]

---

[19] Du Quesnay (1984) 40–1: 'The last phrase [of verse 29] is a masterpiece of understatement', see also Gowers (2012) 4–5. Reckford (1999) 526 thinks that Horace is 'keeping diplomatic silence' by not revealing what he knows.

[20] Freudenburg (2001) 8 and 55 observes that throughout *Sat.* 1.5 Horace refuses to take us anywhere close to Maecenas, and that our desire to know more is a game played on us from beginning to end.

[21] *optimus* does not have to be taken with *Maecenas*, even if it is frequently understood to describe Horace's patron in affectionate terms; see the comments of Gowers (2012) and Brown (1993) on 1.5.27.

[22] The sudden and comical application of conjunctivitis medicine by the poet has been interpreted by Cucchiarelli (2001) 70 as a 'physiology of *recusatio*'. The mirroring phrasing of *huc...Maecenas* (1.5.27) and *hic...ego* (1.5.30) further underscores the contrast between the importance of the delegates' mission and the triviality of Horace's personal experience. See Ehlers (1985) 71; Cucchiarelli (2001) 68; Freudenburg (2001) 53.

[23] Contra Reckford (1999) 533–6, 550, who argues that, by establishing a parallel between the volatile 'friendship' of the triumvirs and the genuine *amicitia* between Horace and friends (cf. 1.5.39–44), *Sat.* 1.5 expresses Horace's hope that he could help to mend the relationship between Antony and Octavian, thus restoring peace.

74 POLITICS AND DIVINIZATION IN AUGUSTAN POETRY

In her commentary on the poem, Gowers draws our attention to the way that *Satire* 1.5 'frame[s] world events in disarmingly domestic terms'.[24] The poet's irreverent deflation of Octavian's involvement in contemporary politics has been understood by Dufallo as a means by which Horace makes Octavian's authority seem down-to-earth and therefore desirable.[25] Through this kind of rhetoric, the poet quietly presents Octavian's unreachable, powerful status—the precise nature of which remains elusive—as ordinary social reality which men like Horace cheerfully accept. Indeed, the poet's self-presentation as one who is laughably unable to participate in the business of negotiation disguises the triumvirs' domination as the buffoonish inadequacy of an individual. The whimsical de-escalation of political tension in *Satire* 1.5 thus creates the impression of '(big) business as usual'; and the removal of Octavian from the surface of the poem reinforces the idea that civil war is some vague notion in the far-off distance. At the same time, however, by depicting himself as being only ever in the shadows of a different, more remote world, the poet identifies politics—the very thing which determines lives—as the preserve of an intangible few, amongst whom the readers detect a silhouette in the shape of Octavian.[26]

The way in which Horace adumbrates Octavian's unreachable superiority by pointedly leaving him out of a poem can also be observed in *Epode* 4, which has a dramatic date close to that of *Satire* 1.5.[27] Set in a time shortly before Octavian's campaign against Sextus Pompey in 36 BC, *Epode* 4 aims its invective at an apparently objectionable upstart who has risen from a freedman to the rank of *tribunus militum* serving in Octavian's army. As in *Satire* 1.5, Octavian at no point makes an appearance in *Epode* 4; but his presence can be inferred from the final four verses, which depict the contempt that the people in the street felt toward this upstart's elevation to a position of power within Octavian's camp (*Epod.* 4.17–20). As Watson points out, this scene shines a positive light on the triumvir: by ventriloquizing the Roman citizens' perception that Octavian should have no truck with the likes of this repug-

---

[24] Gowers (2012) 5.   [25] Dufallo (2015).

[26] Kennedy (1992) 31–5 argues that it is precisely the poems which present themselves as apolitical that are the most actively political, since their superficial apoliticality allows power to be accumulated and exercised beyond the notice of those involved.

[27] The book of the *Epodes* was composed between 42 and 30 BC. The date of composition for individual poems are discussed in the introductory essays of the commentaries of Mankin (1995) and Watson (2003); see also Carrubba (1969) 3. A number of the poems (such as *Epodes* 1 and 4) have a 'pre-Actium' dramatic date, but that does not mean that they can only be read from this temporal perspective. Their appearance in the unified collection published after Actium allows them to be approached from what Kraggerud (1984: 44–65) calls a *Doppelperspektive*—that is, as documents of their own time *and* from a post-Actian revisionist viewpoint. Here I hope to show that the virtual absence of Octavian in these 'early' *Epodes* becomes all the more salient when we read them with the knowledge of his eventual victory in mind.

DIVINIZATION AND THE TRANSFORMATION OF ROME   75

nant upstart, Horace implicitly asserts Octavian as the nobler cause in the war against Sextus.[28] Watson's accurate assessment of *Epode* 4 as an indirect endorsement of Octavian's faction laced with anti-Sextan propaganda forms the basis of my reading of the poem. But I wish to suggest further that *Epode* 4 does not stop at lending Octavian a subtly supportive voice at a tense political moment. The poem, I argue, paints the absent Octavian as an entirely different political entity, thereby creating a distance between him and others who are involved in the civil war; and this in turn allows Horace to insinuate that there is a fundamental distinction between Octavian and those who are jostling for power and status in a volatile and disorderly society.[29]

The justification for this reading can be found in the poem's opening, in which Horace emphatically lays out the irreconcilability between him and the upstart (*Epod.* 4.1–6):

> Lupis et agnis quanta sortito obtigit,
> > tecum mihi discordia est,
> Hibericis peruste funibus latus
> > et crura dura compede.
> licet superbus ambules pecunia,   5
> > fortuna non mutat genus.

Great is the enmity assigned by Nature to wolves and lambs; no less is that between me and you—you with your flanks scarred by Spanish ropes, and legs by iron fetters; you may strut about as proudly as you like on account of your money—but fortune does not alter breeding.

Horace's hatred of his enemy ultimately comes down to the man's supposed low birth (*genus*, 4.6) and good fortune (*fortuna*, 4.6).[30] Embedded in the poet's bitter attack on the upstart's rise in society is an emphasis on the fixed nature of certain things. The passage begins with an age-old proverbial opposition found in the animal kingdom (4.1); this is followed by a reminder of the upstart's indelible past as a slave (4.3–4); and the verbal attack continues with Horace asserting the immutability of one's birth-rank (4.5). Cumulatively, these poetic images insist that there is a natural order of things that cannot be altered by circumstance. Furthermore, as the lexicon of animal species in the

---

[28] Watson (2002) 219–20 and (2007) 97.

[29] A number of studies have noted that the chaotic uncertainty of the 30s permeates the *Epodes*; see Nisbet (1984); Fitzgerald (1988) 177, 183; Watson (2003) 149 and (2007) 97.

[30] Mankin (1995) 110.

76 POLITICS AND DIVINIZATION IN AUGUSTAN POETRY

opening line (*Lupis et agnis*, 4.1) morphs into the language of class distinction five lines later (*genus*, 4.6),[31] Horace symbolically stratifies political classes into different *genera*, allowing the polysemy of the word *genus* to insinuate that the difference between him and the upstart is like that between human and animal. The upstart may perceive that he has soared above his rank, but Horace rejects not only the validity but even the possibility of his elevation. In its venting of a vitriolic contempt for the upstart, the opening of *Epode* 4 enshrines true elevation as something unaffected by the turns of *fortuna* and beyond the reach of certain men.

This exclusionary act affects how we might construe Octavian's non-appearance at the end of the poem, where, as mentioned above, Horace depicts passers-by showing their disdain at the upstart's enlistment in Octavian's army (4.17–20):

> 'quid attinet tot ora navium gravi
>   rostrata duci pondere
> contra latrones atque servilem manum
>   hoc, hoc tribuno militum?'   20

What's the point of sending so many ships' bows beaked with heavy rams against a rabble of pirates and slaves, when this man—yes, this one here—is a senior officer?

Just as the conflict between Octavian and Antony is framed in *Satire* 1.5 as a dispute between estranged friends, here the imminent civil war between Octavian and Sextus is filtered through the citizens' eyes as a race to the bottom between sordid types like the upstart and 'a rabble of pirates and slaves'. Notably, the absence of both Octavian and Sextus in the citizens' idea of civil war underscores the extent to which political struggle between men who hold Rome's future in their hands happens beyond the grasp of the ordinary. Moreover, by having the Roman citizens expressing their disapproval of the upstart's association with the new Caesar, Horace presents Octavian's lofty and virtuous status as not only public opinion but even something that the Roman people would wish to remain unchanged.[32]

---

[31] *genus* can of course also denote the species of animals (*OLD* s.v. 6a). Note also the correspondence between *sortito* in line 1 and *fortuna* in line 6.

[32] Watson (2002) 223 interprets the focalization through the citizens differently: he argues that by making citizens voice their damning assessment of the political situation, Horace manages to maintain his own independence of judgement.

DIVINIZATION AND THE TRANSFORMATION OF ROME   77

This attempt to distance Octavian from the depravity of others goes some way to restore his image at the time. It is well documented that prior to the battle of Naulochus, Sextus, who claimed Neptune as his adoptive father (cf. *Neptunius | dux*, Hor. *Epod.* 9.7–8; App. *B Civ.* 5.100; Cass. Dio 48.48.5), had the support of the people at Rome (Cass. Dio 48.31.5–6; Suet. *Aug.* 16.2).[33] Meanwhile, the *Divi filius* struggled to compete with the popularity and tactics of his rival, and was the target of the anger of the Roman masses who endured famine under Sextus' blockade of the grain supply from Sicily (Suet. *Aug.* 16.1).[34] By having the Roman citizens assuming the moral superiority of Octavian's side, Horace's poem repositions the triumvir as 'the people's choice' when in fact he was far from popular. But more importantly, it should be noted that while the citizens try to distinguish the upstart from his nobler commander, there is no such distinction in their assessment of the Pompeian faction, who are regarded indiscriminately as a group of pirates and lawless slaves (4.19). This characterization of the Pompeian army is of course a slight on Sextus' self-stylization as the son of Neptune. It also reduces the status of Sextus to that of an armed slave and thus no better than the upstart, who is a freedman-turned-army-officer. By establishing this parallel between Sextus and the upstart while removing Octavian from their level, Horace implies that the new Caesar is a better and loftier entity, belonging to a different *genus*. In fact, the poem's earlier assertion, *fortuna non mutat genus* (4.6), now applies to the conflict between Octavian and his rival as much as it does to the inordinate rise of the upstart. The *fortuna* of war does not change one's *genus*: pirates and bandits led by a Neptunian pretender are exactly that, whereas the aboveness of Octavian is (or at least should be) unassailable. The absence of Octavian therefore, far from being incidental, serves to underline that the new Caesar not only rises above the civil-war cesspit but that his aboveness is immutable and indisputable.

One difficulty remains, however. Critics of this *Epode* have noted 'the disturbing similarities' between the upstart and Horace,[35] since the poet himself had once served as *tribunus militum* at Philippi and afterwards enjoyed a comparable elevation to position of prominence within Octavian's circle.[36]

---

[33] The image of Neptune and his symbolic trident appeared on Sextan *denarii* that circulated widely in Italy, see e.g. *RRC* 511/2 and 511/4.

[34] See further Powell (2008) 97–8, 259–61; Miller (2009) 24; Welch (2012) 43–91.

[35] Watson (2003) 150.

[36] See further Carrubba (1969) 56–7; Henderson (1987); Oliensis (1991) 118 and (1998) 66–7; Williams (1995) 312. The interweaving of Rome's political instability and the poet's psychological and corporeal anxieties has been well studied by Henderson (1987); Fitzgerald (1988); and Gowers (2016) 103–30.

78 POLITICS AND DIVINIZATION IN AUGUSTAN POETRY

It has been suggested that the convergence between the upstart and Horace can be seen as the poet deliberately courting a charge of hypocrisy, a move fitting for an iambist who relishes self-deflation.[37] Nevertheless, the poem's final revelation that the upstart occupies a military office associated with Horace's previous opposition to Octavian evidently implicates the poet in the confusion between self and other, friend and enemy, which is inherent in the very concept of civil war.[38] The reading of *Epode* 4 presented above brings out another of the poem's blurred dichotomies, namely that between transformation and immutability. The upstart of this poem is clearly a transformed figure, yet he is thought of as fundamentally unchangeable (cf. *fortuna non mutat genus*). Horace too is a changed man—a convert to the Octavianic cause—but he also has an unalterable past: he was on the 'wrong side' at Philippi. By contrast, Octavian and the worthiness of his cause are, as the poem implicitly claims, immutable. By thus cultivating an aura of unimpeachable distinction around Octavian, *Epode* 4 makes the new Caesar transcend the partisan confusion and societal volatility of the triumviral period, making him an altogether different kind of political entity from his rivals.

In the three pre-Actium poems discussed so far, we have seen Horace carefully carving out a position of exceptional pre-eminence for the new Caesar against a backdrop of societal upheaval. Through images of concealed capability (*Sat.* 1.3), unreachable authority (*Sat.* 1.5), and hierarchical aboveness (*Epod.* 4), the poet draws attention to Octavian's outsized political influence while setting him apart from the power struggle and civic unrest happening on the ground. Indeed, Octavian's status is such that the poet appears to have anxieties about how his own rise in social status would be perceived, now that he is no longer fighting for the republican cause but instead reaping the benefits from being part of Octavian's circle.[39] As we shall see, Horace's uncertainties about his own role as poet and political subject become even more pronounced in the poems set around the time of Actium. The poet's use of divinizing discourse in these poems sensitizes readers to the idea that the glaring disparity between Caesar and his peers might soon reconstitute into something more alarming.

---

[37] Watson (2003) 152.   [38] Fitzgerald (1988) 183; Giusti (2016b) 133.
[39] On the conflict between Horace's various social identities, see esp. Fitzgerald (1988) 190.

DIVINIZATION AND THE TRANSFORMATION OF ROME   79

All Aboard the Ship of Caesar

Epode 1, which takes the form of a *propemptikon* addressed to Maecenas prior to his departure to Actium, heightens Octavian's significance for the Roman world in its opening movement. Caesar hovers at the edges of the poem, about to disappear into the known; but the poet's self-positioning in relation to Octavian's impending absence highlights the extent to which Caesar has distant control over the poet's life while the poet has none over Caesar's (*Epod.* 1.1–10):

> Ibis Liburnis inter alta navium,
>   amice, propugnacula,
> paratus omne Caesaris periculum
>   subire, Maecenas, tuo:
> quid nos, quibus te vita si superstite,   5
>   iucunda, si contra, gravis?
> utrumne iussi persequemur otium
>   non dulce, ni tecum simul,
> an hunc laborem, mente laturi decet
>   qua ferre non mollis viros?   10

You will go, my friend, on Liburnian vessels among the tall bulwarks of ships, prepared to undergo every risk of Caesar's at your own risk, Maecenas. What about me, to whom life is delightful if you survive, but otherwise heavy? Shall I, as bidden, follow peaceful pursuits, which are not sweet if not shared with you? Or shall I endure this hardship, determined to bear it with the spirit that men ought to show if they are not weaklings?

Maecenas is about to follow his commander, Octavian, into war and put his own life at risk for him (cf. *omne Caesaris periculum | subire...tuo*, 1.4); and Horace feels that he is duty-bound to do the same for Maecenas (1.1–4; cf. *te...forti sequemur pectore*, 1.11–14).[40] Given the nature of their relationship, the poet's outlook on life (1.5–6), joyful or gloomy, ultimately hinges on

---

[40] Kraggerud (1984) 29–30 argues that the wording of lines 3–4, set against the exemplary actions of Maecenas and Horace, evoke the *coniuratio totius Italiae*, the oath of loyalty to Octavian taken by Italy and the western provinces in 32 BC (which does not survive) after the declaration of war against Cleopatra. This suggestion, as Watson (2003) 55 rightly points out, is highly speculative albeit very attractive.

80   POLITICS AND DIVINIZATION IN AUGUSTAN POETRY

what happens to Caesar, whose actions fall outside of the poem's visual range and can only be inferred from what Maecenas does. The physical distance that is about to be opened up between Horace, Maecenas, and Octavian thus throws into sharp relief a hierarchical order at the top of which sits Caesar.[41]

The impending disappearance of Octavian and Maecenas from Horace's life also makes the poet realize that things cannot go on as normal without them. Life's true sweetness, so Horace claims, can only be experienced in the company of Maecenas (*non dulce, ni tecum simul*, 1.8); otherwise it is just mandatory fun (cf. *iussi*, 1.7). The word *iussi* does not need to be interpreted strictly as a command from a patron;[42] but its usage here clearly connotes Horace's recognition of Maecenas' superiority. The crescendo of deliberative questions stretching over six verses (1.5–10) underlines the poet's inability to be his own master in the absence of his friend–benefactor, which in turn highlights the extent to which Maecenas—and by extension, Octavian—has become a kind of centre of gravity. Indeed, by suggesting that he simply cannot find true pleasure in life without having his superiors around, Horace makes the towering status of Caesar a sine qua non for the well-functioning of Rome's sociopolitical system.

The idea that Horace ultimately links his livelihood to the safety of Caesar finds fuller expression later in *Ode* 3.14. There, Augustus' triumphal return from the Cantabrian campaign, after narrowly escaping death (3.14.1–4), provides an occasion for the poet to reflect on his own security under Caesar (3.14.13–16).[43] Here in *Epode* 1, Caesar is one step removed from the poet: only Maecenas, who acts as an intermediary, is explicitly presented as the provider of joy and security for Horace. Nonetheless, the poet's framing of his *vita otiosa* as something that is wholly dependent on these men already draws attention to what might lie ahead for Rome on the eve of the battle of Actium. Moreover, by emphasizing the link between his *otium* and the activities of Maecenas and Octavian, Horace subtly invests a divine quality in these men. The poet's idea of 'sweet pleasure' (*otium…dulce*) evokes the Epicurean goal of *ataraxia*,[44] which in turn assimilates the men in whose company Horace finds true *otium* to Epicurus, a 'god' in the eyes of Lucretius (cf. *deus ille fuit, deus, inclute Memmi, DRN* 5.8). Equally importantly, Horace also seems to be

---

[41]   On this hierarchy, see also Oliensis (1998) 80–1.   [42]   White (1993) 267–8.

[43]   Lowrie (2015) 331–2 rightly suggests that the Augustan poets' formulation of civic safety as being embodied in the leader enquires into Rome's (over)dependence on Augustus. See further discussion of *Ode* 3.14 in Chapter 3. Horace expands on the interrelatedness of Roman security and Augustus' personal safety in *Ode* 4.5 (esp. 4.5.27); see discussion in the Epilogue.

[44]   On Horace's familiarity with Epicurean philosophy, see most recently Yona (2018). Virgil makes a similar allusion to the Epicurean ideal of pleasure in *G.* 4.563–4 (*illo Vergilium me tempore dulcis alebat | Parthenope studiis florentem ignobilis oti*); see most recently Freer (2019) 80.

DIVINIZATION AND THE TRANSFORMATION OF ROME   81

in dialogue with Virgil's First *Eclogue*, in which (as we saw in the previous chapter) a powerful young man grants *otium* to Tityrus and is subsequently worshipped as a 'god' (cf. Verg. *Ecl.* 1.6). The presence of the young man (cf. *praesentis*, *Ecl.* 1.41; *illum vidi iuvenem*, 1.42) sets in motion the return of Tityrus' idyllic life, allowing him to find pleasure in herding and singing once again. Here in *Epode* 1, the impending absence of Octavian and Maecenas looks to deprive the poet of his ability to pursue *otium*. By thus evoking these deified benefactors in his attempt to communicate with Maecenas, Horace underlines the fact that Maecenas is no ordinary man, and Octavian even less so. As Caesar's ships set sail for Actium, the intertextual activities of the poet's formulation of his *otium* underline the idea that the relationship between Horace and Octavian is about to be reconfigured, and that Octavian's near-numinous status may stretch to breaking point the conventional social dynamic and political structure of republican Rome.

This re-ordering of relations becomes apparent in *Epode* 9. Set in the heady aftermath of the battle of Actium, *Epode* 9 depicts the poet toasting Octavian's victory against the backdrop of sympotic activities (cf. *Epod.* 9.1–10, 33–8).[45] For the first time in Horace's poetry, Caesar's presence can be detected throughout the poem, especially in its sympotic frame, which will be discussed in more detail shortly. On the other hand, however, the person of Octavian himself is still, in some sense, removed from the poem. In line 2, he is already 'victor…Caesar', subsumed under that glorious moniker; in line 18, his name is 'sung', invoked as if in a hymn or prayer—though the singer is not the poet, but a group of 'Galli' (*Galli canentes Caesarem*).[46] Furthermore, Horace again creates a stark distance between his realm of activity and Octavian's to the point that the latter virtually disappears out of sight and seems to transcend the republican world altogether. The clearest indication of this can be found in the poet's extravagant comparison of Octavian to great republican generals of the past (9.23–6):

> io Triumphe, nec Iugurthino parem
> bello reportasti ducem
> neque Africanum, cui super Carthaginem   25
> virtus sepulcrum condidit.

Hail, Triumph! You did not bring back such a general from the Jugurthine War, nor was Africanus such, whose valour built a tomb over Carthage.

---

[45] The poem's sympotic frame has been much discussed: see esp. Bartels (1973); Slater (1976); Macleod (1982); Loupiac (1998); Cucchiarelli (2006); Giusti (2016b).

[46] The 'Gauls' refer to the Galatians of Amyntas, who defected to Octavian's side right before the battle of Actium (Serv. ad *Aen.* 6.612).

82 POLITICS AND DIVINIZATION IN AUGUSTAN POETRY

Horace's assertion that Octavian ranks higher (*nec...parem*, 9.23) than Marius and 'Africanus' after the victory at Actium is no straightforward eulogy. As I alluded to in the previous chapter, in 101 BC the seven-time consul Marius received offerings and libations along with the gods for defeating Jugurtha.[47] The popular cult of Marius redefined the limit of what kind of honours could be given to a republican statesman until the rules were rewritten again during the dictatorship of Julius Caesar. Likewise, both Scipio Aemilianus and Publius Cornelius Scipio were thought to have achieved divine status for demonstrating extraordinary *virtus* in their service to the Republic (cf. Cic. *Rep.* 6.13, 26). Moreover, as Cole has shown, the very idea of a merit-based apotheosis appeared to have been embedded into Roman political thought by Cicero through the figure of Scipio Aemilianus (cf. Cic. *Rep.* 2.4, 17–20).[48] The *Africanus* in Horace's poem may refer to either the Younger or the Elder Scipio (or both).[49] But regardless of the exact identity of Horace's *Africanus*, the famous generals of this passage are undoubtedly icons of divinized republican statesmen. By asserting that Marius and *Africanus* are no match for Octavian, Horace elevates the victor at Actium to a position that is unprecedented in the history of Rome. The new Caesar's 'aboveness' removes him from the realm of other men, including the greatest statesmen of the Roman Republic; and the underlying implication of this poetic image is the idea that Octavian could no longer be contained or defined within the traditional political framework of the Republic, but that he appears to stand outside and beyond it.

The serious, and not entirely positive, impact this could have on the political future of Rome is hinted at by Horace. Giusti's recent study has drawn our attention to the relevance of Sallust's *Bellum Iugurthinum* as an intertext of *Epode* 9 (cf. *Iugurthino...bello*, 23–4), and has pointed out that Sallust saw the war against Jugurtha as a reaction to the *superbia* which had become widespread in the moral crisis of the late Republic following the destruction of Carthage (cf. *tunc primum superbiae nobilitatis obviam itum est*, 'then for the first time resistance was offered to the insolence of the nobles', Sall. *Iug.* 5.1).[50] In light of the Sallustian intertext, Horace's suggestion that Marius is not equal to Octavian elevates the latter to a position of superiority, which can be seen as either the kind of *superbia* that the Jugurthine War was meant to challenge or the sort of claim to superiority that fuels civil conflict.[51] In this way, the

---

[47] See Chapter 1, n. 42.   [48] Cole (2013) 92–4, 98–102.

[49] The Younger Scipio, Aemilianus: Watson (2003) 330. The Elder Scipio, Publius Cornelius: Kraggerud (1984) 104–5. Conflation of both: Cairns (1983) 83–4.

[50] Giusti (2016b) 143.

[51] Giusti (2016b) 144 n. 68.

poem on the one hand glorifies the achievements of Octavian by suggesting that he has surpassed the limit of greatness established by previous republican generals, while on the other hand problematizing Octavian's unmatched singularity, subtly framing it as something that does not resolve the civil war, but rather reinscribes its inevitability.

The notes of alarm concerning what Octavian's unparalleled status would mean for Rome both encapsulate the underlying anxiety running through *Epode* 9, and open up the interpretation of the poem's much-discussed sympotic frame. While *Epode* 9 clearly exudes a celebratory mood, there is an undercurrent of uncertainty evident from its very first lines. The poem begins with Horace wondering when he would be able to go to Maecenas' house so that they could drink together in Octavian's honour (9.1–4). This opening immediately raises questions about the whereabouts of Horace and Maecenas, and, more subtly, whether the poet's relationship with his friend–benefactor would stay the same after Actium. Later in the poem, when Horace turns his thoughts to the defeated Antony, the picture is again one of uncertainty as the poet tries to guess where in the world Antony would go into hiding (9.29–32). At the end of the poem, readers encounter another sympotic occasion: this time, the party appears to be in full swing already, possibly taking place onboard of a warship (9.33–8).[52] The sense of dislocation conjured up by the poem's sympotic frame, combined with reminders of the fluidity of the postwar situation, underscores the worry and unpredictability bubbling beneath the poem's ostensibly celebratory surface.

This tension between triumphant excitement and latent anxiety in *Epode* 9 culminates in the poem's final sympotic image: *curam metumque Caesaris rerum iuvat | dulci Lyaeo solvere* ('It's a joy to loosen our worry and fear for Caesar's affairs with the help of sweet Lyaeus', 9.37–8). It has been noted that the linguistic ambiguity in the expression *curam metumque Caesaris rerum* ('our worry and fear *for* Caesar's cause' or 'our worry and fear *of* Caesar's cause') leaves the poem on a troublingly equivocal note.[53] Moreover, given the poem celebrates Octavian's victory over the unruly and degenerate forces of

---

[52] Critics have been unable to agree on whether *fluentem nauseam* ('flowing nausea', 9.35) refers to seasickness (Bücheler 1927: 320–1) or hangover (Fraenkel 1957: 71–5). Seasickness would imply that Horace and Maecenas were at Actium, a notion which divides scholarly opinion: see for example the contrasting positions of Setaioli (1981) 1716–28 and Watson (2003) 310–12. My view on whether Horace and Maecenas were present at Actium is similar to that of Kraggerud (1984) 67 and Williams (1968) 214: that is, this information is simply not ascertainable. I am, however, more than partial to Cucchiarelli (2006)'s suggestion that idea of a symposium taking place on a warship would point to a superimposition of the private and the public spheres, which finds fuller expression in the poetry and politics of the Principate.

[53] Mankin (1995) 181.

84 POLITICS AND DIVINIZATION IN AUGUSTAN POETRY

Antony and Cleopatra (cf. 9.11–16), critics have quite rightly found it strange
that Horace now evokes the image of excessive drinking (cf. *capaciores adfer
huc, puer, scyphos*, 9.33)—in other words, the unrestrained aspect of Bacchus—
to alleviate anxiety about Octavian, the supposed civilizer of the East.[54]

One way of understanding the poem's conclusion is, as Giusti suggests, to
view Horace's embrace of 'sweet Lyaeus' as an act of ideological conversion—
an 'early, almost embryonic example' of a recognizable Bacchic poetics in the
Odes, where the *furor* and transgression of the inspired poet convey a guilty
will to power and thus indicate the poet's political reconciliation to the new
regime.[55] However, as I pointed out above, the tension that resides in *Epode* 9
makes it difficult to read the poem's conclusion only as an attempt to recon-
ciliate. Instead I would suggest that this final image, infused with ambiguity
and contradiction, also conveys the idea that Horace is unable to determine
what kind of force Caesar is becoming and what the future holds for Rome.
The victory at Actium has propelled Caesar to new heights unparalleled in
republican history, removing him from the realm of even great men; but the
flipside of this turn of events, as Horace earlier implies, is that no one knows
for sure whether this spells the end of Rome's troubles or the beginning of yet
more. The double-meaning of *curam metumque Caesaris rerum* (9.37), to my
mind, underscores this unknowability. The sympotic frame of the poem further indicates that Caesar could either turn out to be a Bacchic civilizer, a
Liber Pater incarnate who brings about peace and freedom to Rome; or he
could turn out to be an unrestrainable Dionysus, one who transgresses
boundaries and whose power is unpredictable.[56] Seen against this background, the poet's own descent into excess at the end of *Epode* 9 implies that
the line between celebrating Caesar as a restorer of happier times, and

[54] Giusti (2016b) 136; Watson (2003) on 9.38. As Giusti points out, the double symposium of the
poem's opening and closing movements draws out the duality of Bacchus as on the one hand the
peacemaker and civilizing conqueror of the East, who was assimilated to Octavian in his victory over
Egypt, and on the other hand the deity of wine and orgiastic cults, equated with Antony in his unrestrained drunkenness.

[55] Giusti (2016b) 138. On Bacchic poetics in the *Odes*, see Silk (1969); Batinski (1990–1) 362, 374;
Schiesaro (2009). See further discussion of the 'Bacchic Odes' in Chapter 3.

[56] *Epode* 9 develops an association between Octavian and free-spirited celebration in stages. In the
poem's opening address to Maecenas, Horace suggests that they should celebrate Octavian's victory at
Actium just as they celebrated his victory over Sextus (9.7–10): here the poet claims that Sextus had
threatened to enslave Rome (9.7–9). Two lines later, Horace presents another image of slavery: a
Roman soldier—most probably Antony—enslaved by Cleopatra (9.11–14). Through this pair of
images of slavery, Horace implies firstly that both Actium and Naulochus should be construed as wars
of liberation (rather than civil wars); and secondly, that Octavian is the liberator of Rome. The proposed symposium thus establishes a connection between free-flowing wine consumption and civic
freedom, *otium* and Actium, Bacchus and Octavian. The switch of Bacchus from Antony to Octavian
also serves to rehabilitate the deity as a 'freer' in a different sense.

acceding to Caesar's transgression of appropriate limits, is becoming increasingly blurred. In this way, the conclusion of *Epode* 9 gestures at the unknowable direction of politics as a result of Actium, and encapsulates the unnerving experience of facing up to a new political reality.

Epode 9 thus sits an important juncture in the figuration of Octavian's power in divine terms, as the poem deploys this set of imagery to adumbrate the worries occasioned by the stark disparity between Octavian and his subjects-to-be in the aftermath of Actium. Unlike the deeply pessimistic *Epodes* 7 and 16—which present themselves as spoken from the midst of civil war, but may function as reminders of the disaster from which Octavian had saved the Roman state once the book of the *Epodes* was published in 30 BC— *Epode* 9 is framed as a definitively post-Actian composition, and radiates (initially, at least) triumphal optimism about Rome's future.[57] However, by the end of the poem, optimism is set alongside apprehension, allowing the open-endedness of the poem's conclusion to convey that the Roman subject— including those who are within Octavian's circle—is unable to figure out how the future might turn out.[58] *Epode* 9 shows that Caesar's restoration of peace to Rome and his leading of Rome onto a path of constitutional uncertainty are two sides of the same coin. That Horace allows these contradictory notions to co-exist is salient, as it suggests that it is entirely possible to see Octavian as having saved the Republic and destroyed republicanism at the same time. To engage in this kind of 'doublethink', as Horace does in *Epode* 9, is precisely what is required to make sense of the Augustan Principate.

How to Talk about Caesar after the War

I have argued thus far that the outsized authority Octavian possesses, his staggering aboveness in Roman society, and the deeply unequal power relations between him and his supposed peers, which are always already there in Horace's early poetry, are reinscribed in *Epode* 9 as the remarkable qualities of

---

[57] The date of composition for *Epodes* 7 and 16 has generated much debate. On *Epod.* 7, see Setaioli (1981) 1710–12; Kraggerud (1984) 44–65; Watson (2003) 266–71. On *Epod.* 16, see Kraggerud (1984) 136; Cavarzere (1994) 187–8; Watson (2003) 487–8. The crux of the issue is that most critics are content with *c.*39–38 BC as the date of composition for both *Epodes* 7 and 16, whereas Kraggerud (1984) and Mankin (1995) date *Epode* 7 to 32 BC, and *Epode* 16 to around the time of Actium. In the context of the published book, however, *Epodes* 7 and 16 may be read from a *Doppelperspektive* (Kraggerud 1984: 44–65; see n. 27 above).

[58] Additionally, Fitzgerald (1988) 179 suggests that the reversal of chronology occasioned by the placement of *Epod.* 16 after *Epod.* 9, which symbolically reverses Rome's rising fortune after Actium, perhaps indicates that Octavian's return to Rome is awaited with some trepidation.

86 POLITICS AND DIVINIZATION IN AUGUSTAN POETRY

an unprecedented political leader. In doing so, the poet of the *Epodes* looks
ahead to Rome's shift towards a new political climate in which the extraordinary status of Octavian is its defining characteristic.

In the first poem of Book 2 of the *Satires*, published a year or so after
Actium, Horace renders this aspect of the new Principate more visible by
framing it in a series of disarmingly personal discussions about how to write
poetry in the post-Actian age. As a number of studies have pointed out, *Satire*
2.1 is extremely aware of the 'rules' of post-Actian Roman society.[59] From the
outset, libel law and the 'laws' of the satiric genre are inextricably tied up: *Sunt
quibus in satura videar nimis acer et ultra | legem tendere opus* ('There are
some to whom I seem too ferocious in my satire and to be straining my work
beyond what is legitimate', *Sat.* 2.1.1–2).[60] Freudenburg notes that the poet's
subsequent consultation with the jurist Trebatius on what would constitute a
suitable subject for his new book blurs the boundaries between fiction and
reality to such an extent that Trebatius' initial recommendation seems to
underline a tacit expectation that poetry in the post-Actian age should glorify
Octavian's recent military success: *aude | Caesaris invicti res dicere, multa
laborum | praemia laturus* ('dare to tell of the deeds of invincible Caesar; your
efforts will be amply rewarded', 10–12).[61] Muecke in her commentary points
out that Horace here elevates Octavian's status by giving him the epithet *invictus*, which usually belongs to a god like Jupiter (Hor. *Carm.* 3.27.73), or a hero
such as Ennius' Scipio (*Scipio invicte*, Enn. *Var.* 3 = *op. inc.* V Sk.).[62] By the
end of the poem, however, Caesar is not merely the godlike hero of martial
epic, but also—as quoted above at the beginning of this chapter—a literary
critic and courtroom judge (82–6). I highlighted earlier that the expression
iudice...Caesare ('Caesar as judge', 84) intimates that the authority of both
law and literature now coalesce in Octavian; and the image conjured up by
solventur...tabulae ('the tablets will be cancelled', 86) carries alarming

---

[59] See most recently Freudenburg (2021) 51–3. The volume of secondary literature on *Sat.* 2.1 is
considerable. Muecke (1993), Tatum (1998), Michel (1999), McGinn (2001) 95–101, and Lowrie
(2009) are the standout studies of the poem's sustained engagement with Roman laws and the varied
implications of this engagement. Doblhofer (1966) 22–45 examines the poem's panegyrical elements;
Rudd (1966) 124–31, Coffey (1976) 81–97, and Oliensis (1998) 41–6 bring out well the issue of poetic
authority. The poem's dialogue with Callimachus is noted by Coffta (2002) 38–43. On the broader
intertextual relationship between *Sat.* 2 and Callimachus' *Iambi*, see Cucchiarelli (2001) 168–78. The
programmatic function of *Sat.* 2.1 for the organization and thematic principles of Book 2 is well discussed by Knorr (2004) 168–81.

[60] Tatum (1998) 689; Lowrie (2009) 331; Freudenburg (2021) on 2.1.2.

[61] Freudenburg (2001) 76–7. See also Muecke (1993) on 2.1.22. Additionally, Freudenburg (2001)
78–82 and (2021) on 2.1.10–12 notes that lines 10–11 recall Virgil's proposal to write an Augustan epic
at *G.* 3.46–7.

[62] Muecke (1993) on 2.1.11. The placement of this Ennian fragment is uncertain: Skutsch (1985)
752 deems it 'very probable' that it belonged to Ennius' *Scipio*; see further Morelli (2016) 67.

DIVINIZATION AND THE TRANSFORMATION OF ROME   87

overtones of the dissolution of laws before Caesar's authority. Adding to these observations, I now draw attention to the word sandwiched between *solventur* and *tabulae*: the disarming but hardly innocent *risu* ('amid laughter', 86). Whereas the law used to determine what was libellous, now laughter—that most subjective of literary responses—is the new barometer. Caesar's smile will get the poet off (cf. *tu missus abibis*, 'you will go away let off', 86): the opinion of one man is all that matters. Taking on the roles of war-hero, literary critic, and judge simultaneously, Octavian is no ordinary statesman.[63] On the one hand, this implicit characterization of Octavian as dictator hints at Rome's shift towards autocratic rule; on the other hand, it suggests quite flatteringly that there is a new, more exceptional Scipio, to whom Horace is expected to play the part of the panegyrist Ennius.[64] By evoking these two ideas simultaneously, Horace's poem signals that under Octavian Rome is both undergoing a stark constitutional transformation and re-experiencing a more glorious age of the Republic. It is this tacit transmission of the ideology of the emergent regime that, I would suggest, marks *Satire* 2.1 as the product of a new political climate and the beginning of a different kind of relationship between poet and Caesar. Whereas Horace in *Epode* 9 carved out a sympotic space for himself to reflect on the future of Rome, the poet's main worry now is how to keep Caesar smiling. The different outlooks of these two poems underscore the crucial point that, within a year or so after Actium, the future direction of Rome is already no longer a citizen's concern: simply knowing your place and be mindful of what you can say are all that is required to thrive in this new age.

So how does one keep a smile on Caesar's face? The answer is not so easy. Earlier in the poem, Trebatius warns that 'some friend of the great' will strike the poet if he were not careful with his words (*metuo, et maiorum ne quis amicus | frigore te feriat*, 'I'm afraid that one of your great friends may strike you with a chill', 61–2); to which Horace counters that he has nothing to fear because he had 'lived among the great' (*me | cum magnis vixisse invita fatebitur usque | invidia*, 'reluctant Envy will keep on admitting that I lived among great men', 75–7). As Lowrie rightly observes, 'Caesar is Horace's trump card: the "great" even beyond the "friend of the great" Trebatius warns Horace not to offend.'[65] Yet the poet also acknowledges that, if Octavian does not like

---

[63] Lowrie (2009) 345–6, 348.
[64] Freudenburg (2001) 91–2. Note also lines 16–17, *attamen et iustum poteras et scribere fortem, | Scipiadam ut sapiens Lucilius* ('you could describe [him] as both just and brave, as wise Lucilius did of Scipio'), where Octavian is indirectly compared to Scipio Aemilianus by Trebatius.
[65] Lowrie (2009) 343.

88 POLITICS AND DIVINIZATION IN AUGUSTAN POETRY

something, 'he will kick out in every direction while safe himself' (*recalcitrat undique tutus*, 20).[66] The arbitrariness of Octavian's absolute power, I suggest, is prefigured by the expression with which the present discussion began: *aude | Caesaris invicti res dicere* ('dare to tell of the deeds of invincible Caesar', 10–11). *Aude* is ironic, because praising Caesar is just about the safest thing to do in post-Actian Rome;[67] but it also implies that there is danger involved, because Caesar might just find something he does not like about the praise. However, there is nothing one can do about this situation: the palpable Jovian resonance of the epithet *invictus*, which recalibrates the relationship between poet and Caesar in the post-Actian age as that between human and divine, implies that Caesar can do what he likes, just like the king of the gods himself. Rome's authoritarian turn is thus hinted at by Horace through divinizing language; but importantly, the actual words do not come from the poet's own mouth, as lines 10–11 are the advice of Trebatius. By attributing these words to Trebatius, a man rooted to the old republican world and its laws,[68] Horace discreetly implies that even the most ardent republicans can and should see that a new world order now looms large.[69]

One conclusion we may draw at this midway point is that, since the disparity between Octavian and others is figured in increasingly stark human-and-divine terms, the shift in the divinizing language of Horace's triumviral poetry dramatizes Rome's transition from Republic to Principate. As the Roman state emerges from the violent disorder of civil war and reconstitutes into something that bears the signs of a nascent autocracy, poetic images of Octavian's unreachable authority and hierarchical aboveness (*Sat.* 1.3 and 1.5, *Epod.* 1 and 4) are transfigured into a portrait of Caesar as insurmountable dictator, whose jurisdiction is such that the rules of social interaction and literary composition are set to be rewritten. Secondly, as well as dramatizing Rome's constitutional shift, Horace's divinizing language also underscores an ideological shift on the part of the poet-subject. Whereas divinizing imagery in the earlier poems portrays unequal power relations in symbolic terms, in

---

[66] In her excellent study of an apparent reference at *Sat.* 2.1.18–20 to a law in the Twelve Tables regarding quadrupeds, Lowrie (2009) argues that Horace's figuration of Octavian as a moody horse, who kicks out at bad handling but is not liable for his actions, foregrounds the idea that Caesar is beyond the power of the law.

[67] See also Freudenburg (2001) 75 n. 92 and (2021) on 2.1.10.

[68] On Trebatius' legal career, see Bauman (1985) 2, 123–36; Muecke (1993) 99–100; Freudenburg (2021) 49–50, 56. Tatum (1998) 697 writes: 'in *Sat.* II 1, Trebatius embodies the principles of jurisprudence.'

[69] Further, by making Trebatius the giver of advice on how to praise Caesar, Horace narrowly avoids sycophantically eulogizing Octavian himself, thus asserting his poetic independence however circumscribed.

DIVINIZATION AND THE TRANSFORMATION OF ROME   89

Epode 9 and *Satire* 2.1 this language is used to advocate in abstract terms the necessity of facing up to a new reality and the unavoidable submission to raw political power. In other words, this discourse in Horace's poetry ceases to be rhetorical, and instead becomes a tool for coping with, and dissecting the workings of, a new political regime.

Later, in *Satire* 2.6, divinizing language is in operation again, and this time Horace attributes it to people on the street—the masses, as it were. In this poem, Octavian and friends, who were once the main actors of 'big business' (cf. *magnis...rebus, Sat.* 1.5.28), are now thought of as the 'gods' of Roman society by those who are eager to read their minds (*nam te | scire, deos quoniam propius contingis oportet*, 'you ought to know, because you're in closer contact with the gods', 2.6.51–2; cf. also 2.6.54). Meanwhile, the poet is judged to be a mere 'mortal' when he confesses his lack of access to the divine (*iurantem me scire nihil mirantur ut unum | scilicet egregii mortalem altique silenti*, 'when I swear I know nothing they marvel at me as if I am, can you believe, the one and only mortal of uncommonly deep silence', 2.6.57–8). Set against the backdrop of post-Actian land settlement in the winter of 31–30 BC (cf. 2.6.55–6),[70] the poem's characterization of Octavian as a 'policy-god',[71] whose plan is undisclosed to the people, hints at the worrying opacity of the nascent Principate. As for Horace, when he presents the passer-by's pestering of him for inside information as an attempt to engage in a quasi-oracular 'consultation' (*quicumque obvius est, me consulit*, 'whoever comes across me seeks my opinion', 2.6.51), the expectation placed upon the poet to act as a 'seer' not only looks ahead to Horace's vatic pose in the *Odes* but also points to a new role for the poet as the elusive mouthpiece of an inscrutably powerful regime.

Virgil's *Georgics*: Losing Caesar

Virtually contemporaneous with Book 2 of Horace's *Satires*, Virgil's *Georgics* also reflects on Octavian's extraordinary status in the wake of his victory at Actium through discussions of his divinization, which the poet presents as all but certain, though not unproblematic. The poem's ambivalence towards the anticipated apotheosis of Octavian has been understood by some scholars as a

---

[70] Cass. Dio 51.3–4; Aug. *R.G.* 3.3, 16, 15.3; Suet. *Aug.* 17.3. See Muecke (1993) 204 and Freudenburg (2021) on 2.6.55–6 on the land settlement of 31–30 BC.
[71] I borrow this term from Freudenburg (2006) 24.

reflection of Virgil's attempt to come to terms with Octavian's supremacy while confessing Roman anxieties about ruler cult and its potential effect on the Roman constitution.[72] Others have taken the poet's recurrent deliberations on Octavian's divine destiny as a series of political lessons on how to exercise power, aimed directly at the new Caesar, who now possesses the authority 'to initiate, maintain, and bring an end to all manners of phenomena, especially agriculture, poetry, and war'.[73] Different approaches place different degrees of emphasis on the didactic force of Virgil's poem;[74] but nevertheless they share an understanding that the *Georgics*, like Horace's *Epode* 9 and *Satire* 2.1, is constitutive of a wider debate in the post-Actian transitional period about Octavian's power, and that, as such, the poem is acutely aware of its own mediating role both within Virgil's poetic corpus and in Rome's transition from Republic to Principate.[75]

My reading of the *Georgics* pursues this line of interpretation further by suggesting that discussions of Octavian's divinization in the poem function as a means by which Virgil considers the effectiveness and relevance of not just didactic poetry, but poetic mediation more generally, in the face of an emergent Augustan regime. Specifically, I want to illustrate that Virgil initially seeks to direct Octavian on how to achieve divinity and presents him with a model of divinization based on *cura terrarum*, which encapsulates an idealized relationship between ruler, farmer/subject, and poet. As the poem proceeds, however, it becomes clear that the poet's proposal diverges significantly from what is being pursued by Octavian, and this leads eventually to a reflection on the efficacy and nature of poetry in the forthcoming Augustan age. By presenting the divinization of Octavian as a topic unable to be affected by Virgilian didactic, the *Georgics* underscores not only the extent to which Rome is drifting seemingly unstoppably towards a new political reality, but also the diminishing scope for artistic negotiation in the post-Actian world.

---

[72] See esp. Perkell (1989) 150–2; Cole (2001) 69–74; Nelis (2013) 245–6. Gale (2000: 26–31, 35–6, 194; 2003: 325–32, 348–9; 2013: 288–90, 296) has consistently argued that Virgil's discussions of deification and political ambition in the *Georgics* evince a Lucretian ambivalence, which hints at an underlying concern about the divine aspirations of Octavian.

[73] See esp. Nappa (2005) 2–8; quotation comes from p. 7.

[74] Contrast, for example, Nappa (2005) with Batstone (1997); the latter contends that Virgil's poem ultimately only teaches us about the impossibility of obtaining meaning.

[75] Cole (2001) 68–70 and Nappa (2005) 30–3, 39–43, 65–7, 217–32.

DIVINIZATION AND THE TRANSFORMATION OF ROME 91

Divinization and *cura terrarum*

Perhaps the most startling aspect of the *Georgics'* depiction of Octavian is that from the outset Virgil asserts that the new Caesar will almost certainly become a god. The poem opens with a summary of its four books (*G.* 1.1–5), followed by a two-part prayer, in which the poet first addresses a catalogue of agricultural deities (1.5–23), and then Octavian (1.24–42), who, as Virgil makes immediately clear, is an overwhelmingly powerful figure even though he is not a god yet (1.24–5): *tuque adeo, quem mox quae sint habitura deorum | concilia incertum est* ('And you above all, it is unclear what company of the gods shall soon claim you'). The word *mox* delays Octavian's moment of formal divinization, perhaps hinting at a posthumous deification;[76] and the type of divinity he will eventually become is left unclear. But in using *mox*, which conveys a sense of imminence, Virgil underscores the idea that Octavian is almost knocking on the doors of godhood.[77] The next section of the prayer suggests that, depending on what responsibility Octavian chooses to exercise (cf. *velis*, 1.26), he might become the god of land and weather (1.26–8), or the god of the sea (1.29–31), or a new constellation (1.32–5). A fourth possibility— becoming the *rex* of Tartarus (1.36–9)—is firmly rejected. The uncertainty surrounding Octavian's future here lies in what *kind* of divinity he will become and how. The fact that he *will* be divinized is never in doubt.

In the final three lines of the prayer, Virgil directly appeals to Octavian and, rather audaciously, chooses a divine role for him (1.40–2):[78]

> da facilem cursum atque audacibus adnue coeptis,   40
> ignarosque viae mecum miseratus agrestis
> ingredere et votis iam nunc adsuesce vocari.

Grant me an effortless journey and give assent to my bold undertaking, and along with me pity the farmers who do not know the way, come, and even now become accustomed to be called upon by prayers.

The auspicious nod (*adnue*, 1.40) asked of Octavian invests him with a power that traditionally belongs to Jupiter (cf. Hom. *Il.* 1.514, 524, 527). In view of Jupiter's conspicuous absence in the two-part prayer, this image suggests that

---

[76] White (1993) 174; Cole (2001) 71.

[77] Compare Virgil's 'soon' (*mox*) with Horace's 'late' (*serus*) in a similar attempt to delay Augustus' deification: *serus in caelum redeas* (Hor. *Carm.* 1.2.45).

[78] The idea that Octavian is already the subject of prayers even before his deification evokes the senatorial decree of 30 BC requiring priests and priestesses to pray for Octavian (Cass. Dio 51.19.7).

92 POLITICS AND DIVINIZATION IN AUGUSTAN POETRY

Octavian has taken the place usually reserved to the supreme god.[79] Equally strikingly, Octavian seems to have replaced the Muses as well. Both Hesiod and Aratus appeal to the Muses for the success of their didactic works (cf. Hes. *Op*. 1; Arat. *Phaen*. 16–18), but Virgil asks only for the blessing of Caesar for his new poetic project. Positioned as such a major determinant of both human existence and poetry, the poet's request for Octavian to show sympathy towards uninformed farmers (1.41) becomes significant, as it focuses in on the kind of influence Virgil would like Octavian to exert. The display of sympathy is a major theme in the *Georgics*, connecting poet, farmer, and ruler;[80] here especially Virgil appears to suggest that through shared compassion he and Octavian might provide enlightenment, and the latter is placed in the role of an agricultural protector. The semantically homogenous sequence of *cursum* (1.40), *viae* (1.41), and *ingredere* (1.42) further intertwines the progress of poet, farmer, and ruler, giving the impression that by allowing the *Georgics* to advance Octavian can enact poetic enlightenment for farmers as well as his own course to divinity.[81] The new Caesar may not be divinized yet, but in this formulation Virgil already (*iam nunc*, 1.42) makes him a god in his poetry.[82]

Importantly, the request for showing compassion towards the farming community looks directly back to the first of three divine roles proposed to Octavian by the poet earlier in the prologue when Virgil envisaged him as the god of land and weather (1.25–8). Readers do not learn how Octavian will become the god of the sea—he simply 'comes' as one (cf. *an deus immensi venias maris*, 1.29);[83] while the idea that Octavian 'might add himself as a new star' (*novum... sidus te... addas*, 1.32) appears too politically awkward to

---

[79] See also Thomas (1988) 68; Nelson (1998) 111; Morgan (1999) 93–4; Cole (2001) 71; Hejduk (2020) 48. Contra Nappa (2005) 33, who sees Octavian as a parallel to Jupiter rather than supplanting the god's position. Compare Jupiter's absence here with Hor. *Carm*. 1.12.51–2 *tu secundo | Caesare regnes*, where *secundus* is both 'second in command' and 'under the auspices of'. It should be noted that when Jupiter appears for the first time in the *Georgics*, the supreme god is far from kind to farmers: *pater ipse colendi | haud facilem esse viam voluit* ('the Father himself willed that the ways of farming be not at all easy', 1.121–2).

[80] See Perkell (1989) 46–50; though she finds this plea for pity 'discordant' with the tone of the rest of the prologue (p. 150).

[81] My reading here shares some similarities with the notion of 'poetic simultaneity' discussed by Volk (2002) 13–24. *cursum* (1.40) can evoke the notion of poetic progress; see *OLD* s.v. 9. Erren (2003) 42 reads *da facilem cursum* (1.40) as a 'Fahrtmetapher'. Nelis (2008) 504 points out that *ingredior* is often used with *via* to mean 'take the first steps on a path or journey'; see *OLD* s.v. 2. Tandy (1985) 54–5 and Hardie (2002) 178 argue that *ingredere* is often used of rising stars and so looks ahead to Octavian's catasterism, which has been suggested earlier in line 32, *anne novum tardis sidus te mensibus addas* ('or whether you add yourself to the slow months as a new star').

[82] Virgil's insinuation that Octavian is already like a god to him finds further and more explicit expression in Lucan's address to Nero (*sed mihi iam numen*, 1.63).

[83] Nappa (2005) 31 also finds the images of Thule's servitude and the 'purchase' of Octavian by Tethys troubling (cf. 1.30–1).

DIVINIZATION AND THE TRANSFORMATION OF ROME   93

contemplate, since this image alludes to not only the divinization of Hellenistic monarchs (with *novum sidus* evoking the ἄστρον νέον of Callimachus' *Coma Berenices*, cf. *Aet.* fr. 110.64 Harder [= 110.64 Pf. = 213.64 Mass.])[84] but also the apotheosis of the dictator Julius Caesar.[85] By contrast, only the first divine role as the god of land and weather is presented as wholly desirable (1.25–8):

> urbisne invisere, Caesar,   25
> terrarumque velis curam, et te maximus orbis
> auctorem frugum tempestatumque potentem
> accipiat cingens materna tempora myrto.

Whether you might choose to visit cities, Caesar, or look after the lands, and the greatest earth would accept you as the guardian of crops and the lord of seasons, with your temples wreathed with your mother's myrtle.

Octavian's choice of watching over cities and terrains, and the world's acceptance of him as an authority, are paratactically set side by side as corresponding events. His welcomed dual-role as *auctor frugum tempestatum potens* (1.27) is imbued with connotations of deification.[86] As the one who causes crops to grow, Octavian would take over the function of Ceres just as Epicurus' benefaction transcends those of Ceres and Liber (Lucr. *DRN.* 5.7–21);[87] and as the lord of the seasons, he would assume the role of Jupiter similar to the weather-controlling Zeus in the prologue to Aratus' *Phaenomena* (10–13).[88] Both the idea of stepping up to become a divinity for farmers, and the notion of taking over the of Jupiter/Zeus, are present in the final lines of the prayer as I have shown above. Moreover, given that *cura terrarum* (1.26) is a central topic for the *Georgics* (cf. *cura boum*, 1.3) and *cura* is frequently used to mean the 'cultivation' or 'care' of animals throughout the poem (e.g. 1.216, 1.228,

---

[84] Thomas (1986) 177 and (1988) ad 1.32–5. Cf. Catull. 66.63–4 *me | sidus in antiquis diua novum posuit.*

[85] The curious celestial location proposed for the new star of Octavian (cf. 1.33–5) receives attention from Whitcomb (2018).

[86] Nelis (2013) 261 notes that A*U*ctorem *fru*G*U*m tempe*STa*t*U*Mque potentem (1.27) appears to anticipate the future title 'Augustus'. See also Thomas (1988) on 1.27.

[87] Gale (2000) 29. Virgil's request for Octavian to pity farmers who do not yet know the way of life also recalls Epicurus' enlightenment of the mind.

[88] Note also that *urbis…invisere* recalls Arat. *Phaen.* 2 μεσταὶ δέ Διὸς πᾶσαι μὲν ἀγυιαί. Divine visitations are often conveyed by the verb *invisere*, cf. Verg. *Aen.* 4.144 *Delum maternam invisit Apollo;* Catull. 64.384–5 *praesentes namque ante domos invisere castas | heroum et sese mortali ostendere coetu.* Powell (2008: 260) notes that Octavian's double command over *fruges* and *tempestates* precisely reverses his public image before the victory at Naulochus as the bringer of famine and victim of heaven-sent storms.

94 POLITICS AND DIVINIZATION IN AUGUSTAN POETRY

2.405, 2.415, 3.138, 3.157, 3.404, 4.118),[89] Virgil's request for Octavian to take pity on the farmers lies precisely in his power to protect the land and influence their lives and daily tasks. The correspondence between this divine role proposed by Virgil and the poet's final request for Octavian to sympathize with the farmer who depend on him points to a model of divinization favoured by the poet, namely by means of *cura terrarum*. The attainability of this form of divinization is further highlighted by the temporal relationship between the opening and closing of Virgil's address to Octavian. As *mox* (1.24) becomes *iam nunc* (1.42), it underlines that Octavian—if he should choose to act as the benefactor of farmers which he is capable of being—can already consider himself divine (cf. *votis... adsuesce vocari*, 1.42). The final line of the poem's opening prayer thus emphatically communicates to Octavian that divine status and godlike power for him need not be uncertain or delayed: the future can be now.[90]

My contention in the remainder of this discussion is that this provisional model of divinization is subsequently challenged or overlooked at several crucial junctures in the poem.[91] The hymnic list of possibilities in the prologue already gives the impression of wishful thinking, sowing the seed for Octavian going off-piste later in the *Georgics*. As it turns out, scenes of his divinization in the finale of Book 1, the opening of Book 3, and the poem's *sphragis* combine to suggest that Octavian would not subscribe to *cura terrarum* as a means of achieving divinization; and the failure of the poem's *didaxis* for Octavian—written in from beginning and confirmed later by Octavian's disregard for it—points to Virgil's gradual realization of his inability to effect meaningful change with his poetry as Rome enters a new political era.[92] I argued above that Horace in *Satire* 2.1 insinuates that the forthcoming age of Augustus will have a profound impact on poetic composition, especially on what can be said about the new Caesar and how it should be said (cf. *aude | Caesaris invicti res dicere*, Hor. *Sat.* 2.1.10–11). As we shall see, the urgent reflection on the fast-changing relationship between poet and Caesar,

---

[89] Gale (2000) 160 n. 45.

[90] Therefore, it is not so much 'poetic simultaneity' (Volk 2002: 13–24), but 'poetic instantaneity'. This is of course one of the many possible readings of Virgil's final requests in the prologue. For alternative interpretations, see e.g. Gale (2000) 26–31; Hardie (2002) 182–4; Nelis (2008) 502–3.

[91] That Virgil discusses Octavian's deification at key turning-points of the poem further underlines the tied-up progress of his poetry and the apotheosis of Caesar.

[92] Gale (2000) 24, 57, 146–7, 159–62, 173–4 points out that this strategy of destabilizing or rendering ambiguous what at first appears to be an encouraging and unproblematic notion is typical of Virgil's mode of writing in the *Georgics*, and that even the meaning of *cura* becomes complicated as the poem proceeds.

DIVINIZATION AND THE TRANSFORMATION OF ROME   95

art and authority, in *Satire* 2.1 finds correspondence in the *Georgics*, as Virgil too shines a light on these issues by leaving readers in the *sphragis* of his poem with an unforgettable image of Octavian soaring unstoppably towards Olympus while the poet contemplates ambivalently on his own literary career.

Divinization and *cura triumphorum*

The invocation of the gods in the *Georgics*' prologue is structurally mirrored at the end of Book 1, where Virgil appeals to a number of deities to allow Octavian to rescue the Roman world from destruction. While scholars routinely note the poet's stark pessimism here, it has not been sufficiently emphasized that this prayer appears to be conceived in direct tension with the prologue of Book 1, puncturing the poet's earlier wishful thinking. Furthermore, although the dramatic setting of this prayer recalls the turbulent triumviral period, there is good reason to see it as being concerned with the present, like the poem's prologue. Prior to this prayer, Virgil firstly recalls the portents that accompanied the death of Julius Caesar and the civil wars (1.466–92),[93] and then looks ahead to a time when a farmer, tilling the fields which once hosted the battle of Philippi, will one day unearth rusty weapons and the bones of fallen warriors (1.493–7).[94] Between visions of the past and the future, a suggestive gap is thus left open for the poet to speak urgently about the present (1.498–514):

> di patrii Indigetes et Romule Vestaque mater,
> quae Tuscum Tiberim et Romana Palatia servas,
> hunc saltem everso iuvenem succurrere saeclo   500
> ne prohibete. satis iam pridem sanguine nostro
> Laomedonteae luimus periuria Troiae;
> iam pridem nobis caeli te regia, Caesar,
> invidet atque hominum queritur curare triumphos,
> quippe ubi fas versum atque nefas: tot bella per orbem,   505
> tam multae scelerum facies, non ullus aratro
> dignus honos, squalent abductis arva colonis,
> et curvae rigidum falces conflantur in ensem.

[93] On historical flashbacks in the *Georgics*, see Nelis (2013) 255.
[94] On the ambivalence of Virgil's picture of the future, see Lyne (1974) 61; Gale (2000) 34–5.

96 POLITICS AND DIVINIZATION IN AUGUSTAN POETRY

> hinc movet Euphrates, illinc Germania bellum;
> vicinae ruptis inter se legibus urbes   510
> arma ferunt; saevit toto Mars impius orbe,
> ut cum carceribus sese effudere quadrigae,
> addunt in spatia, et frustra retinacula tendens
> fertur equis auriga neque audit currus habenas.

Gods and heroes of my country, Romulus, and Mother Vesta, who guard the Tuscan Tiber and Roman Palatine, do not prevent this young man at least from rescuing a world turned upside down! Long enough already we have atoned for Laomedon's perjuries at Troy with our blood; long enough heaven's realms have envied your presence amongst us, Caesar, and they complain of your care for earthly triumphs, where indeed right and wrong are reversed: so many wars in this world, so many shapes of evil; no worthy honour for the plough: neglected fields robbed of farmers and curved sickles fused into solid blades. Here the Euphrates agitates; there Germany threatens war; neighbouring cities breaking laws to take up arms amongst themselves, as impious Mars rages across the entire world: just like when the chariots stream from the starting gates, add to their speed each lap, and the charioteer, tugging vainly at the bridles, is dragged on by the horses, and the chariot is not responding to the reins.

The manner in which Virgil invokes *Caesar* after an appeal to various other gods parallels the book's opening prayer to Octavian.[95] The poet's claim that heaven wants Octavian for itself (1.503–4) reinforces another prominent aspect of the poem's prologue—namely that his divinization is inevitable.[96] However, whereas the imminence of Octavian's divinization (cf. *mox*, 1.24) piques Virgil's interest in the prologue, here it becomes a source of anxiety. The gods' resentment of Caesar's presence among men and their complaint about his preoccupation with earthly things suggest that there is the risk that they want Caesar to become one of them *too* soon—that is, to die before his time. Not only is the timing of Octavian's divinization now out of the poet's control, Octavian's interest in earthly triumphs (*hominum ... curare triumphos*, 1.504) also diverges from what is asked of him by the poet in the book's opening prayer, as it contrasts sharply with the kind of *cura terrarum* which Virgil presents as more preferable.[97] Indeed, the images of disused or misused farming

---

[95] See also Perkell (1989) 150–2; Gale (2002) 32; Nelis (2008) 505–10.

[96] Note the similar phrasing of *caeli...regia* in 1.503 and *deorum concilia* in 1.24–5.

[97] The claim that 'to care for earthly triumphs' actually delays divinization is also contrary to the contemporary Roman perception of a strong link between triumphal and divine glory. On the connotation of divinity in the Roman triumph, see Beard (2007) 237–8.

DIVINIZATION AND THE TRANSFORMATION OF ROME   97

tools and fields deprived of farmers (1.506–8) virtually call out for the kind of *cura terrarum* envisaged by Virgil for Octavian in the poem's prologue.

Set against this backdrop of the poet losing sway over Octavian's actions, the final simile (1.509–14) gains extra force. Comparing a febrile world descending into chaotic violence to a charioteer losing control of his runaway vehicle, this simile underscores firstly the perils facing Octavian should he continue to pursue worldly triumph.[98] Secondly, it undermines Virgil's request in the prologue for an 'effortless journey' (*facilem cursum*, 1.40), since one of the meanings of *cursus* is a chariot ride;[99] and so the uncontrollable chariot may hint at the poet's failing progress in persuading Octavian to follow the course set out for him. As Caesar morphs into a figure who is preoccupied with a military *cursus* over which neither the poet nor Caesar himself has full control, the final scene of *Georgics* 1 highlights that Virgil's attempt to mediate a symbiotic relationship between Octavian and those who rely on his *cura terrarum* is already faltering, and that there appears to be an irreconcilable divergence between Virgil's *didaxis* and Caesar's own trajectory.

The Triumph of Caesar

The so-called 'proem in the middle'[100] at the beginning of *Georgics* 3 highlights again that military achievement is being pursued by Octavian. Momentarily suspending didactic in favour of panegyric, Virgil now looks ahead to enshrining Octavian in a temple as if he were a deity, and even fantasizes about a triumph of poetry that rivals Caesar's literal triumph. The interconnectedness of the poet's literary future and Octavian's divinity is further dramatized in an ekphrasis of the engraved doors and sculptural decorations of the temple (3.26–36). Virgil claims that he will adorn the temple's doors with battle scenes from the Ganges, the Nile, Asia, the Niphates, and Parthia (3.26–31)—locations which not only recall Octavian's recent victories but also anticipate further Roman campaigns in its wake.[101] No lessons are to be

---

[98] e.g. Gale (2000) 35–6, (2013) 290 argues that the simile alludes to the death of Phaethon. The similarity with Phaethon can also be added to the proem of *G.* 1 through Ovid's reading of the Phaethon myth in *Met.* 2, where Phaethon crashes in that space in the zodiac (between Scorpio and Libra, *Met.* 2.195–200) where Virgil had imagined Octavian to ascend to heaven as a star at *G.* 1.32–5; see Barchiesi (2009).

[99] See also Nelis (2008) 508.

[100] The terminology and concept are originally developed by Conte (1980) 122–36; (1992); (2007) 219–31.

[101] See Mynors (1990) 26; Erren (2003) 576–7; Miller (2009) 3; Nelis (2013) 259. Furthermore, Freudenburg (2001) 86 notes that this idealized vision of Octavian conquering far-off places echoes Horace's brief dallying with epic ideas at *Sat.* 2.1.13–15.

98   POLITICS AND DIVINIZATION IN AUGUSTAN POETRY

taught in this vision of the future; beyond the scope of the present poem, Virgil can only envisage himself taking on the role of the imperial artist and a celebrant of Caesar's triumph (3.10–18):

> primus ego in patriam mecum, modo vita supersit,   10
> Aonio rediens deducam vertice Musas;
> primus Idumaeas referam tibi, Mantua, palmas,
> et viridi in campo templum de marmore ponam
> propter aquam, tardis ingens ubi flexibus errat
> Mincius et tenera praetexit harundine ripas.   15
> in medio mihi Caesar erit templumque tenebit:
> illi victor ego et Tyrio conspectus in ostro
> centum quadriiugos agitabo ad flumina currus.

I'll be the first to return to my country, if life lasts, bringing the Muses with me from the Aonian peak; I'll be the first, Mantua, to bring you Idumaean palms, and I'll set up a temple of marble by the water, on that green plain, where great Mincius wanders in slow curves and clothes his banks with tender reeds. For me, Caesar will be in the middle and own the temple. In his honour, I, the victor, conspicuous in Tyrian purple, will drive a hundred four-horse chariots by the river.

The centre of the Virgilian poem–temple will be occupied by Octavian (3.16), and this will be realized in Book 8 of the *Aeneid*. There, Octavian stands *in medio* (*Aen.* 8.675; cf. *G.* 3.16) on the shield of Aeneas which has the Actian victory as its focal point;[102] and after the battle, the victor surveys a procession of conquered nations (reminiscent of those mentioned here at 3.26–31) from yet another temple—the Palatine Temple of Apollo (*Aen.* 8.720).[103] Indeed, later in this passage of the *Georgics*, Virgil envisages an image of Apollo as part of the decorative programme of his poem–temple (*stabunt et Parii lapides…Troiae Cynthius auctor*, 3.34–6).[104] Various critics have suggested that the reader is here encouraged to connect Virgil's proposed artistic monument with the construction of contemporary architectural projects,

---

[102] Casali (2006) 200 notes that the shield may be read as a surrogate *Aeneid* and Vulcan a surrogate Virgil (*Aen.* 8.439–41): '*tollite cuncta*' inquit '*coeptosque auferte labores*, | Aetnaei Cyclopes, et huc advertite mentem: | *arma acri facienda viro*. Both the shield and the temple are ekphrastic objects.

[103] On comparisons between *G.* 3.26–31 and *Aen.* 8.714–28, see Mynors (1990) 184. See further discussion of the Shield of Aeneas in Chapter 4.

[104] Gros (1993) argues that the *Parii lapides* (3.34) can be either freestanding statues in the temple or its precinct, or figures on the pediment. See also Erren (2003) 581.

DIVINIZATION AND THE TRANSFORMATION OF ROME   99

perhaps especially the Palatine temple.[105] If so, by drawing this parallel Virgil already looks towards the moment when state art and poetic art will become two sides of the same coin: the god who occupies the middle of Virgil's epic-in-the-making is also the man who will soon stand at the centre of the religious and political framework of Rome. Seen in this light, the poet's depiction of Octavian as a divinity housed in a metaphorical temple is itself a metaphor for the evolving relationship between Octavian and those who will soon become his subjects, delicately portraying Rome's cultural revolution towards one-man rule as a disarmingly jubilant scene of thankful worshippers paying tribute to their victory-god.[106]

Leading the celebration of Caesar is Virgil himself, a self-styled *victor* (3.17), gladly driving chariots (3.18) and parading the rewards of *cura triumphorum* in a manner that looks directly back to the failing *auriga* at the end of Book 1.[107] The transfiguration of the image of the poet—from that of a power-broker between Octavian and those who depend on him, to a chief-celebrant of the cult of Caesar—not only embellishes in poetic terms the shift of power away from the poet into the hands of Octavian,[108] but also rehabilitates the concept of ruler cult, making the language of divinization and the idea of willing subordination concurrent with the burgeoning of the new regime. By aestheticizing Rome's transition from republicanism to autocracy in this way, Virgil makes himself complicit in it. For the poet for whom '*right now* it is a delight to lead the solemn procession to the sanctuary [of Caesar]' (*iam nunc sollemnis ducere pompas | ad delubra iuvat*, 3.22–3; cf. *votis iam nunc adsuesce vocari*, 1.42), his postponement of the proposed epic—*mox tamen ardentis accingar dicere pugnas | Caesaris* ('Soon I will prepare myself to speak of Caesar's fierce battles', 3.46–7)—is merely symbolic. The use of *mox* here

---

[105] See Drew (1924); Kraggerud (1998) 13; Miller (2009) 3. Of course Virgil's temple could be referencing several structures at once. Koortbojian (2013) 44 suggests that the phrase *in medio...Caesar* (3.16) alludes to the prominent position of the cult statue in the Temple of Divus Julius. Harrison (2005a) 185 thinks that Virgil's description of the temple's location—riverside and *in campo* (3.13)—recalls the Mausoleum of Augustus. Lundström (1976), Hardie (2002) 194–8, and Heslin (2015) 257–60 all argue, quite plausibly, that Virgil's temple recalls the *Aedes Herculis Musarum*, established by M. Fulvius Nobilior around 187 BC. That Virgil's metaphorical temple is located in Mantua (cf. the local river, Mincio/*Mincius*, at line 15) does not necessarily mean that the poet only has his homeland in mind. As Heslin (2015) 253 rightly says, the setting is Mantuan, but it 'draws on metropolitan models'. By placing the temple in Mantua, Virgil may be bringing all of Italy into the picture: note the ambiguity of *patria* earlier in the passage (cf. *primus ego in patriam... | Aonio rediens deducam vertice Musas*, 3.10–11), where it could mean either Mantua, or Rome, or Italy.

[106] Note at *Aen.* 8.722, *victae gentes* walk in front of Apollo–Caesar.

[107] *quadriiugos* and *currus* (3.18) recall *quadrigae* (1.512) and *currus* (1.514) respectively, while *agitabo* (3.18) contrasts with *fertur* (1.514).

[108] On the redefinition of the relationship between poet and *Caesar*, see also Lowrie (2009) 150, 155–6; Miller (2009) 3–6, 140, 147–8; Bergmann et al. (2012) 12–14.

100 POLITICS AND DIVINIZATION IN AUGUSTAN POETRY

recalls the postponement of Octavian's deification in the *Georgics*' opening prayer (cf. 1.24–5); but much like in that prayer, the line between the present and the future is becoming increasingly blurred: *iam nunc* Rome is moving into a new political era.

Divinization and Didactic Efficacy

The relationship between Octavian's divinization and Virgil's poetic career comes into direct focus again in the *sphragis* to the *Georgics*. This passage, as we saw in Chapter 1, offers a kind of 'parallel chronology' of the lives of *Caesar* and *Vergilius* while reflecting on the contrasting activities each character is preoccupied with. Here the portrait of Octavian clearly and deliberately looks back on his earlier appearances in the poem's prologue and the finale of Book 1 (4.559–62):

> Haec super arvorum cultu pecorumque canebam
> et super arboribus, Caesar dum magnus ad altum   560
> fulminat Euphraten bello victorque volentis
> per populos dat iura viamque adfectat Olympo.

These things I sang about the care of fields, herds, and trees, while mighty Caesar thundered in battle by the deep Euphrates, implemented a victor's laws on willing nations, and took the path towards the heavens.

The juxtaposition of the thematic enumeration of the *Georgics* (4.559–60) and Caesar's thundering (*Caesar...magnus...| fulminat*, 4.560–1) brings the poem to a full circle. In the prologue, Virgil imagines Octavian as *tempestatum potens* (1.27) and asks him to give a Jupiter-like approval to his new undertaking (*audacibus adnue coeptis*, 1.40). Now, as the poem approaches its conclusion, Octavian appears in the guise of the supreme god again: the verb *fulminat* invests in him the traditional power of Jupiter (cf. βροντᾶν οὐκ ἐμόν, ἀλλὰ Διός, Callim. *Aet.* fr. 1.20 Harder [= 1.20 Pf. = 1.20 Mass.]), while at the same time hinting at his control over the physical processes of the weather and so picking up *tempestatum* in the prologue.[109] Moreover, having been asked to 'embark' (*ingredere*, 1.42) on a course to divinity, Octavian now

---

[109] Note the iconography on *BMCRE* I (East), 628–30, a series of post-Actian *denarii* of 29–27 BC which depict on the reverse a laureate ithyphallic terminal figure of Octavian atop a winged thunderbolt. See also *RIC* I² 269a.

DIVINIZATION AND THE TRANSFORMATION OF ROME 101

'attempts a journey to Olympus' (*viamque adfectat Olympo*, 4.562).[110] As this image of Octavian making his way to the sky coincides with the presentation of the unfolding structure of the *Georgics* (4.559–60), the *sphragis* suggests that 'while' (*dum*, 4.560) the poem is being written, Octavian is gradually fulfilling the role of Jupiter assigned to him in the poem's prologue.[111]

Yet the depiction of Octavian's activities here also underlines a process of divinization that is ostensibly different from the one suggested by the poet in the prologue. Octavian is seen firstly conquering the East (*Euphraten...victor*, 4.561), then imposing civic order (*volentis | per populos dat iura*, 4.561–2), and finally heading towards Olympus (4.562).[112] His campaign on the Euphrates and the implementation of legal authority provide a direct response to the finale of Book 1, where imminent dangers along the Euphrates (*hinc movet Euphrates*, 1.509) and the infringement of law by foreign nations (*ruptis...legibus*, 1.510) threaten to bring down Roman hegemony. The correspondence between these two passages adds force to the description of Octavian here as a *victor* (4.561), characterizing his journey to Olympus as the divinization of a conqueror through his military and civic virtues. As the *sphragis* portrays Octavian taking the matter of his deification into his own hands and finding success with it, the poem's final image of *Caesar* leaves readers with the impression that Virgil's teaching on divinization has not had its desired effect on its principal addressee. Rather than to assume the role of a compassionate protector and become divine by taking part in Virgil's poetic consolation of unenlightened farmers who cannot find their way (*via*, 1.41), it would seem that the thundering *Caesar* has found his own path (*via*, 4.562) to immortality.

The idea that Octavian is diverging from the course set by Virgil is highlighted further through the demarcated lives of *Vergilius* and *Caesar*, as the poet's portrait of his own career contrasts sharply with that of Octavian (4.563–6):

---

[110] On the Gigantomachic connotation of *viamque adfectat Olympo*, see earlier discussion in Chapter 1, as well as Hollis (1996), Gale (2003) 327–8, and Hejduk (2020) 58.

[111] Geue (2018) 23 argues that Virgil's use of *dum* is redolent of political fudging, making a purely temporal relationship out of something far more symbiotic between the poet and Caesar. Seductive as this argument is, Geue has got it wrong in my view: the temporal relationship is important. For further discussion, see Hardie (1986) 50–1 and, again, Volk's idea of 'poetic simultaneity'.

[112] Mynors (1990) on 4.561–2 suggests that *volentis* (561) not only portrays Octavian's *imperium* as agreeable and benign but also implies the rule of an immortal: cf. Xen. *Oec.* 21.12 οὐ γὰρ πάνυ μοι δοκεῖ ὅλον τουτὶ τὸ ἀγαθὸν ἀνθρώπινον εἶναι ἀλλὰ θεῖον, τὸ ἐθελόντων ἄρχειν ('For I reckon this gift is not altogether human, but divine—this power to win willing obedience'). By contrast, Geue (2018: 11 and 23) interprets this description of the 'willingness' of imperial subjects as a sign of the poem's naturalization of the ideology of oppression. See also Giusti (2019) on the *intexti Britanni* at *G.* 3.25, who willingly staging their own subjection.

102 POLITICS AND DIVINIZATION IN AUGUSTAN POETRY

> illo Vergilium me tempore dulcis alebat
> Parthenope studiis florentem ignobilis oti,
> carmina qui lusi pastorum audaxque iuventa,   565
> Tityre, te patulae cecini sub tegmine fagi.

At that time sweet Parthenope was nourishing me, Virgil, joyous in the pursuits of lowly leisure, I who toyed with shepherds' songs, and, in youth's boldness, sang of you, Tityrus, in the spreading beech-tree's shade.

Juxtaposed against the heaven-reaching dynamism of Octavian, Virgil's apparent fondness for *otium* (4.564), in conjunction with the nostalgic mention of his youth (*iuventa*, 4.565) and the citation of the opening line of the First *Eclogue* (4.566), pointedly emphasizes that the poet has been left behind to languish in an idealized past.[113] The *Eclogues* and the *Georgics*, now retrospectively fashioned into a single oeuvre,[114] appear insignificant and even incompatible with the concerns of the new *kosmokrator*. That the poet is fully aware of the limitation of his poetry is also embedded in the way in which Virgil describes his past poetic activity as *ludere* (4.565). This verb evokes the Callimachean tradition of light verse,[115] and Virgil alludes to this idea in the prologue to *Eclogue* 6, where Tityrus's choice 'to play' (*ludere*, *Ecl.* 6.1) with the 'rustic Muse' (*agrestis Musa*, *Ecl.* 6.8) is contrasted with the gravity of the themes of epic poetry (*reges et proelia*, *Ecl.* 6.3). In fact, the same verb is used in *Eclogue* 1 when Tityrus reveals that the *otium* restored to him by his saviour enabled him 'to play' with bucolic songs (*ipsum | ludere quae vellem calamo permisit agresti*, 'he allowed me to play what I wished on the rustic reed', *Ecl.* 1.9–10). The use of *lusi* in the *sphragis* of the *Georgics*, therefore, not only draws a parallel between Virgil and Tityrus—the significance of which has already been discussed in Chapter 1—but also characterizes the poet's art as trivial in a world where Caesar dominates. Set against the portrait of Octavian in the first half of the *sphragis*, Virgil's dismissal of his poetic endeavour as mere 'play' ostensibly conveys his reservation about his poetry's capacity to address the most powerful man of the post-Actian world.[116] As the *Georgics'* attempt of persuading Octavian to 'care for the land' comes to an end, the poet simply watches the *princeps* conquering his way to divinity.

---

[113] On the contrast between the active and the contemplative life throughout the *Georgics*, see esp. Perkell (1989) 25–89 and Gale (2003) 329–32.

[114] Fowler (1989) 82.

[115] Clausen (1994) on *Ecl.* 1.10. See also Wagenvoort (1956) 30–42 on the topos of *ludus poeticus* in Latin literature.

[116] See also Perkell (1989) 58–9.

DIVINIZATION AND THE TRANSFORMATION OF ROME 103

Virgil's discussions of Octavian's divinization in the *Georgics* therefore encapsulates an evolving attempt to work out the status, influence, and limitations of both Caesar and poet in post-Actian Roman society. While this negotiation is played out primarily on a personal level and is underpinned by Virgil's interests in the didactic efficacy of the *Georgics* and his own literary career, the diminishing effect of the poet's intervention in Octavian's path to divinity speaks more broadly about the changing relationship between art and authority in the embryonic days of the Augustan Principate. Around the time when the *Georgics* was published, official celebrations and representational media were primed to adulate Octavian as a divine *triumphator* upon his return to Rome. The archaeological evidence from Nicopolis near the site of Actium shows that Octavian attributed his victory to not only Apollo but also Mars and Neptune, thereby establishing a connection with martial divinities in addition to his patron god.[117] In terms of coinage, one issue of *denarii* minted between *c*.29 and early 27 BC depicts Octavian in the role of a victorious god of war.[118] Furthermore, as I discussed in Chapter 1, in the period between the news of the victory at Actium reaching Rome and the triple triumph of 29 BC, the Senate lavished Octavian with numerous 'god-equalling' honours. In light of this set of evidence, which points to a systematic effort by non-poetic media to highlight the connection between triumphal and divine glory, Virgil's gradual acknowledgement of the inefficacy of his poetic *didaxis* can be seen to convey an anxiety about the status and relevance of non-official art. The *Georgics'* opening hymnic appeal to the quasi-divine Octavian implies the possibility of establishing an efficacious relationship with the addressed god who is (or at least might be) listening. However, at end of the poem, this dialogic possibility disappears and is replaced by a far more descriptive account of the all-conquering authority of Caesar. I would suggest that this change in the *mode* of interaction encapsulates Virgil's abandonment of the hope that poetry can retain any meaningful creative agency in post-Actian Rome. Indeed, as the poet depicts himself undergoing a dramatic transformation from one who hopes to influence Caesar's divine future, to a constructor of panegyrical monument and a mirror-image of Caesar as *triumphator*, it

---

[117] See Murray and Petsas (1989) 76; Zachos (2003) 74–6; Lange (2009) 104–5; Miller (2009) 56 n. 6.

[118] *RIC* I² 271. It depicts a statue of Octavian on top of a column, nude except for a billowing cloak, carrying a sword in one hand and a spear in the other—two weapons often identified with Mars. The column could be a close-up of the four-column monument set up by Octavian in the Forum Romanum after his conquest of Egypt (cf. Serv. ad *G.* 3.29). See further Pollini (1990) 348 and Lange (2009) 162–3.

104   POLITICS AND DIVINIZATION IN AUGUSTAN POETRY

renders the poem's thinking on the divinization of Octavian closer to that of the emergent regime and its official discursive channels, thereby signalling that poetry too must play a part in the accumulation of Augustan power.

Caesar's Laws

In both Horace's *Satire* 2.1 and the *sphragis* of Virgil's *Georgics*, the poets' divinizing language introduces a new aspect of Octavian's power by painting him as a legal authority. For Horace, the Jupiter-like 'invincible Caesar' (*Sat.* 2.1.11) is the ultimate 'judge' (*iudice*, 2.1.84), whose verdict, if favourable, is as good as a get-out-of-jail-free card. For Virgil, the 'thundering' Caesar (*fulminat*, *G.* 4.561) is the embodiment of Rome's worldwide jurisdiction, whose subjects willingly submit themselves to his authority in the wake of the victory at Actium (*victorque volentis | per populos dat iura*, 4.561–2). In both instances, Octavian's newly acquired status as a supreme legal force has serious implications on the subject's autonomy: earning Caesar's approval and embracing his superiority give one the freedom to go about their business, whether that is composing bitingly satirical poetry or simply getting on with their daily lives. But freedom earned through subordination exists in name only; moreover, and rather tellingly, neither Horace or Virgil even contemplates what would happen if the legal authority of Caesar is challenged.

Appearing not long after *Satire* 2.1 and the *Georgics*, Propertius' elegy 2.7 (*c.*25 BC),[119] which celebrates the abrogation of an Octavianic marital legislation, again draws attention to the blurred lines between Roman law and Caesar's power through its divinizing language. In fact, Propertius' elegy sensitizes readers to the idea that Caesar's authority could encroach on the individual's autonomy.[120] As in *Satire* 2.1 and the *sphragis* of the *Georgics*, Propertius' poem opens with a comparison of Caesar and Jupiter (2.7.1–6):

---

[119] On the date of publication for the extant Book 2 of Propertius, see Hutchinson (2006) 2–8.

[120] The *lex* mentioned in 2.7 cannot be used to securely date the poem's time of composition, since the existence and supposed effects of this *lex* are unclear. Badian (1985) argues that this *lex* was introduced shortly before Actium and was repealed in 28 BC, thus giving Prop. 2.7 a dramatic date of post-28 BC. But others are less certain: see Beck (2000); James (2003) 229–31; Fedeli (2005) 221–3; Spagnuolo Vigorita (2010) 1–9 and 19–27.

DIVINIZATION AND THE TRANSFORMATION OF ROME   105

Gavisa es certe sublatam, Cynthia, legem
  qua quondam edicta flemus uterque diu,
ni nos divideret; quamvis diducere amantes
  non queat invitos Iuppiter ipse duos.
'at magnus Caesar.' sed magnus Caesar in armis: 5
  devictae gentes nil in amore valent.

You certainly rejoiced, Cynthia, at the abrogation of the law whose promulgation made us both weep a long while, for fear it separate us; though Jupiter himself could not divide two lovers against their will. 'Yet Caesar is mighty.' But it is in arms that Caesar is mighty: conquering nations counts for nothing in love.

Jupiter's failure to separate lovers (2.7.3–4) acts as a foil for Propertius to define the limit of Caesar's power through a dialogue (2.7.5–6).[121] The first part of the dialogue, *at magnus Caesar* (2.7.5), which implicitly compares the *princeps* to Jupiter, opens up the possibility that Caesar might prove successful where Jupiter has to yield. But the rejoinder, *sed magnus Caesar in armis* (2.7.5), dispels such alarmist thinking, asserting that the power which Octavian obtained through conquest (*devictae gentes*, 2.7.6) does not grant him jurisdiction over civilian lives. Propertius' ostensibly anti-establishment pose has polarized the response of scholars.[122] A number of critics, in particular Stahl, have argued that these lines amount to an attack on the intrusion of the regime into the private sphere, since the elegist exposes and then celebrates the limitations of Caesar's control.[123] But Cairns has suggested the poet's persona here is so deliberately anti-social that it can be seen as a negative reinforcement of an implicitly pro-Augustan stance.[124] Meanwhile, Gale has proposed that, since the *lex* is clearly presented as a contentious issue, the point of the poem is therefore to provoke its contemporary readers into making their individual evaluations of Caesar's action and power.[125]

In a more recent study, Roman has offered what I think is the most persuasive argument thus far: that the divided views of modern scholars reflect the

---

[121] It is not immediately clear whether this is an imaginary self-dialogue or a dramatic dialogue between the poet and Cynthia. Stahl (1985) 146 argues for the latter; Heyworth's *OCT* likewise treats the exchange as one between Propertius and his *puella*.

[122] See esp. Wilkinson (1960) 1098; Boucher (1980) 135–6; Stahl (1985) 139–56; Gale (1997); Berry (2005) 195–8; Fedeli (2005) on 2.7; Cairns (2006) 325–6; Heyworth (2007a) 109–14.

[123] Stahl (1985) 139–56.   [124] Cairns (2006) 325–6.

[125] Gale (1997). Gale's position has since been challenged by Heyworth (2007a) 114.

106 POLITICS AND DIVINIZATION IN AUGUSTAN POETRY

politically indeterminate position which Propertius carefully crafts for himself in this poem.[126] Building on this, I suggest further that the poet's indeterminate position is so designed to evade having to make clear what he thinks of the new regime. As we read the poem, we might note that Cynthia is the one who is overjoyed with Caesar's failure (*Gavisa es*, 2.7.1), not Propertius (at least not explicitly). Of course, the poet plays the role of the defiant lover and is clearly pleased that Caesar's *lex* met resistance; but at the same time he shows himself to be well aware of what Caesar *is* capable of in other areas of life, and accepts it as a matter of fact. By not committing himself to an unambiguous position on Caesar's power, Propertius shifts the focus away from what his political stance is, to why he is unable to commit to one stance; and this, in turn, draws attention the capricious political climate of the early Principate, which this passage hints at. The sharp contrast between the lovers' prolonged consternation (*flemus...diu*, 2.7.2) and the suddenness of their newfound happiness reflects a certain unpredictability of life in early Augustan Rome. The rapid exchange between the poet and his interlocutor creates the impression that everything could change in the flash of a moment. And the dialogic style enlivens the idea that Caesar's status and what he would do with it are now topics of (bedroom) conversations. The creeping jurisdiction of Caesar into private lives is resisted for now; indeed, this elegy shows that low-level dissent is even tolerated by the regime. The lovers may have won this battle, but amid their celebrations Propertius subtly underlines that Roman society is more than a little on edge about how Caesar is going to exercise his power in this new age.

By the time we reach the last book of Propertius' poetry (*c*.16 BC), it becomes patently clear that the limitations on Caesar's power have been breached. The poet's depiction of the *princeps* as a god in his final elegy (4.11), which examines the effects of the Augustan moral legislation, underscores the regime's increasingly authoritarian control over individual action. Elegy 4.11 centres on Augustus' deceased stepdaughter, Cornelia, who speaks from beyond the grave (*meum...sepulcrum*, 4.11.1) about her virtues as a wife and a mother,[127] presenting herself as the paragon of the familial values promoted

---

[126] Roman (2014) 167 calls this Propertius' 'autonomist position'.

[127] The elegy opens with Cornelia addressing her husband from her tomb (*Desine, Paulle, meum lacrimis urgere sepulcrum*, 'Cease, Paullus, to burden my tomb with tears', 4.11.1); at one point she even alludes to the inscribed epitaph on her tombstone (*ut lapide hoc uni nupta fuisse legar*, 'so that I may be read on this stone to have been married to one husband', 4.11.36). On the affinities between this poem

DIVINIZATION AND THE TRANSFORMATION OF ROME   107

by the recently passed *leges Iuliae*.[128] For the bulk of the poem, however, Cornelia casts herself in the role of a defendant before the judges of the Underworld: *at si quis posita iudex sedet Aeacus urna,* | *is mea sortita iudicet ossa pila…*| *ipsa loquar pro me* ('but if some Aeacus sits as judge with the urn alongside, let him judge my bones when my case comes up…I plead my own defence', 4.11.19–20 and 27).[129] In her defence speech, Cornelia claims that she has lived her life according to the 'laws' of her family (*mi natura dedit leges a sanguine ductas*, 'nature gave me laws drawn from my blood', 4.11.47), which primarily refer to her lineage and upbringing rather than Augustus' legislation;[130] but her next sentence—*nec possis melior iudicis esse metu* ('and you could not be better out of fear of a judge', 4.11.48)—does bring Augustus into the picture, as the idea of a woman behaving morally only out of fear for the punishment of the court evokes the new *quaestio* of Augustus, which began public trials for adultery.[131] As Cornelia envisages herself facing a posthumous trial, her implicit assertion that she is afraid of neither the judgement of the Underworld nor the Augustan *quaestio* thus establishes a bleak parallel between the two courtrooms, which tacitly casts Augustus as a kind of *iudex* figure on female morality. Admittedly, unlike Horace's *Satire* 2.1 (cf. *iudice… Caesare*, 84), Propertius' text does not make lexically explicit that Augustus is a *iudex*; in any case, the point made by Cornelia here is that the fear of posthumous/criminal trial is not as effective in regulating women's behaviour as the high standards of a distinguished family. Nonetheless, by framing the moral codes of her family as 'laws' (*leges*, 4.11.47), Cornelia's language blurs the line between individual motivation and sociopolitical pressure, illustrating the way in which the perception of the self is increasingly shaped by one's compliance with the *leges* of Augustus—the rules of the regime.

---

and inscribed Latin epitaphs, see Hutchinson (2006) 231 and his comments at 4.11.1, 13–14, 17; also Fedeli (1965) 244; Wyke (2002) 113; Lowrie (2009) 351–3.

[128] On Cornelia's exemplarity as the ideal Augustan *matrona*, see Stahl (1985) 262; Harrison (2005b) 128; Lowrie (2009) 356. The *lex Iulia de maritandis ordinibus* was passed in 18 BC, followed a year later by the *lex Iulia de adulteriis coercendis*.

[129] On the way in which Prop. 4.11 challenges the unities of time and space, and disrupts the consistency of its mode of communication, see Lowrie (2009) 349–59; Dufallo (2007) 87–8; Hutchinson (2006) 231–2.

[130] See the commentaries of Camps (1965), Hutchinson (2006), Coutelle (2015), and Fedeli et al. (2015) on 4.11.47.

[131] See the commentaries of Hutchinson (2006) and Fedeli et al. (2015) on 4.11.48. Note also the unspecificity of *possis*: the 'you' is universal—all aristocratic women have been impacted by the new marriage legislation.

108   POLITICS AND DIVINIZATION IN AUGUSTAN POETRY

By foregrounding in this way the erosion of public and private spheres among the Roman aristocracy, Cornelia's invocation of Augustus as *deus* in the next part of her speech powerfully underscores the extent to which the *princeps*' political authority encroaches on and determines individual lives. Claiming that she has led a life that would not sully the reputation of her family (4.11.49–50), Cornelia compares herself to exemplary Roman women whose respectable character were witnessed by divinities: Claudia Quinta had Cybele as a witness (4.11.51–2), Aemilia had Vesta (4.11.53–4), and now Cornelia can call on Augustus (4.11.57–60):

> maternis laudor lacrimis urbisque querelis,
> > defensa et gemitu Caesaris ossa mea.
> ille sua nata dignam vixisse sororem
> > increpat, et lacrimas vidimus ire deo.   60

I am praised by my mother's tears and the city's grief; my bones are defended by the groan of Caesar. He laments that living I was a worthy sister to his own daughter, and we have seen tears fall from a god.

Augustus is *deus* not because he possesses some supernatural power, but because his endorsement—like that of the goddesses Cybele and Vesta—is uncontestable and definitive.[132] That the tears of Caesar (*lacrimas*, 4.11.60) signify the final seal of approval is further evidenced by the close imitation of this Propertian elegy by the poet of the *Consolatio ad Liviam*, in which the deceased Drusus puts forward the fact that he has elicited tears from divine Caesar as the final evidence of his worthiness and the ultimate reason that his mother, Livia, should not be too saddened by his death: *denique laudari sacrato Caesaris ore | emerui, lacrimas elicuique deo* ('Lastly, I have earned praised from Caesar's sacred lips and drew tears from a god', *Cons. ad Liv.* 465–6).[133] With such weight attached to his emotional response, and invoked as a divine authority on moral virtues, Augustus becomes more than just Cornelia's stepfather: as Hutchinson notes, 'Caesar partly matches the private *maternis* [4.11.57], but also forms a public climax that goes beyond *urbis*

---

[132] Note also the continuation of legal language: Cornelia construes the lamentation she received as a legal argument (*defensa*, 4.11.58); see also Hutchinson (2006) on 4.11.57–8 and Osgood (2014) 138. *laudor* (4.11.57) may well allude to the *laudatio funebris*, see Coutelle (2015) ad loc. and Fedeli et al. (2015) 1349–50.

[133] Hallett (1985) 83 treats this and other verbal evocations of Prop. 4.11 in the *Consolatio ad Liviam* as 'evidence for the attention and favor accorded Propertius, 4.11 in the imperial court'.

DIVINIZATION AND THE TRANSFORMATION OF ROME   109

[4.11.57].'[134] The very public nature of his lamentation, here underscored by the plural verb *vidimus* (4.11.60),[135] places his private paternal role in the public eye, making him a kind of *pater patriae*—the title which Augustus will receive officially from the Senate in 2 BC. In fact, the crescendo latent within the sequence of *maternis* (4.11.57), *urbis* (4.11.57), *Caesar* (4.11.58), and *deo* (4.11.60) animates a process of divinization, whereby Augustus undergoes a transformation from *paterfamilias*, to *pater patriae* and, eventually, 'god'. Augustus' tears are not merely a display of personal grief, but a public statement from Rome's first citizen. In other words, there is a political significance accorded to Augustus' personal, emotional reaction. Like the 'laughter' of 'Judge Caesar' in Horace's *Satire* 2.1.84 (*Caesare risu iudice*), the 'tears' of 'God Caesar' are just as subjective and decisive. The Propertian elegy's depiction of Augustus as a *deus*, I would therefore suggest, encapsulates the extent to which Rome has drifted irreversibly towards autocracy, highlighting the vast scope of Augustus' virtually tyrannical jurisdiction over Roman aristocratic life.

Furthermore, in elegy 4.11 Cornelia makes no qualification about Caesar's status as *deus*, unlike the poet–*amator* in elegies 2.7 and 3.4. In elegy 2.7, Propertius' claim that Caesar is mighty only 'in arms' (*in armis*, 5) and not 'in love' (*in amore*, 6) limits Augustus' power to the military world, undercutting the poem's initial comparison of the *princeps* to Jupiter. Later in 3.4, as we saw in the previous chapter, Propertius portrays Augustus as a god of war only: *Arma deus Caesar dites meditatur ad Indos* ('Divine Caesar is planning war against rich India', 3.4.1); and the opening line of the next poem (3.5) reinforces the impression that Augustus has no power in the private business of lovers: *Pacis Amor deus est; pacem veneramur amantes* ('Amor is the god of peace: we lovers worship peace', 3.5.1). In sharp contrast to these earlier poems, the absence of any qualification on Augustus' status as *deus* here in Propertius' final elegy draws attention to the removal of limitations previously placed on Augustus' jurisdiction. Without having to define in what respect Caesar is considered divine, Cornelia's invocation of Augustus simply as a god-in-the-public-eye conveys the idea that there is no more restriction on his power.

Ventriloquized through the voice of Augustus' apparently faultless stepdaughter, elegy 4.11 thus frames the corrosion of individual autonomy under

---

[134] Hutchinson (2006) on 4.11.57–8.
[135] The genuine plurality of *vidimus* is strengthened by the earlier setting of the city (*urbis*, 4.11.57).

110 POLITICS AND DIVINIZATION IN AUGUSTAN POETRY

the Principate as an exemplary *modus vivendi*, presenting the unchecked power of Augustus as an irrefutable reality of Roman aristocratic life. As such, it is little wonder that critics are divided on the poem's political stance. Reitzenstein, Stahl, and Cairns, amongst others, have understood elegy 4.11 as a poetic tribute to Augustan moral values.[136] By contrast, La Penna, Hallett, Hubbard, Sullivan, Johnson, Janan, and Heyworth have all found Cornelia's virtues uninspiring and subsequently interpreted the poem (to a greater or lesser extent) as a tacit condemnation of Augustan gender codes.[137] I would suggest again that modern scholarship's polarizing response to the poem is the product of Propertius' careful design, and argue further that the depiction of Augustus as a tearful *deus* encapsulates the poet's strategy of calculated indeterminacy. The image of a lamenting divinity entails a deliberate paradox: gods are not meant to cry, so claims Ovid in *Fasti* 4.521 (*neque enim lacrimare deorum est*); but in Virgil's *Aeneid*, Venus cries to Jupiter about the near-destruction of Aeneas' fleet (*Aen.* 1.228–9), while Hercules weeps at the inevitable death of Pallas (*Aen.* 10.464–5).[138] The tears of Augustus, therefore, show him at his most elegiac, most human moment; but on the other hand they reinforce his status as a god who weeps over human mortality.[139] Poised between human and divine, Augustus' in-between state draws attention to the unusual position he occupies within the Roman political hierarchy and the authority he wields over his subjects. However, by making Cornelia the sole speaker of the poem, Propertius evades making clear where he stands on the issue of Augustus' power. In the absence of the poet's voice, the discourse of Augustan virtue takes over Propertian elegy. As Lowrie points out, the epitaphic character of Cornelia's speech, along with the poem's presentation of a lifetime of achievement in the first-person and Cornelia's self-fashioning as an *exemplum* to be imitated by posterity (4.11.43–4 and 67–8), all demonstrate strong resemblance to the narrative mode of Augustus' *Res Gestae*.[140] It is perhaps in this final act of silent acquiescence, through which the autonomous territory of love elegy is transformed into a stomping ground for the master narrative of his age, that Propertius pays his greatest 'tribute' to the power of Augustus.

---

[136] Reitzenstein (1969); Stahl (1985) 262; Cairns (2006) 358–61.

[137] La Penna (1951) 86–8; Hallett (1973) 119–20; Hubbard (1974) 145–9; Sullivan (1976) 44; Johnson (1997) 171–6; Janan (2001) 159–63; Heyworth (2007a) 125–6.

[138] On the falsity of Ovid's claim, see Fantham (1998) on Ov. *Fast.* 4.521. Note also the weeping Heracles in Bacchyl. 5.155–8, with Maehler (2004) ad loc.

[139] Heyworth (2007a) 125 also notes that the tears of the *deus* 'raises questions about his divinity'.

[140] Lowrie (2009) 357; see also Hallett (1985) 79–80.

Conclusions

This chapter has focused on the ways in which the poets mobilized divine imagery in their depiction of the new Caesar around the time when Rome was undergoing a political transition; and has argued that the language of divinization functioned as a means for the poets to articulate a number of latent concerns as they tried to come to terms with the new political order. Through their varied representations of Caesar as an increasingly unreachable and irresistible authority in matters public and private (including warfare, literature, and marriage), the poets' divinizing imagery not only encapsulate the widening disparity in power and status between Caesar and those around him as Rome recovered from the civil war but also underline the shifting relationship between art and authority, as well as the gradual encroachment on individual and creative autonomy, under the Principate.

The unfolding portrait of Octavian as a divine ruler across Horace's two books of *Satires* and the book of *Epodes* idealizes Octavian's role in the civil war and embellishes his position in post-Actian Rome; but at the same time, the poet hints at the prospect of inevitable compliance with Caesar's raw political power. By suggesting that Octavian has already surpassed deified republican heroes as he takes on the role of commander, statesman, and lawgiver simultaneously, Horace's divinizing language subtly draws attention to the troubling concentration of power in Octavian after the victory at Actium.

In Virgil's *Georgics*, the poet's attempted discussion with Octavian on the issue of his divinization becomes a proxy for working out both the political future of Rome and the direction of poetry under the Principate. The shifting relationship between Virgil and Caesar in the course of the *Georgics* dramatizes the poet's inability to slow down Rome's march towards a glorious but ultimately uncharted territory. By conflating the loss of his poetic efficacy with the emergence of Octavian as a self-determining force, Virgil underscores the rapidly changing relationship between creative power and state power in the post-Actian world.

Like Virgil and Horace, Propertius' depiction of the new Caesar as a divine figure also directs the reader's gaze towards the profound cultural and political shifts taking place under the Principate. In particular, the poet focuses on the tension between Caesar's expanding realm of power and the autonomy of the elegiac world. Interacting with Horatian and Virgilian depictions of Caesar as the embodiment of order and Roman jurisdiction, Propertius' presentation of the regime's attempt to impose tougher laws on marriage as a tense negotiation between divine authority and mortal resistance foregrounds a growing anxiety about how Caesar is going to exercise his new powers. The appearance of Augustus as a *deus* in Propertius' final elegy emphatically renders apparent the dissolution of difference between the legal power invested in the *princeps* and Caesar's unchecked personal power.

3

Conquest and Immortality in Horace's *Odes*

When Octavian ordered the doors of the Temple of Janus to be shut on 11 January 29 BC,[1] a highly symbolic act which officially marked Rome's victory over Egypt and the return of peacetime, he could hardly have imagined that he would spend the best part of the next decade sweating over the stability of the Roman empire and his own grip on power.

It all started well enough for the new Caesar. The triple triumph held in August 29 BC, which celebrated his victories in Dalmatia, Actium, and Alexandria, conveyed effectively the homecoming of an invincible general. Soon afterwards, starting from 28 BC, a series of constitutional changes—later described by the emperor himself as a transfer of power back to the Senate—was implemented to signal the restoration of the Republic (*R.G.* 34.1), even though the man now known as 'Augustus' held on to extraordinary power by maintaining his *imperium* over the provinces.[2] Meanwhile, a more literal restoration of Rome's religious sites also began to take place (*R.G.* 20.4; Hor. *Carm.* 3.6.1–3).[3] These outward signs of peace across the empire, coupled with the apparent return of republicanism and religious piety, emphatically reinforced Augustus' status as Rome's saviour, leader, and restorer after more than a decade of civil war.[4]

---

[1] On the date: *Fasti Praenestini* (11 January); *R.G.* 13; Cass. Dio 51.20; Syme (1978) 25.

[2] This constitutional amendment is commonly referred to as the 'First Settlement'. The language of *R.G.* 34.1 clearly demonstrates that this transfer of power was a gradual process, rather than a single act in 27 BC as reported by Cass. Dio 53.2.6–22.5. See also Rich and Williams (1999); Levick (2010) 68–9.

[3] *R.G.* 20.4 claims that eighty-two temples in Rome were restored in 28 BC. It is far more likely that the restoration work *began* in 28 and continued through the mid-20s and beyond, see Kraggerud (1995) 56–9; or the restorations of 28 amounted simply to refurbishment, and are to be distinguished from the more ambitious and extended (new) designs which they initiated, see Zanker (1988) 104–14, esp. p. 103. For discussion of *R.G.* 20.4, see Cooley (2009) 194–5.

[4] In addition, Augustus was awarded the *corona civica* for saving citizens; see Gradel (2002) 49–50 on the Jovian connotation of the wreath. Laurels were placed on the doorposts of his residence; see Pöschl (1991) 260 and Galinsky (1996) 354–5.

Politics and Divinization in Augustan Poetry. Bobby Xinyue, Oxford University Press. © Bobby Xinyue 2022.
DOI: 10.1093/oso/9780192855978.003.0004

114   POLITICS AND DIVINIZATION IN AUGUSTAN POETRY

Yet almost as soon as Augustus implemented these changes, problems began to surface. Unrest on both the western and eastern frontiers of the empire occupied his attention for much of the 20s. Back at home, his tenure of power and prominent position within the new political order became a source of concern. It was not until 20 BC, when the Roman legionary standards lost by Crassus at the battle of Carrhae (53 BC) were finally retrieved from the Parthian empire, that the *princeps* could make a claim to *pax Augusta* and cement his *imperium*.

This chapter examines the ways in which the three books of lyric poetry composed by Horace during this period, known collectively as the *Carmina* (or the *Odes*), responded to these events and interacted with the political discourse of the time.[5] Horace's discussions of Augustus' divinization in these poems, as I shall demonstrate, are best interpreted within the broader context of Augustan imperialism and the regime's attempt to control the political narrative of post-civil war Rome. But before we dive into Horace's poetry, let us first look closely at how the subject of Augustus' divinity became intertwined with the constitutional development of the Principate and the Augustan imperialist project in the 20s.

Conquest, Ruler Cult, and Augustan Power

From the end of 27 to early 24 BC, the volatile situation in northern Spain required the personal involvement of the *princeps* (and this campaign turned out to be the last time Augustus led Roman forces in person).[6] He headed the effort for one year only (26 BC) before retiring to Tarraco due to an illness so critical that it apparently almost cost his life (cf. Hor. *Carm.* 3.14.2). When the unrest in Spain reached what could only be described as a pause in 25 BC,[7] Augustus ordered the doors of the Temple of Janus to be shut again (*R.G.* 13; Cass. Dio 53.26.5)—the second time in five years—thereby claiming the pacification of (the western part of) the empire in a way that the Roman troops could not achieve on the Spanish battlefields.[8] To further underscore the sig-

---

[5] 23 BC is generally given as the date of publication for *Odes* 1–3, though Hutchinson (2002) 517–37 contends that the three books were initially published separately between 25 and 23 BC.

[6] Augustus' return from Spain provided the occasion for *Ode* 3.14.

[7] See Gruen *CAH* X, 165.

[8] Banti–Simonetti VII, 142–5, nos. 1369–72: *dupondii* and *asses* dated to 26–25 BC from an unknown mint in Spain show a caduceus behind the head of Augustus and a palm in front. Pollini (1990) 351 argues that the caduceus symbolizes peace, and the palm branch victory; therefore, Augustus is to be seen as *victor* and *pacifer*.

CONQUEST AND IMMORTALITY IN HORACE'S *ODES*   115

nificance of the campaign, Augustus concluded his autobiography with this event and published it soon after (Suet. *Aug.* 85.1). When he returned to Rome in 24 BC, Augustus chose the privilege of wearing garlands and triumphal dress on the first day of every year (cf. Cass. Dio 53.26.5; Flor. 2.33.53) in lieu of celebrating a triumph. The war in Spain clearly had a deep and long-lasting effect for both the *princeps* and Rome. Not only did it mark a turning-point in Augustus' life (both in terms of his mortality and his political career), it also provided a timely (though hardly justified) reminder, and a felicitous perpetuation, of his image as the *triumphator* of the Roman empire.

Around this time, however, questions concerning the specifics of Augustus' power were being raised. In 23 BC, Augustus gave up his consulship, but retained his chief position in the Senate and obtained the *tribunicia potestas* ('tribunician power'), which, among other things, enabled him to propose laws to the Senate whenever he wished.[9] The move was characteristic of the way Augustus carefully framed his extraordinary status in relatively uncontentious terms. Nonetheless, it caused alarm among the Roman aristocracy, who apparently plotted a conspiracy in response.[10] The concerns about Augustus' power most probably also had something to do with the signs of ruler cult springing up in Rome. The construction of the Mausoleum in 28 BC showed that the model of Hellenistic kingship was at least visible, if not actively pursued, in Augustus' self-commemorative methods.[11] Dio (53.27.3) also preserved the story that Agrippa, who supervised the renovation of the Campus Martius, wished to call the new temple on this site the 'Augusteum' and place a statue of Augustus in it.[12] Precedents for temples of this kind were again associated with Hellenistic monarchies;[13] and although Augustus eventually rejected naming the structure the 'Augusteum', allowing it to be called the 'Pantheon' instead, the very fact that he came close to having a temple named after him suggested that his unparalleled status in Rome continued to spark ideas about divinization and cult. Indeed, for the Roman elites who cultivated an appreciation of the symbolic discourses inherited from the Greek world and the Near East, and who were the primary readers of Horace's

---

[9] This constitutional amendment is commonly known as the 'Second Settlement'. See further Lacey (1996) 100–16; Gruen (2005) 36–43; Ferrary (2001) 115–21 = (Edmondson 2009) 99–103.

[10] On the conspiracy, see Cass. Dio 54.3.4–8; Vell. Pat. 2.91.2; Syme (1986) 387–9.

[11] On the Mausoleum, see Zanker (1988) 72–7 and von Hesberg (1996) 234–7. Virgil alludes to it at *Aen.* 6.873; Horace at *Ode* 3.30.1–2; Propertius at 3.2.18–22. For discussions of these literary allusions, see esp. Galinsky (1996) 352; Gibson (1997); Simpson (2002) 63; Ingleheart (2015) 298–9.

[12] Dio dates the completion of the temple to 25 BC.   [13] Crook *CAH* X, 82.

116 POLITICS AND DIVINIZATION IN AUGUSTAN POETRY

poetry, it would be naïve to imagine that they did not notice the proliferation of divine imagery in their surroundings.[14]

Outside Rome, however, the worship of Augustus was a different story. In the Greek East, cults in honour of Augustus were established from 29 BC (if not earlier).[15] In Italy too, there was evidence to suggest that Augustus received cult through private initiatives. Gradel examined a large collection of inscriptions from the reign of Augustus which appear to testify to the existence of altars, priests, and sacrifices dedicated to the living *princeps*, thus casting doubt on the reliability of Dio's claim that there was no emperor worship in Italy (51.20.6–8).[16] In fact, it would seem that even though explicit artistic assimilation of Augustus to a god came to an end in Rome,[17] elsewhere—and especially in the Greek East—Augustus was given divine status throughout the 20s and beyond.

This situation was, however, complicated by Parthia's retention of standards and captives taken from the army of Crassus in 53 BC, which, as Gruen succinctly puts it, remained 'an open sore and an implicit denial of Rome's omnipotence'.[18] Indeed, Roman military operations in the 20s did not always yield victory. Messalla's pacification of the rebels of Gallia Aquitania in 27 BC (cf. Tib. 1.7) was offset by the ineffectiveness of Augustus' Cantabrian campaign and the failure of Aelius Gallus' expedition into the Arabian peninsula (Cass. Dio 53.29; Strabo 16.4.22–4).[19] The mixed success of Roman forces hardly lent credence to Augustus' grand claim of *per totum imperium populi Romani terra marique...pax parta victoriis* ('peace secured by victories throughout the whole empire of the Roman people on land and sea', *R.G.* 13),[20] and even less to his flaunting of Greek titles such as αὐτοκράτωρ ('master') or σεβαστός ('reverenced') in the eastern provinces.

---

[14] A number of studies have established that the Romans of the late Republican and early Augustan periods were attuned to the ideas and symbols of Alexandrian ruler divinity: see Weinstock (1971); Cole (2013); Koortbojian (2013) 1–10; Pandey (2018) 39–41.

[15] Bithynia and Asia were given permission to set up a cult in his honour soon after the victories at Actium and Alexandria (Cass. Dio 51.20.7). In 29 BC, a temple dedicated to the joint cult of Augustus and Roma was built in Pergamum (Suet. *Aug.* 52; Tac. *Ann.* 4.37). See Bowersock (1965) 116 and Price (1984a) 58.

[16] Gradel (2002) 75–7, 89–97. However, Gradel's main argument that divinity was a 'relative category' has been shown by Levene (2012) to be misleading. Flower (2017) 299–310 rejects the existence of the cult of Augustus' *genius* during his lifetime, but concedes (p. 307) that personal expressions of divine worship of the *princeps*, such as paying homage to Augustus' *numen*, must have existed amongst citizens and in private homes.

[17] Pollini (1990) 350; Galinsky (1996) 314; Feeney (1998) 111.   [18] Gruen *CAH* X, 159.

[19] Poetic allusions to the Arabian campaign are found in Hor. *Carm.* 1.29.1–3, 1.35.10; Prop. 2.6.16, 2.10.15–18; Verg. *Aen.* 8.704–6. On this campaign, see von Wissmann (1976); Sidebotham (1986); Marek (1993); Sartre (2005) 66–7.

[20] On the close association between *pax* and *victoria* in the Augustan rhetoric of empire, see most recently Cornwell (2017) 121–54.

CONQUEST AND IMMORTALITY IN HORACE'S *ODES*   117

Importantly, Parthia was the intended target of Julius Caesar's last campaign before his death (cf. Plut. *Caes.* 58.6);[21] and the most recent Roman attempt on the Parthian empire, led by Antony in 36–34 BC, was unsuccessful (Plut. *Ant.* 37.2, 40.4). Antony's defeat could easily have been interpreted as his failure to live up to his own image as the 'New Dionysus': the Greek god was often thought of as the *triumphator* of the east.[22] Therefore, the conquest of Parthia was no ordinary geopolitical tussle, and certainly no 'cheap fantasy' dreamed up by poets for the *princeps*.[23] It most probably had a very personal significance for Augustus, especially in terms of maintaining his image as the *triumphator* and his godlike authority over provincial subjects.

Although the exact foreign policy pursued by Augustus during this period remains a matter of debate,[24] it is telling that when Augustus did eventually retrieve the standards from Parthia in 20 BC through diplomatic solutions,[25] the event was celebrated in a way that better suited a successful *military* operation (καὶ αὐτοὺς ἐκεῖνος ὡς καὶ πολέμῳ τινὶ τὸν Πάρθον νενικηκὼς ἔλαβε, 'Augustus received them as if he had conquered the Parthian in a war', Cass. Dio 54.8.2). The Senate voted Augustus a triumphal arch and the returned standards would eventually be installed in the Temple of Mars Ultor ('Mars the Avenger'). The construction of this temple was meant to fulfil a vow made by Octavian to avenge the death of Julius Caesar before the battle of Philippi. But now, as the intended home for the Parthian standards, the meaning of this temple was reconfigured so as to celebrate Rome's revenge on a long-standing foreign enemy. In this way, the association of the word *ultor* (in the temple's name) was redirected away from civil war to foreign conquest.[26] No longer engulfed in internal conflict, Rome was to leave behind its troubled past and enter an age of imperial peace.

The victory over Parthia thus came at a particularly opportune moment. It quelled growing questions about Augustus' leadership, especially of the Roman military, and reinforced his position as the master of the Roman

---

[21] See further discussion by Sonnabend (1986) 179–85.

[22] On the role of Dionysus in Hellenistic ruler cult, see Chaniotis (2003) 434; Pfeiffer (2016) 27–8.

[23] Griffin (1984) 198.

[24] Campbell (1992) 220–8 and Gruen *CAH* X, 158–63 argue for a reserved cordiality with reliance upon diplomacy, while Brunt (1990) 456–64 and Wissemann (1982) suggest that Augustus may have intended to annex Parthia if the opportunity arose. My view on the issue accords with that of Powell (2010) 168–9, who argues that the almost continuous internal unrest of the Parthians throughout the 20s must have been a source of worry for Rome. Therefore it would seem more likely than not that Parthia was seen as a potential target of Roman military operation.

[25] It should be noted that Augustus' diplomacy was backed by force: early in the summer of 20 BC, Tiberius brought a large legion to Armenia. See Halfmann (1986) 158.

[26] For further discussions of Augustus' monumentalization of the Parthian settlement, see Rich (1998); Rose (2005) 28–36; Cornwell (2017) 121–39.

118 POLITICS AND DIVINIZATION IN AUGUSTAN POETRY

empire. The success against Parthia allowed Augustus to reassert his control over Rome and its subjects—a control which, as we have seen, was underpinned by his self-fashioning as a perpetual *triumphator* and leaned on the symbolic discourses of ruler divinity. These expressions of Augustan power converged strikingly on the so-called Prima Porta statue. The Parthian handover of Roman standards featured conspicuously on Augustus' breastplate, at the top of which a chariot of the Sun could be seen to illumine Roman military victories across the empire. Augustus was shown wearing military costume, but crucially he was barefoot—an iconographical detail usually associated with the depiction of Olympian gods and deified heroes.[27] Victor, emperor, and god: the Prima Porta statue encapsulated the response of art to the overlapping discourses of conquest and divinity in the construction of Augustan power.

Lyric, Imperialism, and Divinization

Scholars have for some time now accepted that Horace's experiment with Greek lyric in the *Odes* was deeply intertwined with Augustan imperialism. As many have argued, the ways in which Horace maps imperial space,[28] crafts poetic landscape,[29] and delineates the contours of Roman identity in the wake of the civil war,[30] are all 'shaped by an evolving consciousness of expanding imperial terrain'.[31]

This interplay between Horatian lyric and Augustan empire not only sensitizes us to the cultural imperialism embodied by the *Odes*, but also binds the poet and the *princeps* in a relationship where they complement each other while competing for control. Indeed, Horace thematizes this in the first and final poem of the collection. The last two lines *Ode* 1.1 read: *quodsi me lyricis vatibus inseres,* | *sublimi feriam sidera vertice* ('But if you rank me among the lyric bards [of Greece], I shall soar aloft and strike the stars with my head', 1.1.35–6); while in *Ode* 3.30 the poet claims: [sc. *dicar*] *princeps Aeolium carmen ad Italos* | *deduxisse modos* ('[I shall be spoken of as] the First Man to have brought Aeolian verse to the tunes of Italy', 3.30.13–14). The triumphal connotation of the second passage, derived from the verb *deduxisse* (3.30.14),[32]

---

[27] See esp. Zanker (1988) 188–92.   [28] Oliensis (1998) 102–53; Powell (2010).
[29] Lowrie (2010) on the imagery of the *antrum* ('cave') in *Odes* 1–3 as a refuge from civic violence.
[30] Morgan (2005a); Feldherr (2010).   [31] Rimell (2015) 83.
[32] Cf. Verg. *G.* 3.11 *deducam*, and Virgil's self-stylization in the same passage as *victor* (*G.* 3.17); also Hor. *Carm.* 1.37.31, where the same verb (*deduci*) is used to evoke the image of Cleopatra being paraded in a triumphal procession.

vividly presents the composition of Latin lyric poetry as the mastering of Greek culture, which is envisaged as the spoil of conquest; and the poet's self-portrait as *princeps* (3.30.13) only adds to the sense that Horace sees himself as a cultural counterpart to the Roman ruler.[33] The claim to poetic fame in *Ode* 3.30 also answers Horace's avowal of ambition in *Ode* 1.1. There, the true marker of the poet's achievement would come in the form of being ranked among revered Greek predecessors (*lyricis vatibus*, 1.1.35), which is presented by Horace as a kind of personal apotheosis (*feriam sidera*, 1.1.36). And the subtle emphasis on Romanization, embedded in the use of the Latin term *vates* (1.1.35)—rather than the Greek-derived *poeta*—to describe Greek poets,[34] points to the idea that Horace can set about his *own* imperialist project without having to participate in the regime's operations. Horatian lyric qua cultural product of the 20s BC can thus be said to refract, and wrestle with, the preoccupations of the Roman empire and the political ambitions of its *princeps*.

Looking at Horace's depictions of Augustus' divinization within this framework, a different set of understandings may emerge. Previous studies have observed that in the *Odes* Augustus' path to divinity is closely linked to the poems' frequent exteriorization of past civil war as future foreign conquest.[35] As a result, Augustus' divinization is presented by Horace as dependent on, and moving in parallel with, Rome's recovery from near constitutional collapse to the re-establishment of imperial order. While I broadly agree with this account, it should be emphasized that this notion of 'recovery by conquest' is to some extent a *narrative* constructed by Augustus. Augustus continually cultivated visual and symbolic representations of triumph, divinity, and vengeance to produce a glorious vision of Roman imperial order under his leadership. This dramatic picture of Rome's transformation—from being mired in civil war to conquering the world again—underpins Augustus' political authority and strengthens his hold on power. Since Horace positions himself as not only the counterpart but also a rival of Augustan *imperium*, the poet's thinking on Augustus' divinization must be more than just a metaphor for Roman imperialism: rather, as this chapter will show, it should emerge as a site of negotiation between political control and poetic authority.

---

[33] Miller (2009) 312; see also Ziogas (2015) 116–17, who examines the question of poetic *auctoritas* more broadly through a reading of the poet-as-*princeps* theme in Virgil and Ovid. The claiming of literary primacy is a recurrent motif in Augustan poetry, see Hinds (1998) 52–63.

[34] Carey (2016) 177.

[35] Oliensis (1998) 112 speaks of 'the relegation of violence to the outskirts'. See also Lowrie (1997) 262.

120 POLITICS AND DIVINIZATION IN AUGUSTAN POETRY

Taking this view, I shall argue firstly that Horace uses the motif of Augustus' divinization to crystallize—and disrupt—the connection between the narrative of Roman transformation and Augustan power. It will be suggested that, while the poet's discussions of Augustus' divinity appear on the whole to tow the official line of a new imperial order emerging under Augustus, Horace also disrupts this narrative by rendering ambiguous the distinctions between triumph and defeat, Roman and foreign, self and other (most notably in 1.35 and 1.37). In doing so, Horace not only pulls at the seams of the regime's reinvention of civil war as foreign conflict, but even obliquely interrogates the construction of Augustan power.

Building on this, the second part of this chapter moves to examine how the discussion of Augustus' divinization operates as a proxy for Horace's reflections on the relationship between his poetry and the discourse of the regime. Assessing this relationship requires more than deciding whether Horace's representation of Augustus as a god-to-be points to poetic collusion with official propaganda,[36] or is merely lip service offered by a former republican.[37] The polyphony, inherited forms, and varied modes of Horatian lyric enable the poet to achieve both (and more) at once in his negotiation of power with Augustus.[38] As Lowrie and Oliensis have shown, throughout the *Odes* Horace mobilizes a wide range of lyric voices and stances to assert his independence and authority, all the while composing ostensibly panegyrical poetry which elevates and reinforces Augustan sublimity.[39] The tension between lyric and eulogy, form and content, aesthetic ideal and imperial ideology, which has been well noted by Fowler and since developed further by Roman,[40] lies at the heart of the poet's discussion of Augustus' divinization. Therefore, building on the idea that lyric expression and Augustan discourse can be an uncomfortable bind and yet must coexist, I will suggest that Horace—especially in the 'Bacchic Odes' (e.g. *Carm.* 2.7, 2.19, 3.25) and the so-called 'Roman Odes' (*Carm.* 3.1–6)—presents the motif of Augustus' divinization as something that tests both the limits of his lyric poetry and his credentials as a nationalistic *vates*. By framing the topic of Augustus' divinity in this way, Horace subtly transforms this motif from a panegyrical theme into an expression of his

---

[36] Powell (2010), esp. p. 190.   [37] Cole (2001), esp. p. 90.
[38] On Horace's extension and expansion of the lyric tradition, see Harrison (2007a) 168–206. On the interplay between different Greek lyric models in the *Odes*, see Feeney (1993) and Barchiesi (2007). On the Pindaric mode of Horatian lyric, see Fitzgerald (1987) 139–59; Race (2010); Carey (2016). On Horace's engagement with and inventive variation of sympotic lyric, see Davis (2007).
[39] Lowrie (1997) 3–4; Oliensis (1998) 102–53.   [40] Fowler (1995); Roman (2014) 201–20.

CONQUEST AND IMMORTALITY IN HORACE'S *ODES*   121

relinquishment of artistic control and ideological autonomy—an expression of acquiescence to Augustan power.

From Civil War to Foreign Conquest

In sharp contrast to the thoroughly ahistorical world of *Ode* 1.1, wherein Horace exercises his literary *imperium* seemingly unaffected by post-war realities,[41] *Ode* 1.2 is inundated with images evoking the civil war.[42] Lowrie notes well that Horace pursues a particular strategy throughout the *Odes* whenever the civil war comes into focus: the poet identifies a more suitable foreign opponent, as often eastern; invokes a saviour, who turns out to be Augustus; and calls for expiation of a moral disorder.[43] This is especially true for *Ode* 1.2. From its outset (*Iam satis*, 'Now enough', *Carm.* 1.2.1), the poem alludes extensively to the finale of *Georgics* 1 (*satis iam*, *G.* 1.501), evoking its dark vision of a faltering Roman world;[44] and the flashback culminates with Horace claiming that Roman citizens should have fought the Parthians instead of each other (*civis acuisse ferrum | quo graves Persae melius perirent*, 'citizens sharpened the sword which should rather have slain the deadly Parthians', 1.2.21–2). The poet's call to address this past sin (*vitio parentum*, 'parents' crime', 23) then turns into a search for a saviour (25–30, esp. 29–30 *cui dabit partis scelus expiandi | Iuppiter?*, 'to whom will Jupiter assign the task of expiating our crime?').[45] After considering a number of divine candidates— namely Apollo, Venus, and Mars (30–40), all of whom occupy a central place in the Augustan religious reforms[46]—the search comes to a dramatic and satisfactory conclusion with the appearance of Mercury–Augustus (41–52):

---

[41] Oliensis (1998) 106.

[42] Horace's description of portents (1.2.1–20) is thought to be relevant to the poem's dramatic date, often given as January 27 BC when the Tiber flooded; see Nisbet and Hubbard (hereafter N–H) (1970) 17–19 and Clark (2010). But Mayer (2012) rightly warns that using this description to date the poem is unreliable, as these images of violent portents appear to be generic rather than temporally specific.

[43] Lowrie (1997) 178. Several other studies have also drawn attention to the poem's expiatory character, see Bickerman (1961) 8; Cairns (1971) 68–70; Miller (2009) 49.

[44] We find in both texts an account of the portents that attended Julius Caesar's assassination (*G.* 1.466–88; cf. *Carm.* 1.2.1–20); the idea that civil strife is a lamentable crime (*G.* 1.489–92, 505–6; cf. *Carm.* 1.2.21–4); and a plea to Vesta (*G.* 1.498; cf. *Carm.* 1.2.26–8).

[45] On Jupiter's role in the poem, see Hejduk (2020) 112–13.

[46] On the Augustan connection of these gods, see Kiessling and Heinze (1930) on 1.2.33–4; Commager (1962) 187; N–H (1970) on 1.2.33–6; Miller (2009) 48.

122   POLITICS AND DIVINIZATION IN AUGUSTAN POETRY

> sive mutata iuvenem figura
> ales in terris imitaris almae
> filius Maiae patiens vocari
> > Caesaris ultor:
> serus in caelum redeas diuque   45
> laetus intersis populo Quirini,
> neve te nostris vitiis iniquum
> > ocior aura
> tollat; hic magnos potius triumphos,
> hic ames dici pater atque princeps,   50
> neu sinas Medos equitare inultos
> > te duce, Caesar.

Or you [come], o winged son of kindly Maia, if you imitate a young man on earth by transforming your own appearance and can tolerate being called Caesar's avenger; may you delay your return to heaven and dwell happily among the people of Romulus for a long time; and may no breeze come too soon and carry you aloft, alienated by our sins. Here rather may you enjoy glorious triumphs, here may you be glad to be called Father and First Citizen, and may you not allow the Parthians to ride unpunished while you are our leader, Caesar.

The exteriorization of violence from the centre to the outskirts of the empire sets in motion Rome's transition from internal strife to imperial conquest.[47] The same Parthians who should have been dealt with when the Romans were at war with each other are now the target of an Augustan military campaign (51–2). Horace's Augustus only 'tolerates' (*patiens*, 43) being called 'Caesar's avenger' (*Caesaris ultor*, 44; cf. Aug. *R.G.* 2), as if he were unwilling to be associated with the civil war;[48] and the implication is surely that he would rather be thought of as the one who will inflict punishment on the Parthians, here described as 'unpunished' (*inultos*, 51). Indeed, the redirection of vengeful energy from the assassins of Julius Caesar to the marauding Parthians anticipates the events of 20 BC, when (as discussed above) the Temple of Mars Ultor will shed its association with civil war to become a symbol of Roman imperial power.[49] By thus suggesting that Augustus was reluctant to participate in the civil war and would rather embark on foreign conquest, Horace

---

[47] Oliensis (1998) 111–12.

[48] Also noted by Clay (2016) 289–90; whereas the commentaries of N–H (1970) and Mayer (2012) suggest that *patiens* conveys the god's condescension towards being assigned to life on earth.

[49] Commager (1962) 186–7; Seager (1980) 105–6; Mayer (2012) 73.

CONQUEST AND IMMORTALITY IN HORACE'S *ODES*   123

adds force the transformation of Augustus from a *iuvenis* (41) who was eager to participate in Rome's internecine conflict, to a *pater atque princeps* (50) under whom Rome would reunify.

While the call for vengeance against Parthia is jingoistic to the extreme, the meaning and tone of Horace's plea for Augustus to remain among his people is more difficult to pin down. The poet's attempt to persuade Augustus to delay his departure from earth (45–8; especially *hic...hic*, 49–50) clearly recalls Virgil's plea to Octavian at the end of *Georgics* 1 (compare especially *Carm.* 1.2.49 with G. 1.503–4). But Horace adds his own touch by imagining Augustus as the incarnation of Mercury. Considering that Augustus flaunted his rejection of a state cult in his name, the appearance of Augustus here as a 'de-divinized' god may evoke his public opposition to his divinization. On the other hand, Clay has argued that this unusual poetic conceit, which she calls 'une apothéose inversée', may be seen as Horace's attempt to moderate Augustus' ambitions, counteracting the appearance of Augustus' patron deity, Apollo, earlier in the poem (30–2).[50] In this way, the poet's wish for Augustus to remain mortal highlights the political astuteness of the *princeps*, while also hinting at the prospect of unchecked Augustan power.

Horace's apparently eccentric identification of Augustus with Mercury has attracted significant scholarly attention over the years. Amongst the wide-ranging views, seeing the motif as a spontaneous poetic invention has many proponents.[51] However, in many ways Mercury is particularly suited to being associated with Augustus. Mercury/Hermes is well known throughout ancient literature for his ability to adopt different guises, which Horace alludes to with the phrase *mutata...figura* (1.2.41); and Augustus' public image certainly undergoes transformation after the civil war, as suggested by his accelerated maturation from *iuvenis* (41) and *Caesaris ultor* (44) to *pater atque princeps* (50). Moreover, as the messenger of the gods and mediator of human-divine relations, Mercury's traditional image can be used to convey Augustus' importance to Rome as the facilitator of *pax deorum*.[52] Indeed, Mercury's appearance later in *Ode* 1.10 as an unthreatening reconciliatory figure—noted for his ability to diffuse hostile situations (as he escorts Priam to Achilles, cf. 1.10.11–16)—further suggests that his cameo in *Ode* 1.2 has the potential

---

[50] Clay (2016) 290.

[51] See e.g. Scott (1928); La Penna (1963) 82–3; Syndikus (1972) 52–3; White (1993) 178–80, 317–18; Lyne (1995) 48 n. 25; Miller (2009) 51.

[52] Commager (1962) 188 notes Horace's emphasis on Mercury's descent from 'kindly' Maia (*almae*, 1.2.42); Clay (2016) argues that the Horatian Mercury's moderating influence derives from one of the functions of the Greek Hermes as the god of boundaries or limits.

124 POLITICS AND DIVINIZATION IN AUGUSTAN POETRY

to evoke Augustus' claim of restoring peace to Rome after the civil war.[53] The peculiarity of this incarnational conceit, therefore, has little to do with Mercury per se or his suitability as Augustus' divine counterpart. Rather, it is the poet's choice of Mercury ahead of other more obvious candidates that is unexpected.

While Augustus is more frequently associated with Apollo or Jupiter, evidence of the assimilation between Augustus and Mercury is not lacking. We find this motif on the official coinage and private art of the early Principate, even if the latter probably only circulated narrowly.[54] More significant perhaps is the suggestion offered by Nisbet and Hubbard: that the comparison of ruler with Mercury appears to have a Ptolemaic origin, since we have not only Ephippus' report of Alexander dressing up as Hermes (cf. Athenaeus 537e) but also the assimilation of Ptolemy V to Hermes/Thoth on the Rosetta Stone.[55] The commentators go on to say: 'The idea could have come to Rome at any time after Caesar's dictatorship, yet it might be relevant that Octavian had recently conquered an Antony–Osiris in Egypt.'[56] What is strongly implied by Nisbet and Hubbard is that Augustus' victory over the last husband of the last of the Ptolemies could have heightened Horace's sensitivity to the Ptolemaic practice of identifying a ruler with Hermes (or a cognate deity). By presenting Augustus somewhat unexpectedly as Mercury incarnate, Horace could thus be suggesting that the victory over Antony–Osiris and the annexation of Egypt have turned Augustus into a new Ptolemaic divine ruler. What is more, as this divine newcomer caps the appearance of Apollo, Venus, and Mars earlier in the poem, the dramatic entry of Mercury–Augustus into both the Roman pantheon and the ode itself works as a way for Horace to insinuate that a new form of power and political culture has arrived at Rome. We might note that Horace's Mercury enters the poem as a thoroughly Greek figure—a winged master of disguise (*ales...imitaris*, 42) reminiscent of the god's appearances in Homer's epics and the Homeric hymn. However, by the end of the poem he is distinctly Roman: he is *pater*, *princeps*, and *Caesar*. This closural reassertion of Romanness is preceded by a series of images evoking ideas associated with the process of acclimatization: a change in appearance (*mutata...figura*, 41), relocation (*in terris*, 42), imitation (*imitaris*, 42),

---

[53] P. A. Miller (1991) 384–8; J. F. Miller (2009) 51. Additionally, Lyne (1995) 120 suggests that the identification of Mercury with Augustus in 1.2 sets the stage for the deity's rescue of the poet at Philippi later in *Ode* 2.7.

[54] See the reverse of *RIC* I² 257 and *BMCRE* (East), 596–8, a series of *denarii* minted between c.31–29 BC. See Zanker (1988) 269 on a Mercury–Augustus agate.

[55] N–H (1970) on 1.2.41–4.   [56] N–H (1970) on 1.2.41–4.

CONQUEST AND IMMORTALITY IN HORACE'S *ODES*   125

adjustment (*patiens*, 43), re-emergence under a different name (*Caesaris ultor*, 43), and, finally, integration (*intersis*, 46).[57] The transfiguration of Greek Hermes as Roman Caesar entwines Augustus' victory in Ptolemaic Egypt with the advent of Hellenistic political culture in Rome. In this way, Horace's incarnational conceit brings out the extent to which ruler cult has found a new form at the heart of the Roman empire as Augustus goes about subjugating one enemy after another.

The motif of Augustus' divinity in *Ode* 1.2, therefore, can be seen to interrogate the effect of Augustan conquest on the Roman political constitution. A similar configuration can be discerned in *Ode* 1.12. This poem begins with a Pindaric question reminiscent of the opening of the Second *Olympian*: *Quem virum aut heroa lyra vel acri | tibia sumis celebrare, Clio? | quem deum?* ('What man or hero do you choose to celebrate with lyre or shrill pipe, Clio? What god?', 1.12.1–3; cf. τίνα θεόν, τίν' ἥρωα, τίνα δ' ἄνδρα κελαδήσομεν; 'what god, what hero, what man shall we celebrate?', Pind. *Ol.* 2.2).[58] In an attempt to answer these questions, Horace identifies a number of *laudandi* as he moves from the Olympian gods (13–24), to deified heroes (25–32), and then to exemplary republican generals and nobles (37–48)—pausing at one point to consider who from Rome's colourful past should be commemorated (33–6).[59] But in the end, only one man deserves celebration, Augustus, who comes into view in the poem's concluding prayer to Jupiter (49–60):[60]

> gentis humanae pater atque custos,
> orte Saturno, tibi cura magni   50
> Caesaris fatis data: tu secundo
> > Caesare regnes.
> ille seu Parthos Latio imminentis
> egerit iusto domitos triumpho,
> sive subiectos Orientis orae   55
> > Seras et Indos,
> te minor laetum reget aequus orbem:
> tu gravi curru quaties Olympum,

[57] Recent proponents of this view include Miller (2009) 47 and Clay (2016) 292.

[58] For further discussion of Pindaric elements in 1.12, see Jocelyn (1993) and Hardie (2003).

[59] Earlier scholarship tends to organize the poem's *laudandi* into a tripartite scheme: lines 13–24 praise gods, 25–36 heroes, 37–48 men. Brown (1991) 328–30 amends this scheme by suggesting that lines 33–6, where Horace mentions not only early Roman kings but also Cato Uticensis, should constitute a preface to the parade of great men (lines 37–48). This scheme has since been adopted by Hardie (2003) 386 and Mayer (2012) 128–9, amongst others.

[60] Augustus' appearance at the end of the poem clearly makes him the single answer to the poem's opening triple-question; see further West (1995) 59–60; Feeney (1998) 113; Hejduk (2020) 122.

126 POLITICS AND DIVINIZATION IN AUGUSTAN POETRY

> tu parum castis inimica mittes
> fulmina lucis. 60

Father and protector of the human race, o son of Saturn, the care of mighty
Caesar has been entrusted to you by fate: may you reign over your kingdom
with Caesar as your vice-regent. Whether he drives the Parthians who threaten
Latium into submission with a justified triumph, or the Chinese and Indians
who live close to the eastern shores, he will rule in fairness over a happy world
as a subordinate to you. You will shake Olympus with your weighty chariot;
you will hurl your wrathful thunderbolts upon unchaste groves.

As in *Ode* 1.2, Augustus is again tasked with the subjugation of the Parthians
(53–4), whose apparent threat to Latium (53) is used as a pretext for further
imperial expansion. Meanwhile, the words *secundo Caesare* (51–2) and
te minor (57) effectively set a limit on Augustus' power, confining him (as Horace
does in *Ode* 1.2) to the human world for now.[61] However, the emphasis on the
Romanness and humanness of Augustus is offset by comparisons of the *princeps* with Greek monarchs and Jupiter.[62] The imagined Roman encounter with
the Chinese and Indians (55–6), though far from realistic, brings to mind the
eastern conquests of Alexander. The protection Augustus provides to his
subjects mirrors that which he receives from Jupiter (*custos*, 49; *cura*, 50)—a
specular relationship evoking the Greek equivalence between Zeus and rulers
based on their shared protective function.[63] Furthermore, the parallel between
Augustus and Jupiter as chariot-drivers—the former 'driving' (*egerit*, 54) the
Parthians in a triumph, the latter shaking Olympus 'with his weighty chariot'
(58)—looks back to the poem's Olympian opening, and recalls the racing-
chariot of Theron, the Greek tyrant and subject of Pindar's victory ode.[64] Thus
the final three stanzas of *Ode* 1.12 are loaded with hints that the all-conquering
Augustus is approaching the status of a divine monarch.

Some critics have sought to play down the significance of these hints of
kingship. For example, Brown has argued that the appearance of the Jupiter-like
Augustus as the poem's final *laudandus* simply looks head to a 'new—and

---

[61] Weinstock (1971) 304 and Galinsky (1996) 218 suggest that Horace here may be engaging in
some polemics against exaggerated views of Augustus' power.

[62] Note the correspondence between *regnes* (52) and *reget* (57); as well as the application of *pater* to
both Jupiter and Augustus in 1.2; see Cole (2001) 77.

[63] Hardie (2003) 401. The Alexandrian poets too express the idea that the Ptolemies are under the
protection of Zeus; see Callim. *H.* 1.73–4, 79–80; Theoc. *Id.* 17. 73–4. On the Greek and Hellenistic
theories of kingship, see Fears (1977) 125–9.

[64] Hardie (2003) 373. On Pindar's anticipation of the cult of Theron of Acragas, see Currie (2005)
192, 287.

CONQUEST AND IMMORTALITY IN HORACE'S *ODES*   127

greater—era in Roman history'.[65] However, the verb used by Horace to characterize Augustus' power, *reget* (57), which looks back to the *regnum* of early Rome (34), rather implies a return to the days of Romulus. In any case, as Horace searches through history for a suitable *laudandus*, it is noticeable that the poet struggles to talk about the Republic (33–6):

> Romulum post hos prius an quietum
> Pompili regnum memorem an superbos
> Tarquini fascis, dubito, an Catonis
>   nobile letum.

After them [i.e. the deified heroes], I hesitate whether to sing of Romulus first, or the peaceful reign of Numa Pompilius, or the overbearing *fasces* of Tarquinius, or the illustrious death of Cato.

Brown interprets this impressionistic survey of famous Romans as a means by which Horace indicates the richness of potential themes before choosing his subjects.[66] I would suggest alternatively that Horace's *aporia*, especially in light of Augustus' representation at the end of the poem, rather dramatizes the apprehension of someone trying to work out the nature of the current regime and its relation to the past. Not knowing whether to begin a eulogy of Rome's illustrious history with the reign of Romulus, or the abolition of monarchy, or the fall of the Republic, is a sign that the ideological landscape of one's surroundings is undergoing rapid and substantial change. Horace's rhetorical *dubitatio* at this crucial juncture in the poem, along with the poet's tactful allusion to Rome's constitutional collapse (*Catonis* | *nobile letum*, 35–6),[67] creates the impression that he knows neither how the past should be viewed, nor what can safely be said in the present political moment. Once the catalogue of famous Romans gets going, Horace veers from praising individual acts of heroism (37–44) to eulogizing dynastic success (*fama Marcelli*, 46),[68] culminating with the mention of the Julian Star (*Iulium sidus*, 47) which looks ahead to the introduction of Augustus in the poem's final stanzas.[69] By carefully

---

[65] Brown (1991) 331.   [66] Brown (1991) 335.

[67] Hardie (2003) 392 notes that *nobile letum* is double-edged ('illustrious death' or 'famous oblivion').

[68] Note Peerlkamp's emendation of *Marcellis* for *Marcelli*. Some critics have understood Horace to refer to Marcellus, son of Octavia and nephew of Augustus, rather than M. Claudius Marcellus (five-time consul and winner of *spolia opima*). Peerlkamp's emendation reaches at the idea that Horace meant both Marcelli. See further discussion by N–H ad loc.

[69] This move towards Rome's 'political dynasties' is also noted by Schmidt (1984) 144–6 and White (1988) 351–3. See Pandey (2018) 55–8 for further discussion of the juxtaposition of *sidus Iulium* with *fama Marcelli*, and a similar juxtaposition at Prop. 3.18.31–4.

128   POLITICS AND DIVINIZATION IN AUGUSTAN POETRY

articulating Rome's shift towards dynastic power in this way, Horace draws
further attention to the political evolution taking place under the Principate.
Ode 1.12 clearly pays tribute the idea of a new imperial order under Augustus;
but the poem's presentation of the *princeps* as a Jovian monarch breaking
tradition from the republican past underlines the poet's reservations about
the Rome's transformation under Augustus.

The Illusion of Triumph

The vision of the Roman empire conjured up by *Odes* 1.2 and 1.12, one
which relies on Augustus to exteriorize violence from the centre to the
periphery in order to prevent a repeat of the civil war, appears again in *Odes*
1.21 and 1.35. The former, a short hymn to Latona and her children, concludes with a hopeful image of Augustus' patron deity, Apollo, diverting war
and malevolent forces away from the Romans and their *princeps* to the
Parthians and Britons instead (*hic bellum lacrimosum . . . a populo et principe
Caesare in | Persas atque Britannos . . . aget*, 'he will drive mournful warfare
away from the people and the leader, Caesar, and toward against the Persians
and Britons', 1.21.13–16).[70] Likewise in *Ode* 1.35, which again looks ahead to
Augustan campaigns against Britons and eastern foes (1.35.29–32), the poet
draws on a notion seen previously in *Ode* 1.2: that the crime of the civil war
(*cicatricum et sceleris pudet | fratrumque*, 'the shame of our scars and crimes
and our brothers', 1.35.33–4; cf. 1.2.21–30) must be atoned for by rechannel-
ling destructive aggression towards foreign enemies (*o utinam <u>nova</u> | incude
diffingas retusum in | Massagetas Arabasque ferrum*, 'O please, turn blunted
blades *re*forged on *new* anvils on Arabs and the Massagetae', 1.35.38–40).
As critics have noted, Horatian lyric's extradition of violence to the margins of
empire in these poems continues the displacement of victimhood from citizens to foreigners, which has been in operation since *Ode* 1.2; and this poetic
strategy resonates with the way in which Augustus himself—and later Virgil
in Book 8 of the *Aeneid* (cf. 8.675–713)—'transforms' the civil war into a
conflict between Rome and an eastern enemy.[71]

Important though this observation is, it requires some qualification.
Horace's depiction of future conquests is so interlaced with a suspicion of the

---

[70] The coupling of the *populus* and the *princeps* (1.21.14), with the latter replacing the Senate, is
redolent of totalitarian rule; see also N–H (1970) ad loc.; Miller (2009) 268.
[71] Oliensis (1998) 112–13; Feldherr (2010) 229.

CONQUEST AND IMMORTALITY IN HORACE'S *ODES*   129

morality of imperialism and an emphasis on the unpredictability of power and fortune, that the very idea of a divinely favoured *imperium Augusti* (which *Odes* 1.2 and 1.12 appear to avow) begins to come under scrutiny. *Ode* 1.29, for example, scolds the philosopher Iccius for abandoning his learning in search of foreign riches and exotic spoils.[72] The poem's personal attack has been read by many as playful,[73] but as Mayer's commentary points out,[74] the line between ironic banter and moral critique is not always clear (1.29):

> Icci, beatis nunc Arabum invides
> gazis, et acrem militiam paras
>   non ante devictis Sabaeae
>   regibus, horribilique Medo
> nectis catenas? quae tibi virginum   5
> sponso necato barbara serviet?
>   puer quis ex aula capillis
>   ad cyathum statuetur unctis,
> doctus sagittas tendere Sericas
> arcu paterno? quis neget arduis   10
>   pronos relabi posse rivos
>   montibus et Tiberim reverti,
> cum tu coemptos undique nobilis
> libros Panaeti Socraticam et domum
>   mutare loricis Hiberis,   15
>   pollicitus meliora, tendis?

What now, Iccius? Have you got your eye on the rich treasure of the Arabs? Are you preparing a fierce campaign against the previously unconquered kings of Sabaea, and forging chains for the fearsome Mede? What foreign maiden will be your slave when you have killed her betrothed? What boy from the royal court with scented hair will be stationed by your ladle, trained as he was to aim Chinese arrows with his father's bow? Who would deny that rivers can flow back up steep mountains, and the Tiber be reversed, when you, who promised better things, now intend to swap the famous books of Panaetius and the school of Socrates for some Spanish breastplate?

---

[72] On the date of the poem, *c*.26–25 BC, see N–H (1970) 338.
[73] N–H (1970) 339; West (1995) 136–41; Maurach (2001) 342; contra Connor (1987) 151–3.
[74] Mayer (2012) 192.

130 POLITICS AND DIVINIZATION IN AUGUSTAN POETRY

Iccius' envy for wealth (*invides*, 1) makes it clear that his motive for military action has little to do with the desire to the extend Roman command.[75] The foreign maiden (*barbara*, 6) and the perfumed boy 'from the royal court' (*ex aula*, 7), whom Iccius want as his house-slaves, emblematize the infiltration of eastern decadence and foreign luxury into the very heart of Rome. The alarming degeneration of Iccius' character (*pollicitus meliora*, 16) is highlighted further by the preposterous image of the Tiber reversing its course (*Tiberim reverti*, 12), which recalls the river's flooding of Rome in *Ode* 1.2 (*Tiberim retortis . . . undis*, 1.2.13–14) and underscores in a physical sense the dilapidation of Roman integrity and moral rectitude. Foreign war is meant to help Romans expiate the sin of civil war by uniting them in a fight against a common enemy. But here in 1.29, Rome's imperial ambition, reified by a philosopher's eagerness to swap books for armoury (13–16), appears to send its citizens back (cf. *relabi*, 11; *reverti*, 12) to the days of profound upheaval and moral delinquency.[76] As Horace draws a pointed connection between foreign conquest and moral impiety in a poem that evokes a number of contemporary or proposed Roman military expeditions (cf. 1–4, 15),[77] it would appear that the poet is contesting the view that foreign war will ensure domestic recovery and usher in a new glorious age. Indeed, as we saw in Propertius 3.4, the elegist further problematizes the connection between foreign wealth, eastern conquest, and Augustan power: *Arma deus Caesar dites meditatur ad Indos,* | *et freta gemmiferi findere classe maris* ('Divine Caesar is planning war against rich India, cutting the straits of the pearl-bearing sea with his fleet', Prop. 3.4.1–2). The prominence of *dites* and *gemmiferi* in the opening lines of the elegy insinuates that Roman imperialism under 'divine Augustus' is about more than just bringing peace to Rome.

Ode 1.35, which meditates on the changeable nature of Fortuna,[78] then makes the point that the pursuit of power and triumph is completely futile. In his address to Fortuna at the beginning of the poem, Horace attributes to the goddess the power 'to raise mortal body from the lowest level or to turn proud triumphs into funeral processions' (*vel imo tollere de gradu* | *mortale*

---

[75] Horace's own distaste for wealth and avaricious audacity is expressed in 1.31.6, 10–15. *Epistles* 1.12 similarly condemns the greed of Iccius, see Putnam (1995).

[76] Some, e.g. Commager (1962) 228 and Connor (1987) 151–3, even suggest that the poem is anti-imperialist.

[77] There are allusions to the failed Arabian expedition of Aelius Gallus (1–4); the intended conquest of Parthia (*Medo*, 4); and the recent operation in Spain (*loricis Hiberis*, 15).

[78] Horace's Fortuna takes on the characteristic arbitrariness usually associated with Tyche, see Mayer (2012) 215.

CONQUEST AND IMMORTALITY IN HORACE'S *ODES* 131

corpus vel superbos | vertere funeribus triumphos, 1.35.2–4). If the equal likelihood of apotheosis and death does not make the imperialist pause, then the sudden turning of victory into funeral by Fortuna certainly makes a mockery of any attempt to conquer. In any case, as the poet goes on to suggest, since every people on earth—from the Scythians to the Latins—are subject to life's unpredictability (*te profugi Scythae, | urbesque gentesque et Latium ferox* ... *metuunt*, 'the retreating Scythians, cities and peoples, and warlike Latium [all] fear you', 9–12), the equalling power of Fortuna effaces the difference between self and other. Set against this background, the poem's final prayer for Augustan military success in Britain and the East (29–40, see above), which operates on the differentiation between 'us' and 'them', may be more ironic than it seems.

An example of Fortune's unpredictability is then provided in *Ode* 1.37, the last of a well-recognized Horatian 'Actium trilogy' consisting also of *Epodes* 1 and 9.[79] In this dithyrambic ode which celebrates Augustus' victory over Cleopatra,[80] the Egyptian queen is said to be 'drunk on sweet fortune' when she planned destruction on Rome (*fortunaque dulci | ebria*, 11–12). The poem's focus on Cleopatra—with Antony completely elided from the narrative—caps Horace's strategy of converting Rome's civil war into a conflict against a foreign enemy, a shift of perspective redolent of the Augustan narrative of the battle of Actium.[81] Yet, the poem's portrayal of Cleopatra's courage and dignity in the final moment of her life, when she chose suicide over the humiliation of becoming a captive (21–32), brings to mind the exemplary actions of the heroes of the Roman Republic.[82] Horace's glorification of Cleopatra also points to the idea—latent in a double-reading of *deliberata morte* (29)—that in choosing death Cleopatra conversely overcomes death (*de liberata morte*, 'freed from death'). Indeed, an alternative interpretation of the poem's final word, *triumpho* (32), as 'I triumph' (rather than as an ablative noun belonging to the construction *deduci superbo* ... *triumpho*, 'to be led along in a proud

---

[79] *Ode* 1.37 is well served by secondary literature, often antithetical: see esp. Johnson (1967); Davis (1991) 233–42; Lowrie (1997) 138–64; Oliensis (1998) 136–44.

[80] On the poem's dithyrambic characteristics, see esp. Hardie (1976) and Giusti (2016b) 137–8. Other genres also leave their mark: see Syndikus (1972) 333–4 on Pindaric epinician; Leeman (1985) 231–3 on tragedy; and Hunter (2006) 48–50 on Euripides' *Bacchae* specifically.

[81] Lowrie (1997) 145; Feldherr (2010) 224. Moreover, the similarity between Cleopatra's threat to Rome (6–8), and the menacing nature of the foreign enemies whom Horace identifies as suitable targets of future imperial campaigns (e.g. *Parthos Latio imminentis*, 'the Parthian threatening Latium', 1.12.53), conveniently frames the battle of Actium as the beginning of Rome's reassertion of her power upon the world.

[82] Commager (1962) 92; Pöschl (1991) 113–16.

132 POLITICS AND DIVINIZATION IN AUGUSTAN POETRY

triumph'),[83] further accentuates the confusion between victory and defeat, immortality and death as the poetry-book edges towards its conclusion.

In an illuminating study of the intersection of sympotic poetics and civil-war politics in *Ode* 1.37, Feldherr argues that Horace's poem binds Cleopatra and Augustus in a mirroring relationship through an alternating identification of each character with the god Dionysus, who exercises a distorting force on the poem's initial attempt to redefine civil war as foreign war.[84] Feldherr's reading of the poem as a self-debilitating interrogation of the (Roman) 'self' and the (Egyptian, eastern, foreign) 'other' draws our attention to the way that *Ode* 1.37 caps a broader movement in the second half of the book, whereby (as described above) Horace gradually turns the screw on the Augustan vision of a new imperial order which the poet initially presents as desirable in *Odes* 1.2 and 1.12. In the poem about the philosopher Iccius, Horace comes close to stating that foreign conquest precipitates exactly the kind of moral dilapidation that almost destroyed Rome in the civil war; while in *Ode* 1.35, the poet spells out in no uncertain terms the unpredictability of fortune and power, and frames it within the context of the Augustan imperial project. By questioning the morality and effectiveness of conquest in these poems, Horace challenges both the rationale of expiating past sins through foreign wars, and the attainability of perpetual *imperium*. Coming at the end of this poetic sequence, the confusion of identities in *Ode* 1.37 not only disrupts the difference between victorious Roman Caesar and conquered Egyptian enemy but even exerts a destabilizing effect on Horace's representation of Mercury–Augustus in *Ode* 1.2, which occupies a mirroring position to *Ode* 1.37 in the book.[85] The god incarnate of 1.2 is ostensibly Roman, but he also embodies the *translatio* of Ptolemaic ruler cult to Rome; whereas the figure who appears most Roman at the end of 1.37, who is immortalized by the poet, is not Augustus, but a Ptolemaic queen. The heroizing Romanization of Cleopatra works as a foil for the equally disorienting image of Augustus as Mercury incarnate. Insomuch that the 'triumph' of Cleopatra interrogates Augustus' transformation of civil war into foreign conquest, the Hellenizing portrayal of Augustus as a god-on-earth emblematizes Rome's self-alienation in the pursuit of *imperium*.

---

[83] Feldherr (2010) 231; anticipated by Oliensis (1998) 140. Additionally, Lowrie (1997) 141 n. 3 notes that *non* applies to every word in the final line: 'she is not humble, she is not a woman, it was not a triumph.'

[84] Feldherr (2010) 228–30.

[85] For other readings of 1.2 and 1.37 in conjunction, see Pöschl (1991) 74; Lowrie (1997) 142–4; Feldherr (2010) 223–4.

CONQUEST AND IMMORTALITY IN HORACE'S *ODES*   133

Bacchic Poetics and Augustan Power

This chapter has so far argued that, on one level, the symmetry between Augustus' path to divinity and Rome's transformation from civil-war disorder to imperial power in *Odes* 1 serves to reinforce the Augustan discourse of *pax parta victoriis*. Indeed, a number of poems from Book 1 actively extend the notion that Rome must aim its violence outwards in order to avoid a repeat of the civil war. At the same time, however, the poet uses the motif of Augustus' divinization to interrogate Rome's ongoing transformation under the Principate. In the more solemn 'public' *Odes* 1.2 and 1.12, Horace subtly establishes a link between further imperial conquest and Rome's shift towards monarchy. In the more convivial 'private' world of *Ode* 1.37, when the influence of Bacchus takes over, Horace's immortalization of Cleopatra disrupts the neat dichotomies underpinning the discourse of Augustan triumph, through which the poet distances himself from the regime's attempt to redefine and exteriorize the violence of the civil war.[86] This marked shift from a Pindaric mode of communal lyric (1.2 and 1.2), to a more erratic and conflicted mode of private sympotic lyric (1.37), pointedly re-interiorizes a discordancy that contravenes Rome's triumphant transformation under Augustus.

In the second book of the *Odes*, Horace makes further use of sympotic and Bacchic imagery to render apparent the difficulty involved in reconciling official discourse with his lyric programme. *Ode* 2.7, which celebrates the repatriation of the poet's ex-republican friend Pompeius, sets up the relationship between Horace and Augustus, as well as the tension between the civil-war past and the Augustan present, through Bacchic symbolisms.[87] The significance of the poem's divine imagery is foregrounded when Horace recounts that he was rescued by Mercury during the defeat at Philippi (13–14), while his friend Pompeius was unable to extricate himself from the battle.[88]

---

[86] The placement of 'public' and 'private' in apostrophe is (as is now common in Greek and Latin literary scholarship) intended to allude to lyric poetry's frequent self-representation as being sung at a large and communal, or a smaller and more intimate, occasion. Whether a poem was indeed performed (or was simply imagined as being performed) in front of a public or private audience can only be determined securely through external evidence. For an overview of the performative contexts of Greek lyric, see Carey (2009); on Pindaric victory odes, see Agócs et al. (2012); on dithyrambs, see Kowalzig and Wilson (2013); on the audience and *laudandi* of Alcaeus' sympotic lyric, see Budelmann (2012) 188.

[87] This 'Pompeius' has been variously identified as an associate of Sextus or a minor relation of Pompey Magnus; see esp. Citroni (2000) 28–9. The true identity of this character is not, as Harrison (2017) 102 reasserts, as important as the fact that someone with such a prominently anti-Caesarian name and matching loyalties has been allowed to return to Rome, which may be interpreted as a compliment to Augustus' *clementia*.

[88] Mercury's intervention here has a clear epic colouring, but also appears to imitate a similar scene of the poet's rescue in Archilochus fr. 95 West; see N–H (1978) 107–8 and Harrison (2017) 107. The

134   POLITICS AND DIVINIZATION IN AUGUSTAN POETRY

Although Mercury's intervention here is usually understood as one of a number of instances in the *Odes* where Horace presents the god of the lyre as his divine protector (cf. 1.10.1–6; 2.17.29),[89] the deity's incarnation as Augustus in *Ode* 1.2 demands that the possibility of mythologizing roleplay be left open.[90]

The final three stanzas of 2.7 then depict a sympotic scene in which Horace asks his wine cups to be filled with the 'memory-dulling Massic' (*oblivioso levia Massico | ciboria exple*, 21–2) and submits to the power of Bacchus (26–8):

> non ego sanius
> bacchabor Edonis: recepto
> dulce mihi furere est amico.

I shall revel no more sanely than Thracian Edonians: it is a delight for me to go wild when I got my friend back.

Wine induces oblivion (21) and ecstasy (*bacchabor* 27, *furere* 28) simultaneously: it enables the poet to blur the past and enjoy the present.[91] When reminders of Horace's previous opposition to Augustus come back to haunt him,[92] the poet first mythologizes the events at Philippi in such a way that the Homeric resonance of his recollection makes the entire experience seem distant and unreal.[93] But to truly move on from the civil war, the poet, like the Edonian women, must surrender control to Bacchus and be 'under the influence', as it were, to find joy in the present moment—much like at the end of *Epode* 9 (lines 37–8) where 'sweet Lyaeus' provided Horace with comfort in the anxiety-ridden aftermath of Actium.[94] The mention of the Edonian Bacchants is particularly significant because it evokes Aeschylus' *Edonians*,

---

motif of the abandoned shield at 2.7.10 recalls similar scenes from Archilochus (fr. 5 West), Alcaeus (fr. 428a Lobel–Page = fr. 201B Voigt), and Anacreon (fr. 381b Campbell); for a recent reassessment of the motif both in Greek lyric poetry and in Horace, see Smith (2015), and previously De Martino (1992).

[89] Fraenkel (1957) 163–6; P. A. Miller (1991); J. F. Miller (2009) 44–53.

[90] Schmidt (2002) 279 suggests, unconvincingly, that Mercury's rescue of the poet in 2.7 recalls the intervention of the *iuvenis* in *Ecl.* 1.

[91] See Harrison (2017) on 2.7.21. Feldherr (2010) 226 rightly suggests that 'telling the story of forgetting always opens the door to memory'; see also O'Gorman (2002) 97, who speaks of 'the return of the repressed'. By contrast, Smith (2015) 271–3 reads Horace's *oblivio* as emblematic of the amnesty under which Pompeius has returned.

[92] Some have argued that Horace is critical of Brutus and the Republican cause in 2.7; see further N–H (1978) 106–21; Moles (1987).

[93] On the mythologization of civil war in 2.7, see esp. Davis (1991) 89–98; Citroni (2000) 39–45; O'Gorman (2002) 98. There are many epic parallels of the image of the hero being whisked away from the battlefield by a god, see N–H (1978) on 2.7.13 with references and Harrison (2016) 93–7. The latter also detects echoes of Odysseus' shipwreck (Hom. *Od.* 5.288–431) in Horace's metaphorical sea-storm of war (2.7.15–16).

[94] See my reading of these lines of *Epod.* 9 in Chapter 2.

CONQUEST AND IMMORTALITY IN HORACE'S *ODES*   135

which tells the failed attempt by Lycurgus to suppress the worship of Dionysus and the king's downfall at the hands of the god.[95] Despite the play's fragmentary state, it is clear that Lycurgus' resistance to the importation of a foreign cult constitutes an important thematic element.[96] By evoking this story at the end of a poem in which Horace's former resistance to Augustus is painted in mythological colours, the poet's self-identification with the Edonian Bacchants not only dramatizes his succumbing to the Augustan cause but also alludes to the immense power of the new ruler. As a present-day conqueror of the east, Augustus too, much like Dionysus, cannot be resisted, but must be embraced.[97]

That the poet needs the help of Bacchus in his negotiation of the Augustan present becomes clearer, and starker, in two other thematically related poems. Both the poet's submission to Dionysiac influence and the implicit assimilation of Bacchus with Augustus re-emerge in *Ode* 2.19. Schiesaro has argued that this poem conveys the idea that the composition of Augustan panegyric requires the poet to overcome his own reservations, literary or otherwise.[98] This is especially evident in the way that Bacchus' image undergoes a dramatic change in the course of the poem. At the start of 2.19, the god appears rather unusually as a teacher of songs (*Bacchum in remotis carmina rupibus | vidi docentem*, 'I have seen Bacchus teaching songs on distant cliffs', 1–2);[99] then he assumes his more familiar role as the inspirer of frenzy, filling the poet's mind with unpredictable energy (*Euhoe, recenti mens trepidat metu | plenoque Bacchi pectore turbidum | laetatur*, 'Euhoe! My mind trembles with fresh fear, and with my heart filled with Bacchus, it experiences a disturbing joy, 5–7); and by the end of the poem, in another unexpected representational turn, Bacchus emerges as an Olympian combatant in the war against the Giants (21–4).[100] Horace's reinvention of Bacchus as a symbol of divine retribution in the story of the Gigantomachy—a trope often used as an allegory for Augustus' victory over Antony and Cleopatra (cf. *Ode* 3.4.42–80; Verg. *Aen.* 8.675–713)—initiates the process of Bacchus' rehabilitation as an Augustan deity.[101] Through his Romanization and 're-domestication' of

---

[95] De Martino (1992) 49.   [96] See further West (1990) 26–7.

[97] See also Citroni (2000) 36–7; Harrison (2016) 97–8. Similarly, Moles (1987) 71 reads the poem as Horace giving Pompeius practical advice on the political attitude he should now take.

[98] Schiesaro (2009), esp. pp. 66–7, 75–6.

[99] Henrichs (1978) 205 points out that the emphasis on vision (*vidi*), suggestive of divine epiphany, followed by praise of the god, finds parallel in Hellenistic aretalogy.

[100] Pöschl (1973) 228 and Harrison (2017) 225–6 see a parallel between the multiplicity of Bacchus' image and the poet's own literary *variatio* and generic fluctuations.

[101] Batinski (1990–91); Koster (1994) 51–70; Stevens (1999) 287–90; Cucchiarelli (2011b) 264. On the Virgilian Gigantomachy, see Hardie (1986) 97–109; on its use in *Ode* 3.4, see Lowrie (1997) 238–42.

136 POLITICS AND DIVINIZATION IN AUGUSTAN POETRY

Bacchus,[102] Horace demonstrates his willingness to praise Augustus. But to make such a move, Horace needed a Bacchic-inspired frenzy in the first place (5–7). Embracing Augustan power, as it turns out, requires one to abandon level-headedness and good sense.

In *Ode* 3.25, a companion piece to *Ode* 2.19, Horace again allows himself to be swept up by the energizing force of Bacchus (*Quo me, Bacche, rapis tui | plenum?*, 'Where are you hurrying me, Bacchus, full as I am of you?', 1–2), and later compares himself to a Maenad (*non secus . . . Euhias*, 'no different to a Maenad', 9–10) as he did previously at 2.7.26–7 (*non . . . sanius . . . Edonis*, 'no saner than the Edonians'). The poet claims that Bacchic frenzy would enable him to complete a most challenging literary task—the immortalization of Augustus (3–8):

> quibus
> antris egregii Caesaris audiar
>   aeternum meditans decus   5
> stellis inserere et consilio Iovis?
>   dicam insigne recens adhuc
> indictum ore alio.

In what caverns shall I be heard as I practise setting the eternal glory of peerless Caesar among the stars and in the council of Jupiter? I shall sing a momentous theme, one that is modern and has never yet been sung by another's lips.

Hardie suggests that Horace calls for Dionysiac excess because Augustus is full of confounding contradictions: he is a mortal in the company of the gods, a king who restored the Republic; and in order to come to terms with such paradox and sublimity, the poet must possess a correspondingly heightened and irrational disposition, which only Bacchus can provide.[103] In addition, this passage also implies that the composition of Augustan panegyric (*egregii Caesaris . . . | aeternum . . . decus*, 4–5) tests the limits of Horatian lyric, since it is exactly the sort of topic which the poet in *Ode* 1.6 claims that he finds difficult to handle, artistically and morally: *tenues grandia, dum pudor | imbellisque lyrae Musa potens vetat | laudes egregii Caesaris . . . deterere* ('[I am] too slight for grand themes, while modesty and powerful Muse of the unwarlike lyre forbid me from diminishing the praise of peerless Caesar', 1.6.9–12).[104]

---

[102] I borrow this term from Fuhrer (2011) 383.   [103] Hardie (2016) 20.
[104] Schiesaro (2009) 64–6.

The word *pudor* (1.6.9) carries some weight here. Mayer's suggestion to interpret *pudor* as 'diffidence' or 'sense of inadequacy' concerning one's literary competence,[105] while reasonable, underplays the ethical and socio-behavioural dimension of the word.[106] In *Satire* 1.6, *pudor* is a kind of moral virtuosity that helps Horace to observe and maintain certain societal boundaries (*infans . . . pudor*, 'speechless shame', *Sat.* 1.6.57; *pudicum,* | *qui primus virtutis honos, servavit,* 'he kept me modest—and that is virtue's first honour, *Sat.* 1.6.82–3).[107] Similarly, at *Epistles* 2.1.258–9 (*nec meus audet* | *rem temptare pudor quam vires ferre recusent,* 'nor does my modesty dare to attempt a task which my strengths refuse to bear'), the *pudor* that prevents Horace from writing a panegyric of Augustus is not merely diffidence, but also a sense that it is reprehensible to disregard restraints and ignore one's limitations. It is precisely because divinizing Augustus in poetry transgresses certain sociopolitical boundaries that Horace in *Ode* 3.25 characterizes this activity as *dulce periculum* ('sweet danger', 18).[108] By thus associating the immortalization of Augustus with surrendering control to Bacchic frenzy and making moral and literary transgressions, Horace not only hints at the irrationality that lies at the heart of the Augustan political mythology[109] but also suggests that ideological sobriety and poetic authority must be relinquished in order to eulogize the *princeps*.

Poetic Limitations in the 'Roman Odes'

The idea that the poetic immortalization of Augustus tests the limits of both Horatian lyric and the poet's ideological autonomy also figures in the opening Alcaic sequence that launches the third book of the *Odes*. Commonly known as the 'Roman Odes',[110] the first six poems of Book 3 constitute Horace's most sustained and explicit engagement with the official policies of Augustus. However, as Lowrie rightly observes, Horace often presents Augustus' policies

---

[105] Mayer (2012) 93.

[106] On *pudor* as a Roman social emotion, see Kaster (1997) 4: '*pudor* denotes a displeasure with oneself caused by vulnerability to just criticism of a socially diminishing sort.'

[107] Gowers (2012) 234.

[108] Reading *Odes* 1.18, 2.19, and 3.25 as a narrative sequence, Lowrie (1997) 324 concludes: '3.25 gives the story's conclusion after the fact: Bacchus, the god of wine and the symposium, enables Horace to cross his own boundaries, and to praise Caesar.'

[109] Heyworth (2016) 255–6: 'One of the purposes of these two expressions of Bacchic influence in 2.19 and 3.25 is to mark the poet as beyond reason in what he says in the accompanying panegyric.'

[110] Several comprehensive studies are dedicated solely to the 'Roman Odes', see esp. Witke (1983); Schenker (1993). The aesthetic unity and thematic homogeneity of this poetic sequence have encouraged Heyworth (1995) 142–4 to treat it as one continuous poem.

138 POLITICS AND DIVINIZATION IN AUGUSTAN POETRY

as his own recommendations or 'warnings whose message has already been heeded', so as to assert his poetic independence and gain the rhetorical upper hand by not directly recounting the *res gestae* of Augustus.[111] The first Roman Ode, for example, condemns excessive ambition and greed (3.1.9–44), extolling instead the virtues of the simple life (3.1.45–8).[112] By doing so, Horace frames Augustus' self-restraint and promotion of frugality (Suet. *Aug.* 72–3) as principles that answer the poet's desire for a moral revival. In the second Roman Ode, Horace's praise of *virtus* as an immortalizing quality (3.2.17–24) allows the poet to sidestep direct panegyric of Augustus, while still acknowledging the recent achievement of the *princeps*, who was awarded the so-called *clipeus virtutis* in 27 BC (Aug. *R.G.* 34).[113] Similarly, Horace's call for an urgent repair of Rome's dilapidated temples in *Ode* 3.6 sets up the poet as the impetus and authority behind the rebuilding programme initiated (or about to be initiated) by Augustus.[114] The *princeps* is not mentioned in any of these three poems, even though his achievements and policies are presented as fundamental to Rome's recovery after the civil war. By sidestepping direct praise of Augustus and his policies, Horace creates a distance between his poetry and the regime's political programme.

In the poems in which Augustus does appear, Horace's panegyric is still not straightforward. While *Odes* 3.3, 3.4, and 3.5 on the whole speak favourably of Augustus' rule, twice proclaiming his deification as the anticipated reward for his rehabilitation of Roman *imperium* (3.3.11–12; 3.5.1–4), it is noticeable that the poet's praise of Augustus is never fully reconciled with these poems' central narratives, which retreat into an epicized legendary past. Oliensis has argued that Horace's use of mytho-historical narratives in these three odes (Juno's prophecy of Rome in 3.3, the Gigantomachy in 3.4, and the story of Regulus in 3.5) opens up a gap between the Augustan present and the exemplary past that is wide enough to render the supposed poetic message untranslatable.[115] Meanwhile, Lowrie has shown that even though the mythic narratives of the 'Roman Odes' (especially the Gigantomachy of 3.4) have a patriotic slant, their meaning is obfuscated by the poet's repeated emphasis of the

---

[111] Lowrie (1997) 258–65, esp. p. 260.

[112] On the poem's engagement with Epicurean philosophy, see Cairns (1995) 120–4; Lyne (1995) 162–3.

[113] There is a copy of the shield from Arles, see EJ² 22. The 'Roman Odes' contain several references to the four qualities depicted on the shield: *virtus* (3.2.17–24), *clementia* (3.4.41–2), *iustitia* (3.3.1–8), and *pietas* (3.6.1–8). See further Williams (1969) 37; Jameson (1984) 233; West (2002) 3–10, 26–7; Nisbet and Rudd (hereafter N–R) (2004) on 3.2.17–20;

[114] Lowrie (1997) 258; Witke (1983) 73–7. On the date of composition of 3.6, see Fenik (1962) 86–7; West (2002) 64–6; N–R (2004) 97.

[115] Oliensis (1998) 131–2.

tension between epic content and lyric form.[116] Most recently, Hejduk has suggested that although Horace develops a parallel between Augustus and Jupiter in the 'Roman Odes', the poet's depiction of Jupiter often 'problematizes the ostensibly simple message of glorifying Augustus'.[117] In what follows, I develop further this well-founded scepticism about the congruity between Augustan eulogy and exemplary narrative in the 'Roman Odes'. I argue that, although these narratives should—by allegorical analogy— immortalize Augustus' achievements, Horace uses them instead to demarcate his lyric programme from political panegyric, thereby reasserting *his* control over the use of exemplary narratives in the face of Augustan appropriation. Luke Roman has recently argued that in the 'Roman Odes' there is a discernible juxtaposition between Augustus' sphere of power and Horace's own space of autonomy, and that through this juxtaposition the poet 'clarifies the boundaries of the political and poetic realms'.[118] Here I suggest further that Horace not merely presents a clear separation of political and poetic realms, but even frames this demarcation as withholding his artistic consent to Augustan power.

Ode 3.3

The third Roman Ode gives an indication of the way in which Horace dissociates mythologizing narrative from Augustan achievement. The poem begins with a catalogue of figures who have obtained, or will eventually obtain, divine status by their virtue. Amongst them is Augustus (9–16):

> hac arte Pollux et vagus Hercules
> enisus arces attigit igneas,   10
>   quos inter Augustus recumbens
>   purpureo bibet ore nectar.[119]
> hac te merentem, Bacche pater, tuae
> vexere tigres indocili iugum
>   collo trahentes; hac Quirinus   15
>   Martis equis Acheronta fugit.

---

[116] Lowrie (1997) 245–57.
[117] Hejduk (2020) 124; see further pp. 123–9.   [118] Roman (2014) 219.
[119] The MSS variant *bibit* should be jettisoned: the future tense *bibet* is clearly right, as Horace later in 3.5.2–3 writes *praesens divus **habebitur** | Augustus.*

140   POLITICS AND DIVINIZATION IN AUGUSTAN POETRY

By such art did Pollux and far-travelled Hercules prevail and reach the citadels of fire, and reclined between them Augustus will drink the nectar with his purple lips. By such art, father Bacchus, your tigers carry you deservingly, dragging the yoke on their untameable necks. By such art did Quirinus escape from Acheron on the horses of Mars.

In republican Rome, Hercules, Bacchus, and the Dioscuri are conventionally regarded as benefactors of mankind;[120] and by the mid-40s BC, they are often grouped together with Romulus-Quirinus (as Horace does here) as men who became gods on account of their beneficent work (cf. Cic. *Leg.* 2.19; *Nat. D.* 2.62, 3.39; *Tusc.* 1.28).[121] But catalogues of this kind are also a standard feature of Hellenistic encomia: following his conquest of Persia, Alexander is often compared to the well-travelled Herakles and Dionysus by panegyrists and court poets.[122] Moreover in Theocritus' *Idylls* 17.13–22, we find a scene of Olympian feast in which Ptolemy I Soter is flanked by Alexander on one side and Herakles on the other.[123] The presence of Augustus in the company of Hercules and Bacchus thus sets him up as a new Alexander, destined to earn his divinization through heroic conquest and achievement.[124] Indeed, his appearance here brings to mind a *triumphator*, as *purpureo . . . ore* (12) evokes the painted face of the victorious general in a procession.[125] By opening the poem with this mytho-historical catalogue, Horace draws attention to the close connection between the mythologization of conquest and the immortalization of Augustus.

The main narrative of *Ode* 3.3 then creates the impression that the poet is engaged in making precisely this connection. The poem's central episode is a soliloquy by Juno, in which the goddess sets out the terms of Romulus' apotheosis and looks ahead to present-day Roman *imperium* (18–68). This speech is modelled on a now-lost scene of Olympian debate in Ennius' *Annales*, where the goddess must have consented to Romulus' entry to

---

[120] See Brink (1982) on Hor. *Ep.* 2.1.5–17; also Doblhofer (1966) 122–8; Eidinow (2000) 467.

[121] See Cole (2013) 85–103 for Cicero's importance in establishing Romulus as the defining model of the Roman deification.

[122] Bellinger (1957) 99–100; Doblhofer (1966) 134–8.

[123] See further Heyworth (2016) 241–2.

[124] On the recognizable features of Alexander in sculptural and numismatic depictions of Augustus, see Kleiner (2005) 208 and Galinsky (2005) 341. Pliny the Elder also records that Augustus signed documents with an image of Alexander (*HN* 37.10), and that statues of Alexander were dedicated in the Forum of Augustus and the Temple of Mars Ultor (*HN* 34.48).

[125] Eidinow (2000). Contra Sutherland (2002) 177, who suggests that *purpureo ore* conjures up wine and the symposium.

CONQUEST AND IMMORTALITY IN HORACE'S *ODES*   141

heaven.[126] In Horace's poem, Romulus' apotheosis is presented as a precursor to that of Augustus: the sight of Romulus sitting among the gods supping nectar (*illum ego lucidas | inire sedes, ducere nectaris | sucos . . . patiar*, 'I shall allow him to enter the illumined abodes, to drink the juice of nectar', 33–6) clearly recalls the poem's earlier image of Augustus (11–12, above).[127] Furthermore, Juno's prophetic vision of the Parthian empire being under Roman jurisdiction (*triumphatisque possit | Roma ferox dare iura Medis*, 'may warlike Rome have the power to rule over the conquered Medes', 43–4) brings to mind the proposed Augustan conquest of Parthia encouraged by Horace in *Odes* 1.2 and 1.12.

Importantly, however, Juno's speech about Roman conquest is imbued with a sense of excessive transgression (53–6):

> quicumque mundo terminus obstitit,
> hunc tanget armis, visere gestiens,
>   qua parte debacchentur ignes,   55
>   qua nebulae pluviique rores.

Whatever limit is set to the world, let her [i.e. Rome] touch it with weapons, eager to see the part where fire, cloud, and rainy dew rage uncontrollably.

Rome will not simply reach the boundary of the world, but test it with force (*armis*, 54); and *debacchentur* (55), which accentuates the unpredictable conditions of regions unknown,[128] frames Roman conquest as a transgression of normal habitable spheres. In addition to this sense of spatial transgression, there is also a hint of literary transgression: *armis* especially gestures towards the passage's indebtedness to its epic predecessor. Set against the comparison of meteorological forces to frenzied Bacchants (with *debacchentur* evoking *bacchabor* in 2.7.27), this image of Roman transgression reminds readers of Horace's claim in *Odes* 2.19 and 3.25 that he would require a Dionysiac excess to overcome lyric reservations and enter the epicized world of Augustan panegyric. Therefore, even though Juno's speech presents a vision of Roman conquest that corresponds with the poem's opening image of Augustus as a divine conqueror, the lyric poet implies that this kind of triumphalist mytho-

---

[126] This lost Ennian episode must also have been the model for Juno's speech at the end of the *Aeneid* (12.791–842). See further Feeney (1991) 125–6; Lowrie (1997) 228, 247–8; Harrison (2007a) 187–8.

[127] On Romulus' prefiguration of Augustus, see Suet. *Aug.* 7; Cass. Dio 53.16.7; Commager (1962) 212; West (2002) 38; N–R (2004) 36.

[128] N–R (2004) ad loc.

142 POLITICS AND DIVINIZATION IN AUGUSTAN POETRY

historical narrative is something of a literary transgression for him. Indeed, *Ode* 3.3 concludes with a highly metaliterary comment that suggests that the poem's central narrative is generically deviant (69–72):

> non hoc iocosae conveniet lyrae:
> quo, Musa, tendis? desine pervicax   70
>   referre sermones deorum et
>   magna modis tenuare parvis.

This will not suit my playful lyre. Where are you going, my wilful Muse? Stop retelling the talk of gods and reducing great matters to small measures.

As Harrison notes, this closural moment of self-consciousness makes explicit that the epic elevation and serious tone achieved in the course of the poem are inappropriate for Horatian lyric.[129] By dissociating his lyric poetry from an epicized narrative of Roman *imperium* in this way, the final stanza of *Ode* 3.3 frames in light-hearted literary-critical terms Horace's attempt to withhold his art from mythologizing Augustus.

Ode 3.4

In *Ode* 3.4, the exemplary narrative is the war between Olympian gods and the Giants, a myth that occupies a central place in Augustan poetic accounts of the civil war.[130] Yet Horace's telling of the story is more ambiguous than it should be.[131] The most perplexing aspect of the Horatian Gigantomachy is that it is ostensibly *not* about the glory of Augustus. Lowrie argues persuasively that the first part of Horace's narrative, which focuses on the Giants' defeat by the Olympians (42–64), is couched within a rhetoric that glorifies primarily the guiding influence of the Muses, not the achievement of Augustus (*vos lene consilium et datis et dato | gaudetis, almae,* 'you give gentle counsel, and you delight in having given it, kindly ones', 41–2).[132] Moreover,

---

[129] Harrison (2007a) 188. Coffta (2002) 120–3 suggests in addition that this highly Callimachean ending may be read as a reassertion of poetic tension.

[130] See esp. Verg. *Aen.* 8.685–706.

[131] Commenting on the difference between Pindaric and Horatian uses of mythological *exempla*, Hardie (2008) 87 writes: 'In Pindaric appeals to general knowledge . . . the point at issue is explicit, whereas in our passage it is far from clear what point is being exemplified.'

[132] Lowrie (1997) 221–2; see also Hejduk (2020) 128. Hardie (2008 and 2010) argues that the Horatian Gigantomachy is primarily a philosophically inspired epinician to Jupiter (2008: 110; 2010: 193–7), situated within a larger 'kletic hymn' to the Muses (2008: 80–6).

CONQUEST AND IMMORTALITY IN HORACE'S *ODES*   143

the poem does not draw a clear enough analogy between Augustus and Jupiter, and as a result the reader is left wondering how to interpret the story's moralizing maxim: is the statement—*vis consili expers mole ruit sua* ('power without good sense comes crashing down under its own weight', 65)—meant to highlight the proper use of power by Jupiter and Augustus and the role they (and the Muses) had in curtailing imprudent and destructive forces?[133] Or is it a warning (for Augustus?) against the danger of exercising unrestrained power?[134] The poem goes on to recount a number of mythological *exempla* to demonstrate that overreaching ambition can be punished by the gods (66–80). But Horace does not attribute this edifying catalogue to the Muses, who have disappeared from the poem by this point. In their absence, the poet and the *princeps* come into direct contact, at which point Horace's counsel about *vis* (65, above) steers dangerously close to the man who holds supreme power in the poet's day.[135]

That the Gigantomachy is mobilized ambivalently by Horace is not as unexpected as it may initially seem. Already in the first Roman Ode, the poet reminds readers that, although the Gigantomachy pays tribute to Jupiter and his representatives on earth, the story also warns rulers about their use of power: *regum timendorum in prioprios greges,* | *reges in ipsos imperium est Iovis,* | *clari Giganteo triumpho,* | *cuncta supercilio moventis* ('dreaded kings have power over their own flocks; kings themselves are under the power of Jove, who, in the glory of his triumph over the Giants, moves the whole universe with the flick of his brow', 3.1.5–8). Indeed, even the comparison between ruler and Jupiter can go both ways. Here the image of the fear-inspiring kings (*regum timendorum*, 5), set against Jupiter's haughty flick of the eyebrow (*supercilio*, 8), paints a stark picture of authoritarian power.[136] In *Ode* 1.12, Horace's depiction of Augustus as the earthly representative of Jupiter does not simply endorse the power of the *princeps*, but also hints at the monarchic turn of Augustan Rome. If it is not uncharacteristic for Horace to use the Gigantomachy in a double-edged manner, then the way in which *Ode* 3.4 situates this narrative somewhere between a eulogistic mythologization of

---

[133] Lefèvre (1993) 167–8; Miller (1998); West (2002) 40–53; Hardie (2010) 244–50, 277–98. Others have happily read the Gigantomachy of 3.4 as a generally flattering allegory of the events at Actium and Alexandria; see e.g. Wilkinson (1951) 69–52; Nisbet (1962) 194–202; Syndikus (1973) 70–1; Santirocco (1986) 120–1.

[134] Hornsby (1962) 101, 104; Commager (1962) 203.

[135] Lowrie (1997) 242 speaks of how the statement about *vis* 'baldly targets Caesar'. Oliensis (1998) 134 notes that for most of 3.4 the Muses form a kind of 'communicating wall', enabling Horace to address Caesar without confronting him.

[136] Hejduk (2020) 124–5 notes further that this image of intimidating rulers clashes with Augustus' self-presentation as the benevolent first citizen.

144 POLITICS AND DIVINIZATION IN AUGUSTAN POETRY

the civil war and a warning about the dangers of exercising unregulated *vis* may suggest that Horace is contesting the status of the Gigantomachy as a metaphor for Augustan power.

Finally, the fact that Horace's Gigantomachy may be read as a story about the dangers of losing restraint—or, put another way, the perils of transgression— also draws attention to its potential as a metapoetic statement on literary excess. Indeed, Horace is particularly concerned with poetic ambition in the first half of the poem, which presents readers with a mythologized autobiography of the poet as a favourite of the Muses (6–28).[137] This autobiography is prefaced by a moment where Horace questions his sanity (*an me ludit amabilis | insania?*, 'Or is a loveable delusion toying with me?', 5–6), and followed by an account of an imaginary journey to the frontiers of the Roman empire (29–36), where Horace envisages himself coming into contact with peoples and nations who usually appear in the context of Augustan conquest (*Bosphorum...litorisAssyrii...Britannos...Concanum...Gelonos...Scythicum*, 30–6).[138] This image of the poet—as one who is affected by a delightful frenzy (5–6), empowered by divine poetic forces to reach for new heights (*in arduos | tollor Sabinos*, 'I am borne aloft to the Sabine hills', 21–2), and daring to go to places where he usually would not (30–6)—brings to mind Horace's self-representation in the two 'Bacchic Odes' (2.19 and 3.25), where similar motifs are used to suggest the transgression of poetic boundaries. Taking these self-portraits together, the poet's mythical autobiography in 3.4 may be read as Horace stepping into the role of an imperial lyricist, while the imagined tour of foreign places intertwines the poet's literary ambition with Augustan conquest.[139] Set against this background, the epicized Gigantomachy which occupies the second half of 3.4 may, on the one hand, be seen as a demonstration of the poet's new literary persona.[140] On the other hand, its central message— namely, overweening ambition is punished and transgressive *vis* is destined to

[137] Davis (1991) 101–7 reads the poet's autobiography as an act of 'authentication', through which Horace displays his suitability as a chosen panegyrical poet, a role which he takes on later in this poem. On the image of the ποιητὴς θεοφιλής in Greek lyric and Horace's allusion to it, see Krasser (1995) 73–4; Hardie (2008) 85–6.

[138] Bosporus: 2.20.14. The 'Assyrian shore' refers to the area near the Euphrates: 2.9.21 (*Medumque flumen*, 'the Median river'). Britons: 1.21.15, 1.35.30, 3.5.3. Geloni: 2.9.23, 2.20.19; Lowrie (1997) 212 argues that the Geloni in the *Odes* are a 'symbol of empire'. The Concani are a Cantabrian tribe, and their appearance here has usually been understood as an allusion to Augustus' campaigns in northern Spain, see Syme (1987) 57 n. 48; N–R (2004) ad 3.4.34. Scythians: 1.35.9, 2.11.1, 3.8.23, 3.29.28, 4.5.25, 4.14.42, 4.15.24. On the coherence of Horace's mention of the Scythians and the Geloni, see Powell (2010) 141–50.

[139] The tour of 3.4 reworks the poet's immortal flight in *Ode* 2.20.14–20: see Lowrie (1997) 212; Sutherland (2002) 190; Harrison (2017) 241.

[140] Koster (1998) 160.

CONQUEST AND IMMORTALITY IN HORACE'S *ODES* 145

fail—simultaneously undoes the imperial poet's performance. Oliensis suggests that, by assimilating himself with the Giants whose pretentions are flattened by Jupiter's thunderbolt, Horace demonstrates to Augustus—the earthly Jupiter—that he recognizes and accepts his subordinate place within the new political order.[141] However, one might also say that the assimilation between the poet's marked generic extravagance and the uncontrolled *vis* of the Giants points to the idea that assuming the role of an imperial poet is to misuse or abuse the *vis* of poetry. Horace claims that the gods favour 'controlled power' (*vim temperatam di quoque provehunt* | *in maius*, 'the gods also advance controlled power', 66–7); and if Augustus really is a *deus* (or is to be seen as one), then he too would appreciate the poet's more restrained use of poetic power. By implicitly fashioning his composition of the Gigantomachy as an act of literary transgression that only an overambitious imperial eulogist would embark on, Horace peddles his credentials as a nationalistic *vates* while marking the limits of his lyric poetry.

Ode 3.5

A comparison between Jupiter and Augustus, which *Ode* 3.4 pointedly evades, is finally made explicit in the opening of *Ode* 3.5, where the familiar concept of expiating past sins through foreign conquest also returns (1–12):

> Caelo tonantem credidimus Iovem
> regnare: praesens divus habebitur
>   Augustus adiectis Britannis
>   imperio gravibusque Persis.
> milesne Crassi coniuge barbara   5
> turpis maritus vixit et hostium—
>   pro curia inversique mores!—
>   consenuit socerorum in armis,
> sub rege Medo Marsus et Apulus,
> anciliorum et nominis et togae   10
>   oblitus aeternaeque Vestae,
>   incolumi Iove et urbe Roma?

---

[141] Oliensis (1998) 136.

146 POLITICS AND DIVINIZATION IN AUGUSTAN POETRY

We have come to believe that Jupiter rules because he thunders in the sky; Augustus will be held a god in our midst when Britons and dread Persians are added to the empire. How is it that the soldier of Crassus has lived in disgrace as the husband of a barbarian wife, and that the Marsian and the Apulian have grown old—shame on the Senate and our changed ways!—among the weapons of our enemies, their fathers-in-law, serving the king of the Medes, and forgetting their own shields, names, togas, and eternal Vesta, while Jupiter lives and the city of Rome still stands?

This emotionally charged opening identifies Rome's revenge on Parthia as the prerequisite for Augustus' divinization.[142] The expression *praesens divus* (2), which is the Latin equivalent of the Greek θεὸς ἐπιφανής, evokes the Hellenizing depiction of the *princeps* in *Ode* 1.2 as god incarnate. There, Horace asks Augustus to stay on earth and help Romans to purge their past sins by redirecting violence toward the Parthians; here in 3.5, the poet makes clear that the unavenged defeat of Crassus is what stands between Augustus and immortality. Importantly, the image of ex-Roman soldiers married to barbarian wives (5), forgetful of Roman values as they lived out their lives in enemy camp (11–12), strongly evokes Antony's time in Egypt (cf. Verg. *Aen.* 8.688).[143] By presenting Crassus' disgraced soldiers as precursors to the nativized Antony, Horace establishes a distorting parallel between the putative Parthian campaign and Augustus' war against Antony and Cleopatra, through which the poet implicitly recasts the civil war as a campaign that prevented further Roman humiliation. Horace thus sets up Augustus as the guardian of Roman honour, whose divinization will mark the culmination of Rome's revival; and the poem is primed to explore how the Parthian situation will be addressed.

The rest of 3.5 takes up this issue through the famous story of Regulus. His exemplary contempt for surrender and courageous willingness to confront the Carthaginian enemy make him, as Lowrie puts it succinctly, 'not merely an illustrious counterpoint that shows up the present degradation, but a

---

[142] The future indicative *habebitur* (3.5.2) adds force to this assertion. The verb's passive voice is not a distancing device (contra Galinsky 1996: 318 and N–R 2004 ad loc.), but generates a matter-of-fact objectivity. It contrasts with the subjective, distant, and abstract *credidimus* (3.5.1), as Hejduk (2020) 129 rightly says. Luther (2003) 13–17 suggests that *habebitur* is a faux future because Augustus' divinization is '*de facto* bereits Wirklichkeit' (p. 13). But contemporary evidence does not bear out this out. The apotheosis of Augustus is by no means, as Luther thinks (p.17), 'eine bereits bestehende (oder vom princeps als bestehend propagierte) politische Situation'.

[143] Anticipated, but not articulated in these terms, by Binder and Heckel (2002) 83.

CONQUEST AND IMMORTALITY IN HORACE'S *ODES* 147

model for action *now*.[144] Indeed, the notion that this republican hero is to be seen as an exemplum of good leadership for the present Augustan age is evident from the very first word of Regulus' speech: *signa ego Punicis | adfixa delubris . . . vidi* ('Standards nailed onto Punic temples I have seen', 18–21)—an image that parallels the Parthian retention of Roman standards. However, despite the clear sense that the past is meant to illuminate the present,[145] there is substantial divergence between the poem's two central figures, Regulus and Augustus. Commenting on the poem's depiction of Regulus, Oliensis writes:

> In direct contrast to the quasi-deified Augustus invoked at the start of the ode, Horace's Regulus wins glory by performing and enforcing his own humiliation, keeping his "virile countenance" trained not on the heavens but on the earth (*virilem | torvus humi posuisse vultum*, C. 3.5.43–4). . . . Whereas Augustus is destined to be a "present god" (*praesens divus*, 2), Regulus preserves Rome by permanently absenting himself. And yet Augustus' brilliant presence is finally eclipsed by Regulus' sublime self-effacement.[146]

To add to Oliensis's observation, the contrast between these two figures is also marked by the different means of obtaining immortality ascribed to them: Augustus is to achieve divine status through self-aggrandizing conquest, whereas Regulus has gained perpetual fame by self-sacrifice. While Horace does not present these two methods of winning immortality as being in conflict, the poet certainly does not reconcile them either. Furthermore, Regulus' image in the poem as a defeated general who courageously embraces a certain death is more similar to Horace's Cleopatra (1.37) than Augustus.[147] It is this un-Augustan Regulus, who is immortalized in death rather than on the battlefield, that the poem presents as a model for the *princeps*.

The point I am making here is not that Horace is being deliberately subversive, but rather that the exemplary narrative of 3.5, like the image of Cleopatra in 1.37, disrupts the difference between triumph and defeat, glory and humiliation, immortality and ignominy—distinctions that underpin the construction of self and other, and the discourse of a new Augustan imperial order. It is by making the exemplarity of this heroic story less clear-cut, and less politically

---

[144] Lowrie (1997) 243; original emphasis. Sutherland (2002) 194–5 adds that Regulus' speech may be seen as a *mise en abyme*, urging the poem's audience respond to the poem as a whole in the way that the Senate did to Regulus' appearance before them.
[145] Morgan (2005b) 320 calls 3.5 an 'unusually time-conscious piece': Regulus is said to have a 'foresighted mind' (*mens provida*, 13) and fears for 'the time to come' (*veniens in aevum*, 16).
[146] Oliensis (1998) 141–2.   [147] Porter (1987) 166; Oliensis (1998) 141.

148 POLITICS AND DIVINIZATION IN AUGUSTAN POETRY

convenient for Augustus, that Horace asserts his poetic authority over the use of immortalizing narrative, denying it from becoming part of the Augustan language of power. In this way, *Ode* 3.5 encapsulates an evolving programme within the 'Roman Odes' where Horace's use of mytho-historical narratives gives the impression that they would exemplify and immortalize Augustus' achievements, but in the end deviate from this very rhetorical purpose. Furthermore, by framing these epicized exemplary narratives as either literary transgressions or moments of losing authorial control, Horace demarcates his lyric poetry from immortalizing eulogy. As we reach *Ode* 3.5, this apparent discordance, which has been building up in the course of the 'Roman Odes', points ever more clearly to a sustained poetic evasion of the mythologization of Augustus.

Coming to Terms with Divine Power

Whereas the 'Roman Odes' dramatize the poet's inhibition about reconciling his lyric authority with imperial praise by creating a series of fault-lines between mythologizing narrative and Augustan power, *Ode* 3.14, on the surface of it, appears to have overcome this reservation. Beginning with an emphatic assimilation of Augustus and Hercules (*Herculis ritu*, 1), the poem celebrates Augustus' recent Cantabrian campaign by presenting it as a defining moment for the empire and Roman citizens of every kind, as well as an occasion for the poet to reflect on how far Rome has come from the turbulent days of the civil war.

From the outset, Horatian lyric is put to public use as the poet imagines himself officiating the homecoming of Augustus as if a quasi-religious event, where the *princeps* is cast as a deified hero manifest (1–12):

> Herculis ritu modo dictus, o plebs,
> morte venalem petiisse laurum
> Caesar Hispana repetit penatis
> victor ab ora.
> unico gaudens mulier marito   5
> prodeat iustis operata divis,
> et soror cari ducis et decorae[148]

---

[148] Manuscript variant: *clari*.

CONQUEST AND IMMORTALITY IN HORACE'S *ODES* 149

> supplice vitta
> virginum matres iuvenumque nuper
> sospitum; vos, o pueri et puellae   10
> iam virum expertae, male ominatis
>   parcite verbis.

People of Rome! Caesar, who was just said to have sought a crown of bay at the cost of his life, comes home victorious like Hercules from the Spanish shore. Let the lady who rejoices in her incomparable husband come forth, performing due ritual to the righteous gods; and along with her, the sister of our dear leader and, adorned with suppliant garlands, the mothers of young women and men recently saved from death. You boys, and you girls, who have had no experience of a man, avoid any words of ill omen.

By comparing Augustus' Cantabrian War to Hercules' defeat of Geryon in Spain, Horace's use of mythological exemplum in the first stanza conveys that the *princeps*, like Hercules, is to be seen as a civilizer of the world and guardian of Rome, further legitimizing Augustus' place in the catalogue of deified heroes in *Ode* 3.3.[149] The highly religious language in the second and third stanzas (*decorae | supplice vitta*, 7–8; *o pueri et puellae . . . male ominatis | parcite verbis*, 10–12) then creates the impression that Augustus is to be worshipped like Hercules.[150] Virgil later tells that, after Hercules had overcome Geryon and herded his cattle to Italy, the hero arrived at Evander's settlement (the future site of Rome) and was immediately perceived as the long-anticipated deity who would save the Arcadians from the monster Cacus (*attulit et nobis aliquando optantibus aetas | auxilium adventumque dei*, 'and time finally gave us the help and the presence of a god we hoped for', Verg. *Aen.* 8.200–1). The Virgilian Hercules, like Horace's Herculean Augustus, is referred to as a *victor* (Verg. *Aen.* 8.204; Hor. *Carm.* 3.14.4); and Evander's description of the rituals performed in honour of Hercules' victory over Cacus includes details such as requesting youths to participate (8.273–4), ritual

---

[149] The phrase *morte venalem . . . laurum* (3.14.2) obliquely refers to Augustus' precarious health during the Cantabrian campaign (Cass. Dio 53. 25–8): his brush with death further recalls Hercules' experience on the pyre on Mount Oeta before being swept up to heaven (Apollod. *Bibl.* 2.7.7). Morgan (2005a) 191 argues that this shift from near-fatal mortality to Herculean invincibility in the poem's opening dramatizes the turbulent emotions that Romans had experienced while Augustus was in Spain.

[150] The association between Hercules and Augustus was firmly established in 29 BC when the latter arranged his triple triumph to begin immediately after the festival of Hercules at the Ara Maxima on 12 August. The opening of 3.14 thus also implies that the present occasion is on par with the momentous celebration of 29 BC.

150   POLITICS AND DIVINIZATION IN AUGUSTAN POETRY

wreathing (8.273–4, 285–6), and making communal offerings to the gods (8.278–9)—all of which find parallels here in Horace's poem (3.14.6, 8, 10–12).[151] By transforming Augustus' *reditus* into a sacred occasion for the city, and assimilating it with the worship of Hercules, Horace implies that Augustan conquest is as central to the welfare of Rome as the proper observance of religious practice.[152] The poem's sacralization of the homecoming of Augustus thus inscribes imperialism into the religious fabric of Rome, making foreign conquest an indispensable part of civic life, and Augustan *imperium* an essential aspect of social cohesion.[153] Above all, by directly addressing the Roman people (*o plebs*, 1; *vos, o pueri et puellae*, 10) in a manner not seen since the first Roman Ode (*Odi profanum vulgus et arceo;* | *favete linguis:* . . . *Musarum sacerdos* | *virginibus puerisque canto*, 'I hate the uninitiated crowd and keep them away. Grant me your silence . . . I sing to girls and boys as priest of the Muses', 3.1.1–4),[154] Horace endows himself with the authority of a ceremonial officiant and puts his lyric in service of sanctifying Augustan power.

The shift to the setting of a private symposium in the second half of 3.14 not only mirrors the public festive atmosphere in the poem's first half but also highlights the extent to which Augustan conquest has infected an individual's response and perspective. In particular, the poet's request for wines that survived the Social War and the slave revolt of Spartacus (18–19) underlines how one's sense of history is now shaped by Rome's transformation from civil strife to imperial peace under Augustus. Indeed, Horace's claim that Augustus' rule has banished his 'dark worries' (*atras* . . . *curas*, 13–14) and 'fear' of violent conflict (*nec tumultum* | *nec mori per vim metuam*, 14–15) looks directly back to the final sympotic scene of *Epode* 9 and clears up the 'worry and fear' which Caesar occasioned immediately after Actium (*curam metumque Caesaris rerum iuvat* | *dulci Lyaeo solvere, Epod.* 9.37–8).[155] By retrospectively eliminating the ambivalence of *Epode* 9, the poet implies that Rome has been on a path to stability and renewal ever since Actium, and that the present occasion proves it.

---

[151] Klingner's Teubner edition of the *Odes* prints *sacris* for *divis* (3.14.6), and *nominatis* for *ominatis* (3.14.11); these variants have no significant material impact on the interpretation of lines 6–12. On Horace's apparent awareness of Virgil's ambition to compose epic poetry, see Kidd (1977); Harrison (2007b) 8–9; Rumpf (2009).

[152] N–R (2004) 180–1 argue that Horace's description of the public event is a combination of *adventus* and *supplicatio*. The latter was a national day either of prayer for the future or of thanksgiving for the past, see Wissowa (1912) 423–7. Women played an important part in the rituals of the *supplicatio* (Livy 27.51.9); and the custom of celebrating the *supplicatio* wreathed in garlands (3.14.7–8) was reported in Livy 34.55.4.

[153] Morgan (2005a) has also argued that *Ode* 3.14 promotes the Augustan message of unity and social cohesion by alluding to the worship of Hercules in Italy as the god of community.

[154] See also Lowrie (1997) 57.   [155] See further discussion in Chapter 2.

However, just as when Horace appears to be indulging in a moment of heady triumphalism, the poet draws attention to the indelibility of the past by saying a little more than he should. Anticipating that an uncompromising doorman might cause a delay to his party, Horace complains: *non ego hoc ferrem calidus iuventa | consule Planco* ('I would not have put up with this sort of thing in my hot-blooded youth when Plancus was consul', 27–28). As often noted, *consule Planco* (28), the final phrase of the poem, dates Horace's pugnacious youth to the year of the battle of Philippi, when he fought on Brutus' side against Octavian: by concluding the ode with the recollection of this event, Horace's eulogy of Augustus is confounded at the last moment. We see that in *Ode* 2.7, where a similar sympotic occasion is staged, Horace tries to forget the past with the aid of wine (*oblivioso . . . Massico*, 2.7.21); but here in 3.14, as Oliensis points out, wine seems to have the opposite effect (*Marsi memorem duelli*, '[wine that] remembers the Marsic War', 3.14.18).[156] The power of Bacchus in *Odes* 2.19 and 3.25 enables Horace to overcome his reservations and transgress literary and political boundaries, allowing him to immortalize Augustus; but in *Ode* 3.14, the wine may have loosened Horace's tongue a bit too much. Surrounded by the *otium* afforded by Caesar's conquests, Horace's nostalgic reminiscence of his previous resistance to the current regime paints his acquiescence to Augustan power as an act of willing self-disempowerment that a citizen has to perform in exchange for *pax Romana*—an ideological compromise that jars with all kinds authoritarian connotations. What began as a fulsome eulogy of the Herculean conquest of the *princeps*, thus ends with the suggestion that the peace guaranteed by the Augustan *imperium* comes at a price. As a result, the portrait of Augustus as a divine *triumphator* becomes associated with not only the conquest of foreign enemy but also the subjugation of the citizenry's non-conformity, the disappearance of political difference, and the erasure of resistance.

Conclusions

In a recent essay, Hollard notes that the *Odes* encapsulate the Augustan political myth of *res publica restituta* by reconciling two things that are irreconcilable: the return of traditional Roman religion and the divinization of Augustus.[157] In making this observation, Hollard shows that the motif of Augustus' divinity constitutes an important element of Horace's critique of the political

---

[156] Oliensis (1998) 148.   [157] Hollard (2016) 59.

152   POLITICS AND DIVINIZATION IN AUGUSTAN POETRY

discourse of the Principate. Much of this chapter has been devoted to exploring this possibility, illustrating that the *Odes* frequently and in varied ways interrogated the construction of Augustan power through discussions of Augustus' divinization.

The chapter began by suggesting that visual and symbolic representations of Augustus' divinity played a significant role in creating a narrative of Rome's transformation from civil strife to imperial order under Augustus. The point of this analysis was to highlight that the motif of Augustus' divinization is a site where Horace's authority as a poet comes into contact with Augustus' attempt to control political discourse. The two main arguments conceived in this chapter were both concerned with this issue.

Firstly, I argued that, while a number of *Odes* cheerfully synchronize Augustus' divinization with Rome's exteriorization of civil war as foreign conquest, Horace also disrupts this narrative of a new Augustan imperial order by probing the effect of Augustan conquest on the Roman constitution, and blurs key distinctions that underpin the Augustan construction of self and other. In doing so the poet interrogates, and subtly distances himself from, the discourse of Augustan power. Following on from this, my second argument was that this tension between Horatian lyric and Augustan discourse is embodied and played out on a more extensive scale in the 'Bacchic Odes' and the 'Roman Odes'. In these poems, Horace implies that in order for Augustus to be immortalized in his poetry, he would not only have to overcome certain poetic limitations but also relinquish his ideological independence, which the poet performs in *Ode* 3.14, though not without wistful melancholy. By presenting this twofold argument, I hope to have shown that in the course of the *Odes*, the motif of Augustus' divinity goes from being a symbol of Roman *imperium* to an expression of acquiescence to Augustan power; and that this semantic shift underlines a sustained attempt by Horace to negotiate artistic and political autonomy while Augustus sought to control the political narrative of the first decade of his rule.

In closing this study of the *Odes* with a reading of 3.14, I also wanted to bring out the idea that this process of negotiation ends with Horace acknowledging that ultimately Rome needs Augustus. This reading should have some implications for the interpretation of the final poem of the collection. As discussed above, *Ode* 3.30 sees Horace making a claim to poetic immortality (*non omnis moriar*, 6) in a manner that clearly responds to his avowal of such an ambition in the very first ode.[158] This ode has usually been interpreted as

---

[158] On the poet's 'progression' from *Ode* 1.1 to 3.30, see esp. D'Elia (1995) 160–2; Lowrie (1997) 212; Coffta (2002) 98–104; Harrison (2007c) 28–30; Roman (2014) 216–18.

CONQUEST AND IMMORTALITY IN HORACE'S *ODES*   153

an assertion of poetry's power to transcend physical limitations and a self-aggrandizing statement of Horace's achievement vis-à-vis those of Augustus (*dicar...princeps*, 10–13).[159] The poem's famous opening (*Exegi monumentum aere perennius*, 'I have completed a monument more lasting than bronze', 1) even creates the impression that Horace will surpass Augustus in matters concerning immortality, as scholars detect an allusion to Augustus' Mausoleum in the word *monumentum*.[160] The enormous Greek-style tomb provides the most striking example of Augustus' attempt to determine his posthumous fate during his lifetime.[161] By suggesting that his lyric monument will outlast physical structures such as Augustus' Mausoleum, the poet intimates that he will outdo the *princeps* in obtaining true immortality.

At the same time, however, Horace's final competitive act is paradoxically self-undermining and draws attention to his ineluctable reliance on Augustan power. Having claimed that his poetry will outdo monuments and transcend physical limitations, Horace then predicates his poetic immortality on the survival of the Roman state cult—specifically on the performance of its rituals in an architecturally defined setting: *usque ego postera | crescam laude recens, dum Capitolium | scandet cum tacita virgine pontifex* ('I shall continue to grow, fresh with the praise of posterity, as long as the priest climbs the Capitol with the silent virgin', 7–9).[162] Even when Horace confidently appoints himself as the *princeps* of Latin lyric (13), this bold gesture underlines that the scope of individual ambition and the expression of individual achievement are determined by the language of Augustan power. We may also recall that when Horace announces his ambition to obtain poetic immortality in *Ode* 1.1, it is already implied there that the poet's celestial fame ultimately depends on the judgment of his patron Maecenas: *quodsi me lyricis vatibus inseres, | sublimi feriam sidera vertice* ('But if *you* place me amongst the lyric bards of Greece, I shall soar aloft and strike the stars with my head', 1.1.35–6). The concluding image of *Ode* 3.25 offers another reminder of the dynamic between Horace's bid for immortality and Augustus' all-determining divine power. Philip Hardie has suggested that the poet's coronation by Bacchus at the end of the poem (*sequi deum | cingentem viridi tempora pampino*, 'to follow the god who

---

[159] See e.g. Lowrie (2009) 118–19; Miller (2009) 312.

[160] Anticipated by Woodman (1974); explicated by Gibson (1997); Simpson (2002) 63; Ingleheart (2015) 298–9.

[161] It is worth remembering that Augustus' *Res Gestae* was inscribed on tablets that stood outside the Mausoleum after the emperor's death in AD 14.

[162] Roman (2014) 218 reads 3.30.7–9 differently: he argues that the Capitoline state cult symbolizes an eternal Rome (and Horatian poetic monument) that will survive independent of any given ruler. Schwindt (2005) 17–18 thinks that Horace here attempts to reconcile the transience of time with the permanence of time.

154 POLITICS AND DIVINIZATION IN AUGUSTAN POETRY

wreathes my temples with green vine-leaves', 3.25.19–20) symbolizes the moment Horace identifies himself with Augustus through the figure of Bacchus, as the trinity of poet, *princeps*, and god are conjoined in a moment of immortalization, capping a poetics of ascent which began with the poet's mental and emotional escalation as he sought Bacchic inspiration to divinize Augustus (3.25.3–5, above).[163] That is one way of reading the poet's self-representation as an empowered Bacchant. Another way is to see it as part of a broader pattern beginning with *Ode* 1.1, whereby Horace's assertions of poetic immortality are always implicitly circumscribed by Augustan power. In *Ode* 3.25, the poet can only 'follow' the god (*sequi*, 3.25.19), who dictates the course of the poet's coronation. Likewise, while *Ode* 3.30 sets out as an assertion of poetic immortality and individual accomplishment, it morphs into an implicit admission of how poetry is guaranteed and circumscribed by the longevity of Augustan *imperium*. Indeed, by describing himself as a poetic *princeps* who has conquered his way to literary prominence (3.30.13–14, above), it may be said that in the end Horace can only seek to ensure his own survival by subscribing to the very discourse which legitimizes Augustus' power. By closing his first lyric collection in this way, Horace underscores the extent to which one's perception of individual power is becoming contiguous with one's relationship to Augustan power.

---

[163] P. R. Hardie, 'Heavenly Emotions' (a seminar delivered in 2018 at the Institute of Classical Studies, London).

4

Divinization and the Inevitability of Augustan Rome

In 17 BC, six years after the death of Gaius Claudius Marcellus, Augustus formally adopted the young sons of his daughter Julia and her husband Agrippa, Gaius and Lucius (Cass. Dio 54.18). The identification of a new generation of Caesars in a direct line of descent underlined the idea of genealogical pre-eminence, which can be seen in Augustus' self-presentation around this time. Scholars have noted the return of the image of Julius Caesar and the *sidus Iulium* on the obverse of coins minted from *c.*20 BC onwards,[1] with the denarius issued by L. Lentulus in 12 BC being the most striking example of this new design, where Augustus is shown fixing a star on the head of a semi-nude (cult) statue of his deified father.[2] The revival of this numismatic motif, coupled with the adoption of Gaius and Lucius, not only reinforced Augustus' own claim to divine ancestry and the sense that he is susceptible to an apotheosis similar to that of Julius Caesar,[3] but also conveyed the continuation of Julian greatness from one Caesar to the next, forging a visual language of the divine destiny of the *gens Iulia*.[4]

Coinage is one of several places where we can identify a broader attempt by Augustus to present himself and the burgeoning Julian dynasty as already possessed of unsurpassed greatness. The retrospective, even teleological, view that the supremacy of the *princeps* was divinely preordained, could also be observed in the arrangement of statues in the Forum Augustum, which sought to position Augustus as the culmination of Roman history. Under construction from possibly as early as the late 20s and mostly finished by 2 BC, this highly ideological space featured a temple to Mars Ultor, which housed

---

[1] *BMCRE* I (Spain), 323–8, 357.
[2] *RIC* I² 415. On the probable correspondence between this numismatic image and Caesar's cult statue in the Temple of Divus Julius, see Koortbojian (2013) 45. Pandey (2018) 67–8 also notes the visual parallel between the Lentulus coin and the denarius of P. Sepullius Macer (44 BC); the latter depicts Julius with the star on the obverse.
[3] Pandey (2018) 65.   [4] Weinstock (1971) 377–8; Williams (2003) 7.

Politics and Divinization in Augustan Poetry. Bobby Xinyue, Oxford University Press. © Bobby Xinyue 2022.
DOI: 10.1093/oso/9780192855978.003.0005

156 POLITICS AND DIVINIZATION IN AUGUSTAN POETRY

cult statues of Mars, Venus, and Deified Julius Caesar. The temple itself was flanked by a pair of hemicycle galleries that displayed statues of Aeneas and Romulus surrounded by Alban kings, Julian ancestors, and *summi viri* (Suet. *Aug.* 31.5).[5] However, the focal point of the entire structure was none other than Augustus himself. At the centre of the Forum, facing the Temple of Mars Ultor, there stood a quadrigate statue inscribed with the title which Augustus received in 2 BC, *pater patriae*, an honour which the emperor himself later described as the high point of his career (Aug. *R.G.* 35). Trevor Luke has argued that the deification of Augustus was strongly hinted at by the 'visual theology' of the quadriga, which strategically situated Augustus in a hierarchically arranged gathering of founders, heroes, and gods, wherein the *princeps* was assimilated to the latter.[6] Luke suggests that the path from the entrance of the Forum Augustum to the Temple of Mars Ultor may be viewed as a linear journey through Roman history and in hierarchical status to ever-loftier honorands, ending with the deities Mars, Venus, and Deified Julius Caesar: thus positioned on this path towards the temple, the quadriga of Augustus—depicted as if it had completed the final stage of its journey—effectively implied that the *princeps* was destined to become like the gods in the temple which his chariot faced.[7]

This interpretation of the Forum Augustum opens up the possibility of seeing the Forum's statuary arrangement as a monumental visual parallel to the iconography of the divinity of the *gens Iulia* on contemporary coinage, as both art forms position the apotheosis of Augustus as the climactic endpoint of a grand historical process. By thus making divinization a seemingly inevitable dénouement, Augustus becomes the highly anticipated *deus ex machina* of a historical drama; and as a corollary, history itself, when viewed from this perspective, constitutes a 'path' towards the glory of the *gens Iulia* personified by Augustus' apotheosis. The visual language of divinization, expressed in both the statues of the Forum Augustum and on the official coinage from the second decade of Augustus' rule, sets up a dialectical relationship, whereby the present reshapes the past and the past exists in service of the present—a dynamic that turns historical contingency into inevitability.

---

[5] For detailed analysis of the Forum Augustum, see Zanker (1970); Geiger (2008).

[6] Luke (2014) 176 for the quotation, 266–72 for extended discussion. 'Theology' is defined by Luke (2014) 2 as creatively crafted religious performances and narratives used by Roman elites to establish and maintain their own social and political pre-eminence, and to address the crises or concerns of their times.

[7] Luke (2014) 271–2. Furthermore, it appears that the chariot was left empty, which may have evoked the disappearance and subsequent apotheosis of Romulus, as well as the Hellenistic tradition of establishing cults for 'descending' ruler–deities; see Luke (2014) 266–7.

DIVINIZATION AND THE INEVITABILITY OF AUGUSTAN ROME   157

This chapter examines how the formulation of Augustus' divinization as the culmination of Rome's political myth finds expression in poetry and is critiqued by it. My main focus is Virgil's *Aeneid*. It has long been recognized that while Virgil's epic engages with the symbolic language of Augustan power throughout, the poem can hardly be said to unequivocally endorse Augustus' supremacy. Critics who see the 'Parade of Heroes' in *Aeneid* 6 as a prefiguration of the statuary arrangement in the Forum Augustum argue that Virgil's narrative differs from, and implicitly competes with, Augustus' plan to reorder history; and that in doing so Virgil asserts authorial agency before material art refigures poetic image into unalterable monumental form.[8] Miller's analysis of the figure of Apollo in the *Aeneid* shows that the poem's Apolline prophecies and interventions are depicted in such a way so as to highlight the extent to which official ideology shapes poetic discourse.[9] The symbolism of the *sidus Iulium* too has undergone discerning re-assessment, as Pandey's recent study argues that the recurrent sidereal imagery in the *Aeneid* (and elsewhere) depicts the tension between dynastic and meritocratic justifications of Julian supremacy, rather than straightforwardly privileging the idea that Augustus' greatness is divinely preordained.[10]

While there will be some overlap between the subject of this chapter and the scholarship considered above, the present investigation offers new perspectives by focusing on how the *Aeneid*'s prophecies of Augustus' divinization constitute an important locus for accessing the poem's critique of its artistic involvement in the Augustan reinvention of history.[11] While the *Aeneid*'s major prophecies appear to look ahead to the inevitability of Augustan glory, it is well noted that Virgil also highlights the multivalency and contingency of the historical trajectory of the *gens Iulia*. In his seminal

---

[8] Feldherr (1999); Pandey (2018) 142–70.

[9] Miller (2009) 95–184, esp. p. 97. Likewise, Feeney (1991) 157 argues that the *Aeneid*'s representations of the divine 'have many powerful points of contact with the cults being fostered or established by Augustus.' See also Paschalis (1986); Casali (2009).

[10] Pandey (2018) 58–64. By contrast, Williams (2003) argues that Virgil uses the iconography of Caesar's comet and the star of Venus to glorify the Julian line, particularly Augustus, and to underline the expectation of Augustus' apotheosis. This mode of optimistic reading is anticipated by Wagenvoort (1956) 1–29; Bömer (1951); West (1993). Closely connected to the interpretation of the poem's sidereal imagery is the question of how (well) the *Aeneid* addresses the issue of succession, on which see Rogerson (2017).

[11] Readers of the *Aeneid* encounter Augustus' divinity mainly through the poem's prophetic visions about the future Rome. Indirect articulations of Augustus' divinization can also be observed in the poem's strategic referencing of the Ptolemaic ruler cult, see Hardie (2006b); or through Virgil's use of mythological typology, which brings into focus the interrelated roles of Hercules, Aeneas, and Augustus, see Gransden (1976) passim, esp. pp.14–20. An aspect of this chapter is to examine how these themes and techniques impinge on one another and operate in conjunction with the poem's more explicit prophecies about Augustus.

158   POLITICS AND DIVINIZATION IN AUGUSTAN POETRY

work on prophecies in the *Aeneid*, O'Hara has shown compellingly that there is a tendency within the poem's prophetic scenes to emphasize long-term optimistic future, but partially suppress or only hint at short-term tragedies and calamities.[12] Building on this observation, but without committing to the bipolarity of optimistic and pessimistic readings, I suggest firstly that the tension between inevitability and contingency in the poem's prophetic scenes may be interpreted as Virgil's way of showing to readers that there are two ways of viewing Augustus' rise to power—two ways of thinking about the past and the future of Rome: either as predestined, or as a process that is rarely straightforward, often unknowable, and even ambiguous.

Secondly, I wish to suggest that in these prophetic episodes where the Augustan age is envisaged as the culmination of Roman history, Virgil subtly emphasizes that the perception of history as 'fate' relies heavily on representation and readerly cooperation. A well-known instance of this kind of poetic self-reflection can be found at the end of Book 8, where Aeneas marvels at the images forged on the shield Vulcan made for him: *rerumque ignarus imagine gaudet | attollens umero famamque et fata nepotum* ('ignorant of the subject matter he delights in the image, lifting onto his shoulder the fame and the fate of his descendants', 8.730–1). As Feldherr notes, the pointed juxtaposition of *fama* and *fata*—both derived from the verb for speaking, *fari*—draws attention to the issue of how words become real.[13] And Pandey adds that Aeneas' uninformed elation (*ignarus...gaudet*) at the shield's sublime imagery (*imagine*) underlines how a carefully crafted representation can generate ideological fervour, enabling the acceptance of fiction as reality, and the transformation of *fama* into *fata*.[14] Indeed, Aeneas' reaction to the images on the shield may be seen as a paradigm for how readers of the *Aeneid* might respond to the epic itself;[15] and this metatextual phenomenon, as many have observed, is anticipated in the poem's very first ekphrasis (1.450–93).[16] There, Aeneas offers a selective, sympathetic, and even optimistic interpretation of the Trojan War frieze on the Temple of Juno at Carthage—in spite of the artwork's depiction of Trojan suffering and its function as an adornment on an

---

[12] O'Hara (1990), esp. pp. 128–75, correlates the experience of the poem's characters—buoyed and deceived at the same time by prophecies—with that of the Roman readers, for whom optimistic future under Augustus is set in tension with loss and darkness encountered recently in the civil war.

[13] Feldherr (2014) 282; see also Hardie (2012) 9.   [14] Pandey (2018) 201.

[15] Lyne (1987) 209. The multiplicity of audiences in the *Aeneid*'s descriptive or visual narratives is well noted by Boyd (1995) 74–6.

[16] Horsfall (1973) 7–8; Segal (1981) 75–6; Leach (1988) 72, 314–18; Fowler (1991); Barchiesi (1997a) 273–8; Bartsch (1998) 337; Perkell (1999) 45–6; Pandey (2018) 16–18.

DIVINIZATION AND THE INEVITABILITY OF AUGUSTAN ROME   159

anti-Trojan monument. Perkell notes well that this episode demonstrates that
'Vergil has placed in paradigmatic position the possibility (or even the fact) of
misreading art that, in subject matter, is very much like the poem we are
reading'.[17] But more than that, it also draws attention to the blurred lines
between representation and retrospection, and the implication of both artist
and viewer/reader in any (unreliable) reconstruction of the past. Expanding
on this kind of reading of the *Aeneid*'s ekphrastic and *mise en abyme* passages,
this chapter seeks to illumine the poem's reflections on its own involvement,
as well as the reader's complicity, in the mythologization of Augustan supremacy as predestined fate. It will be seen that Virgil underlines the presence of
his art and the role of the viewer especially in passages which proclaim the
divine destiny of Augustus. In doing so, the poet gestures at how the *Aeneid*
and its readers all play a part in rendering Augustan supremacy 'inevitable'. By
thus emphasizing reinvention's dependence on representation and readerly
cooperation, Virgil's epic encapsulates the tensions and complicities between
art and power, ruler and subject.

The final section of this chapter ('Coda') traces the immediate impact of the
Aeneid's depiction of Augustus' divinization through a reading of Horace's
Carmen Saeculare and Propertius 4.6. These two poems, I suggest, respond to
the Augustan teleological view of Roman history by reformulating in their
own ways the *Aeneid*'s prophecies about Augustus. That Horace and
Propertius vocalize the apparent inevitability of Augustan supremacy *through*
Virgil's epic highlights the extent to which the *Aeneid* is co-opted by the
regime as its definitive ideological narrative. The poetic response of the
Carmen Saeculare and Propertius 4.6 thus long anticipate Ovid's pointed
praise of Virgil as 'that fortunate author of your *Aeneid*' (*ille tuae felix Aeneidos
auctor*, Ov. *Trist.* 2.533), where the exiled poet's striking usage of the posses-
sive *tuae* hints at the epic's appropriation by Augustan discourse.[18]

---

[17] Perkell (1999) 46. On ekphrasis as a site of confrontation between different ways of representing
and imagining reality, see Barchiesi (1997a) 275–8. Several other passages of the poem (and even
entire books of the *Aeneid*) have been understood to encapsulate the poet's artistic endeavour, or mirror the epic's overall content, or miniaturize aspects of the *Aeneid*'s major themes. See e.g. Hardie
(1986) 53–66 and Nelis (2001) 99–112 on the song of Iopas in Book 1; Hershkowtiz (1991) and Quint
(1993) 53–65 on Book 3; Galinsky (1966) and Morgan (1998) on the Hercules and Cacus episode in
Book 8; Fowler (2000a) on the Nisus and Euryalus episode in Book 9.
[18] See further Barchiesi (1997b) 27; Ingleheart (2010) ad loc.

160 POLITICS AND DIVINIZATION IN AUGUSTAN POETRY

Certainty and Ambiguity in Jupiter's Prophecy

Jupiter's prophecy in Book 1 provides a programmatic indication of the way in which Augustus' divinization will be presented in the rest of the *Aeneid*. Claiming to be the voice of *fata* (1.262), the god foretells to Venus the everlasting rule of Aeneas' descendants (1.267–85) and lends his personal authority to it (*his ego nec metas rerum nec tempora pono:* | *imperium sine fine dedi*, 'for them I impose no limits of space or time: I have given empire without end', 1.278–9).[19] This vision of the imminent glory of the *gens Iulia* is bookended by a pair of predictions of apotheosis. At the start of his speech, Jupiter sets things in motion by anticipating Aeneas' ascension to heaven (*sublimemque feres ad sidera caeli* | *magnanimum Aenean*, 'you will raise the great-souled Aeneas on high to the stars of heaven' 1.259–60); at the other end, the god envisages the divinization of a certain Caesar (1.286–96):

> nascetur pulchra Troianus origine Caesar,
> imperium Oceano, famam qui terminet astris,
> Iulius, a magno demissum nomen Iulo.
> hunc tu olim caelo spoliis Orientis onustum
> accipies secura; vocabitur hic quoque votis.   290
> aspera tum positis mitescent saecula bellis:
> cana Fides et Vesta, Remo cum fratre Quirinus
> iura dabunt; dirae ferro et compagibus artis
> claudentur Belli portae; Furor impius intus
> saeva sedens super arma et centum vinctus aënis   295
> post tergum nodis fremet horridus ore cruento.

From this splendid lineage will be born a Trojan Caesar, who will bound his power with Ocean, his fame with the stars; he will be a Julius, a name derived from the mighty Iulus. One day, anxious no more, you will welcome him to heaven laden with spoils of the East; he too shall be invoked in prayers. Then, wars will cease and the ages of harshness will soften: white-haired Faith and Vesta, Quirinus along with his brother Remus, will make laws. The Gates of War, grim with iron and closely fitted bars, will be closed; inside, impious Madness, sitting on savage weapons and hands bound back by a hundred bronze knots, with face covered with blood, will roar ferociously.

---

[19] On universalizing expressions in the *Aeneid*, see Hardie (1986) 293–335. On the effect of Jupiter's powerful rhetoric, see Syed (2005) 44 and Hejduk (2020) 67–8. But O'Hara (1990) 132–6 finds Jupiter's words overly optimistic.

As is often the case with prophecies, Jupiter here makes the deification of Caesar seem inevitable and yet full of alarming uncertainties. For a start, it is impossible to say for sure who this 'Trojan Caesar' is (1.286), as scholars are unable to agree on whether this figure is Augustus, or Julius Caesar, or design-edly ambiguous.[20] To avoid revisiting an issue already well served by modern critical insight, I simply put forward my view that Virgil's text does not insist on identifying this character as *either* Augustus *or* Julius; but if one chooses to interpret *tum* (1.291) strictly as a marker of chronological transition,[21] then the 'Trojan Caesar' can only be Julius.

On top of this issue, the prophecy is unclear about what *kind* of diviniza-tion is being envisaged for Caesar. A lot hinges on the phrase *spoliis Orientis onustum* ('laden with spoils of the East', 1.289). This phrase could refer to Julius Caesar's eastern conquests of 48–47 BC;[22] or, if one takes the *Troianus Caesar* to be Augustus, it could refer to his victory over Antony and Cleopatra,[23] or his more recent diplomatic success over the Parthians which brought back the lost Roman standards.[24] Whatever the precise point of reference, this tri-umphal image implies that the divinization envisaged here is one based on merit and achievement, rather than ancestral lineage.[25] However, Jupiter's prophecy also appears to suggest a dynastic model for Caesar's divinization. The parallel between *feres ad sidera...Aenean* ('you will raise Aeneas to the stars', 1.259–60) and *hunc tu olim caelo... | accipies* ('one day you will welcome him to heaven', 1.289–90) implies that Caesar will be divinized primarily for being a descendant of Venus, for his genealogical privilege. The conflation of these two modes of divinization—meritocratic and dynastic—hints at the convergence of Roman power with Julian power, echoing the way that Roman *imperium* (1.279) is mapped onto Caesar's *imperium* (1.287) in the course of the prophecy. Indeed, the sense of geopolitical transgression embedded in the phrase *imperium sine fine* (1.279) lends its force to Caesar's divinization, which may be seen as a transgression of ontological boundaries—an extension of Julian supremacy *sine fine*. Whoever this Caesar may be, his future sits

---

[20] For Augustus: R. D. Williams (1972) on 1.286; Kinsey (1981); Binder (1988) 269; Kraggerud (1992) and (1994); Harrison (1996). For Julius Caesar: West (1993) 16; Dobbin (1995); Pandey (2018) 156 n. 46. Either or both could be meant: Austin (1971) on 1.286; O'Hara (1994); Galinsky (1996) 251–2; M. F. Williams (2003) 15–16.

[21] As argued by Dobbin (1995).

[22] They include the victories at Alexandria (48 BC) and against Pharnaces (47 BC), and the tri-umph held for both victories in 46 BC (Livy *Epit.* 115; Suet. *Iul.* 37). See further Dobbin (1995) 13–20.

[23] Williams (1972) ad loc. The *spolia* could also refer to the dedication of war spoils at Actium and Rome; see Page (1894) ad loc.; Taylor (1931) 175.

[24] Austin (1971) ad loc.

[25] Similar to what Horace suggests in the catalogue of deified heroes in *Ode* 3.3.9–16.

162   POLITICS AND DIVINIZATION IN AUGUSTAN POETRY

ambiguously between an achievement-based divinization, which is conceived as the reward for expanding Roman rule, and a lineage-based divinization, which is associated with monarchical dynasties and ultimately un-Roman. In this way, Jupiter's prophecy complicates the vision of Caesar's rise to power, creating a tension between the historical process towards Rome and the predestined supremacy of the Julians.[26]

Inevitability and Contingency: The Journey towards Rome

The books that narrate Aeneas' journey from Troy to Cumae, during which the hero receives multiple prophecies foretelling the future glory and divinization of his descendants, amplify the apparent inevitability of Augustan supremacy. However, through repeated reminders of the ambiguity, unreliability, and lacunosity of oracular signs, these books of the *Aeneid* also sensitize readers to the unknowability of the future and, more importantly, the ideological inclination that is required to view the unknowable or the yet-to-happen as predestined.

An indication of this dynamic can be observed in the events surrounding the omens at the end of Book 2. When a flame suddenly appears above Ascanius' head during the fall of Troy, Aeneas is struck with fear (*nos pavidi trepidare metu*, 'terrified, we hurried about with fear', 2.685), while his father delightedly asks Jupiter for further signs of confirmation (2.687–91), which soon arrive in the form of a thunderbolt followed by a shooting star (2.692–8). Seeing this, Anchises immediately prays to the star (*sanctum sidus adorat*, 2.700) and confidently interprets it as a sign that augurs a bright future for his descendants and the Trojan race (*di patrii; servate domum, servate nepotem. | vestrum hoc augurium, vestroque in numine Troia est*, 'gods of my homeland, look after this house, look after my grandson. This is your omen, and Troy is under your divine watch', 2.702–3). Virgil's *sanctum sidus* is often thought to be an allusion to the comet that appeared at the funeral games of Julius Caesar, which subsequently became a visual sign of the divinity of the *gens Iulia*.[27] However, it is worth emphasizing—as Rogerson and Pandey have done

---

[26] Indeed, the prophecy ends on an equivocal note as its description of the new peaceful age (1.291–6) makes no reference to utopian pleasure and fecundity, but instead offers a curious portrait of *Furor* barely contained. See further Bartsch (1998) 332; Hejduk (2009) 283–91 and (2020) 63–4.

[27] See e.g. Williams (2003) 4–7.

DIVINIZATION AND THE INEVITABILITY OF AUGUSTAN ROME 163

recently—that this scene pointedly juxtaposes two contrasting reactions to omens.[28] Whereas Anchises immediately embraces the supernatural signs as divine indications of a hopeful future and eagerly surrenders himself to whatever course the future may take (*sequor et qua ducitis adsum*, 'I follow, and, wherever you lead, I am there', 2.701), Aeneas' initial panic highlights not only the ambiguity of signs but also the difficulty of knowing what will happen next for the Trojans. Anchises' inclination to see the *sidus* as a prefiguration of the future glory of Trojan descendants underlines the willing cooperation required from a viewer in the transformation of an image into a symbol of power. Compared to Aeneas' response, which is notable for its complete lack of a grand vision (as he is only concerned with the events that just happened), Anchises' response mirrors that of the 'optimistic' Roman reader. By focusing on Anchises' reaction to the star, Virgil underlines that the interpreter has a role to play in the creation of meaning, and that a reader can be complicit in the construction of Augustan power.

The tension between the unknowability of the future and the apparent inevitability of forthcoming greatness, which underpins the scene of omens in Book 2, is sustained in the poem's account of Aeneas' journey from Troy to Cumae. In the course of Book 3, as well as later in Book 5, Virgil develops this tension into two contrasting ways of viewing the historical trajectory from the Trojan past to the Augustan present—as either predestined or contingent. An especially informative episode is Apollo's oracle at Delphi, during which the Trojan hero learns that 'the house of Aeneas and his sons' sons and their sons born after them will rule over the whole earth' (*hic domus Aeneae cunctis dominabitur oris | et nati natorum et qui nascentur ab illis*, 3.97–8).[29] As Miller aptly puts it, this scene initiates 'Apollo's (and Virgil's) master narrative... of gradually unfolding [the] future' to the Trojan remnant.[30] Both the wording and the conviction of this Apolline prophecy bear the hallmark of Jupiter's pronouncement of the fated rule of Rome (cf. *domus Assaraci... dominabitur*, 1.284–5; *nascetur*, 1.286); and the anticipated achievement of the descendants of Aeneas (*nati natorum*, 3.98) is reaffirmed by Apollo later in his speech to

---

[28] Rogerson (2017) 121; Pandey (2018) 58–64, 155–6, 199–201.

[29] As Harrison (1981) 215 n. 10 shows, Apollo here seems to quote a prediction made by Poseidon at *Iliad* 20.307–8, but modifies it by stressing that it is the *race* of Aeneas that will rule *all men* (rather than the *might* of Aeneas that will rule over *the Trojans* as in Homer's text). See also Hardie (1998) 56.

[30] Miller (2009) 124.

164   POLITICS AND DIVINIZATION IN AUGUSTAN POETRY

Aeneas' *natus*, Ascanius, when the young man had completed his first act of conquest (9.641–4).[31]

At the same time, however, as is fitting for oracular communication, Apollo does not disclose the identity of the *nati natorum*, thereby leaving the door open for the sudden and unexpected introduction of Silvius as the heir to Aeneas in Book 6 (6.760–6).[32] Notably, the description of Silvius as <u>regem</u> <u>regumque parentem</u>, | unde genus Longa nostrum <u>dominabitur</u> Alba ('king and father of more kings, through whom our race will rule over Alba Longa', 6.765–6), effectively evokes the wording of Apollo's prophecy (cf. *dominabitur*, 3.97; *nati natorum* 3.98). Moreover, the Trojans' reaction to the Delphic oracle—*mixtoque ingens exorta tumultu* | *laetitia* ('there arose great joy mixed with apprehension', 3.99–100)—underscores not only the opacity of Apollo's instruction for them to seek their 'motherland' (3.94–6) but also the more general sense that their journey towards a supposedly brighter future is fraught with uncertainties. Indeed, the final major event of Book 3, the death of Anchises, is foretold by none of the book's prophetic authorities, as Aeneas regrettably acknowledges (3.712–13). By ending the most oracular-driven book of the *Aeneid* with prophetic communication's failure to foretell, Virgil alerts readers to a troubling aspect of the discourse of Rome's fated rise, whereby events that may undermine the impression of unhindered progress are conveniently suppressed. Importantly, critics have suggested that Apollo's prophetic guidance of the Trojans appears to be a Virgilian invention.[33] If this is the case, then the poem's portrayal of Apollo as a supporter of the *gens Iulia* from its early days must belong to a broader discourse that seeks to retrospectively legitimize Augustus' identification of Apollo as his divine patron.[34]

The ideological underpinning of seeing things through the lens of fate is highlighted further in a number of scenes where Aeneas unmistakably prefigures Augustus. The episode of the hero's stopover at Leucas and Actium following the Trojans' encounter with Celaeno clearly looks ahead to events in Augustus' life (3.274–88).[35] The way Apollo's temple at Leucas dramatically

---

[31] Apollo's description of Ascanius as *dis genite et geniture deos* ('born of the gods and will become father to gods', 9.642) evokes the formulation of *nati natorum et qui nascentur ab illis* (3.98); see further below. On the Delphic episode's allusion to Callimachus' *Hymn to Delos*, see Barchiesi (1994) 438; Miller (2009) 110.

[32] See below for detailed discussion of the 'Ascanius or Silvius' issue.

[33] Paschalis (1986) 47; Miller (1994) 103.

[34] The importance of Apollo to the *gens Iulia* prior to the civil war is far from clear. Ancient sources even disagree on whether Apollo was the watchword for the triumvirate's side (Val. Max. 1.5.7) or Brutus' side (Plut. *Brut.* 24.4–7) at the battle of Philippi. See further Moles (1983); Gosling (1986); Gurval (1995) 98–100.

[35] Miller (2009) 124.

DIVINIZATION AND THE INEVITABILITY OF AUGUSTAN ROME   165

emerges from the clouds (*et Leucatae nimbosa cacumina montis* | *et formidatus nautis aperitur Apollo*, 'Mount Leucas's cloud-capped peaks and Apollo's shrine, dreaded by sailors, come in view', 3.274–5) borrows the language of divine epiphany;[36] and the same verb, *aperitur* (3.275), is used later to describe the appearance of the *sidus Iulium* above Augustus' head before the battle of Actium (*patriumque aperitur vertice sidus*, 8.681), which is settled by an epiphany from Apollo (8.704–6). By establishing a close correspondence between these two moments which lie centuries part, Virgil hints at the idea that even a passing moment in the long history of Rome is now susceptible to ideological rereading. A more explicit formulation of this idea can be observed in the next scene, when Aeneas and his men, upon finding their way to Actium,[37] hold athletic games (3.279–80) and dedicate war spoils (3.286–8). This episode immediately brings to mind Augustus' foundation of the Actian games and his self-memorialization in the same region.[38] Similarly in Book 5, the rites and funeral games instituted by Aeneas for his deified father (*divinique...parentis*, 5.47) are depicted as precursors to those instituted by Augustus for Julius Caesar.[39] These moments of prefiguration not only reinscribe the battle of Actium and Apollo's patronage of Augustus as part of Rome's national myth but also create the impression that the history of Rome was always going to culminate in Augustan supremacy. By foregrounding the Augustan lens through which Aeneas' journey to Italy is viewed, Virgil gradually renders apparent the extent to which his poetry must negotiate with the regime's narrative of its destined supremacy.

Retelling and Representation: (i) The Role of the Poet

When Aeneas finally arrives in Cumae at the beginning of Book 6, he makes a vow promising that he will one day build a temple for Apollo. Through this vow, Virgil underlines that the perception of history as a predestined course is

---

[36] Nelis (2001) 62 argues that Virgil here alludes to Apollo's appearance before the exhausted Argonauts (cf. Ap. Rhod. *Argon.* 2.676).

[37] Virgil does not seem to take into account the geographical distance between Leucas and Actium, but treats the two locations poetically as one. See Horsfall (2006) on 3.279–80.

[38] On the dedications at Actium and Nicopolis, see Zachos (2003) 65–9.

[39] Serv. ad *Aen.* 5.45. In Book 5, Aeneas seems to envisage annual *ludi funebres* taking place at temples dedicated to his father (5.54, 59–60, 93). This brings to mind the deification of Julius Caesar, the construction of the Temple of Divus Julius immediately after the funeral games (Cass. Dio 47.18.4), and the evidence that the commemorative games honouring Caesar eventually became a permanent fixture on the imperial calendar. See further Bailey (1935) 291–301; Panoussi (2009) 161–3.

166 POLITICS AND DIVINIZATION IN AUGUSTAN POETRY

inseparable from and heavily reliant upon representation, specifically the *Aeneid* (6.69–74):

> tum Phoebo et Triviae solido de marmore templum
> instituam festosque dies de nomine Phoebi.   70
> te quoque magna manent regnis penetralia nostris:
> hic ego namque tuas sortis arcanaque fata
> dicta meae genti ponam, lectosque sacrabo,
> alma, viros....

Then I will set up to Phoebus and Trivia a temple of solid marble, and festal days in Phoebus' name. A great shrine awaits you too in the heart of our kingdom; for here I will place your oracles and the mystic utterances you told to my people, and I will ordain chosen men, O kindly one....

This vow looks ahead, first and foremost, to Augustus' construction of the Palatine temple and the transferral of the Sibylline books from the Capitoline to the Palatine.[40] But it also establishes a crucial parallel between Aeneas and Virgil through its allusion to the opening of *Georgics* 3, where the poet once promised to build a metaphorical 'marble temple' in honour of Augustus (*templum de marmore*, G. 3.13), which in turn further correlates Augustus with Apollo (as the twin recipient of temples).[41] With the vows of Aeneas and Virgil fulfilled by the construction of the Palatine temple and the composition of the *Aeneid* respectively, the architectural metaphor of *Georgics* 3, which assimilates poem to temple, now lends the *Aeneid* a material presence, figuring the epic as a constituent of the Augustan visual programme and a key part of the discourse of Augustan power. Aeneas' vow thus brings Augustus and Virgil into contact; and as poet and *princeps* each finds their counterpart in Aeneas, this passage crystallizes the reliance and negotiation between art and power.

A precursor to this kind of poetic self-reflection can be found in the scene depicting the first encounter between Dido and Aeneas in Book 1, when the Trojan hero finally sheds the concealing mist in which Venus had shrouded him. Importantly, this scene of revelation is presented as if it were a moment of divine epiphany (1.588–93):

---

[40] Miller (2009) 139; Horsfall (2013) ad loc.
[41] Deremetz (1995) 157–61; Kofler (2003) 53–61; Miller (2009) 140.

DIVINIZATION AND THE INEVITABILITY OF AUGUSTAN ROME   167

> restitit Aeneas claraque in luce refulsit
> os umerosque deo similis; namque ipsa decoram
> caesariem nato genetrix lumenque iuventae   590
> purpureum et laetos oculis adflarat honores:
> quale manus addunt ebori decus, aut ubi flavo
> argentum Pariusve lapis circumdatur auro.

Aeneas stood there, shining in the bright daylight, like a god in shoulders and face; for his own mother had imparted to her son lustre to his hair, the glow of youth, and a joyfulness and distinction to his eyes: such glory an artist's hands add to ivory, or when silver or Parian marble is covered in glittering gold.

Aeneas' godlike luminosity assimilates him to Sol–Apollo (1.588–9),[42] while the comparison of his divinely enhanced physical features to magnificent works of art (1.589–93) lends this description an obvious ekphrastic quality, foregrounding the intervention of the artist.[43] Indeed, Dido's reaction to Aeneas' sudden appearance—*obstipuit primo aspectu Sidonia Dido* ('at first Sidonian Dido was struck by his sight', 1.613)—heightens the sense of dramatic illusion, further blurring the boundary between image and reality. Aeneas' divine aura, which so amazes Dido and which Virgil compares to the effect the hands of a skilful craftsman can bring to a representation, emphasizes the compelling power that art can have on the viewer's perception of reality. Like the embellishing design of Venus, the artist can 'add glory' (1.592) to their material, alter its outward appearance (*flavo* |...*lapis circumdatur auro*, 1.592–3), and persuade the unsuspecting viewer to mistake it for something grander and more momentous.[44] By framing this scene of man-manifesting-as-god as an intensely metapoetic moment that underscores the sublimity of divine imagery, Virgil draws attention to the role his poetry will

---

[42] Note also: (a) Dido's initial appearance to Aeneas is similar to that of Diana, the goddess of the moon (1.498–504); (b) later in the Carthaginian hunting scene, Aeneas is again compared to Apollo (4.141–50). The conjunction of sun and moon, as Hardie (2006b) 30 well observes, anticipates a doomed, illicit love affair. On the allusion to the *sidus Iulium* in the phrase *caesariem nato genetrix* (1.590), see Williams (2003) 13; Hardie (2006b) 35.

[43] On the Homeric tenor of this scene (cf. *Od.* 6.229–35; 23.156–62), see Clausen (1987) 26–8; Smith (2005) 29–31.

[44] It is also worth pointing out that both the concealing *nubes* (which rendered Aeneas invisible) and the divinizing lustre are the works of Venus. Indeed, there appears to be no temporal disjunction between the disappearance of the mist (cf. 1.586–7) and Venus' embellishment of her son in the next scene. The goddess plays a crucial role in bringing into existence the poem's first idealized image of Aeneas.

168 POLITICS AND DIVINIZATION IN AUGUSTAN POETRY

play in changing the perception of another man-god, Augustus, who (as we shall see) undergoes a similar kind of divinization from charismatic hero to Apolline *roi-soleil* on a 'real' artefact crafted by Vulcan-as-poet later in Book 8 (678–81, 720–3).[45]

By highlighting the role of the artist in the mediation of perception, this episode also throws into sharp relief the epic's first major depiction of Caesar's divinization earlier in Book 1. There, Virgil introduces Jupiter's pronouncement of fate with a word that evokes the unfurling of a book-scroll: *volvens fatorum arcana* ('*unrolling* the mysteries of fate', 1.262).[46] The Latin poem and the prophetic scroll converge at the very moment when Caesar's apotheosis is about to be unfolded. Through this image, which gives Jupiter's words a physical presence, Virgil suggests that his own art is implicated in rendering 'real' the divine destiny of the *gens Iulia*—an idea which will resurface emphatically in the poet's description of Aeneas' shield. As the poem proceeds, these moments of poetic self-referentiality turn the epic's focus inward to reflect on its own role in the crafting of power.

Retelling and Representation: (ii) The 'Parade of Heroes'

The so-called 'Parade of Heroes' or *Heldenschau* of *Aeneid* 6 (756–892) is by definition telling history in the future tense.[47] Entering into a dialogue with both Ennius' *Annales* and the visual programme of the Forum Augustum,[48] Anchises' narrative tableaux organize centuries of forthcoming dynastic successions and constitutional changes into an authoritative account of fate (*te tua fata docebo*, 'I shall teach you your fate', 6.759). Aeneas is not just the primary audience of the parade; he is also the surrogate reader of a narrative that shares clear affinities with the epic itself. The didactic tenor of Anchises' speech (*docebo*, 6.759) further implies that this episode intends to teach a way of seeing the past in light of the present.[49]

---

[45] On Vulcan as a surrogate author, see Barchiesi (1997a) 278–9; Putnam (1998) 163; Casali (2006).

[46] Austin (1971) ad loc.

[47] The forward chronological movement of the *Heldenschau* serves simultaneously as historical retrospective; see further Pandey (2018) 153–6.

[48] On the passage's engagement with Ennius' *Annales*, see Hardie (1986) 76–83 and (1993) 103–5; Goldschmidt (2013) 166–79.

[49] On the didacticism of this episode, see Gransden (1984) 109; Hardie (1986) 69–70; Henry (1989) 69–70 (on *docebo*) and 136–7; Kondratieff (2012) 134; Horsfall (2013) on 6.759. The statuary *summi viri* in the Forum Augustum may also have a didactic function, according to Favro (1998) 126–8.

DIVINIZATION AND THE INEVITABILITY OF AUGUSTAN ROME   169

Anchises' account begins with a catalogue of Alba Longan kings, which leads to a eulogy of Romulus (6.778–90). He then skips ahead seven centuries and introduces a certain 'Caesar', who is said to be destined for heaven (*hic Caesar et omnis Iuli | progenies magnum caeli ventura sub axem*, 'here is Caesar and all the offspring of Iulus about to reach the great vault of heaven', 6.789–90).[50] Then immediately in the next line, Augustus makes a dramatic entry (6.791–805):

> hic vir, hic est, tibi quem promitti saepius audis,
> Augustus Caesar, divi genus, aurea condet
> saecula qui rursus Latio regnata per arva
> Saturno quondam, super et Garamantas et Indos
> proferet imperium; iacet extra sidera tellus,   795
> extra anni solisque vias, ubi caelifer Atlas
> axem umero torquet stellis ardentibus aptum.
> huius in adventum iam nunc et Caspia regna
> responsis horrent divum et Maeotia tellus,
> et septemgemini turbant trepida ostia Nili.   800
> nec vero Alcides tantum telluris obivit,
> fixerit aeripedem cervam licet, aut Erymanthi
> pacarit nemora et Lernam tremefecerit arcu;
> nec qui pampineis victor iuga flectit habenis
> Liber, agens celso Nysae de vertice tigris.   805

Here is the man—here he is—whom you so often hear promised to you: Augustus Caesar, born of a god, who will bring back the ages of gold to the fields of Latium once ruled by Saturn. He will extend Rome's power beyond the Indians and the Garamantes to a land past the stars, beyond the paths of the year and the sun, where sky-bearing Atlas spins on his shoulder the orb studded with burning stars. Already awaiting his arrival, the Caspian kingdoms and Maeotia's land shudder at the gods' prophecies; and the seven mouths of the Nile agitate in turmoil. Indeed, Hercules did not cross so much of the earth, even though he shot down the bronze-hoofed doe, tamed the groves of Erymantus and made Lerna tremble with his bow. Nor did the

---

[50] The identity of this Caesar is uncertain. Some have argued that this Caesar must be Augustus, because lines 789–90 are so overwhelmingly positive, whereas Julius Caesar is depicted in a negative light later at 6.826–31; see e.g. Williams (1972) ad loc. Others, however, have maintained that Julius Caesar is meant at 6.789; and that the poem's inconsistency in its depiction of Julius Caesar is intended to highlight the instability of history and meaning; see e.g. O'Hara (1990) 163–72 and (2007) 91–5; Pandey (2018) 156.

170 POLITICS AND DIVINIZATION IN AUGUSTAN POETRY

conqueror Bacchus, who drove his tiger-drawn chariot down from the high
peak of Nysa and guided the yoke with reins made of ivy.

The initial portrait of Augustus (6.791–7) not only presents him as the culmination of Roman achievement but even insinuates that the entire historical
process of Rome has been building up to Augustan supremacy. Virgil achieves
this by framing this image of Augustus as a kind of answer to Jupiter's prophecy in Book 1, as well as to the mysterious characters of *Eclogues* 1 and 4.[51]
The description of Augustus' imperial expansion here (*super et Garamantas et
Indos | proferet imperium*, 6.794–5) responds specifically to Jupiter's vision for
the future of Rome (cf. *imperium sine fine*, 1.279).[52] The proclamation of a
forthcoming Augustan Golden Age (*aurea condet | saecula*, 6.792–3) now
provides a reference point for both the peaceful *saeculum* envisaged by Jupiter
(cf. *aspera tum positis mitescent saecula bellis*, 1.291) and the identity of the
miraculous *puer* in *Eclogue* 4—the inaugurator of the Golden Age in that
poem.[53] Furthermore, Virgil's Augustus—here introduced with the words *hic
vir* (6.791)—answers the description of the mysterious young man in *Eclogue*
1 as *iste deus* ('that god', *Ecl.* 1.18); and this act of literary self-referentiality, as
Geue well notes, is highlighted by the words *tibi quem promitti saepius audis*
(6.791): we have indeed heard all about him before.[54] By presenting the arrival
of Augustus as something that has long been anticipated, Virgil frames political change as predestined history, thus naturalizing the emergence of the
Principate and the rule of Augustus.[55]

But the poet does not stop here: the comparison of Augustus with Hercules
and Bacchus (6.798–805) then embeds the divinization of the *princeps* as also
part of Rome's predestined history. The comparison here operates primarily
on a spatial level, whereby Augustus is envisaged to outdo Hercules and
Bacchus with his worldwide conquest (*nec... tantum telluris*, 6.801). However,
the introduction of these two mythological figures also brings to mind the
issue of deification. Both Hercules and Bacchus are famous for instituting
their cult upon overcoming their enemy: Virgil himself treats the theme of

---

[51] Treating these three texts in conjunction has a long tradition in Virgilian scholarship: see e.g.
Taylor (1931) 112–14; Williams (2003) 21.
[52] The repetition of *extra... extra* (6.795–6) re-enlivens the idea of *sine fine*. The emphasis on the
Augustan empire stretching *beyond* the path of the sun (6.796) evokes and caps the encomia of
Alexander, which often claim that the Macedonian king subdued the *oikoumene* bound by the reach of
the sun; see further Buchheit (1971) with references.
[53] Some critics find Virgil's depiction of Augustus as the founder of a new Golden Age more
ambivalent than it appears. Ryberg (1958) 129 argues that lines 792–4 present Augustus as a Jupiter-
figure, and Jupiter is more associated with the Iron Age. Thomas (2001) 3–7 adds that the meaning of
condere as a temporal marker can often be ambiguous.
[54] Geue (2013) 67–8.   [55] See further Geue (2013) 64–8.

DIVINIZATION AND THE INEVITABILITY OF AUGUSTAN ROME   171

the foundation of Hercules' cult following the hero's victory over Cacus in Book 8 of the *Aeneid*;[56] while Euripides' *Bacchae* centres on Dionysus' establishment of his cult in Thebes against the resistance of Pentheus, and the play at one point associates Dionysus with the recreation of the Golden Age (Eur. *Bacch.* 704–11), which parallels the brief mention of Augustus' restoration of the Golden Age in our passage (6.792–3).[57] By claiming that Rome's present-day ruler will surpass these two deified conquerors (*pacarit*, 6.803; *victor*, 6.804), Virgil sets up divinization as the anticipated culmination of Augustus' achievements, prefiguring the visual theology of the *princeps*' apotheosis inside the similarly mytho-historical setting of the Forum Augustum.[58]

This image of Augustus as the divinely ordained, destined-to-be-deified Roman conqueror reconciles an encomiastic account of one man's path to unparalleled power with the seductive rhetoric of Rome's irresistible rise, conflating personal glory with national achievement. However, elsewhere in Anchises' speech, the idea that Roman history would converge gloriously and inevitably with Augustus as the head of the *gens Iulia* appears to be more problematic. Most notably, by starting and ending the 'Parade of Heroes' with Silvius and Marcellus—the Italian son of Aeneas, and the putative successor of Augustus, respectively—Anchises' tableaux of Roman history are bookended by complications in dynastic handover.[59] Rogerson points out that the displacement of Ascanius by Silvius as the heir of Aeneas (6.760–6) seriously disrupts what had, until that moment, seemed like a clear momentum of the succession of the *gens Iulia*.[60] This uncertainty surrounding who would succeed Aeneas, as Rogerson goes on to say, underlines not only the multivalence of prophecies but also the contingency of the hopes invested in the young.[61] Likewise, the appearance of the prematurely deceased Marcellus at the end of the *Heldenschau*, who is depicted as if a second Ascanius (*puer Iliaca quisquam de gente*, 'boy of the Trojan line', 6.875), reinscribes loss, doubt, and unpredictability into the fate of the Julians in a way that Augustus would seek to suppress in the

---

[56] Gransden (1976) passim, esp. pp. 14–20; Morgan (1998); see also Prop. 4.9.

[57] Mac Góráin (2021) 95–6.

[58] On the correspondence between the Virgilian and Augustan 'Halls of Fame', see Zanker (1988) 193–5; Geiger (2008) 50–1; Pandey (2018) 158–64.

[59] Rogerson (2017) 15–36; see also Feeney (1986) 15–16.

[60] Rogerson (2017) 16. On the discrepancies between the narratives of *Aen.* 6 and elsewhere in the poem, see also Zetzel (1989) and O'Hara (2007) 88–95. By contrast, Bettini (2005) 89–95 argues that the *Heldenschau* leaves open the originator and genealogical sequence of the Alban dynasty so as to reconcile the canonical version of the Trojan–Alban myth (cf. Livy 1.3.4), whereby Romulus traces his ancestry back to the son of Aeneas and Lavinia, with the genealogical claims of the ruling *Iulii*, who had their roots in Alba Longa.

[61] Rogerson (2017) 33. See also Feeney (1986) 16, who concludes that the *Heldenschau* ultimately tells 'nothing more than the mixed uncertainties of actual history'.

172   POLITICS AND DIVINIZATION IN AUGUSTAN POETRY

design of the Forum Augustum. Compared with Propertius' near-contemporary treatment of Marcellus' death in elegy 3.18, which emphasizes the futility of pursuing glory,[62] Virgil's rhetoric is decidedly more effusive and sympathetic as he presents the death of Marcellus as a loss of potential greatness (6.872–81). However, while Propertius concludes his elegy by predicting that Marcellus' connections to both the Claudii and the Iulii would guarantee him an apotheosis like that of Julius Caesar (Prop. 3.18.31–4; especially, *qua Siculae victor telluris Claudius et qua | Caesar ab humana cessit in astra via*, '[a route] by which Claudius, conqueror of the Sicilian land, and by which Caesar passed from the human road to the stars', 3.18.33–4), Virgil offers nothing of the sort. As Feeney argues, Marcellus in the *Aeneid* embodies an emphatic 'stifling of promise', which in turn asks questions of whether Augustus would be able to carry things through.[63] The appearance of Marcellus, therefore, much like the unexpected introduction of Silvius at the start of the *Heldenschau*, indirectly challenges the notion that the future of the Principate and the *gens Iulia* could be planned.[64] As a result, the divinization of Augustus becomes the final specific event predicted by the poem, beyond which there seems to be only loss and uncertainty.

Indeed, Virgil even suggests that the entire premise of the 'Parade of Heroes' could turn out to be false by concluding the episode with Aeneas exiting the Underworld through the Gates of Sleep (6.893–9). Although the *Heldenschau* is framed as a narrative of *fata* from the outset (cf. *te tua fata docebo*, 6.759), at the end of his journey Aeneas is said to be inflamed with a love for *fama* (*famae venientis amore*, 6.889) and leaves Hades via where 'spirits send false dreams to the sky' (*falsa ad caelum mittunt insomnia Manes*, 6.896).[65] The juxtaposition of *falsa* and *ad caelum* here (6.896) looks back to *fama*, evoking its double-meaning as pre-eminent glory (*ad caelum*) and unreliable tale (*falsa*), which in turn underlines the idea that the entire *Heldenschau* is a motivated retelling of Roman history.[66] By playing the role of the surrogate reader to Anchises' unfolding of Roman history, Aeneas'

---

[62] See especially Prop. 3.18.11–12, *quid genus aut virtus aut optima profuit illi | mater, et amplexum Caesaris esse focos?* ('what has been the use to him of his lineage or excellence or his noble mother, and the fact that he embraced Caesar's hearth?'); with Heyworth and Morwood (2011) ad loc. For further comparative readings of Marcellus' portrayal in Propertius and Virgil, see Nethercut (1970); Falkner (1977).

[63] Feeney (1986) 16. By contrast, Glei (1998) 123–4 suggests that the death of Marcellus is framed as a warning from the gods against excessive ambition.

[64] See also Glei (1998) 125–6.

[65] Molyviati-Toptsis (1995) 646 also notes the transition from *fata* to *fama*. Tarrant (1982) 53 reads 6.896 as expressing Virgil's own sense of 'the evanescence of mortal aspiration'.

[66] Likewise, Molyviati-Toptsis (1995) 643 suggests that the ending of the *Heldenschau* retrospectively highlights the ambiguity and distortion of factual truth in Anchises' speech.

DIVINIZATION AND THE INEVITABILITY OF AUGUSTAN ROME   173

internalization of this account of Augustan inevitability as tantalizing *fama*—at once inspiring and illusory—not only draws attention to the slippage between representation and reality in both Virgil's epic and Augustus' Rome, but also highlights the readerly collusion that is required to imbibe history's unpredictability as apparent destiny.[67]

The Reinvention of History: Augustus on the Shield of Aeneas

This chapter has so far made two main observations about the *Aeneid*'s treatment of the divinization of Augustus as one of its central long-term prophecies. Firstly, while these prophecies on the whole articulate the notion that Augustan supremacy is predestined, and frame the *gens Iulia*'s rise to power as the materialization of divine will, the poem's occasional and pointed reinstatement of historical contingency asserts a means of viewing the past that is not steered by the apparent inevitability of Augustan rule. In this way, Virgil's poem offers an alternative to the regime's re-ordering of Roman history as a fated path to present glory. Secondly, the ways in which passages prefiguring Augustus' divinization intersect with metapoetic reflection (1.588–93; 6.69–74), or constitute part of a larger narrative that is emblematic of the *Aeneid* itself (such as the 'Parade of Heroes'), underscore the idea that the reinvention of history as 'fate' is heavily reliant on representation—including and especially the present epic. Through these moments, Virgil highlights the implication of his own art in the regime's construction of its myth.

Book 8's description of the artwork on Aeneas' shield, which stands as another miniaturized *Aeneid* (like the *Heldenschau* of Book 6), continues to straddle the line between critique and collaboration. But here Virgil goes further by depicting how his poem enfolds the reader into its retelling of the past, through which the poet gestures at the *Aeneid*'s complicity in the distortion of history. It is well recognized among scholars that the shield operates as a means by which Virgil underlines and interrogates the artificiality of his poem.[68] As both a material object and a narration of history, the shield draws our attention to the slippage between reality and representation, fact and fiction, in Virgil's epic.[69] The scene of the battle of Actium best demonstrates

---

[67] Zetzel (1989) 274 similarly concludes that Virgil implicitly 'insist[s] that the reader apply critical intelligence to the facts of his narrative'.

[68] On the relationship between artefact and artist, and how it emblematizes the dynamic between text and author, see esp. Hardie (1998) 75–9 and Fowler (2000b) 29–30.

[69] See further Barchiesi (1997a) 275–6; Feldherr (2014) 282, 293; Pandey (2018) 195–6.

174   POLITICS AND DIVINIZATION IN AUGUSTAN POETRY

this; indeed, for many critics, this scene has become a touchstone for assessing the *Aeneid*'s interaction with the regime's narrative of the civil war.[70] On the shield, Augustus is seen leading Italian ships into battle, emerging from it victorious with Apollo's help, and then presiding over a triumphal procession (8.678–728). Virgil's depiction of the naval battle as a new Gigantomachy, where Roman forces and Olympian gods are pitted against monstrous Egyptian deities (8.696–706), clearly resonates with the Augustan reinvention of the civil war as a victory for the forces of order over chaos.[71] But more than that, the way in which Augustus is introduced into the scene reflects the text's concern with its ability to rewrite the past and assert it as real (8.680–1):

> stans celsa in puppi, geminas cui tempora flammas
> laeta vomunt patriumque aperitur vertice sidus.

High he stood on the stern, while his blessed temples erupted with twin flame-plumes, and his father's star appeared above his head.

Augustus' elevated position on the shield (*stans celsa*, 8.680) not only encourages readers to see the *princeps* as a Jupiter-like figure in the absence of the god himself,[72] but also introduces a vertical perspective that mimics what Feldherr calls 'divine viewing', whereby the elevated position from which gods view human action renders the events depicted on the shield 'real' and so transforms Virgil's representation of the battle into a synchronous event.[73] Augustus' image is further enhanced by the appearance of twin flames and the comet of Caesar (8.681). Some critics have pointed out that the poetic imagery here is not a straightforwardly eulogistic response to official iconography, since the twin flames on Augustus' temples (*geminas...flammas*, 8.680) may be understood as part of a series of ambivalent fiery omens within the *Aeneid* that augur violent conflict as much as forthcoming greatness.[74] Yet by

---

[70]   Rowland (1968); Johnson (1976) 111–14; Williams (1981); DuBois (1982) 41–8; Thomas (1983); Hardie (1986) 336–76; Lyne (1987) 207–9; Gurval (1995) 209–47; Bartsch (1998) 330–2; Putnam (1998) 119–88; Casali (2006); Miller (2009) 69–75, 206–10; Feldherr (2014).

[71]   See esp. Hardie (1986) 104, 122–3, 349–50, 352–3; also Bartsch (1998) 330–1; Miller (2009) 69–70. Quint (1993) 31–46 adds that the teleological form of epic narrative itself enacts a form of control over the chaotic forces of history. In reality, the battle of Actium was something of an anticlimax; see Pelling *CAH* X, 54–9 and Lange (2011).

[72]   Thomas (2001) 50.   [73]   Feldherr (2014) 294–5.

[74]   Cf. the flames rising from Ascanius' head (2.681–4); the burning hairs of Lavinia (7.73–80); the 'twin crests' and mysterious sign that Mars adds to Romulus' head (*geminae stant vertice cristae | et pater ipse suo superum iam signat honore*, 'twin crests crown his helmet, and the father himself now marks him with his own honour of divinity, 6.779–80); and the flames resembling the blood-red glow of a comet above Aeneas' head as he prepares for war (10.270–5). In the last instance, the image's

DIVINIZATION AND THE INEVITABILITY OF AUGUSTAN ROME   175

incorporating the *sidus Iulium* into the shield's design, producing in effect an image on metal, Virgil evokes visual representations of the comet on contemporary coinage which depict Divus Julius and Augustus together.[75] In doing so, the poet implies that his poetic *imago* (8.671) of Augustan glory is just as real as an actual physical insignia of the fated divinity of the *gens Iulia*.

The tension between the passage's self-conscious probing of its artifice on the one hand, and its apparent function as a visual and poetic counterpart to the Augustan mythologization of the civil war on the other, can also be observed in the shield's depiction of Augustus during the triple triumph (*triplici... triumpho*, 8.714), where the *princeps* is seen inspecting the parade from the vantage point of Apollo's temple on the Palatine (8.720–3):

> ipse sedens niveo candentis limine Phoebi   720
> dona recognoscit populorum aptatque superbis
> postibus; incedunt victae longo ordine gentes,
> quam variae linguis, habitu tam vestis et armis.

He himself, seated at the snowy-white threshold of gleaming Apollo, inspects the gifts of his peoples and hangs them high on the door-posts, while vanquished nations approach in a long line, varied in their language as in their clothing and weapons.

The implicit comparison of Augustus with Sol–Apollo not only alludes to the idea of universal empire comprising all lands under the sun but also, as Hardie points out, evokes the practice of Ptolemaic rulers identifying themselves with Osiris, who represents the sun (Diod. Sic. 1.11.1).[76] As the conqueror of the last Ptolemaic monarch (Cleopatra) and Antony–Osiris, Augustus supersedes them and becomes the ultimate *roi-soleil* in the tradition of Hellenistic ruler cult.[77] But crucially, our passage situates this form of ruler cult in Rome, on the Palatine (8.720); and through this act of relocation Virgil domesticates divinization and integrates it as part of Rome's new political landscape. At the centre of this image, Augustus inspects (*recognoscit*, 8.721) gifts and subjects from all corners of the world; yet he is also the object of a readerly gaze fixed on the shield. The double status of Augustus as both internal viewer and viewed object creates a *mise en abyme* for the poem's readers, as they 'look

---

explicit menace is well noted by e.g. Lyne (1987) 32 and Pandey (2018) 83–4; though others, e.g. West (1993) 13 and Williams (2003) 9, take a more generous view of the simmering violence.

[75] See also Weinstock (1971) 377–8; Williams (2003) 5–7; Pandey (2018) 64–5.

[76] Hardie (2006b) 30.   [77] Hardie (2006b) 36–7.

176 POLITICS AND DIVINIZATION IN AUGUSTAN POETRY

upon Augustus looking upon his subjects' and find themselves amongst those paying divine honour to the *roi-soleil*.[78] The Roman reader's encounter with this artwork also evokes the first meeting between Dido and Aeneas in Book 1, where the Trojan hero's godlike luminous appearance (1.588) dazzles the unsuspecting Carthaginian queen like some gleaming, sublime artefact (1.592–3). Thus finding themselves in the position of both worshipper and victim, the Roman reader is pulled into the poem's self-reflection on the role it plays in the glorification of Augustan power.

Finally, the shield's seamless transition from battle scene to triumphal scene further creates the impression that Augustus' rise to power follows a natural order of things: victory, celebration, authority.[79] However, this image of Augustus viewing the procession from the new imperial complex, receiving offerings (8.721) as soon as he had concluded his warfare (8.689–95), not only wilfully disregards the two intervening years between Actium (31 BC) and the triple triumph (29 BC) but also deliberately overlooks the fact that the Palatine temple was still under construction in 29 BC.[80] Some critics are happy to treat Virgil's muddled history as a testament to the elevated profile of Apollo in the decade after Actium.[81] But it might also be said that Virgil's distorted retrospective of the aftermath of the civil war encapsulates the convergence of fact and fiction in the Augustan retelling of the past. As ostensible falsehood and blatant inaccuracy make up the fabric of a new post-truth Rome, the shield's depiction of the civil war underlines the extent to which the past is seen through the victor's perspective—one which steers the subject's gaze teleologically towards the supremacy of Augustus.

Prefiguring Actium: Ascanius and Apollo's Prophecy

The reinvention of the Actian victory as the culmination of Roman power, as well as the (visual) language of predestiny which permeates Augustus' self-fashioning, come into focus again in Book 9, where Ascanius claims his first victim in the Trojan–Rutulian war. Aeneas' son fatally shoots Numanus Remulus with an arrow in response to the latter's taunting of Trojan effeminacy and

---

[78] Pandey (2018) 199. On the *mise en abyme* of viewership, see also Barchiesi (1997a) 276; Feldherr (2014) 283, 289, 298. Further, Stöckinger (2016) 236–7 points out that this scene of gift-giving within the new metropolis of Rome inversely mirrors the 'toxic gift' of the Trojan Horse which led to Troy's destruction; and that this correspondence hints at the completion of a grand historical process.

[79] See also Feldherr (2014) 306.   [80] Also noted by Pandey (2018) 199–200.

[81] e.g. Miller (2009) 210.

DIVINIZATION AND THE INEVITABILITY OF AUGUSTAN ROME   177

oriental culture (9.621–37);[82] and this heroic deed is immediately congratulated by Apollo (9.638–44):

> Aetheria tum forte plaga crinitus Apollo
> desuper Ausonias acies urbemque videbat
> nube sedens, atque his victorem adfatur Iulum: 640
> 'macte nova virtute, puer, sic itur ad astra,
> dis genite et geniture deos. iure omnia bella
> gente sub Assaraci fato ventura resident,
> nec te Troia capit.'

Right then, by chance, long-haired Apollo sat on a cloud in the heavenly region, and from above he saw the Ausonian armies and cities and said to the victorious Iulus: 'Blessings on your new manliness, my boy: this is the path to the stars. You, who are born of the gods and will become father to gods! Justly, all wars fated to come will subside under the descendants of Assaracus. And Troy does not set its limits on you.'

The significance of this episode is well summed up by Hardie: Ascanius' shot is 'the first deliberate intervention in the historical process that leads to Rome by the ancestor of the *gens Iulia*'.[83] On the surface of it, Ascanius' feat and Apollo's epiphany are presented as precursors to the events at Actium. The arrival of Apollo onto the Italian battlefield here (*Apollo | desuper*, 9.638–9) looks ahead (and back) to his intervention at the naval combat (*Apollo | desuper*, 8.704–5); the imagery of Iulus making his way *ad astra* (9.641) recalls the symbolism of the *sidus Iulium* on the shield; and the atmosphere immediately after Ascanius' arrow shot (*laetitiaque fremunt animosque ad sidera tollunt*, 'they roared in joy and raised spirits to the stars', 9.637) breathes a similarly celebratory air as the Augustan triple triumph (*laetitia ludisque viae plausuque fremebant*, 'the streets were roaring with joy, festivities, and applause', 8.717).[84] Set against this background, Apollo's anticipation of deified Julian descendants (*geniture deos*, 9.642), and the god's prediction that Ascanius' offspring would put an end to all warfare (9.642–3), combine to exert an

---

[82] Horsfall (1971) discusses the dependence of Numanus Remulus' speech on the ethnographical tradition; Dickie (1985) presents a comprehensive *Quellenforschung* on the speech. Others focus on the speech's intersection with the discourse of Roman identity in Virgil's time: see Thomas (1982) 98–9; Cairns (1989) 125–6; Quint (1993) 24–6; Casali (2009) 314.

[83] Hardie (1994) 198. Contra Casali (2009) 316, who reads Apollo's words at lines 641–4 as ironic praise.

[84] See further Hardie (1994) 198; Miller (2009) 155.

178   POLITICS AND DIVINIZATION IN AUGUSTAN POETRY

authenticating force on the *gens Iulia*'s claim to dynastic supremacy and the regime's presentation of Actium as the defining moment of Augustan *imperium*.

At the same time, however, this episode again raises questions about the succession of the *gens Iulia*, and its prefiguration of Actium is more ambivalent than it initially seems. Apollo's championing of Ascanius as a proto-Augustus reopens the question of whether Ascanius or Silvius was the ancestor of the *gens Iulia* (cf. 6.763–6). The surprising appearance of Augustus' patron deity in this scene, as Casali argues, could well draw (unwanted) attention to the fact that the version of the *gens Iulia*'s descent from Ascanius–Iulus is a highly politically motivated version of the genealogy, which at the end of Virgil's poem loses out to a pre-Julian version which has Silvius as the ancestor.[85] Moreover, since Virgil makes it abundantly clear (especially in the speech of Numanus Remulus) that Aeneas' enemy are Italians,[86] the present episode not only hints at 'the contradiction between the Trojan and the Italian element in Augustan propaganda'[87] but also asserts itself as a microcosm of civil war. Indeed, later in his speech, Apollo urges Ascanius to refrain from going on a killing spree (*cetera parce, puer, bello*, 'spare the rest from war, my boy', 9.656).[88]

As Rogerson points out, Apollo's instruction for the Trojan *puer* to suspend fighting evokes on the one hand Anchises' address to the ghosts of Caesar and Pompey, who appear in the Underworld as *pueri* engaged in civil war (*ne, pueri, ne tanta animis adsuescite bella . . .* | *tuque prior, tu parce*, 'do not, my boys, do not accustom your spirits to such great wars . . . you be the first to show pity, you', 6.832–4); on the other hand, it also recalls Anchises' doctrine of *parcere subiectis* for subsequent Romans ('spare the defeated', 6.853).[89] This twofold echo of Anchises' speech has some implications. First, it retrojects an element of inevitability onto the recent civil war. The readiness of the Trojan prince to kill more Italians looks toward the failure of Caesar and Pompey to spare each other's men: this correspondence, in turn, suggests that the Roman civil war may be construed as the eventual manifestation of a previously

---

[85] Casali (2009) 318–25.

[86] On the Italian ethnic patriotism of Numanus Remulus' speech, see esp. Horsfall (1971) 1108–13 and Hardie (1994) 188–98.

[87] Casali (2009) 316.

[88] In Hom. *Il.* 17.322–41 (a clear model for our passage), Apollo appears to Aeneas and—in contrast to the Virgilian Apollo—incites the Trojan hero to combat; see Hardie (1994) 207. Casali (2009) 300–5, 319, 324–5 argues that Virgil's Apollo deliberately marginalizes Ascanius from the epic plot, which in turn suggests that the epic is resisting the Julian attempt to integrate Ascanius–Iulus into the ancestral line of the Alban kings and Rome's Trojan history. See also Lyne (1987) 202–3.

[89] Rogerson (2017) 166.

supressed eagerness for internecine conflict. Secondly, since Augustus claims to have shown *clementia* to his former enemies after the civil war, the reader may be reminded of the *princeps* through the injunction of Apollo-as-Anchises. That Augustus could be seen—through the prism of this episode—as either the force that finally reined in civil strife or the perpetuator of a civil-war impulse retroactively renders the shield's depiction of the battle of Actium more equivocal. But more than that, by making the Ascanius–Apollo episode more semantically deviant than is required from a narrative of historical prefiguration, Virgil reinstates ambiguity in the Trojan myth, and restores the multivalency of Rome's past in response to the regime's refashioning of history as destiny.

Conclusions

The intention of this chapter has not been to paint the *Aeneid* as a poem that antagonistically lays bare the Augustan regime's ideological narrative, which would misrepresent Virgil's literary endeavour and its relation to authority. Rather, I hope to have shown that, through its prophecies of Augustus' divinization, Virgil's epic interrogates the relationship between poetry and ideology at a time when the Principate was notably attempting to present itself as the telos of Roman hegemony. In this way, the *Aeneid*'s treatment of this motif may be seen as a form of negotiation with truth and power, highlighting both the poem's ostensible divergence from and, at the same time, 'ineluctable collusion' with the regime's self-fashioning as the predestined culmination of Roman history.[90] Throughout the poem's prophetic discourse, Virgil foregrounds multivalency and ambiguity so as to complicate, or even counteract, the idea that the entire historical process of Rome was destined to lead towards Augustan supremacy. When the poem does articulate this kind of teleological perspective, it explicitly figures itself as a constitutive medium of the Augustan ideological programme. By thus contesting the regime's discourse of predestiny on the one hand, and gesturing at its own involvement in the Augustan retelling of Roman history on the other, the *Aeneid* encapsulates the tension and complicity between art and authority in the age of Augustus.

---

[90] Hardie (1997) 182, discussing the relationship between artist and ruler in the final book of Ovid's *Metamorphoses*.

180   POLITICS AND DIVINIZATION IN AUGUSTAN POETRY

Coda

The way in which Virgil's epic uses the prophecies of Augustus' divinization to explore the relationship between poetic discourse and ideological discourse is picked up in Horace's *Carmen Saeculare* and Propertius 4.6.[91] In the final part of this chapter, I wish to show that the construal of the *Aeneid* by these two later poems as the new national myth of the Principate constitutes not so much a criticism of Virgil's poem, but a comment on how the Augustan discourse of predestined glory is shaping the reception of Virgil's epic. In their reworking of the *Aeneid's* major prophetic scenes, Horace and Propertius each suggest that the regime has co-opted the notion of inevitable supremacy to such an extent that poetry's prophetic discourse can now only be consumed in light of Augustus' rise to power.

The *Carmen Saeculare*

The *Aeneid's* prophetic discourse on Augustan Rome is an important body of intertexts for the *Carmen Saeculare*, since the principal aim of Horace's hymn—whose composition is apparently prescribed in the Sibylline oracle (*Sibyllini monuere versus | virgines lectas puerosque castos | dis... | dicere carmen*, 'the Sibylline verses have commanded chosen girls and chaste boys to sing a hymn to the gods', *Carm. saec.* 5–8)[92]—is to articulate the perpetuation and rebirth of Rome in the time of Augustus.[93] Performed on the final day of the games, the *Carmen Saeculare* has the potential to suggest conclusively that the prophetic visions of the *Aeneid* are being realized and enacted through its performance.[94] Horace introduces Augustus into the poem obliquely as

---

[91] The *Carmen's* dialogue with the *Aeneid* is well established; see esp. Putnam (2000) 80–4, 122–4 and Thomas (2011) 74, 77. On the intertextual relationship between the *Aeneid* and Prop. 4.6, see esp. Hutchinson (2006) on Prop. 4.6. passim; Miller (2009) 80–1, 85–6, 89–92; Pandey (2018) 68–72.

[92] The Sibylline oracle for the Augustan *ludi saeculares* of 17 BC called for 'paeans' to be sung in Latin (ἀειδόμενοί τε Λατῖνοι | παιᾶνες, *Sib. Orac.* 18–19; see also Zosimus 2.6.1; Phlegon: *FGrH* 257: F37). The convenience is suspect, especially as by 17 BC the *libri Sibyllini* were kept on the Palatine and effectively put under Augustus' jurisdiction. See further Beard et al. (1998) 205; Miller (2009) 134.

[93] Unlike the Augustan games, the *ludi saeculares* of the third and second centuries were most likely held in times of crisis and had an expiatory function; see further Beard et al. (1998) 71–2, 111.

[94] Feeney (1998) 36–7; Putnam (2000) 50, 94–5, 149–50; Lowrie (2009) 140. On the unprecedented ritual format of the Augustan *ludi*, see Feeney (1998) 28–38, esp. pp. 29–31. Schnegg-Köhler (2002) offers the most comprehensive study of the religious proceedings of the Augustan *ludi*. Barchiesi (2002) 201–2 well sums up the nature of the Augustan *ludi* and Horace's hymn: '[both] are involved in the production and the workings of ideology.'

DIVINIZATION AND THE INEVITABILITY OF AUGUSTAN ROME 181

'the famous offspring of Anchises and Venus' (*clarus Anchisae Venerisque sanguis*, 50), which pointedly casts the *princeps* as a reincarnation, as well as the descendant, of Aeneas.[95] The hymn's subsequent portrayal of Augustus as 'superior in war, gentle on the fallen enemy' (*bellante prior, iacentem | lenis in hostem*, 51–2) evokes Anchises' speech in the 'Parade of Heroes': *tu... Romane, memento | ...parcere subiectis et debellare superbos* ('You, Roman, remember to spare the defeated and war down the proud', Verg. *Aen.* 6.851–3). While the second half of Virgil's epic does not offer unequivocal testimony to the policy's implementation by Aeneas, the *Carmen Saeculare* on the other hand presents it as the actual practice of Augustus.[96] Critics have noted further that the Virgilian phrase, *Romane, memento*, also appears in the Sibylline oracle predicting the Augustan *ludi* (μεμνῆσθαι, 'Ρωμαῖε, *Sib. Orac.* 3),[97] which in turn lends Anchises' words in the *Aeneid* an even stronger prophetic quality and a direct contemporary relevance. Seen in this light, Horace's hymnic reformulation of Anchises' doctrine as a characteristic attribute of Augustus not only belatedly crystallizes the *Romanus*-figure (cf. *Romane, memento*) in the Virgilian *Heldenschau* but also reframes the Augustan Principate as the ideal state and the culmination of a long mytho-historical process.

The hymn's next two stanzas then rework Anchises' vision of the Augustan Golden Age and world empire (cf. *Aen.* 6.791–9). Here Horace goes further than Virgil by imparting onto Augustus a quasi-oracular authority (*Carm. saec.* 53–60):

> iam mari terraque manus potentis
> Medus Albanasque timet securis,
> iam Scythae responsa petunt superbi   55
>   nuper et Indi.
> iam Fides et Pax et Honos Pudorque
> priscus et neglecta redire Virtus
> audet, apparetque beata pleno
>   Copia cornu.   60

---

[95] The *acta* of the Augustan *ludi* appear to suggest that Augustus was present at the hymn's performance on the Palatine (*CIL* 6.32323, 147–50). The presence of the *princeps* in full view of the ceremony's spectators would have added force to Horace's depiction of Augustus as Aeneas incarnate.

[96] Davis (2001) 122: 'Horace's pro-Augustan reading of the *Aeneid* presents as fact inferences not warranted by Virgil's text.'

[97] Feeney (1998) 36; Putnam (2000) 80; Thomas (2011) 78.

182 POLITICS AND DIVINIZATION IN AUGUSTAN POETRY

Now the Parthians fear our mighty hands, powerful on land and sea, and our Alban axes; now the Scythians and the Indians, who were until recently proud, seek our responses. Now Faith, and Peace, and Honour, and ancient Modesty, and long-neglected Virtue dare to return, and blessed Plenty with her full horn comes into sight.

While Virgil has Anchises claiming that eastern kingdoms 'already awaiting [Augustus'] arrival...shudder at the gods' prophecies' (*huius in adventum iam nunc...| responsis horrent divum*, 6.798–9), Horace paints a contemporary picture (*iam*, 53) of foreign nations seeking 'responses' directly from Rome (*responsa petunt*, 55).[98] The substitution of divine prophecy with Augustan diplomacy suggests more than just that 'Rome itself has become the oracular divinity';[99] it also implies that the *princeps* is now the embodiment of divine agency. Horace transforms the *Aeneid*'s prophetic visions of Augustan Rome into hymnic utterances (cf. the anaphora of *iam* in lines 53–7) that, through their performance, instantly sacralize the present age and the political authority of Augustus.[100] And in doing so, the *Carmen Saeculare* shapes Augustus as the figure in whom inconceivable ideals materialize as hardly conceivable Roman realities.[101] Whereas Virgil mobilizes his epic to critique, as well as to render apparent, this process of materialization, Horace encourages the audience of his hymn to see Rome and Augustus *through* the prism of the *Aeneid*, thereby turning the epic into an instrument with which one can appreciate the emergence of Augustan Rome as divine prophecy manifest. Horace's distillation of the *Aeneid* into a poem about the destiny of Augustan power is by all means a collaboration with autocracy. Yet it also shows that the *Carmen Saeculare* is interested in more than just versifying the regime's ideology, as Horace intervenes in the negotiation between art and power, and makes explicit the singular interpretative framework within which poetic representations of Augustus must be understood.

---

[98] Barchiesi (2002) 109 and Thomas (2011) on *Carm. saec.* 55–6 suggest that *responsa petere* can convey the consultation of a prophetic authority; see *OLD* s.v. *responsum* 2a. Cf. Tityrus' appeal to the divine young man at *Ecl.* 1.44: *hic mihi responsum primus dedit ille petenti*. Prose sources also record that when Augustus established diplomatic relations with nations in the East, foreign ambassadors sought responses from Augustus directly (*R.G.* 31.1; Cass. Dio 54.9.8; Flor. *Epit.* 2.34.61–2; Strabo 15.1.4, 15.1.73).

[99] Putnam (2000) 83 n. 63.

[100] See also Lowrie (2009) 135: 'The poem is unusual...in leading up to the performative accomplishment of its own prayers.'

[101] Note especially that present-tense indicative verbs take over the *Carmen* as soon as Augustus enters the poem at the point where the chorus asks the gods to grant whatever Augustus entreats of them (cf. *impetret*, 51). See further Putnam (2000) 93; Thomas (2011) on *Carm. saec.* 53–60.

DIVINIZATION AND THE INEVITABILITY OF AUGUSTAN ROME 183

Propertius 4.6

Propertius' elegy 4.6 appears soon after the *Carmen Saeculare*, possibly in time for the celebration of the *ludi quinquennales* in 16 BC.[102] The poem presents itself as a thoroughly Callimachean aetiological hymn on the Palatine Temple of Apollo.[103] Through a series of allusions to Callimachus' portrayal of the special relationship between god and monarch in the *Hymn to Apollo* and *Hymn to Delos*, Propertius eulogizes Apollo's role in helping Augustus to secure his victory at Actium.[104] Despite its encomiastic theme, however, the poem is by no means an uncomplicated praise of the *princeps* and his divine patron. As Lowrie points out, Propertius' highly visualized language lends this elegy a 'painterly' quality, which assimilates the poem to a visual artefact like its subject, the Palatine temple, thereby drawing attention to its own artificiality and status as a representation of the regime.[105]

That elegy 4.6 is underpinned by a heighted sensitivity of its relation to the Augustan visual programme also comes across in Propertius' depiction of the battle of Actium, which shows a sustained engagement with Virgil's version of the event in the shield-ekphrasis in *Aeneid* 8. Propertius' description of the moment before the battle emulates that of Virgil's by transforming the twin flames and the Julian star above Augustus' head (cf. *Aen.* 8.680–1) into a triple-flame accompanied by Jupiter's lightning (*astitit Augusti puppim super, et nova flamma* | *luxit in obliquam ter sinuata facem*, '[Apollo] stood above the vessel of Augustus, and a strange flame shone out, bending three times into a zigzag of lightning', 4.6.29–30).[106] The way that the Propertian Apollo addresses his earthly counterpart as 'Augustus, saviour of the world from Alba Longa' (*o Longa mundi servator ab Alba,* | *Auguste,* 4.6.37–8) not only reinforces the version of the Julian genealogy that begins with Ascanius but also evokes the anachronism in Virgil's account of Actium, where the epic poet

---

[102] The *ludi quinquennales* were instituted in honour of the battle of Actium, which were first celebrated in 28 BC, the year of the inauguration of the Palatine temple (Cass. Dio 53.1.4; cf. Hor. *Carm.* 1.31 and Prop. 2.31). See further Günther (2006) 374 and Hutchinson (2006) 2–3 on the poem's date of composition. Cairns (1984) argues that Prop. 4.6 may have been intended for public performance.

[103] Heyworth (1994) 60–6; Coleman (2003); Hutchinson (2006) on 4.6 passim; Petrovic (2008); Miller (2009) 226–34; Acosta-Hughes and Stephens (2012) 257. On the Callimachean tenor of Book 4, see esp. Pillinger (1969); Miller (1982) 371–96; Hutchinson (2006) 11–13.

[104] The poem's dialogue with Callimachus is explicit from the outset (4.6.3–4), where Propertius calls on Callimachus and Philetas to mark the genre of his song (as he did in 3.1.1–4). The elegy's joint hymning of Apollo and Augustus replicates the proximity and special relationship between Ptolemy and Apollo in Callim. *H.* 2.26–7. On the nexus of correspondence between Prop. 4.6.37–42 and Callim. *H.* 4.165–70, see Petrovic (2008) 199–202.

[105] Lowrie (2009) 192.

[106] Camps (1965) ad loc.; Hutchinson (2006) ad loc.; Miller (2009) 86; Pandey (2018) 70–1.

184 POLITICS AND DIVINIZATION IN AUGUSTAN POETRY

also uses the name 'Augustus' even though it did not exist at the time of the battle (cf. *Aen.* 8.678).[107] Indeed, the elegy's main claim—that the Palatine temple was conceived as a victory-monument honouring Apollo's intervention at Actium (*Actius hinc traxit Phoebus monumenta*, 'from this Actian Phoebus derived his monuments', 4.6.67)—accords with the revised Augustan *aetion* for the temple which the Virgilian ekphrasis also promulgates (cf. *Aen.* 8.720–2).[108] The highly intertextual fabric of Propertius' elegy makes it clear that the poem is relying on and interacting with secondary sources, from Virgil's *Aeneid* to Augustan visual culture;[109] and that the poem is highly self-conscious of its status as a latecomer in the representational corpus of the victory at Actium. Indeed, the density and frequency of Propertius' dialogue with prior textual and artistic sources strongly suggest that this elegy is at least as interested in responding to contemporary ideas and representations as asserting its own creative inventiveness.

Approaching the elegy from this perspective, we may gain a different view of the poem's arguably most Virgilian moment, when Propertius dramatizes the Julian star on Aeneas' shield (cf. *patriumque aperitur vertice sidus*, Verg. *Aen.* 8.681) by introducing Julius Caesar as an actual character into the elegy's depiction of the immediate aftermath of the battle (Prop. 4.6.59–60):

> at pater Idalio miratur Caesar ab astro:
> 'sum deus: est nostri sanguinis ista fides.'

But from the star of Venus his father Caesar looks on in wonder: 'I am a god: this victory is proof that you are of my blood.'

Verse 60 has been the subject of intense textual critical scrutiny, but there is no sufficient reason to think that Propertius did not write thus.[110] The hexameter (verse 59) is secure and its meaning comprehensible: Julius Caesar, who is already in heaven, looks down onto Actium. The verb *miratur* (4.6.59), often denoting a mixture of amazement, delight, and admiration (cf. Verg. *Aen.* 1.456, 7.813, 8.870), anticipates a wondrous revelation in the pentameter;[111] and

---

[107] Coleman (2003) 41 sees Augustus' name here as a reference to Apollo's prophetic power. In addition, Apollo's pledge to put his archery in service of Augustus (cf. *tibi militat arcus*, 4.6.39) renders explicit the prefigurative force of the arrowshot in the Apollo–Ascanius episode in *Aeneid* 9.

[108] See also Miller (2009) 227.   [109] Pandey (2018) 71.

[110] This couplet should not be deleted (as suggested by Bernays 2002: 593–8) or obelized: some reference to the winning side seems desirable before *prosequitur* in line 61, which depicts marine deities celebrating the Roman victory. Neither the punishment of the unnamed Cleopatra (4.6.57) nor the wreckage from the battle (4.6.58) would be celebrated in this way.

[111] Richter (1966) 454.

DIVINIZATION AND THE INEVITABILITY OF AUGUSTAN ROME   185

Julius Caesar's words do not disappoint. The positions occupied by *sum* and *est* look ahead to something striking or controversial (cf. Prop. 3.6.20, 4.7.1; Ov. *Her.* 14.4–7),[112] and this turns out to be precisely the case as *sum deus* on this occasion does not introduce an epiphany,[113] but rather emphasizes that Divus Julius suddenly believes in his own divinity as if it had been uncertain even to him until Augustus put the final stamp on it—an irony which Ovid takes even further in the final book of the *Metamorphoses* (15.746–61).[114] While the notion that the victory at Actium reaffirms Julian dynastic supremacy finds its counterpart in the *Aeneid*, Caesar's incongruous cameo in Propertius' poem goes one step further by suggesting, rather unusually, that the greatness—and indeed the realness—of Caesar's divinization is not confirmed until it is authenticated by Augustus. Put differently, Propertius seems to imply that nothing is certain until is proven twice.

This idea has some implications for interpreting the relationship between Propertius 4.6 and Virgil's *Aeneid*. In a recent reading of the elegy, Pandey treats the appearance of Julius Caesar in Propertius' retrospective of Actium as 'a solipsistic *Q.E.D.* stamping a textbook written by the victors'; and she argues that this episode calls attention to the process by which successive representations flatten out complex events by making their outcomes seem fated.[115] I want to build on this observation, but also take it in a different direction. Propertius' elegy is unambiguous about its status as a representational latecomer: it knowingly fashions itself as a poetic account of an already-built monument, and constantly foregrounds Virgil's depiction of Actium as a precursor to its own. Against this backdrop, we might say that Propertius' reformulation of Virgil's Actian narrative allows the elegist to assert himself as the Augustus to Virgil's Caesar—the latecomer who confirms the *Aeneid's* prior representation and authenticates it as 'real'. Just as Augustus verifies as fact Caesar's divine status by his own repetition of conquest, so too does

---

[112] Hutchinson (2006) ad loc.; on the positioning of the verb *esse*, see Adams (1994) 69–76.

[113] Contra Cairns (1984) 167–8. The naval battle is won; the current situation does not call for a divine intervention.

[114] Hutchinson (2006) ad loc. The emendation offered by Richter (1966) 451–65, followed by Fedeli's Teubner edition, should be jettisoned: '*tu deus es: nostri sanguinis ista fides*' misconstrues the dramatic situation even though it seems superficially reasonable to argue that it is Julius Caesar whose divinity underpins that of his adopted son. Butrica (1997) 185–6, on the other hand, makes Apollo the speaker and proposes: *cui deus: 'est vestri sanguinis ista fides.'* This could work, though it raises the question of what the *ista* refers to. In contrast to both Richter and Butrica, Heyworth (2007b) 460–1 opts against substantial emendation, and recommends instead substituting *sanguinis* with *numinis* on the basis that *sanguinis* cannot sufficiently denote divinity in the present context. However, one argument in favour of keeping *sanguinis* would be that *numinis* does not convey as effectively the mischievous insinuation that there is hardly any *sanguis* shared by Julius Caesar and Augustus.

[115] Pandey (2018) 71–2; quotation from p. 71.

186   POLITICS AND DIVINIZATION IN AUGUSTAN POETRY

Propertius—by reformulating and re-presenting Virgil's narrative—confirm the *Aeneid*'s account of Actium as historical reality once and for all.

Yet, as much as this elegy makes a claim for its authenticating force and reinforces the status of Virgil's epic as *the* poetic expression of Augustan supremacy, it is not by any means an undiscerning iteration of the regime's self-fashioning. In fact, Propertius' elegy subtly renders problematic the notion of ever-greater Julian achievement through light-hearted metaliterary play. The elegy's final scene, which depicts a symposium of poets, shifts the reader's attention to Propertius' interest in writing panegyric on his own terms.[116] The imperial conquests sung by jingoistic poets gathered at the party (4.6.77–84) are set in contrast with the aetiological victory-hymn which Propertius had just composed and deemed sufficient (*bella satis cecini*, 'I have sung enough of wars', 4.6.69). The elegist is in their company, but offers no bellicose composition of his own: the internal dynamic of this scene, as Luke Roman rightly observes, invites wider reflections on how Propertius' poetry sits with 'the communal project of Augustan praise'.[117] Moreover, as Propertius recounts his fellow poets' celebration of the recent Parthian victory, the elegist hints at the problem of extending the logic of 'nothing is certain until proven twice'. The songs of the patriotic symposiasts look confidently ahead to the day when Gaius and Lucius—the recently adopted sons of Augustus—undertake a military campaign against the Parthians: *sive aequus pharetris Augustus parcet Eois,* | *differat in pueros ista tropaea suos* ('if favourable Augustus spares the archers of the East, let him postpone those trophies for his boys', 4.6.81–2). However, earlier in his elegy, Propertius shows that Julius Caesar did not have his divine status confirmed until his adopted son, Augustus, had put a conclusion to the war which stretched as far back as Caesar's own lifetime. If Julius Caesar's greatness and divinization needed the authentication of Augustus, then Augustus too would need to wait for his adopted sons to finish his battles for him and confirm his greatness and divinity once and for all, which, as history would have it, they never do. By unpicking in this way the logic of a twice-proved divinization, Propertius' elegy, not unlike Virgil's *Aeneid*, trains the reader's gaze on the implausibility of Augustus' self-presentation as the telos of Roman hegemony.

---

[116] Hutchinson (2006) on 4.6.76; Petrovic (2008) 205–6; Roman (2014) 198–200.
[117] Roman (2014) 200.

Epilogue
To Divinity and Beyond

The Politics of Divinizing Poetics

This study has shown that the motif of Augustus' divinization in the poems of Virgil, Horace and Propertius operates as a means for the poets to work out and critique the relationship between the individual and the state, security and freedom, art and authority during Rome's transition from Republic to Principate. Since this motif is used by the poets to make sense of the shifting constitutional direction of Rome, examine (their implication in) the production of political myths, and articulate the irrepressible and yet indispensable nature of Augustan power, this theme is therefore far more than a schematic trope or a figurative expression of ideological commitment. This poetic discourse, I would conclude, has the semantic range and analytical properties of a language of political science. In the hands of the 'first-generation' Augustan poets, the issue of Augustus' divinity thus becomes a tool for exploring concepts and urgent questions that have come to the fore under the Principate.

While poetic interests in Augustus' divinization cannot be viewed in isolation from the strategies and expressions adopted by Augustus (and those around him) in official policies, this book has sought to suggest that the poets engaged with this subject imaginatively, and variously used it as a point of entry to discussing issues pertaining to the losses and gains of the individual, as well as the tensions and complicities between art and power, amid Rome's collapse and reconstitution under Augustus. The relationship between a divinized benefactor and his beneficiaries not only evolved into a poetic symbol of the dynamic between citizens and *princeps* after the civil war but also became a *locus renovandus* of the poets' attempts to figure out what *libertas* meant in the new political age and at what cost this *libertas* was obtained. The realization that the new Caesar occupied the summit of the Roman world following Actium, and that he was soon to possess even greater, unparalleled authority, provided the backdrop for urgent reflections on the velocity at which Rome was hurtling towards an unknown political territory and what

---

Politics and Divinization in Augustan Poetry. Bobby Xinyue, Oxford University Press. © Bobby Xinyue 2022.
DOI: 10.1093/oso/9780192855978.003.0006

that would mean for poetry and speech. By framing Augustus' divinization as the embodiment of the culmination of Roman *imperium*, Horace's first collection of the *Odes* underlined the extent to which Augustan power rested on the glorification and fabrication of foreign conquest, thus foregrounding the artistic, as well as ideological, negotiations involved in the poet's self-reinvention as the Augustan *vates*. In the *Aeneid*, the predestiny of Augustus' divinization highlighted by the poem's various prophetic speeches and artefacts not only drew attention to the teleological thinking and self-mythologizing strategies underpinning the regime's ideological and visual programme but also allowed Virgil to underline that his own epic, and the poetic art in general, was entangled in the rewriting of the past. In sum, the poetic discourse on Augustus' divinity was concerned with far more than just how Augustus managed his public image and controlled his worship: it cut to the core of the ways in which the Augustan Principate has indelibly changed the dynamics between citizen and political system, culture and authority.

In my analysis, the Augustan poets played a key part in ushering in political change, but they also found ways of gesturing at how the new regime has altered not only the practice of their art but also the fundamental principles and power dynamics on which Rome rested. As much as their rhetoric on the divinity of a powerful ruler had the potential to sanctify autocratic power and naturalize radical societal transformation, the poets' constant (and often anxious) reflections on where they stood in relation to the god-man, how they should approach Caesar's godlike authority, and whether there were any boundaries to Augustus' divine jurisdiction, pointedly drew the readers' attention to the extent to which their *libertas* as citizen and artist was being redefined and compromised under the Principate. Moreover, by framing Augustan power as salvific on the one hand and disempowering on the other, and by presenting the *princeps* as a 'god manifest' whose status both stabilized and disrupted Rome's political order, the poets highlighted the paradoxes of the new regime, hinting at the troubling indispensability of autocratic power for the peace and security of the state. Through their discussions of Augustus' divinity, the poets thus carved out a space for themselves to exercise limited freedom of political thought, and to dissect the nature and implications of Rome's reconstitution under Augustus.

To this extent, this study ultimately traces poetry's creative and contestatory reappropriation of a language of power. As we saw in the Introduction with the passages of Suetonius, Augustus selectively engaged in or rejected the discourse of divinization in order to maintain political control on the one hand, and to curate a particular narrative of his (lack of desire to) rule on the

EPILOGUE: TO DIVINITY AND BEYOND 189

other. This books tells of how this discourse was seized upon by the poets, who likewise deployed it carefully, but turned it into a means through which to work out and interrogate the regime's self-fashioning. On one level, this act of poetic reappropriation subtly flashes literature's ability to intercept or 'read' the operations of an important instrument of mass persuasion for the Augustan regime. On another level, poetry's inventive, disruptive uses of divinizing language constitute an attempt to regain control of the use of that language from Augustus. By prising open and recalibrating divinizing language in this way, poetry reasserts the plurality of meanings in political discourse, and demonstrates that it is ultimately impossible for a regime to define the semantic range of figurative speech.

Towards the Divinization of Augustus

This book has focused mostly on the period stretching from the triumviral years to the end of approximately the first decade of Augustus' rule, a temporal span of roughly a quarter of a century. During this period, the poets' discussions of Augustus' divinity convey the experience of being swept up in a time of uncertainty and coming to terms with a new political reality. As the Principate gradually establishes itself, however, the political uncertainty facing the poets is not so immediate or pressing any more, but lies in the distance: specifically, the issue of what will happen to Rome when Augustus eventually has to confront his mortality. He is, after all, *not* divine. This is a scenario which Tacitus raises with the benefit of hindsight (Tac. *Ann.* 1.4):

> igitur verso civitatis statu nihil usquam prisci et integri moris: omnes exuta aequalitate iussa principis aspectare, nulla in praesens formidine, *dum Augustus aetate validus* seque et domum et pacem sustentavit.
>
> Thus, as the status of the city was overturned, nothing remained of the ancient and unspoilt Roman character: stripped of equality, all waited on the orders of the *princeps*—with no fear for the present, *so long as Augustus, in the vigour of his prime*, upheld himself, his house, and peace.

The *dum*-clause hints at the worry that as Augustus ages—*aetate* here literally means 'in respect to his age'—he may not be able to exert his control as effectively as when he was younger. In the next sentence, this exact situation arises. Tacitus recounts that when Augustus 'was in his advancing years and was wearied with his sickly body' (*postquam provecta iam senectus aegro et corpore*

190 POLITICS AND DIVINIZATION IN AUGUSTAN POETRY

fatigabatur), discontent grew and the prospect of political unrest resurfaced (*aderatque finis et spes novae, pauci bona libertatis in cassum disserere, plures bellum pavescere, alii cupere,* 'the end was coming and so was the hope for a new beginning: a few idly discussed the blessings of freedom, more grew afraid of war, others desired it'). By foregrounding twice the importance of Augustus' health to Roman stability, Tacitus' sweeping account of the first Principate points to the idea that the strength of the Augustan Age was in large part reliant on the strength of Augustus' age (cf. *aetate validus*). I want to suggest below—with the hope of encouraging further investigation—that not only did the Augustan poets make similar observations at the time, but the anticipation of the inevitable end of Augustus' reign became an important element of poetry's discussion of Augustus' divinity, especially in Horace's final book of the *Odes*. By concluding this study with a brief examination of a poetic collection that is very much concerned with the perpetuation of the Augustan Principate—one that reflects a completely different political mood compared to the poetry of the 20s, I wish to drive home the point that poetry's discourse on Augustus' divinity continues to evolve and synchronize itself with the shift of political power.

The *aetas* of Augustus

The publication of *Odes* 4 in 13 BC coincides with Augustus' return to Rome after a three-year absence, during which he campaigned with his stepsons Drusus and Tiberius.[1] In that year, both Horace and Augustus are in their fifties; and the coming of age of a new generation of aristocrats—Paulus Fabius Maximus (4.1), Iullus Antonius (4.2), and of course the Nerones brothers (4.4; 4.14)—only heightens the fact that time is not on Horace's or Augustus' side. Indeed, *Odes* 4 opens with the poet confessing that he is no longer the young man he once was (4.1.1–7); and the entire collection is held together by Horace's constant reflections on his career as lover and lyricist (4.2.27–32; 4.3; 4.6.41–4; 4.11.31–6). The appearance of Virgil in *Ode* 4.12, who had already been dead for six years by the time *Odes* 4 appeared, only further underscores the loss and human fragility among Horace's contemporaries.

While *Odes* 4 is explicit about the poet's ageing, its approach is a lot subtler when it comes to Augustus. At *Ode* 4.14.34–40, for example, Horace notes

---

[1] Augustus launched an operation against the Sygambri in 16 BC in response to Lollius' defeat in Gaul, and did not return until 13 BC. Three years is a long time for someone whose health is notoriously poor, especially during military campaigns (cf. Suet. *Aug.* 8, 13, 28, 59, 81, 91; Cass. Dio 53.25–8).

EPILOGUE: TO DIVINITY AND BEYOND   191

that the day marking the recent victory of Drusus and Tiberius against the Alpine tribes falls precisely on the fifteenth anniversary of the annexation of Alexandria (1 August 30 BC).[2] The presentation of such a political timeline allows Horace to reframe the irretrievable passage of time for Augustus as a 'renewal of Roman energy' by the victorious Nerones.[3] *Ode* 4.4, an apparent companion piece to 4.14,[4] alludes to the fact that Augustus has entered a new stage in life by depicting him as the *paterfamilias* of an auspicious *domus* (*faustis...penetralibus*, 4.4.26; *Augusti paternus...animus*, 4.4.27–8), while referring to Drusus as the *iuvenis* of this household (4.4.24).[5] By transferring onto Drusus an appellation closely associated with Augustus in the triumviral period and the early 20s BC (cf. Hor. *Carm.* 1.2.41; *Sat.* 2.5.62; Verg. *Ecl.* 1.42; *G.* 1.500), Horace implies that a new rank of imperial *iuvenes* would soon succeed the *princeps* as Rome's future leaders. On the other hand, the fatherly image of Augustus presiding over the upbringing of his children implies that the imperial *domus*, however 'auspicious' (cf. *faustis*) it may be, is not immune to the displacement of one generation by the next.

The sense that Augustus' reign is finite is conveyed by the final poem of the collection, in which Horace looks back on the achievements of 'your age, Caesar' (*tua, Caesar, aetas*, 4.15.4). In his analysis of this conspicuous expression, Breed recalls the story told by Suetonius that following Augustus' death there was a senatorial proposal to recognize the period of Augustus' mortal life officially as the *saeculum Augustum* (Suet. *Aug.* 100.3). Taking this as an interpretive cue, Breed goes on to suggest that since *aetas* (like *saeculum*) necessarily implies a discrete period of time, its identification in this Horatian ode with the person of Augustus thus obliquely looks ahead to the inevitable end of both the reign and the life of the *princeps*.[6] This 'symbiotic intrication of the Augustan Age with Augustus' age', as Mitchell well puts it,[7] has an embryonic precedent in *Eclogue* 4. Virgil's poem synchronizes the arrival of the 'final age' of the Sibylline prophecy (*ultima...aetas, Ecl.* 4.4) with the growth of the miraculous child from infancy (*nascenti puero, Ecl.* 4.8) to manhood (*ubi iam firmata virum te fecerit aetas*, 'when the strength of age has made you a man', *Ecl.* 4.37). The overlapping of secular *aetas* with biological *aetas* in Virgil's poem sets in motion a way of perceiving worldly, epochal

---

[2] Note also the 'commemorative' coin series *RIC* I[2] 170–3, showing either Apollo with the legend ACT or Diana with SICIL·, which recall the victories at Actium and Naulochus respectively.

[3] Mitchell (2010) 73.   [4] Thomas (2011) 245.

[5] On the religious connotation of *faustis...penetralibus*, see Putnam (1986) 90; Thomas (2011) ad loc.

[6] Breed (2004) 247. Cooley (2019) argues that there was an increasing recognition among Romans that the period in which they lived was defined by Augustus' personal authority.

[7] Mitchell (2010) 44.

192 POLITICS AND DIVINIZATION IN AUGUSTAN POETRY

transformation through the lens of a powerful individual's life and achievements. But when that age-defining individual turns out not to be age-defying, as in the case of Augustus, Horace's poetic entwining of political era and human lifespan—however eulogistically articulated—rather calls attention to the eventuality that the prosperity Rome is experiencing right now would not last forever.

Pausing Augustan Time

As a counterpoise to the underlying anxieties about ageing, finality, and the passing of time, we find throughout *Odes* 4 a desire for timelessness and an urge to perpetuate the present.[8] This wish to defy temporal constraints is partly reflected in Horace's sustained interest in the idea of overcoming mortality. For example, *Odes* 4.8 and 4.9 emphatically assert poetry as the supreme artistic form that enables its subjects to live on after death.[9] By claiming that heroes and great leaders of the past—including Romulus, Hercules, the Dioscuri, Bacchus, and Homeric warriors—would not have survived in people's memories without poetry (4.8.22–34; 4.9.25–8), Horace implicitly makes Augustus' immortality dependent on his poetry, and asserts the true eternity of his art.[10]

Another way in which the poet's hope for everlastingness manifests itself is through the depiction of the Augustan present as the pinnacle of Rome's good fortunes. We can observe this most clearly in *Ode* 4.2, when Horace advises the young aristocrat and up-and-coming poet, Iullus Antonius, on how to compose an encomium for when Augustus returns from his campaign against the Sygambri (4.2.33–44):

> concines maiore poeta plectro
> Caesarem, quandoque trahet feroces
> per sacrum clivum merita decorus   35

---

[8] See also Lowrie (1997) 49: 'Horatian lyric is equally concerned with a transient and an eternal *here and now*, with the contemporary *now* of history and the timelessness granted by poetry.' Original emphasis.

[9] Note especially the contrast Horace draws between poetry (*carminibus*, 4.8.11) and the plastic art (*incisa notis marmora publicis*, 'marble engraved with public letters', 4.8.13). Harrison (1990) 38 argues that *incisa...marmora* evokes the inscribed epitaphs of the statues in the Forum Augustum.

[10] For further discussions of 4.8.22–34, see Barchiesi (1996) 40; Kovacs (2009) 24; Thomas (2011) 192–6. On the unity of 4.8 and 4.9, see esp. Putnam (1986) 159–60; Barchiesi (1996) 12; Johnson (2004) 93.

EPILOGUE: TO DIVINITY AND BEYOND   193

> fronde Sygambros,
> quo nihil maius meliusve terris
> fata donavere bonique divi
> nec dabunt, quamvis redeant in aurum
>   tempora priscum.   40
> concines laetosque dies et Vrbis
> publicum ludum super impetrato
> fortis Augusti reditu forumque
>   litibus orbum.

You, a poet of grander plectrum, will celebrate Caesar when he, decorated with a well-earned wreath, drags the fierce Sygambri up the Sacred Hill. Nothing greater or better than him have the Fates and the benevolent gods given to the world, nor ever will, even if the ages return to their ancient gold. You will celebrate the joyful days and the City's public games upon the granted return of brave Augustus; you will sing of the Forum bereft of lawsuits.

These three stanzas gradually build up to a picture of utopian timelessness. The temporal specificity of the anticipated *triumphus* (4.2.34–6) makes way for a more general description of a joyful era (37–44). During this transition, the Augustan present is shown to be the culmination of human time: not only is Augustus' greatness unable to be matched by anything before or after (37–9), but even if the fantastical Golden Age were to return (39–40), it would not be as good as now.[11] The desire for the present Augustan moment to perpetuate is felt most strongly in the final stanza. Here the mention of the postponement of legal business (43–4), set against the backdrop of an entire city enjoying days off (41–2), underscores the suspension of time, as well as the overall utopian quality of this description.

The desire for timelessness in this passage becomes even stronger when we situate it within a wider literary and cultural context. The poet's eager anticipation for the *triumphus*, and the energizing effect it is envisaged to have on the populace, evoke not only the Virgilian triple triumph in *Aeneid* 8 (cf. *laetitia ludisque viae plausuque fremebant*, 'the streets were roaring with joy, festivities, and applause', Verg. *Aen.* 8.717) but also Horace's own depiction of Augustus' victorious return from Spain in *Ode* 3.14 (cf. *hic dies vere mihi festus*, 'this day [is] truly festive for me', *Carm.* 3.14.13). In both of these passages, it is strongly

---

[11] Others read verses 39–40 differently. Zanker (2010) 508–9 thinks that this sentence expressly questions whether the Golden Age would return. Heyworth (2016) 256 regards this claim by Horace as 'irrational flattery' and thus undermines its own panegyrical force.

194   POLITICS AND DIVINIZATION IN AUGUSTAN POETRY

implied that the appearance of the *princeps* in Rome is similar to a divine epiphany: Virgil effectively identifies Augustus with Apollo (cf. *ipse sedens niveo candentis limine Phoebi*, 'he himself seated at the snowy-white threshold of gleaming Apollo', *Aen.* 8.720), while Horace compares Augustus to Hercules (cf. *Herculis ritu*, 'in the manner of Hercules', *Carm.* 3.14.1). Here in *Ode* 4.2, it has been suggested by Hardie that Augustus comes across as a *praesens deus* and is assimilated to Dionysus, since the poem exhibits dithyrambic features.[12] While it is doubtful—to this reader at least—that Augustus' image here evokes Dionysus specifically, Hardie's observation that this scene exudes the atmosphere of a citizen body excitedly awaiting a divine epiphany is accurate, especially as *impetratro* in verse 42 has the connotation of a successful appeal to a divine force.[13] Thus, not only is the forthcoming triumphal procession made to resemble past versions, the intertextuality of Horace's divinizing language also likens Augustus to a god who repeatedly visits upon Rome and brings about joy again and again. As Horace speaks about a future event as if it were a repeat of the glory days, we should remind of ourselves that these stanzas are supposed to be literary advice for a younger poet from the next generation. In other words, Horace is meant to inspire new poetic material; but instead we find him slipping into nostalgia. Such repetition and nostalgia are the markers of a desire to stall change, to freeze and savour a moment in time.[14] Away from poetry, we find a similar attempt to pause the progression of time in contemporary coinage. The series of *denarii* and *aurei* minted at Lugdunum commemorating the victories of Drusus and Tiberius show Augustus looking unusually youthful; and his titulature on these coins includes for the first time in more than a decade the words 'Divi filius'.[15] The visual language of Augustus' agelessness on these coins thus forms part of a wider discourse on the perpetuation of Roman power. In this way, poet and moneyers mirror each other in their attempt to defy the inevitable decay of the *aetas* of Augustus, as they each try to make the transient present permanent.

---

[12] Hardie (2015) 281; note especially the dramatization of the impassioned singing of 'io Triumphe' two stanzas later (4.2.49–52). See also Thomas (2011) on 4.2.49–50.

[13] Fedeli and Ciccarelli (2008) ad loc. I would add that *impetrato* looks back to the *boni divi* of line 38 who gave Augustus to the world, and characterizes Augustus' *reditus* as the manifestation of divine benefaction.

[14] *Odes* 4 opens with Horace displaying his sensitivity to pause, recurrence, and the persistence of the past: *Intermissa, Venus, diu | rursus bella moves?* ('Paused for a long time, are you, Venus, starting your wars again?', 4.1.1–2).

[15] See *RIC* I[2] 164 = *BMCRE* I (Gaul), 443–8. The principal motif of the series is the handover of the palm of victory to Augustus by a pair of military figures, often identified as the Nerones brothers, or by a single military figure (see *BMCRE* I [Gaul], 449), probably Drusus. See further Zanker (1988) 225–6.

EPILOGUE: TO DIVINITY AND BEYOND   195

The Divinity of Augustus in *Ode* 4.5

Odes 4 is thus underpinned by tensions between the unstoppable passage of time and the desire for timelessness, between absence and presence, finality and perpetuity. In its eulogization of Augustus' reign, this poetic collection is constantly grappling with the paradox that Rome's hope for everlasting stability and prosperity is pinned to something so transient as the mortal body of its *princeps*. These ideas permeate and intensify in *Ode* 4.5, in which Horace, speaking as if on behalf of the Roman people, asks Augustus to return home quickly from his campaign in Gaul and Spain. This poem has been of great interest to scholars, mainly because it contains an extended description of the worship of Augustus taking place in Italy (cf. 4.5.31–6). Much critical effort has also been applied to understanding the poem's genre and performance context; subsequently, the material on Augustus' divinity has largely been approached from the angle of how it maps onto the poem's overall generic identity.[16] Without disregarding these earlier studies, I wish to bring out a different aspect of *Ode* 4.5's concern with Augustus' divinity. My reading will show that the poem's appeal to Augustus, while of course conveying a nation's yearning for its leader, also carries a whiff of anxiety about a future without the *princeps* and the stability he embodies. Set within this emotionally fraught context, Horace's description of the ritual activities of the cult of Augustus— with its heavy emphasis on longevity and continuity—subtly captures the growing realization of the transience of Augustus' reign and the temporariness of entrusting everything to the mortal powers of one man.

Set in a dramatic period prior to Augustus' return in 13 BC, the sense of anxiety in *Ode* 4.5 is already simmering in its opening two verses: *Divis orte bonis, optume Romulae | custos gentis, abes iam nimium diu* ('Descendant of the kindly gods, best guardian of Romulus' race, you have already been away too long', 4.5.1–2). Critics have been quick to detect the ways in which these lines exhibit the features of a ὕμνος κλητικός ('hymn of invocation').[17] But the immense interest in the poem's generic properties takes attention away from the fact that this opening contains a stark contrast between Augustus' defining attribute as the 'guardian' of the Roman people (*custos*, 4.5.2) and his

---

[16] Du Quesnay (1995); Kamptner (2001); Johnson (2004) 116–18. The once-popular view that this ode was written to be performed does not accord with the current understanding of Horatian lyric as a simulacrum of performance; see Lowrie (2009) 90–4.

[17] Du Quesnay (1995) 151; Kamptner (2001) 286–7; Johnson (2004) 118.

196   POLITICS AND DIVINIZATION IN AUGUSTAN POETRY

prolonged absence from them (*abes*, 4.5.2).[18] The word *nimium* (4.5.2) is key here: it suggests that the period of Augustus' absence has far exceeded the limit of comfort. The image of a divine-born guardian of Rome, who is missed badly by the people, further recalls Ennius' Romulus and the desire felt by the Romans when their king had vanished (Enn. *Ann.* 105–9 Sk.).[19] And this allusion is confirmed when, in the poem's next stanza (4.5.5–8), Horace's eulogy of Augustus as the light for his people evokes (and outdoes) Ennius' praise of Romulus as one who has led the Romans to the shore of light (cf. *tu produxisti nos intra luminis oras*, Enn. *Ann.* 109 Sk.).[20] The implied comparison of Augustus with the deified founder of Rome adds to the divine aura of the *princeps*. But on the other hand, it also brings into focus the parallel between Augustus' prolonged absence and Romulus' disappearance—the latter (as I discussed in the Introduction) has been explained as the king having fallen in harm's way. Through this intertext, the opening of *Ode* 4.5 already hints at the possibility that Augustus' absence may turn out to be permanent.

The poem's next two stanzas (4.5.9–16) then compare Rome's anticipation for Augustus' return (*quaerit patria Caesarem*, 'our country looks out for Caesar', 4.5.16) to a mother waiting for the homecoming of her son, who is described as a *iuvenis* (4.5.9). The syntactically parallel *mater iuvenem* (4.5.9) and *patria Caesarem* (4.5.16) invite direct identification of the *iuvenis* with *Caesar*, thus evoking Augustus' poetic image during a particularly volatile period of Roman history.[21] In these previous instances of Augustus being identified as a *iuvenis*, his presence among the people is especially emphasized by the poet. In *Eclogue* 1, the *iuvenis* is being treated as a divine benefactor by Tityrus because he is present to help when the other gods are nowhere to be found (cf. *Ecl.* 1.41–2). At *Georgics* 1.498–501, Virgil complains that the gods begrudge the presence of the *iuvenis* on earth, and wish to have him in heaven instead. In *Odes* 1.2, Horace himself leads the call for the *iuvenis* to prolong his stay among the Romans in order to restore and grow Roman power (cf. 1.2.45–6). We can make two observations from these earlier passages: firstly, the physical presence of the *iuvenis* brings about stability,

---

[18] Augustus is again *custos* in 4.15.17. The motif of ruler-as-guardian also appears in Theoc. *Id.* 17.104–5, ὧι ἐπίπαγχυ μέλει πατρώια πάντα φυλάσσειν | οἵ ἀγαθῶι βασιλῆι. For *custos* used of tutelary deities, cf. *Carm.* 1.12.49 (Jupiter); 1.28.29 (Neptune); 2.17.30 (Faunus); 3.22.1 (Diana); *Sat.* 2.6.15 (Mercury); *Epist.* 2.1.255 (Janus); *Ars P.* 239 (Silenus).

[19] Skutsch (1985) 258; Du Quesnay (1995) 162–4.

[20] Putnam (1986) 105 and Kamptner (2001) 287 argue that Horace is trying to outdo Ennius in his encomium by presenting Augustus as light itself. Contra Johnson (2004) 127–8, who finds Horace's panegyric rather muted compared to Ennius'.

[21] Johnson (2004) 116. On the familial and communal inclusiveness conveyed by the equation of *mater* with *patria*, see Khan (2000) 550–1.

EPILOGUE: TO DIVINITY AND BEYOND   197

and secondly, the time that the *iuvenis* spends with his people is contingent and beyond their control. Applying these ideas to *Ode* 4.5, Horace's simile becomes more equivocal than it appears. While the comparison of Augustus to a *iuvenis* recalls and underscores his importance to the security and stability at home, it also highlights the idea that the Romans ultimately have very little say on how long their *iuvenis*-turned-*princeps* will stay with them.

The absence of Augustus and the anxiety arising from it become more pronounced in the poem's next three stanzas, which envisage what life will be like once Augustus returns (4.5.17–28). Here the images of abundance, prosperity, and Roman *imperium* not only evoke the picture of *pax Augusta* at verses 49–60 of the *Carmen Saeculare*[22] but also find visual parallels on the Ara Pacis, whose construction began in the same year as the publication of *Odes* 4.[23] However, while Augustus was present at the performance of the *Carmen Saeculare*,[24] and will certainly appear on the upper frieze of the Ara Pacis,[25] here in *Ode* 4.5 Horace deftly draws attention to the fact that at this moment in time Augustus is absent and susceptible to mortal danger (4.5.25–8):

> quis Parthum paveat, quis gelidum Scythen   25
> quis Germania quos horrida parturit
> fetus incolumi Caesare? quis ferae
>   bellum curet Hiberiae?

Who would fear the Parthian, who the frozen Scythian, who the dreaded offspring Germany breeds, as long as Caesar is safe? Who would worry about war in savage Spain?

Quite rightly, Lowrie zeroes in on the loaded phrase *incolumi Caesare* ('as long as Caesar is safe', 4.5.27) and interprets its usage here as a development on the theme of 'group safety embodied in the leader', which originates with Cicero and is expanded upon by Virgil in his Orientalist description of the bee-community in *Georgics* 4 (cf. *rege incolumi*, 'as long as their king is safe',

---

[22] Miller (2009) 289. Currie (1996) 79 connects the 'listing' effect of 4.5.17–24 to epigraphic formulae; see also Johnson (2004) 121.

[23] Du Quesnay (1995) 165. On the imagery of abundance and Golden Age prosperity on the Ara Pacis, see Castriota (1995) 13–14, 124–44; Cornwell (2017) 167–8. On the connection between Augustus' *reditus* in 13 BC and the Ara Pacis, see Lange (2015) 141–2; Cornwell (2017) 156–9.

[24] See discussion in the previous chapter.

[25] On the iconography of the Ara Pacis frieze, see esp. Momigliano (1942b); Moretti (1948); Ryberg (1949); Weinstock (1960); Kleiner (1978); Holloway (1984); Zanker (1988) 121–3; Billows (1993); Rehak (2001); Cornwell (2017) 178–81.

198 POLITICS AND DIVINIZATION IN AUGUSTAN POETRY

G. 4.212).[26] One of the key points of Lowrie's study is that Virgil's projection of this monarchic mentality onto others—whether bees or the Orient—'both reveals and holds at a distance Roman discomfort with the direction politics was taking as a result of civil war'.[27] But here in *Ode* 4.5, Horace's deployment of this motif establishes this mentality as a Roman phenomenon. Moreover, the context in which it is used suggests that this motif is now associated with the security of Rome in wars against foreign enemies;[28] in other words, the stakes attached to Augustus' safety and welfare is much higher. As Horace implies that Roman power itself may be under threat if Caesar is not safe and sound, *Ode* 4.5 not only underlines the extent to which Rome has embraced monarchic rule but also hints at the problem of putting the hopes and fears of an entire nation in one man.

By recognizing that *Ode* 4.5 is more emotionally and politically fraught than it initially appears, it becomes more apparent that Horace's hymnic appeal subtly communicates an acute awareness of Augustus' mortality and a concern for Rome's future in the (eventual) absence of the *princeps*. Set against this backdrop, Horace's closing description of the worship of Augustus takes on a greater significance both in terms of what it adds to the poem, and in terms of its broader political symbolism (4.5.29–40):

> condit quisque diem collibus in suis
> et vitem viduas ducit ad arbores;   30
> hinc ad vina redit laetus et alteris
>   te mensis adhibet deum.
> te multa prece, te prosequitur mero
> defuso pateris, et Laribus tuum
> miscet numen, uti Graecia Castoris   35
>   et magni memor Herculis.
> 'longas o utinam, dux bone, ferias
> praestes Hesperiae' dicimus integro
> sicci mane die, dicimus uvidi,
>   cum sol Oceano subest.   40

Each man spends the day among his own hills and leads the vine to the widowed trees; then, he returns happily to his wine and requests you as a god at the second course. He honours you with many a prayer, pouring libation from the dish, and combines your worship with that of the household gods,

---

[26] Lowrie (2015) 333.   [27] Lowrie (2015) 323.   [28] Lowrie (2015) 334.

EPILOGUE: TO DIVINITY AND BEYOND   199

as Greece does when remembering Castor and mighty Hercules. 'May you bring long holidays to Italy, blessed leader!'—This is what we say early in the morning when we are sober and the whole day is ahead us; this is what we say when we are drunk and the sun is beneath the Ocean.

These three stanzas have been understood as an invitation for Augustus to come home, with the poet depicting how the country is now ready to receive and honour its leader.[29] But Horace has more than just the present political moment in mind. As critics have noted, these stanzas evoke *Eclogue* 9's blissful image of shepherds concluding their day with song (cf. *Ecl.* 9.51–2), as well as the pastoral religiosity of *Eclogue* 1.[30] The Virgilian texture of this passage intensifies its idyllic quality, adding force to the poem's diminishing historical and geopolitical specificity as it culminates in an image of ritual activity being repeated in an idealized rustic world that seems far removed from contemporary reality (cf. 4.5.39–40). By applying this 'Virgilian filter' to his representation, Horace conjures up a mirage of the Roman world that has its own temporal rhythm and is unaffected by unpredictability, one in which Augustus is always 'present' at a pious request (cf. 4.5.31–2) and lives on everlastingly with every repetition of ritual performance (cf. 4.5.37–40). Horace's vision of uninterrupted longevity and timelessness emblematizes the wish for something transient to be eternal. Uncircumscribed by the temporal limitations placed on a ruler's reign, this description of the worship of Augustus is a symbolic image of holding onto unreality.

Beyond Divinization

The interpretation offered above is conceived intentionally to contrast with how these Horatian stanzas have usually been discussed in scholarship. Previous examinations of this passage have tended to focus on two questions. Firstly, is the libation described by Horace performed to Augustus or to the *genius* of Augustus? And secondly, where should we situate this passage in the historical development of the cult of Rome's first emperor? For what is worth, my position on these two questions are as follows.

The libation depicted in verses 33–4 clearly relates to the post-Actian senatorial decree (30 BC) which asked prayer and libation be offered to Augustus at

[29] Du Quesnay (1995) 175, 182.
[30] On these Virgilian resonances, see Putnam (1986) 110–11; Du Quesnay (1995) 173–4; Hunter (2006) 126. For allusions to the *Georgics*, see Thomas (2011) on 4.5.29–32 and 31.

200   POLITICS AND DIVINIZATION IN AUGUSTAN POETRY

all banquets, public and private.[31] All surviving evidence points to the libation being poured to Augustus himself, not the *genius* of Augustus.[32] Ovid (*Fast.* 2.635–8) and Petronius (*Sat.* 60) later also mention this libation: their texts again show that the libation was poured to Augustus himself.[33] The sole indication of a libation being performed to the *genius* of Augustus was a wall painting from Pompeii, which has not survived. No photograph or other reproduction of the fresco exists: all we possess is a description of it by Boyce from 1937 and an interpretation of the fresco image by Mau from more than a century ago.[34] Therefore, as Gradel rightly argues, the works of Boyce and Mau cannot be used as a reliable source to identify this passage of Horace as depicting the worship of the *genius* of Augustus.[35] Some, however, have suggested that Horace's words, *Laribus tuum | miscet numen* (4.5.34–5), encourage the reader to interpret this scene as a prefiguration of the joint cult of the *genius Augusti* and the Lares Compitales, introduced apparently in 12 BC (one year after the publication of the *Odes* 4).[36] This reading encounters two difficulties: firstly, it requires *tuum numen* to mean *genius Augusti*;[37] and secondly, it is by no means clear that a cult of the *genius Augusti* existed in Rome during Augustus' lifetime.[38] In fact, when Horace speaks about the worship of Augustus in *Epistles* 2.1, which is usually dated to 12 BC,[39] the poet again refers to the emperor's *numen* and does not relate it in any way to the Lares: *praesenti tibi maturos largimur honores | iurandasque tuum per numen ponimus aras* ('we load you with timely honours while [you are] here [with us],

---

[31] Fraenkel (1957) 446–7; Fishwick (1991) I, 375; Du Quesnay (1995) 175; Gradel (2002) 207; Flower (2017) 300–1. Thomas (2011) on 4.5.31–6 even observes verbal similarities between Horace's poetic account and the reported language of the decree in Cass. Dio 51.19.7.

[32] Gradel (2002) 77–81; Flower (2017) 299–307. Taylor (1931) 216–17 was the first to argue for the *genius*, claiming that word itself was 'suppressed' by Horace. Other proponents of this theory include Fishwick (1991) I, 375 n.2 and Lott (2014) 10.

[33] See Robinson (2011) on Ov. *Fast.* 2.633–8; Smith (1975) on Petr. *Sat.* 60.7; with further discussions by Gradel (2002) 208–9 and Flower (2017) 307.

[34] Boyce (1937) no. 466; Mau (1908) 278. Mau's discussion was cited by Fishwick (1991) I, 376 in support of his *genius* theory.

[35] Gradel (2002) 209–12.

[36] La Penna (1963) 119; Fishwick (1991) I, 375–6; Johnson (2004) 116; Fedeli and Ciccarelli (2008) 262, 288–90.

[37] Fishwick (1991) initially insists that 'the emperor's *Genius* can perfectly well be called *numen*' (I, 377); but later (I, 386) concedes that the *numen* of Augustus, unlike his *genius*, is 'a divine property (one might almost say *the* divine property) immanent within him.' Original emphasis.

[38] See esp. Flower (2017) 299–310. A cult of Augustus' *genius* during the emperor's lifetime was first posited by Taylor (1931) 184–94; and followed by Galinsky (1996) 301, Tarpin (2002) 137–64, Letta (2003), and Rosso (2015), among others. Unusually, Gradel (2002) 116–30, 162–97 rejects the practice of pouring a libation to Augustus' *genius*, but accepts a *genius* cult at the *compita* in Rome.

[39] On the date of *Epist.* 2.1, see Rudd (1989) 1.

EPILOGUE: TO DIVINITY AND BEYOND   201

and set up altars to swear our oaths in your divinity', *Epist.* 2.1.15–16).[40] In the absence of any evidence for an earlier attempt to introduce the cult of the *numen Augusti*,[41] the sense of *numen* in both *Epistles* 2.1 and *Ode* 4.5 can only be the divine nature of the *princeps*. Therefore, the final stanzas of *Ode* 4.5 present us with an image of Augustus himself—not his *genius*—being worshipped as a god in a private context.[42] To this extent, *Ode* 4.5 contains the earliest representation of Augustus as the subject of a private cult in the extant corpus of Augustan poetry.

Important though it is to establish this kind of historical significance for a particular literary text, taking this approach to Horace's depiction of the worship of Augustus tells us little about what this poetic image communicates; why it occupies such a prominent place in his poetry; and how it intersects with the poet's broader thinking on issues relating to power and authority. I hope that this book has gone some way to address these questions, and has shown along the way that—because the poets' discussions of Augustus' divinity are concerned with more than just the worship of the emperor—the entire poetic discourse on Augustus' divinity is therefore altogether historically significant.

---

[40] The phrase *per numen* (*Epist.* 2.1.16) does not evoke official language because an official use of Augustus' *numen* is not known before Tiberius' dedication of an altar to the *numen Augusti*, which is variously dated to between AD 5 and 10. The commonly accepted date is AD 6; cf. *Fasti Praenestini*, *CIL* 1², p. 231, with discussion by Fishwick (1991) I, 377–8.

[41] This notion was proposed by Weinstock (1971) 213 n. 7. More recently, even the existence of the cult of the *numen Augusti* has been questioned by Gradel (2002) 248.

[42] Also the view of Du Quesnay (1995) 176, Gradel (2002) 247, and Flower (2017) 307.

References

Abbreviations of modern journals follow the list of *L'Année philologique* where available. In other cases, journal names are given in full.

Acosta-Hughes, Benjamin, and Susan A. Stephens. 2012. *Callimachus in Context: From Plato to the Augustan Poets*. Cambridge: Cambridge University Press.

Adams, James. N. 1994. *Wackernagel's Law and the Placement of the Copula 'esse' in Classical Latin*. Cambridge: Cambridge University Press.

Agócs, Peter, Christopher Carey, and Richard Rawles, eds. 2012. *Reading the Victory Ode*. Cambridge: Cambridge University Press.

Ahl, Frederick. 1984. 'The Art of Safe Criticism in Greece and Rome'. *AJPh* 105: 174–208.

Alföldy, Géza. 1972. 'Die Ablehnung der Diktatur durch Augustus'. *Gymnasium* 79: 1–12.

Althusser, Louis. 1970. 'Idéologie et appareils idéologiques d'État (Notes pour une recherche)'. *La Pensée* 151.

Anderson, Robert D., Peter J. Parsons, and R. G. M. Nisbet. 1979. 'Elegiacs by Gallus from Qaṣr Ibrîm'. *JRS* 69: 125–55.

Ando, Clifford. 2011. *Law, Language and Empire in the Roman Tradition*. Philadelphia: University of Pennsylvania Press.

Arena, Valentina. 2012. *Libertas and the Practice of Politics in the Late Roman Republic*. Cambridge: Cambridge University Press.

Atkins, Jed W. 2018. *Roman Political Thought*. Cambridge: Cambridge University Press.

Austin, R. G. 1971. *P. Vergili Maronis Aeneidos Liber Primus*. Oxford: Clarendon Press.

Badian, Ernst. 1985. 'A Phantom Marriage Law'. *Philologus* 129: 82–98.

Bailey, Cyril. 1935. *Religion in Virgil*. Oxford: Clarendon Press.

Barchiesi, Alessandro. 1994. 'Immovable Delos: *Aeneid* 3.73–98 and the Hymns of Callimachus'. *CQ* 44: 438–43.

Barchiesi, Alessandro. 1996. 'Poetry, Praise and Patronage: Simonides in Book 4 of Horace's *Odes*'. *ClAnt* 15: 5–47.

Barchiesi, Alessandro. 1997a. 'Virgilian Narrative: Ecphrasis'. In Martindale 1997: 271–81.

Barchiesi, Alessandro. 1997b. *The Poet and the Prince*. Berkeley: University of California Press.

Barchiesi, Alessandro. 2002. 'The Uniqueness of the *Carmen Saeculare*'. In Woodman and Feeney 2002: 107–23.

Barchiesi, Alessandro. 2005. 'Learned Eyes: Poets, Viewers, Image Makers'. In Galinsky 2005: 281–305.

Barchiesi, Alessandro. 2007. '*Carmina*: *Odes* and *Carmen Saeculare*'. In Harrison 2007d: 144–61.

Barchiesi, Alessandro. 2009. 'Phaethon and the Monsters'. In Philip Hardie, ed. 2009. *Paradox and the Marvellous in Augustan Literature and Culture*. Oxford: Oxford University Press, 163–88.

Bartels, Christfried. 1973. 'Die neunte Epode des Horaz als sympotisches Gedicht'. *Hermes* 101: 282–313.

Bartsch, Shadi. 1998. '*Ars* and the Man: The Politics of Art in Virgil's *Aeneid*'. *CPh* 93: 322–42.

204 REFERENCES

Bather, Philippa, and Claire Stocks, eds. 2016. *Horace's Epodes: Contexts, Intertexts, and Reception*. Oxford: Oxford University Press.

Batinski, Emily. 1990–1. 'Horace's Rehabilitation of Bacchus'. *CW* 84: 361–78.

Batstone, William. 1997. 'Virgilian Didaxis: Value and Meaning in the *Georgics*'. In Martindale 1997: 125–44.

Bauman, Richard A. 1985. *Lawyers in Transitional Politics: A Study of the Roman Jurists in Their Political Setting in the Late Republic and Triumvirate*. Munich: Beck.

Beard, Mary. 2007. *The Roman Triumph*. Cambridge, MA: Harvard University Press.

Beard, Mary, John North, and Simon Price. 1998. *Religions of Rome*. 2 vols. Cambridge: Cambridge University Press.

Beck, Marcus. 2000. 'Properzens Elegie 2,7 und die augusteische Ehegesetzgebung'. *Philologus* 144: 303–24.

Bellinger, Alfred. 1957. 'The Immortality of Alexander and Augustus'. *YCIS* 15: 91–100.

Bergmann, Bettina, Joseph Farrell, Dennis C. Feeney, James Ker, Damien P. Nelis, and Celia Schultz. 2012. 'An Exciting Provocation: John F. Miller's *Apollo, Augustus and the Poets*'. *Vergilius* 58: 3–20.

Berkowitz, Luci. 1972. 'Pollio and the Date of the Fourth *Eclogue*'. *California Studies in Classical Antiquity* 5: 21–38.

Bernays, Ludwig. 2002. 'Bemerkungen zur Elegie 4.6 des Properz'. *Mnemosyne* 55: 593–8.

Berry, Michael. 2005. 'Propertian Ambiguity and the Elegiac Alibi'. In Carl Deroux, ed. 2005. *Studies in Latin Literature and Roman History XII*. Brussels: Latomus, 194–213.

Bettini, Maurizio. 2005. 'Un'identità "troppo compiuta." Troiani, Latini, Romani e Iulii nell'*Eneide*'. *MD* 55: 77–102.

Bickerman, Elias J. 1974. 'Filius Maiae (Horace, *Odes* I.2.43)'. *PP* 16: 5–19.

Billows, Richard. 1993. 'The Religious Procession of the Ara Pacis Augustae: Augustus' *supplicatio* in 13 B.C.'. *JRA* 6: 80–92.

Binder, Gerhard. 1971. *Aeneas und Augustus. Interpretationen zum 8. Buch der Aeneis*. Meisenheim am Glan: Anton Hain.

Binder, Gerhard. 1988. 'Aitiologische Erzählung und augusteisches Programm in Vergils *Aeneis*'. In Gerhard Binder, ed. (1988) *Saeculum Augustum II*. Darmstadt: Wissenschaftliche Buchgesellschaft, 255–87.

Binder, Gerhard, and Hartwig Heckel. 2002. 'Abschied von Regulus. Überlegungen zu Hor. c. 3, 5'. *WJA* 26: 61–97.

Bing, Peter. 2016. 'Epicurus and the *iuvenis* at Virgil's *Eclogue* 1.42'. *CQ* 66: 172–9.

Bömer, Franz. 1951. 'Vergil und Augustus'. *Gymnasium* 58: 26–55.

Boucher, Jean-Paul. 1974. 'Place et rôle de la religion dans les Élégies de Properce'. In Pierre Boyancé, ed. *Mélanges de philosophie, de littérature et d'histoire ancienne offerts*. Rome: École Française de Rome, 79–102.

Boucher, Jean-Paul. 1980. *Études sur Properce: Problèmes d'inspiration et d'art*. Paris: De Boccard.

Bowditch, Phebe L. 2001. *Horace and the Gift Economy of Patronage*. Berkeley: University of California Press.

Bowditch, Phebe L. 2009. 'Palatine Apollo and the Imperial Gaze: Propertius 2.31 and 2.32'. *AJPh* 130, 401–38.

Bowditch, Phebe L. 2011. 'Tibullus and Egypt: A Postcolonial Reading of Elegy 1.7'. *Arethusa* 44: 89–122.

Bowersock, Glen W. 1965. *Augustus and the Greek World*. Oxford: Clarendon Press.

Bowersock, Glen W. 1971. 'A Date in the *Eighth Eclogue*'. *HSPh* 75: 73–80.

Boyce, George K. 1937. *Corpus of the Lararia of Pompeii*. Rome: American Academy.

REFERENCES   205

Boyd, Barbara Weiden. 1995. '*Non enarrabile textum*: Ecphrastic Trespass and Narrative Ambiguity'. *Vergilius* 41: 71–90.

Breed, Brian W. 2004. '*tua, Caesar, aetas*: Horace *Ode* 4.15 and the Augustan Age'. *AJPh* 125: 245–53.

Bremmer, Jan N., and Nicholas Horsfall, eds. 1987. *Roman Myth and Mythography*. London: University of London Institute of Classical Studies.

Brenk, Frederick E. 1995. 'Heroic Anti-Heroes: Ruler Cult and Divine Assimilations in Plutarch's *Lives* of Demetrios and Antonius'. In Italo Gallo and Barbara Scardigli, eds. 1995. *Teoria e prassi politica nelle opere di Plutarco*. Naples: M. D'Auria, 65–82.

Bright, David F. 1975. 'The Art and Structure of Tibullus 1.7'. *GB* 3: 31–46.

Brink, Charles O. 1982. *Horace on Poetry. Epistles Book II. The Letters to Augustus and Florus*. Cambridge: Cambridge University Press.

Brilliant, Richard. 1999. 'Let the Trumpets Roar! The Roman Triumph'. In Bettina Bergmann and Christine Kondoleon, eds. 1999. *The Art of Ancient Spectacle*. New Haven and London: Yale University Press, 221–29.

Brown, P. Michael. 1993. *Horace. Satires I*. Warminster: Aris & Philips.

Brown, R. D. 1991. '*Catonis nobile letum* and the List of Romans in Horace *Odes* 1.12'. *Phoenix* 45: 326–40.

Brunt, Peter A. 1988. *The Fall of the Roman Republic and Related Essays*. Oxford: Clarendon Press.

Brunt, Peter A. 1990. *Roman Imperial Themes*. Oxford: Clarendon Press.

Buchheit, Vinzenz. 1971. 'Epikurs Triumph des Geistes'. *Hermes* 99: 303–22.

Bücheler, Franz. 1927. *Kleine Schriften*, 2 vols. Leipzig and Berlin: Teubner.

Budelmann, Felix. 2012. 'Epinician and the *Symposion*: A Comparison with the *enkomia*'. In Agócs et al. 2012: 173–90.

Burrell, Barbara. 2004. *Neokoroi: Greek Cities and Roman Emperor*. Leiden: Brill.

Butrica, James L. 1997. 'Editing Propertius'. *CQ* 47: 176–208.

Cairns, Francis. 1971. 'Horace, *Odes* 1.2'. *Eranos* 69: 68–88.

Cairns, Francis. 1983. 'Horace *Epode* 9: Some New Interpretations'. *ICS* 8: 80–93.

Cairns, Francis. 1984. 'Propertius and the Battle of Actium (4.6)'. In Woodman and West 1984: 129–68.

Cairns, Francis. 1989. *Vergil's Augustan Epic*. Cambridge: Cambridge University Press.

Cairns, Francis. 1995. 'Horace's First Roman Ode (3.1)'. *Papers of the Leeds International Latin Seminar* 8: 91–142.

Cairns, Francis. 2006. *Sextus Propertius: The Augustan Elegist*. Cambridge: Cambridge University Press.

Cairns, Francis. 2008. 'C. Asinius Pollio and the *Eclogues*'. *PCPhS* 54: 49–79.

Campbell, Brian. 1992. 'War and Diplomacy: Rome and Parthia, 31 BC–AD 235'. In John Rich and Graham Shipley, eds. 1992. *War and Society in the Roman World*. London: Routledge, 220–8.

Camps, William. A. 1965. *Propertius: Elegies Book IV*. Cambridge: Cambridge University Press.

Camps, William. A. 1966. *Propertius: Elegies III*. Cambridge: Cambridge University Press.

Camps, William. A. 1967. *Propertius: Elegies II*. Cambridge: Cambridge University Press.

Carey, Christopher. 2009. 'Genre, Occasion and Performance'. In Felix Budelmann. ed. 2009. *The Cambridge Companion to Greek Lyric*. Cambridge: Cambridge University Press, 21–38.

Carey, Christopher. 2016. 'Negotiating the Public Voice'. In Delignon et al. 2016: 177–92.

Carrubba, Robert W. 1969. *The Epodes of Horace: A Study in Poetic Arrangement*. The Hague: Mouton.

206 REFERENCES

Casali, Sergio. 2006. 'The Making of the Shield: Inspiration and Repression in the *Aeneid*'. *G&R* 53: 185–204.

Casali, Sergio. 2009. 'The Theophany of Apollo in Virgil, *Aeneid* 9: Augustanism and Self-Reflexivity'. In Lucia Athanassaki, Richard P. Martin, and John F. Miller, eds. 2009. *Apolline Politics and Poetics*. Athens: European Cultural Centre of Delphi, 299–327.

Castriota, David. 1995. *The Ara Pacis Augustae and the Imagery of Abundance in Later Greek and Early Roman Imperial Art*. Princeton: Princeton University Press.

Cavarzere, Alberto. 1994. 'Vate me: L'ambiguo sigillo dell'epodo XVI'. *Aevum antiquum* 7, 171–90.

Chaniotis, Angelos. 2003. 'The Divinity of Hellenistic Rulers'. In Andrew Erskine, ed. 2003. *A Companion to the Hellenistic World*. Malden, MA and Oxford: Blackwell, 431–45.

Chaniotis, Angelos. 2011. 'The Ithyphallic Hymn for Demetrios Poliorketes and Hellenistic Religious Mentality'. In Panagiotis P. Iossif, Andrzej S. Chankowski, and Catharine C. Lorber, eds. 2011. *More than Men, Less than Gods*. Leuven: Peeters, 157–95.

Charlesworth, M. P. 1933. 'Some Fragments of the Propaganda of Mark Antony'. *CQ* 27: 172–7.

Chaudhuri, Pramit. 2014. *The War with God: Theomachy in Roman Imperial Poetry*. Oxford: Oxford University Press.

Chillet, Clément. 2016. *De l'Étrurie à Rome: Mécène et la fondation de l'Empire*. Rome: École française de Rome.

Citroni, Mario. 2000. 'The Memory of Philippi in Horace and the Interpretation of *Epistle* 1.20.23'. *CJ* 96: 27–56.

Clark, Anna J. 2007. *Divine Qualities: Cult and Community in Republican Rome*. Oxford: Oxford University Press.

Clark, Raymond. 2010. 'Ilia's Excessive Complaint and the Flood in Horace, *Odes* 1.2'. *CQ* 60: 262–7.

Classen, Carl. 1985. *Recht—Rhetorik—Politik: Untersuchungen zu Ciceros rhetorischer Strategie*. Darmstadt: Wissenschaftliche Buchgesellschaft.

Clausen, Wendell. 1964. 'An Interpretation of the *Aeneid*'. *HSPh* 68: 139–47.

Clausen, Wendell. 1972. 'On the Date of the First Eclogue'. *HSPh* 76: 201–5.

Clausen, Wendell. 1987. *Virgil's Aeneid and the Tradition of Hellenistic Poetry*. Berkeley: University of California Press.

Clausen, Wendell. 1994. *A Commentary on Virgil, Eclogues*. Oxford: Oxford University Press.

Clauss, Manfred. 1996. 'Deus praesens: Der römische Kaiser als Gott'. *Klio* 78: 400–33.

Clay, Jenny Strauss. 2016. 'Horace et le frère cadet d'Apollon'. In Delignon et al. 2016: 285–93.

Coffey, Michael. 1976. *Roman Satire*. London: Methuen.

Coffta, David J. 2002. *The Influence of Callimachean Aesthetics on the Satires and Odes of Horace*. Lewiston, Queenston, and Lampeter: E. Mellen Press.

Cole, Spencer. 2001. 'The Dynamics of Deification in Horace's *Odes* 1–3'. In Sulochana R. Asirvatham, Corinne O. Pache, and John Watrous, eds. 2001. *Between Magic and Religion: Interdisciplinary Studies in Ancient Mediterranean Religion and Society*. Lanham, MD: Rowman and Littlefield, 67–91.

Cole, Spencer. 2006. 'Cicero, Ennius, and the Concept of Apotheosis at Rome'. *Arethusa* 39: 531–48.

Cole, Spencer. 2013. *Cicero and the Rise of Deification at Rome*. Cambridge: Cambridge University Press.

Coleman, Kathleen. 2003. 'Apollo's Speech before the Battle of Actium'. In André F. Basson and William J. Dominik, eds. 2003. *Literature, Art, History: Studies on Classical Antiquity and Tradition in Honour of W. J. Henderson*. Frankfurt: Peter Lang, 37–41.

REFERENCES 207

Coleman, Robert. 1977. *Vergil. Eclogues.* Cambridge: Cambridge University Press.

Commager, Steele. 1959. 'Horace, *Carmina*, I.2'. *AJPh* 80: 37–55.

Commager, Steele. 1962. *The Odes of Horace. A Critical Study.* New Haven and London: Yale University Press.

Connolly, Joy. 2015. *The Life of Roman Republicanism.* Princeton: Princeton University Press.

Connor, Peter. 1987. *Horace's Lyric Poetry: The Force of Humour.* Berwick, Victoria: Aureal Publications.

Connors, Catherine M. 1998. *Petronius the Poet: Verse and Literary Tradition in the Satyricon.* Cambridge: Cambridge University Press.

Conte, Gian Biagio. 1980. *Il genere e i suoi confini: cinque studi sulla poesia di Virgilio.* Turin: Stampatori.

Conte, Gian Biagio. 1992. 'Proems in the Middle'. *YCIS* 29, 147–59.

Conte, Gian Biagio. 2007. *The Poetry of Pathos, Studies in Virgilian Epic* (ed. Stephen J. Harrison). Oxford: Oxford University Press.

Cooley, Alison. 2009. *Res Gestae Diui Augusti. Text, Translation, and Commentary.* Cambridge: Cambridge University Press.

Cooley, Alison. 2019. 'From the Augustan Principate to the Invention of the Age of Augustus'. *JRS* 109: 71–87.

Cornwell, Hannah. 2017. *Pax and the Politics of Peace: Republic to Principate.* Oxford: Oxford University Press.

Coutelle, Éric. 2015. *Properce, Élégies, livre IV.* Brussels: Latomus.

Crook, John A. 1996. 'Political History, 30 B.C. to A.D. 14'. *CAH* X: 70–112.

Cucchiarelli, Andrea. 2001. *La satire e il poeta: Orazio tra Epodi e Sermones.* Pisa: Giardini.

Cucchiarelli, Andrea. 2006. 'La tempesta e il dio (forme editoriali nei *carmina* di Orazio)'. *Dyctinna* 3.

Cucchiarelli, Andrea. 2011a. 'Ivy and the Laurel: Divine Models in Virgil's *Eclogues*'. *HSPh* 106: 155–78.

Cucchiarelli, Andrea. 2011b. 'Virgilio e l'invenzione dell'età augustea (modelli divini e linguagio politico dalle "Bucoliche" alle "Georgiche")'. *Lexis* 29: 229–74.

Cucchiarelli, Andrea. 2012. *P. Virgilio Marone. Le Bucoliche, introduzione e commento.* Rome: Carocci.

Currie, Bruno. 2005. *Pindar and the Cult of Heroes.* Oxford: Oxford University Press.

Currie, H. M. 1996. 'Horace's "Epigraphic Poetry": Some Comments on *Odes* IV'. *Latomus* 55: 78–86.

Damon, Cynthia, and Joseph Farrell, eds. 2020. *Ennius' Annals: Poetry and History.* Cambridge: Cambridge University Press.

Davis, Gregson. 1991. *Polyhymnia: The Rhetoric of Horatian Lyric Discourse.* Berkeley: University of California Press.

Davis, Gregson. 2007. 'Wine and the Symposium'. In Harrison 2007d: 207–20.

Davis, Gregson, ed. 2010. *A Companion to Horace.* Malden, MA and Oxford: Blackwell.

Davis, Gregson. 2012. *Parthenope: The Interplay of Ideas in Vergilian Bucolic.* Leiden: Brill.

Davis, Peter J. 1999. 'Ovid's *Amores*: A Political Reading'. *CPh* 94: 431–49.

Davis, Peter J. 2001. 'The Fabrication of Tradition: Horace, Augustus and the Secular Games'. *Ramus* 30: 111–27.

D'Elia, Salvatore. 1995. 'Orazio: carm. III 30'. In Marcello Gigante and Salvatore Cerasuolo, eds. 1995. *Letture oraziane.* Naples: Università di Napoli, 147–64.

Delignon, Bénédicte, Nadine Le Meur, and Olivier Thévenaz, eds. 2016. *La poésie lyrique dans la cité antique: Les Odes d'Horace au miroir de la lyrique grecque archaïque.* Paris: De Boccard.

208 REFERENCES

Della Corte, Francesco. 1984–91. *Enciclopedia Virgiliana*. Rome: Istituto della Enciclopedia Italiana.

De Martino, Francesco. 1992. 'Scudi "a rendere" (Hor. Carm. 2,7: i preceduti greci)'. *AION* 12: 45–64.

Deremetz, Alain. 1995. *Le miroir des muses. Poétiques de la réflexivité à Rome*. Villeneuve d'Ascq: Universitaires du Septentrion.

Dickie, M. 1985. 'The Speech of Numanus Remulus (*Aeneid* 9.598–620)'. *Papers of the Liverpool Latin Seminar* 5: 165–221.

Dobbin, Robert F. 1995. 'Julius Caesar in Jupiter's Prophecy, *Aeneid*, Book 1'. *ClAnt* 14: 5–40.

Doblhofer, Ernst. 1966. *Die Augustuspanegyrik des Horaz in formalhistorischer Sicht*. Heidelberg: Winter.

Drew, D. L. 1924. 'Virgil's Marble Temple: *Georgics* III.10–39'. *CQ* 18: 195–202.

DuBois, Page. 1982. *History, Rhetorical Description, and the Epic from Homer to Spenser*. Cambridge: Brewer.

Dufallo, Basil. 2007. *The Ghosts of the Past: Latin Literature, the Dead, and Rome's Transition to a Principate*. Columbus: Ohio State University Press.

Dufallo, Basil. 2015. 'Publicizing Political Authority in Horace's *Satires*, Book 1: The Sacral and the Demystified'. *CPh* 110: 313–32.

Dugan, John. 2013. 'Cicero and the Politics of Ambiguity: Interpreting the *Pro Marcello*'. In Catherine Steel and Henriette van der Blom, eds. 2013. *Community and Communication: Oratory and Politics in Republican Rome*. Oxford: Oxford University Press, 211–25.

Du Quesnay, I. M. Le M. 1976. 'Vergil's Fourth *Eclogue*'. *Papers of the Liverpool Latin Seminar* 1: 31–8.

Du Quesnay, I. M. Le M. 1981. 'Vergil's First *Eclogue*'. *Papers of the Liverpool Latin Seminar* 3: 29–182.

Du Quesnay, I. M. Le M. 1984. 'Horace and Maecenas: The Propaganda Value of *Sermones* I'. In Woodman and West 1984: 19–58.

Du Quesnay, I. M. Le M. 1995. 'Horace, *Odes* 4.5: *Pro reditu imperatoris Caesaris Divi Filii Augusti*'. In Harrison 1995: 128–87.

Dyer, R. R. 1990. 'Rhetoric and Intention in Cicero's *Pro Marcello*'. *JRS* 80: 17–30.

Eagleton, Terry. 2002. *Marxism and Literary Criticism*. 2nd edn. London: Routledge.

Eckerman, Chris. 2016. 'Freedom and Slavery in Vergil's *Eclogue* 1'. *WS* 129: 257–80.

Ehlers, W. 1985. 'Das "Iter Brundisinum" des Horaz *Serm*. 1.5'. *Hermes* 113: 69–83.

Eidinow, J. S. C. 2000. '"Purpureo bibet ore nectar": a reconsideration'. *CQ* 50: 463–71.

Elliott, Jackie. 2013. *Ennius and the Architecture of the Annales*. Cambridge: Cambridge University Press.

Erren, Manfred. 2003. *P. Vergilius Maro. Georgica. Band 2 Kommentar*. Heidelberg: Winter.

Falkner, Thomas M. 1977. 'Myth, Setting and Immortality in Propertius 3.18'. *CJ* 73: 11–18.

Fantham, Elaine. 1996. *Roman Literary Culture: From Cicero to Apuleius*. Baltimore and London: The Johns Hopkins University Press.

Fantham, Elaine. 1997. 'The Contexts and Occasions of Roman Public Rhetoric'. In William J. Dominik, ed. 1997. *Roman Eloquence: Rhetoric in Society and Literature*. London: Routledge, 111–28.

Fantham, Elaine. 1998. *Ovid. Fasti Book IV*. Cambridge: Cambridge University Press.

Fantuzzi, Marco, and Theodore Papanghelis, eds. 2011. *Brill's Companion to Greek and Latin Pastoral*. Leiden: Brill.

Farrell, Joseph. 2002. 'Greek Lives and Roman Careers in the Classical *Vita* Tradition'. In Patrick Cheney and Frederick A. de Armas, eds. 2002. *European Literary Careers: The Author from Antiquity to the Renaissance*. Toronto: University of Toronto Press, 24–45.

REFERENCES   209

Farrell, Joseph. 2020. 'The Gods in Ennius'. In Damon and Farrell 2020: 63–88.

Farrell, Joseph, and Damien P. Nelis, eds. 2013. *Augustan Poetry and the Roman Republic*. Oxford: Oxford University Press.

Favro, Diane. 1994. 'The Street Triumphant: The Urban Impact of Roman Triumphal Parades'. In Zeynep Çelik, Diane Favro, and Richard Ingersoll, eds. 1994. *Streets: Critical Perspectives on Public Space*. Berkeley: University of California Press, 151–64.

Favro, Diane. 1998. *The Urban Image of Augustan Rome*. Cambridge: Cambridge University Press.

Fears, J. R. 1977. *Princeps a diis electus: The Divine Election of the Emperor as a Political Concept at Rome*. Rome: American Academy.

Fears, J. R. 1981. 'The Theology of Victory at Rome: Approaches and Problems'. *ANRW* II.17.2, 737–826.

Fedeli, Paolo. 1965. *Properzio. Elegie. Libro IV*. Bari: Adriatica.

Fedeli, Paolo. 1985. *Properzio: il libro terzo delle Elegie*. Bari: Adriatica.

Fedeli, Paolo. 2005. *Properzio: Elegie libro II*. Cambridge: Cairns.

Fedeli, Paolo, and Irma Ciccarelli. 2008. *Q. Horatii Flacci. Carmina Liber IV*. Florence: Le Monnier.

Fedeli, Paolo, Rosalba Dimundo, and Irma Ciccarelli, eds. 2015. *Properzio: Elegie, Libro IV*. 2 vols. Nordhausen: Bautz.

Feeney, Dennis C. 1986. 'History and Revelation in Vergil's Underworld'. *PCPhS* 32: 1–24.

Feeney, Dennis C. 1991. *The Gods in Epic: Poets and Critics of the Classical Tradition*. Oxford: Clarendon Press.

Feeney, Dennis C. 1992. '*Si licet et fas est*: Ovid's *Fasti* and the Problem of Free Speech under the Principate'. In Powell 1992: 1–25.

Feeney, Dennis C. 1993. 'Horace and the Greek Lyric Poets'. In Niall Rudd, ed. 1993. *Horace 2000: A Celebration: Essays for the Bimillennium*. London: Duckworth, 41–63.

Feeney, Dennis C. 1998. *Literature and Religion at Rome: Cultures, Contexts, and Beliefs*. Cambridge: Cambridge University Press.

Feeney, Dennis C. 2002. '*Vna cum scriptore meo*: Poetry, Principate and the Traditions of Literary History in the Epistle to Augustus'. In Woodman and Feeney 2002: 172–87.

Feeney, Dennis C. 2007. *Caesar's Calendar*. Berkeley: University of California Press.

Feldherr, Andrew. 1999. 'Putting Dido on the Map: Genre and Geography in Vergil's Underworld'. *Arethusa* 32: 85–122.

Feldherr, Andrew. 2010. '"Dionysiac Poetics" and the Memory of Civil War in Horace's Cleopatra Ode'. In Brian W. Breed, Cynthia Damon, and Andreola Rossi, eds. 2010. *Citizens of Discord: Rome and Its Civil Wars*. Oxford: Oxford University Press, 223–32.

Feldherr, Andrew. 2014. 'Viewing Myth and History on the Shield of Aeneas'. *ClAnt* 33: 281–318.

Fenik, Bernard. 1962. 'Horace's First and Sixth Roman Odes and the Second Georgic'. *Hermes* 90: 72–96.

Ferrary, Jean-Louis. 2001. 'À propos des pouvoirs d'Auguste'. *CCG* 12: 101–54 = 2009. 'The Powers of Augustus'. In Jonathan Edmondson, ed. 2009. *Augustus*. Edinburgh: Edinburgh University Press, 90–136.

Fishwick, Duncan. 1987–2005. *The Imperial Cult in the Latin West: Studies in the Ruler Cult of the Western Provinces of the Roman Empire*. 3 vols. Leiden: Brill.

Fitzgerald, William. 1987. *Agonistic Poetry: The Pindaric Mode in Pindar, Horace, Hölderlin, and the English Ode*. Berkeley: University of California Press.

Fitzgerald, William. 1988. 'Power and Impotence in Horace's *Epodes*'. *Ramus* 17: 176–91.

Flower, Harriet. 2017. *The Dancing Lares and the Serpent in the Garden: Religion at the Roman Street Corner*. Princeton: Princeton University Press.

210   REFERENCES

Fowler, Don. 1989. 'First Thoughts on Closure: Problems and Prospects'. *MD* 22: 75–122.

Fowler, Don. 1991. 'Narrate and Describe: The Problem of Ekphrasis'. *JRS* 81: 24–35.

Fowler, Don. 1995. 'Horace and the Aesthetics of Politics'. In Harrison 1995: 248–66.

Fowler, Don. 2000a. 'Epic in the Middle of the Wood: *Mise en abyme* in the Nisus and Euryalus Episode'. In Alison Sharrock and Helen Morales, eds. 2000. *Intratextuality: Greek and Roman Textual Relations*. Oxford: Oxford University Press, 89–113.

Fowler, Don. 2000b. *Roman Constructions: Readings in Postmodern Latin*. Oxford: Oxford University Press.

Fraenkel, Eduard. 1957. *Horace*. Oxford: Clarendon Press.

Freer, Nicholas. 2019. 'Virgil's *Georgics* and the Epicurean Sirens of Poetry'. In Xinyue and Freer 2019: 79–90.

Freudenburg, Kirk. 2001. *Satires of Rome: Threatening Poses from Lucilius to Juvenal*. Cambridge: Cambridge University Press.

Freudenburg, Kirk. 2006. 'Playing at Lyric's Boundaries: Dreaming Forward in Book Two of Horace's *Sermones*'. *Dictynna* 3.

Freudenburg, Kirk. 2014. '*Recusatio* as Political Theatre: Horace's Letter to Augustus'. *JRS* 104: 105–32.

Freudenburg, Kirk. 2021. *Horace. Satires Book II*. Cambridge: Cambridge University Press.

Fuhrer, Therese. 2011. 'Inszenierung von Göttlichkeit. Die politische Rolle von Dionysos / Bacchus in der römischen Literatur'. In Renate Schlesier, ed. 2011. *A Different God? Dionysos and Ancient Polytheism*. Berlin and Boston: De Gruyter, 373–89.

Gagé, Jean. 1955. *Apollon romain*. Paris: De Boccard.

Gagliardi, Paola. 1997. *Il dissenso e l'ironia: per una rilettura delle orazioni 'cesariane' di Cicerone*. Naples: D'Auria.

Gaisser, Julia H. 1971. 'Tibullus 1.7: A Tribute to Messalla'. *CPh* 66: 221–9.

Gale, Monica R. 1997. 'Propertius 2.7: *Militia Amoris* and the Ironies of Elegy'. *JRS* 87: 77–91.

Gale, Monica R. 2000. *Virgil on the Nature of Things: The Georgics, Lucretius and the Didactic Tradition*. Cambridge: Cambridge University Press.

Gale, Monica R. 2003. 'Poetry and the Backward Glance in Virgil's *Georgics* and *Aeneid*'. *TAPhA* 133: 323–52.

Gale, Monica R. 2013. 'Virgil's Caesar: Intertextuality and Ideology'. In Farrell and Nelis 2013: 278–96.

Galinsky, Karl. 1966. 'The Hercules-Cacus Episode in *Aeneid* VIII'. *AJPh* 87: 18–51.

Galinsky, Karl. 1972. *The Herakles Theme: The Adaptation of the Hero in Literature from Homer to the Twentieth Century*. Oxford: Blackwell.

Galinsky, Karl. 1996. *Augustan Culture. An Interpretive Introduction*. Princeton: Princeton University Press.

Galinsky, Karl. ed. 2005. *The Cambridge Companion to the Augustan Age*. Cambridge: Cambridge University Press.

Galinsky, Karl. 2006. 'Vergil's Uses of *libertas*: Texts and Contexts'. *Vergilius* 52: 3–19.

Geiger, Joseph. 2008. *The First Hall of Fame: A Study of the Statues in the Forum Augustum*. Leiden: Brill.

Geue, Tom. 2013. '*Princeps* "avant la lettre": The Foundation of Augustus in Pre-Augustan Poetry'. In Mario Labate and Gianpiero Rosati, eds. 2013. *La costruzione de mito augusteo*. Heidelberg: Winter, 49–67.

Geue, Tom. 2018. 'Soft Hands, Hard Power: Sponging Off the Empire of Leisure (Virgil, *Georgics* 4)'. *JRS* 108: 115–40.

Geue, Tom. 2019. *Author Unknown: The Power of Anonymity in Ancient Rome*. Cambridge, MA: Harvard University Press.

REFERENCES   211

Gibson, B. J. 1997. 'Horace, *Carm.* 3.30.1–5'. *CQ* 47: 312–14.

Gildenhard, Ingo. 2011. *Creative Eloquence: The Construction of Reality in Cicero's Speeches.* Oxford: Oxford University Press.

Giusti, Elena. 2016a. 'Did Somebody Say Augustan Totalitarianism? Duncan Kennedy's "Reflections", Hannah Arendt's *Origins*, and the Continental Divide Over Virgil's *Aeneid*'. *Dictynna* 13.

Giusti, Elena. 2016b. 'Dithyrambic Iambics: *Epode* 9 and its General(s') Confusion'. In Bather and Stocks 2016: 131–52.

Giusti, Elena. 2019. 'Bunte Barbaren Setting Up the Stage: Re-Inventing the Barbarian on the *Georgics*' Theatre-Temple'. In Xinyue and Freer 2019: 105–14.

Glei, Reinhold F. 1998. 'The Show Must Go On: The Death of Marcellus and the Future of the Augustan Principate'. In Stahl 1998: 119–34.

Goldschmidt, Nora. 2013. *Shaggy Crowns: Ennius' Annales and Virgil's Aeneid.* Oxford: Oxford University Press.

Gosling, Anne. 1986. 'Octavian, Brutus and Apollo: A Note on Opportunist Propaganda'. *AJPh* 107: 586–9.

Gowers, Emily. 2005. 'The Restless Companion: Horace, *Satires* 1 and 2'. In Kirk Freudenburg, ed. 2005. *The Cambridge Companion to Roman Satire.* Cambridge: Cambridge University Press, 48–61.

Gowers, Emily. 2012. *Horace. Satires Book I.* Cambridge: Cambridge University Press.

Gowers, Emily. 2016. 'Girls Will Be Boys and Boys Will Be Girls, Or, What Is the Gender of Horace's *Epodes*?'. In Bather and Stocks 2016: 103–30.

Gradel, Ittai. 2002. *Emperor Worship and Roman Religion.* Oxford: Oxford University Press.

Gransden, Karl W. 1976. *Virgil. Aeneid Book VIII.* Cambridge: Cambridge University Press.

Gransden, Karl W. 1984. *Virgil's Iliad: An Essay on Epic Narrative.* Cambridge: Cambridge University Press.

Graverini, Luca. 1997. 'Un secolo di studi su Mecenate'. *RSA* 27: 231–89.

Grebe, Sabine. 2004. 'Augustus' Divine Authority and Vergil's *Aeneid*'. *Vergilius* 50: 35–62.

Griffin, Jasper. 1977. 'Propertius and Antony'. *JRS* 67: 17–26.

Griffin, Jasper. 1984. 'Augustus and the Poets: "Caesar qui cogere posset"'. In Fergus Millar and Erich Segal, eds. 1984. *Caesar Augustus: Seven Aspects.* Oxford: Clarendon Press, 189–218.

Griffiths, Frederick T. 1979. *Theocritus at Court.* Leiden: Brill.

Grimal, Pierre. 1951. 'Énée à Rome et le triomphe d'Octave'. *REA* 53, 51–61.

Grisart, A. 1966. 'Tityre et son dieu: des identifications nouvelles'. *LEC* 34, 115–42.

Gros, Pierre. 1993. '*stabunt et Parii lapides*: Virgile et les premiers frontons augustéens d'après *Géorgiques*, iii, v.34'. In Marie-Madeleine Mactoux and Évelyne Geny, eds. 1993. *Mélanges Pierre Lévêque*, vol. 7. Paris: Les Belles Lettres, 155–9.

Gruen, Erich S. 1996. 'The Expansion of the Empire under Augustus'. *CAH* X: 147–97.

Gruen, Erich S. 2005. 'Augustus and the Making of the Principate'. In Galinsky 2005: 33–51.

Günther, Hans-Christian. 2006. 'The Fourth Book'. In Hans-Christian Günther, ed. 2006. *Brill's Companion to Propertius.* Leiden: Brill, 353–95.

Gurval, Robert A. 1995. *Actium and Augustus: The Politics and Emotions of Civil War.* Ann Arbor: University of Michigan Press.

Gurval, Robert A. 1997. 'Caesar's Comet: The Politics and Poetics of an Augustan Myth'. *Memoirs of the American Academy in Rome* 42: 39–71.

Habinek, Thomas, and Alessandro Schiesaro, eds. 1997. *The Roman Cultural Revolution.* Cambridge: Cambridge University Press.

Halfmann, Helmut. 1986. *Itinera principum: Geschichte und Typologie der Kaiserreisen im römischen Reich.* Stuttgart: Steiner.

212 REFERENCES

Hall, Jon. 2009. 'Serving the Times: Cicero and Caesar the Dictator'. In William J. Dominik, John Garthwaite, and Paul A. Roche, eds. 2009. *Writing Politics in Imperial Rome*. Leiden: Brill, 89–110.

Hallett, Christopher H. 2005. *The Roman Nude: Heroic Portrait Statuary 200 BC–AD 300*. Oxford: Oxford University Press.

Hallett, Judith P. 1973. 'The Role of Women in Roman Elegy: Counter-Cultural Feminism'. *Arethusa* 6: 103–24.

Hallett, Judith P. 1985. 'Queens, Princeps and Women of the Augustan Elite: Propertius' Cornelia-Elegy and the *Res Gestae Divi Augusti*'. In Rolf Winkes, ed. 1985. *The Age of Augustus*. Providence: Center for Old World Archaeology and Art, Brown University, 73–88.

Hammer, Dean. 2008. *Roman Political Thought and the Modern Theoretical Imagination*. Norman: University of Oklahoma Press.

Hammer, Dean. 2014. *Roman Political Thought from Cicero to Augustine*. Cambridge: Cambridge University Press.

Hardie, Alex. 1976. 'Horace *Odes* 1,37 and Pindar *Dithyramb* 2'. *Papers of the Liverpool Latin Seminar* 1: 113–40.

Hardie, Alex. 2002. 'The *Georgics*, the Mysteries and the Muses at Rome'. *PCPhS* 48: 175–208.

Hardie, Alex. 2003. 'The Pindaric Sources of Horace *Odes* 1.12'. *HSPh* 101: 371–404.

Hardie, Alex. 2008. 'An Augustan Hymn to the Muses (Horace *Odes* 3.4) Part I'. *Papers of the Langford Latin Seminar* 13: 55–118.

Hardie, Alex. 2010. 'An Augustan Hymn to the Muses (Horace *Odes* 3.4) Part II'. *Papers of the Langford Latin Seminar* 14: 191–317.

Hardie, Alex. 2015. 'A Dithyramb for Augustus: Horace, *Odes* 4.2'. *CQ* 65: 253–85.

Hardie, Philip R. 1986. *Virgil's Aeneid: Cosmos and Imperium*. Oxford: Clarendon Press.

Hardie, Philip R. 1993. *The Epic Successors of Virgil*. Cambridge: Cambridge University Press.

Hardie, Philip R. 1994. *Virgil. Aeneid Book IX*. Cambridge: Cambridge University Press.

Hardie, Philip R. 1997. 'Questions of Authority: The Invention of Tradition in Ovid *Metamorphoses* 15'. In Habinek and Schiesaro 1997: 182–98.

Hardie, Philip R. 1998. *Virgil*. Oxford: Oxford University Press.

Hardie, Philip R. 2006a. 'Culture and Historical Narratives in Virgil's *Eclogues* and Lucretius'. In Fantuzzi and Papanghelis 2006: 275–300.

Hardie, Philip R. 2006b. 'Virgil's Ptolemaic Relations'. *JRS* 96: 25–41.

Hardie, Philip R. 2012. *Rumour and Renown: Representations of Fama in Western Literature*. Cambridge: Cambridge University Press.

Hardie, Philip R. 2016. 'Introduction: Augustan Poetry and the Irrational'. In Philip R. Hardie, ed. 2016. *Augustan Poetry and the Irrational*. Oxford: Oxford University Press, 1–36.

Harrison, E. L. 1981. 'Vergil and the Homeric Tradition'. *Papers of the Liverpool Latin Seminar* 3: 209–25.

Harrison, Stephen J. 1990. 'The Praise Singer: Horace, Censorinus and *Odes* 4.8'. *JRS* 80: 31–43.

Harrison, Stephen J., ed. 1995. *Homage to Horace: A Bimillenary Celebration*. Oxford: Clarendon Press.

Harrison, Stephen J. 1996. '*Aeneid* 1.286: Julius Caesar or Augustus'. *Papers of the Leeds International Latin Seminar* 9: 127–33.

Harrison, Stephen J. 2005a. 'Vergil and the Mausoleum Augusti: *Georgics* 3.12–18'. *AClass* 48: 185–8.

REFERENCES 213

Harrison, Stephen J. 2005b. 'Hercules and Augustus in Propertius 4.9'. *Papers of the Langford Latin Seminar* 12: 117–31.

Harrison, Stephen J. 2007a. *Generic Enrichment in Vergil and Horace*. Oxford: Oxford University Press.

Harrison, Stephen J. 2007b. 'The Primal Voyage and the Ocean of Epos: Two Aspects of Metapoetic Imagery in Catullus, Virgil and Horace'. *Dictynna* 4.

Harrison, Stephen J. 2007c. 'Horatian Self-Representations'. In Harrison 2007d: 22–35.

Harrison, Stephen J., ed. 2007d. *The Cambridge Companion to Horace*. Cambridge: Cambridge University Press.

Harrison, Stephen J. 2016. 'Horace *Odes* 2.7: Greek Models and Roman Civil War'. In Delignon et al. 2016: 89–98.

Harrison, Stephen J. 2017. *Horace. Odes Book II*. Cambridge: Cambridge University Press.

Hejduk, Julia. 2009. 'Jupiter's *Aeneid*: *Fama* and *Imperium*'. *ClAnt* 28: 279–327.

Hejduk, Julia. 2020. *The God of Rome: Jupiter in Augustan Poetry*. Oxford: Oxford University Press.

Hekster, Olivier, and John Rich. 2006. 'Octavian and the Thunderbolt: The Temple of Apollo Palatinus and Roman Traditions and Temple Building'. *CQ* 56: 149–68.

Hellegouarc'h, Jean. 1972. *Le vocabulaire latin des relations et des parties politiques sous la République*. Paris: Les Belles Lettres.

Henderson, John. 1987. 'Suck it and See (Horace, *Epode* 8)'. In Michael Whitby, Philip R. Hardie, and Mary Whitby, eds. 1987. *Homo Viator: Classical Essays for John Bramble*. London: Bristol Classical Press, 105–18.

Henderson, John. 1993. 'Be Alert (Your Country Needs Lerts): Horace, *Satires* 1.9'. *PCPhS* 39: 67–93.

Henderson, John. 1994. 'On Getting Rid of Kings: Horace, *Satire* 1.7'. *CQ* 44: 146–70.

Henrichs, Albert. 1978. 'Horaz als Aretaloge des Dionysus: *credite posteri*'. *HSPh* 82: 203–11.

Henry, Elisabeth. 1989. *The Vigour of Prophecy: A Study of Virgil's Aeneid*. Carbondale and Edwardsville: Southern Illinois University Press.

Hershkowitz, Debra. 1991. 'The *Aeneid* in *Aeneid* 3'. *Vergilius* 37: 69–76.

Heslin, Peter. 2015. *The Museum of Augustus: The Temple of Apollo in Pompeii, the Portico of Philippus in Rome, and Latin Poetry*. Los Angeles: J. Paul Getty Museum.

Heslin, Peter. 2018. *Propertius, Greek Myth, and Virgil*. Oxford: Oxford University Press.

Heyworth, Stephen J. 1994. 'Some Allusions to Callimachus in Latin Poetry'. *MD* 33: 51–79.

Heyworth, Stephen J. 1995. 'Dividing Poems'. In Oronzo Pecere and Michael Reeve, eds. 1995. *Formative Stages of Classical Traditions: Latin Texts from Antiquity to the Renaissance*. Spoleto: Centro italiano di studi sull'Alto medioevo, 117–48.

Heyworth, Stephen J. 2007a. 'Propertius, Patronage and Politics'. *BICS* 50: 93–128.

Heyworth, Stephen J. 2007b. *Cynthia. A Companion to the Text of Propertius*. Oxford: Oxford University Press.

Heyworth, Stephen J. 2016. 'Irrational Panegyric in Augustan Poetry'. In Hardie 2016: 240–62.

Heyworth, Stephen J., and James H. W. Morwood. 2011. *A Commentary on Propertius, Book 3*. Oxford: Oxford University Press.

Hickson-Hahn, Frances. 2000. 'Pompey's *supplicatio duplicata*: A Novel Form of Thanksgiving'. *Phoenix* 54: 244–54.

Hinds, Stephen. 1998. *Allusion and Intertext: Dynamics of Appropriation in Roman Poetry*. Cambridge: Cambridge University Press.

Hollard, Virginie. 2016. 'La fonction politique du poète dans la cité à l'époque d'Auguste: l'exemple d'Horace (*Odes* et *Carmen saeculare*)'. In Delignon et al. 2016: 49–62.

214   REFERENCES

Hollis, Adrian. S. 1996. 'Octavian in the Fourth *Georgic*'. *CQ* 46: 305–8.

Holloway, Ross. 1984. 'Who's Who on the Ara Pacis?'. *Studi e Materiali* (*Studi in onore di Achille Adriani*) 6: 625–8.

Hornsby, Roger. 1962. 'Horace on Art and Politics (*Ode* 3.4)'. *CJ* 58: 97–104.

Horsfall, Nicholas. 1971. 'Numanus Remulus: Ethnography and Propaganda in *Aeneid* 9.598 ff.'. *Latomus* 30: 1108–16.

Horsfall, Nicholas. 1973. 'Dido in the Light of History'. *PVS* 13: 1–13.

Horsfall, Nicholas. 2006. *Virgil, Aeneid 3: A Commentary*. Leiden: Brill.

Horsfall, Nicholas. 2013. *Virgil, Aeneid 6: A Commentary*, 2 vols. Berlin and Boston: De Gruyter.

Hubbard, Margaret. 1974. *Propertius*. London: Duckworth.

Hunter, Richard. 1985. 'Horace on Friendship and Free Speech (*Epistles* 1.18 and *Satires* 1.4)'. *Hermes* 113: 480–90.

Hunter, Richard. 2001. 'Virgil and Theocritus: A Note on the Reception of the *Encomium to Ptolemy Philadelphus*'. *SemRom* 4: 159–63.

Hunter, Richard. 2006. *The Shadow of Callimachus: Studies in the Reception of Hellenistic Poetry at Rome*. Cambridge: Cambridge University Press.

Hurley, Donna W. 2001. *Suetonius: Diuus Claudius*. Cambridge: Cambridge University Press.

Hutchinson, Gregory O. 1981. 'Notes on the New Gallus'. *ZPE* 41: 37–42.

Hutchinson, Gregory O. 2002. 'The Publication and Individuality of Horace's *Odes* Books 1–3'. *CQ* 52: 517–37.

Hutchinson, Gregory O. 2006. *Propertius. Elegies Book IV*. Cambridge: Cambridge University Press.

Huttner, Ulrich. 1997a. *Die politische Rolle der Heraklesgestalt im griechischen Herrschertum*. Stuttgart: Steiner.

Huttner, Ulrich. 1997b. 'Hercules und Augustus'. *Chiron* 27: 369–91.

Iacopi, Irene, and Giovanna Tedone. 2005–6. 'Bibliotheca e porticus ad Apollinis'. *MDAI(R)* 112: 351–78.

Ingleheart, Jennifer. 2010. *A Commentary on Ovid, Tristia, Book 2*. Oxford: Oxford University Press.

Ingleheart, Jennifer. 2015. '*Exegi monumentum*: Exile, Death, Immortality and Monumentality in Ovid, *Tristia* 3.3'. *CQ* 65: 286–300.

James, Sharon L. 2003. *Learned Girls and Male Persuasion: Gender and Reading in Roman Love Elegy*. Berkeley: University of California Press.

Jameson, Fredric. 1971. *Marxism and Form*. Princeton: Princeton University Press.

Jameson, V. B. 1984. '*Virtus* Reformed: An "Aesthetic Response" Reading of Horace, *Odes* III 2'. *TAPhA* 114: 219–40.

Janan, Micaela. 2001. *The Politics of Desire: Propertius IV*. Berkeley: University of California Press.

Jocelyn, H. D. 1993. '*Carm.* 1.12 and the Notion of a "Pindarising" Horace'. *Sileno* 19: 101–29.

Johnson, Timothy S. 2004. *A Symposion of Praise: Horace Returns to Lyric in Odes IV*. Madison: University of Wisconsin Press.

Johnson, W. R. 1967. 'A Quean, a Great Queen? Cleopatra and the Politics of Misrepresentation'. *Arion* 6: 387–402.

Johnson, W. R. 1976. *Darkness Visible: A Study of Vergil's Aeneid*. Berkeley: University of California Press.

Johnson, W. R. 1997. 'Final Exit: Propertius 4.11'. In Deborah H. Roberts, Francis M. Dunn, and Don Fowler, eds. 1997. *Classical Closure: Reading the End in Greek and Latin Literature*. Princeton: Princeton University Press, 163–80.

REFERENCES   215

Judge, Edwin A. 1974. '*Res publica restituta*: A Modern Illusion?'. In James Evans, ed. 1974. *Polis and Imperium: Studies in Honour of Edward Togo Salmon.* Toronto: Hakkert, 279–311.

Kamptner, Margit. 2001. 'Gedanken zu Horaz, carm. 4,5'. *WS* 114: 285–96.

Kapust, Daniel J. 2011. *Republicanism, Rhetoric, and Roman Political Thought.* Cambridge: Cambridge University Press.

Karakasis, Evangelos. 2011. *Song Exchange in Roman Pastoral.* Berlin and New York: De Gruyter.

Kaster, Robert A. 1997. 'The Shame of the Romans'. *TAPhA* 127: 1–19.

Keith, Alison. 2008. *Propertius: Poet of Love and Leisure.* London: Bloomsbury.

Kennedy, Duncan F. 1992. '"Augustan" and "Anti-Augustan": Reflections on Terms of Reference'. In Powell 1992: 26–58.

Khan, H. A. 2000. '*Vt mater iuuenem...sic...quaerit patria Caesarem*: A Note on the Simile at Horace, *Odes* 4, 5, 9–16'. *Latomus* 59: 549–51.

Kidd, D. A. 1977. 'Virgil's Voyage'. *Prudentia* 9: 97–103.

Kiessling, A., and Richard Heinze. 1930. *Q. Horatius Flaccus. Erster Teil: Oden und Epoden.* Berlin: Weidmannsche Buchhandlung.

Kinsey, T. E. 1981. 'Virgil, *Aeneid* I.286–288'. *Liverpool Classical Monthly* 6: 27.

Klein, Richard. 1969. *Prinzipat und Freiheit.* Darmstadt: Wissenschaftliche Buchgesellschaft.

Kleiner, Diana E. E. 1978. 'The Great Friezes of the Ara Pacis Augustae. Greek Sources, Roman Derivatives, and Augustan Social Policy'. *MEFRM* 90: 753–85.

Kleiner, Diana E. E. 2005. 'Semblance and Storytelling in Augustan Rome'. In Galinsky 2005: 197–233.

Knorr, Ortwin. 2004. *Verborgene Kunst. Argumentationsstruktur und Buchaufbau in den Satiren des Horaz.* Hildesheim: Olms-Weidmann.

Knox, Peter E. 2005. 'Milestones in the Career of Tibullus'. *CQ* 55: 204–16.

Koenen, Ludwig. 1993. 'The Ptolemaic King as a Religious Figure'. In Anthony W. Bulloch, Erich S. Gruen, A. A. Long, and Andrew Stewart, eds. 1993. *Images and Ideologies: Self-Definition in the Hellenistic World.* Berkeley: University of California Press, 25–115.

Kofler, Wolfgang. 2003. *Aeneas und Vergil. Untersuchungen zur poetologischen Dimension der Aeneis.* Heidelberg: Winter.

Kondratieff, Eric. 2012. '*Anchises Censorius*: Vergil, Augustus, and the Census of 28 B.C.E.'. *ICS* 37: 121–40.

Konstan, David. 1978. 'The Politics of Tibullus 1.7'. *Rivista di studi classici* 26: 173–85.

Koortbojian, Michael. 2013. *The Divinization of Caesar and Augustus: Precedents, Consequences, Implications.* Cambridge: Cambridge University Press.

Korenjak, Martin. 2003. '*Tityri sub persona*: Der antike Biographismus und die bukolische Tradition'. *Antike und Abendland* 49: 58–79.

Koster, Severin. 1994. *Horaz-Studien.* Erlangen: Universitätsbund Erlangen-Nürnberg.

Koster, Severin. 1998. '*Descende caelo* (Horaz, carmen 3,4)'. In Anna E. Radke, ed. 1998. *Candide iudex. Beiträge zur augusteischen Dichtung.* Stuttgart: Steiner, 147–61.

Kovacs, David. 2009. 'Horace, Pindar and the Censorini in *Odes* 4.8'. *JRS* 99: 23–35.

Kowalzig, Barbara, and Peter Wilson, eds. 2013. *Dithyramb in Context.* Oxford: Oxford University Press.

Kraggerud, Egil. 1984. *Horaz und Actium: Studien zu den politischen Epoden.* Oslo: Universitetsforlaget.

Kraggerud, Egil. 1992. 'Which Julius Caesar? On *Aen.* 1, 286–296'. *SO* 67: 103–12.

Kraggerud, Egil. 1994. 'Caesar Versus Caesar Again: A Reply'. *SO* 69: 83–93.

Kraggerud, Egil. 1995. 'The Sixth Roman Ode of Horace: Its Date and Function'. *SO* 70: 54–67.

216 REFERENCES

Kraggerud, Egil. 1998. 'Virgil Announcing the *Aeneid*: On *Georgics* 3.1–48'. In Stahl 1998: 1–20.

Krasser, Helmut. 1995. *Horazische Denkfiguren: Theophilie und Theophanie als Medium der poetischen Selbstdarstellung des Odendichters*. Göttingen: Vandenhoeck & Ruprecht.

Kronenberg, Leah. 2009. *Allegories of Farming from Greece and Rome: Philosophical Satire in Xenophon, Varro and Virgil*. Cambridge: Cambridge University Press.

Kronenberg, Leah. 2016. 'Epicurean Pastoral: Daphnis as an Allegory for Lucretius in Vergil's *Eclogues*'. *Vergilius* 62: 25–56.

Kropp, Andreas. 2009. 'King–Caesar–God. Roman Imperial Cult Among Near-Eastern "Client" Kings in the Julio-Claudian Period'. In Michael Blömer, Margherita Facella, and Engelbert Winter, eds. *Lokale Identität im Römischen Nahen Osten: Kontexte und Perspektiven*. Stuttgart: Steiner, 99–150.

Krostenko, Brian A. 2005. 'Style and Ideology in the *Pro Marcello*'. In Kathryn Welch and T. W. Hillard, eds. 2005. *Roman Crossings: Theory and Practice in the Roman Republic*. Swansea: Classical Press of Wales, 283–316.

Lacey, Walter K. 1996. *Augustus and the Principate: The Evolution of the System*. Leeds: Francis Cairns.

Laird, Andrew. 2009. 'Virgil: Reception and the Myth of Biography'. *CentoPagine* 3: 1–9.

Lange, Carsten H. 2009. *Res Publica Constituta: Actium, Apollo and the Accomplishment of the Triumviral Assignment*. Leiden: Brill.

Lange, Carsten H. 2011. 'The Battle of Actium: A Reconsideration'. *CQ* 61: 608–23.

Lange, Carsten H. 2015. 'Augustus' Triumphal and Triumph-like Returns'. In Ida Östenberg, Simon Malmberg, and Jonas Bjørnebye, eds. 2015. *The Moving City: Processions, Passages and Promenades in Ancient Rome*. London: Bloomsbury, 133–44.

La Penna, Antonio. 1951. *Properzio*. Florence: La Nuova Italia.

La Penna, Antonio. 1963. *Orazio e l'ideologia del principato*. Turin: Einaudi.

La Rocca, Eugenio. 1992. '*Theoi epiphaneis*: linguaggio figurativo e culto dinastico da Antioco IV ad Augusto'. *SIFC* 10: 630–78.

Leach, Eleanor W. 1974. *Vergil's Eclogues: Landscapes of Experience*. Ithaca: Cornell University Press.

Leach, Eleanor W. 1988. *The Rhetoric of Space: Literary and Artistic Representations of Landscape in Republican and Augustan Rome*. Princeton: Princeton University Press.

Leclercq, René. 1996. *Le divin loisir*. Brussels: Latomus.

Le Doze, Philippe. 2009. 'Aux origines d'une retraite politique: Mécène et la *res publica restituta*'. In Frédéric Hurlet and Bernard Mineo, eds. 2009. *Le Principat d'Auguste. Réalités et représentations du pouvoir. Autour de la Res publica restituta*. Rennes: Presses universitaires de Rennes, 101–18.

Le Doze, Philippe. 2010. 'Les idéologies à Rome: les modalités du discours politique de Cicéron à Auguste'. *Revue historique* 654: 259–89.

Le Doze, Philippe. 2014a. *Le Parnasse face à l'Olympe. Poésie et culture politique à l'époque d'Octavien/Auguste*. Rome: École française de Rome.

Le Doze, Philippe. 2014b. *Mécène. Ombres et flamboyances*. Paris: Les Belles Lettres.

Le Doze, Philippe. 2015. '*Res publica restituta*. Réflexions sur la restauration augustéenne'. *CCG* 26: 79–108.

Le Doze, Philippe. 2019. 'Maecenas and the Augustan Poets: The Background of a Cultural Ambition'. In Josiah Osgood, Kit Morrell, and Kathryn Welch, eds. 2019. *The Alternative Augustan Age*. Oxford: Oxford University Press, 231–46.

Leeman, Anton D. 1985. *Form und Sinn: Studien zur römischen Literatur (1954–1984)*. Frankfurt: Peter Lang.

REFERENCES 217

Lefèvre, Eckard. 1993. *Horaz. Dichter im augusteischen Rom*. Munich: Beck.

Letta, Cesare. 2003. 'Novità epigrafiche sul culto del Genius Augusti in Italia'. In Maria Angeli Bertinelli and Angela Donati, eds. 2003. *Usi e abusi epigrafici*. Rome: Bretschneider, 217–36.

Levene, David. 1997. 'God and Man in the Classical Latin Panegyric'. *PCPhS* 43: 66–103.

Levene, David. 2012. 'Defining the Divine in Rome: In Memoriam S. R. F. Price. *TAPhA* 142: 41–81.

Levick, Barbara. 2010. *Augustus: Image and Substance*. London and New York: Longman.

Liegle, Josef. 1943. 'Die Tityrusekloge'. *Hermes* 78: 209–31.

Loar, Matthew P. 2017. 'Hercules, Mummius, and the Roman Triumph in *Aeneid* 8'. *CPh* 112: 45–62.

Lott, J. Bert. 2014. *The Neighbourhoods of Augustan Rome*. Cambridge: Cambridge University Press.

Louis, Nathalie. 2010. *Commentaire historique et traduction du Divus Augustus de Suétone*. Brussels: Latomus.

Loupiac, Annick. 1998. 'Le trilogie d'Actium et l'*Épode IX* d'Horace: document historique ou *carmen symposiacum?*'. *BAGB* 3: 250–9.

Lowrie, Michèle. 1997. *Horace's Narrative Odes*. Oxford: Oxford University Press.

Lowrie, Michèle. 2009. *Writing, Performance, and Authority in Augustan Rome*. Oxford: Oxford University Press.

Lowrie, Michèle. 2010. 'Horace *Odes* 4'. In Davis 2010: 210–30.

Lowrie, Michèle. 2015. '*Rege incolumi*: Orientalism, Civil War, and Security at *Georgics* 4.212'. In Paolo Fedeli and Hans-Christian Günther, eds. 2015. *Virgilian Studies: A Miscellany Dedicated to the Memory of Mario Geymonat (26.1.1941–17.2.2012)*. Nordhausen: Bautz, 322–42.

Lowrie, Michèle. 2016. 'Le corps du chef: transformations dans la sphère publique à l'époque d'Horace'. In Delignon et al. 2016: 71–86.

Luce, T. J. 1965. 'The Dating of Livy's First Decade'. *TAPhA* 96: 209–40.

Luck, Georg. 1979. 'Notes on Propertius'. *AJPh* 100: 73–93.

Luke, Trevor S. 2014. *Ushering in a New Republic: Theologies of Arrival at Rome in the First Century BCE*. Ann Arbor: University of Michigan Press.

Lundström, Sven. 1976. 'Der Eingang des Proömiums zum dritten Buche der Georgica'. *Hermes* 104: 163–91.

Lushkov, Ayelet. 2020. 'Livy's Ennius'. In Damon and Farrell 2020: 211–27.

Luther, Andreas. 2003. 'Zur Regulus-Ode (Horaz, C. 3,5)'. *RhM* 146: 10–22.

Lyne, R. O. A. M. 1974. '*scilicet et tempus ueniet…* Virgil, *Georgics* 1.463–514'. In Woodman and West 1974: 47–66.

Lyne, R. O. A. M. 1987. *Further Voices in Vergil's Aeneid*. Oxford: Clarendon Press.

Lyne, R. O. A. M. 1995. *Horace: Behind the Public Poetry*. New Haven and London: Yale University Press.

Mac Góráin, Fiachra, 2020. 'Introduction. Dionysus and Rome: Accommodation and Resistance'. In Fiachra Mac Góráin, ed. 2020. *Dionysus and Rome: Religion and Literature*. Berlin and Boston: De Gruyter, 1–37.

Mac Góráin, Fiachra. 2021. 'Augustus and the *Neoi Dionysoi*'. In Filip Doroszewski and Dariusz Karłowicz, eds. 2020. *Dionysus and Politics: Constructing Authority in the Greco-Roman World*. London: Routledge: 89–102.

Macleod, C. W. 1982. 'Horace and His Lyric Models: A Note on *Epode* 9 and *Odes* 1,37'. *Hermes* 110: 371–5.

Mader, Gottfried. 1989. 'Heroism and Hallucination: Cleopatra in Horace C. 1.37 and Propertius 3.11'. *GB* 16: 183–201.

218 REFERENCES

Maehler, Herwig. 2004. *Bacchylides. A Selection*. Cambridge: Cambridge University Press.

Mankin, David. 1995. *Horace. Epodes*. Cambridge: Cambridge University Press.

Manuwald, Gesine. 2007. *Cicero, Philippics 3-9. Edited with Introduction, Translation and Commentary*, Vol. 1: *Introduction, Text and Translation, References and Indexes*; Vol. 2: *Commentary*. Berlin and Boston: De Gruyter.

Manuwald, Gesine. 2011. 'Ciceronian Praise as a Step Towards Pliny's *Panegyricus*'. In Paul Roche, ed. 2011. *Pliny's Praise: The Panegyricus in the Roman World*. Cambridge: Cambridge University Press, 85–103.

Marcone, Arnaldo. 2010. 'Un "dio presente": osservazioni sulle premesse ellenistiche del culto imperiale romano'. In Silvia Bussi and Daniele Foraboschi, eds. 2010. *Roma e l'eredità ellenistica*. Pisa: Serra, 205–10.

Marek, Christian. 1993. 'Die Expedition des Aelius Gallus nach Arabien im Jahre 25 v. Chr'. *Chiron* 23: 121–56.

Martindale, Charles. ed. 1997. *The Cambridge Companion to Virgil*. 1st edn. Cambridge: Cambridge University Press.

Mau, August. 1908. *Pompeii in Leben und Kunst*. Leipzig: Engelmann.

Maurach, Gregor. 2001. *Horaz: Werk und Leben*. Heidelberg: Winter.

Mayer, Roland. 1983. 'Missing Persons in the *Eclogues*'. *BICS* 30: 17–30.

Mayer, Roland. 2012. *Horace. Odes. Book 1*. Cambridge: Cambridge University Press.

McGinn, Thomas. 2001. 'Satire and the Law: The Case of Horace'. *PCPhS* 47: 81–102.

McGowan, Matthew. 2009. *Ovid in Exile: Power and Poetic Redress in the Tristia and Epistulae ex Ponto*. Leiden: Brill.

Meban, David. 2009. 'Virgil's *Eclogues* and Social Memory'. *AJPh* 130: 99–130.

Meister, Felix. 2020. *Greek Praise Poetry and the Rhetoric of Divinity*. Oxford: Oxford University Press.

Michel, Jacques-Henri. 1999. 'La satire 2.1 à Trébatius ou la consultation du juriste'. *RIDA* 46: 369–91.

Millar, Fergus. 1973. 'Triumvirate and Principate'. *JRS* 63: 50–67.

Miller, John F. 1981. 'Propertius 2.1 and the New Gallus Papyrus'. *ZPE* 44: 173–6.

Miller, John F. 1982. 'Callimachus and the Augustan Aetiological Elegy'. *ANRW* II.30.1, 371–417.

Miller, John F. 1994. 'Virgil, Apollo, and Augustus'. In Jon Solomon, ed. 1994. *Apollo: Origins and Influence*. Tucson: University of Arizona Press, 99–112.

Miller, John F. 1998. 'Horace's Pindaric Apollo (*Odes* 3.4.60-4)'. *CQ* 48: 545–52.

Miller, John F. 2009. *Apollo, Augustus and the Poets*. Cambridge: Cambridge University Press.

Miller, Paul Allen. 1991. 'Horace, Mercury, and Augustus, or the Poetic Ego of *Odes* 1-3'. *AJPh* 112, 365–88.

Miller, Paul Allen. 2004. *Subjecting Verses: Latin Love Elegy and the Emergence of the Real*. Princeton: Princeton University Press.

Mitchell, Elizabeth. 2010. 'Time for An Emperor: Old Age and the Future of the Empire in Horace *Odes* 4'. *MD* 64: 43–76.

Moles, John. 1983. 'Fate, Apollo, and M. Junius Brutus'. *AJPh* 104: 249–56.

Moles, John. 1987. 'Politics, Philosophy, and Friendship in Horace's *Odes* 2, 7'. *QUCC* 25: 59–72.

Moles, John. 1993. 'Livy's Preface'. *PCPhS* 39: 141–68.

Molyviati-Toptsis, Urania. 1995. '*Sed falsa ad caelum mittunt insomnia Manes* (*Aeneid* 6.896)'. *AJPh* 116: 639–52.

Momigliano, Arnaldo. 1942a. '*Terra marique*'. *JRS* 32: 53–64.

REFERENCES   219

Momigliano, Arnaldo. 1942b. 'The Peace of the Ara Pacis'. *Journal of the Warburg and Courtauld Institutes* 5: 228–31.

Moore, Timothy. 1989. 'Tibullus 1.7: Reconciliation through Conflict'. *CW* 82: 423–30.

Morelli, Alfredo M. 2016. 'Lo Scipio e la poesia celebrativa enniana per Scipione. Con una appendice sul problema storico dell''ultimo discorso' dell'Africano'. In Bruna Pieri and Daniele Pellacani, eds. 2016. *Si verba tenerem. Studi sulla poesia latina in frammenti*, Berlin and Boston: De Gruyter, 53–78.

Moretti, Giuseppe. 1948. *Ara Pacis Augustae*. Rome: Libreria dello Stato.

Morgan, Llewelyn. 1998. 'Assimilation and Civil War: Hercules and Cacus (*Aen.* 8.185–267)'. In Stahl 1998: 175–97.

Morgan, Llewelyn. 1999. *Patterns of Redemption in Virgil's Georgics*. Cambridge: Cambridge University Press.

Morgan, Llewelyn. 2005a. 'A Yoke Connecting Baskets: *Odes* 3.14, Hercules, and Italian Unity'. *CQ* 51: 190–203.

Morgan, Llewelyn. 2005b. 'Spartan Tarentum? Resisting Decline in *Odes* 3.5'. *CQ* 55: 320–3.

Mouritsen, Henrik. 2011. *The Freedman in the Roman World*. Cambridge: Cambridge University Press.

Muecke, Frances. 1993. *Horace. Satires II*. Warminster: Aris & Philips.

Murray, William M., and Photios M. Petsas. 1989. *Octavian's Campsite Memorial for the Actian War*. Philadelphia: American Philosophical Society.

Myers, K. Sara. 2009. *Ovid. Metamorphoses XIV*. Cambridge: Cambridge University Press.

Mynors, R. A. B. 1990. *Virgil's Georgics. A Commentary*. Oxford: Clarendon Press.

Nappa, Christopher. 2005. *Reading after Actium: Vergil's Georgics, Octavian, and Rome*. Ann Arbor: University of Michigan Press.

Nauta, Ruurd R. 2006. 'Panegyric in Virgil's *Bucolics*'. In Fantuzzi and Papanghelis 2006: 301–32.

Nelis, Damien P. 2001. *Vergil's Aeneid and the Argonautica of Apollonius Rhodius*. Leeds: Francis Cairns.

Nelis, Damien P. 2008. 'Caesar, the Circus and the Charioteer'. In Jocelyne Nelis-Clément and Jean-Michel Roddaz, eds. 2008. *Le cirque romain et son image*. Bordeaux: Ausonius. 497–520.

Nelis, Damien P. 2013. 'Past, Present and Future in Virgil's *Georgics*'. In Farrell and Nelis 2013: 244–62.

Nelson, Stephanie. 1998. *God and the Land: The Metaphysics of Farming in Hesiod and Vergil*. Oxford: Oxford University Press.

Nethercut, William R. 1970. 'The Ironic Priest. Propertius' "Roman Elegies", 3.1–5: Imitations of Horace and Vergil'. *AJPh* 91: 385–407.

Nethercut, William R. 1971. 'Propertius 3.11'. *TAPhA* 102: 411–43.

Nisbet, R. G. M. 1962. '*Romanae fidicen lyrae*: The *Odes* of Horace'. In John P. Sullivan, ed. 1962. *Critical Essays on Roman Literature. Elegy and Lyric*. London: Routledge and Kegan Paul, 181–218.

Nisbet, R. G. M. 1978. 'Virgil's Fourth Eclogue: Easterners and Westerners'. *BICS* 25: 59–78.

Nisbet, R. G. M. 1984. 'Horace's *Epodes* and History'. In Woodman and West 1984: 1–18.

Nisbet, R. G. M., and Margaret Hubbard. 1970. *A Commentary on Horace: Odes I*. Oxford: Clarendon Press.

Nisbet, R. G. M., and Niall Rudd. 2004. *A Commentary on Horace: Odes III*. Oxford: Oxford University Press.

Norden, Eduard. 1924. *Die Geburt des Kindes*. Leipzig: Teubner.

North, John. A. 1975. 'Praesens Divus. [Review of S. Weinstock, *Divus Julius*]'. *JRS* 65: 171–7.

220 REFERENCES

O'Gorman, Ellen. 2002. 'Archaism and Historicism in Horace's *Odes*'. In David Levene and Damien P. Nelis, eds. 2002. *Clio and the Poets: Augustan Poetry and the Traditions of Ancient Historiography*. Leiden: Brill, 81–101.

O'Hara, James J. 1990. *Death and the Optimistic Prophecy in Vergil's Aeneid*. Princeton: Princeton University Press.

O'Hara, James J. 1994. 'Temporal Distortions, "Fatal" Ambiguity, and *Iulius Caesar* at *Aeneid* 1.286–96'. *SO* 69: 72–82.

O'Hara, James J. 2007. *Inconsistency in Roman Epic*. Cambridge: Cambridge University Press.

Oliensis, Ellen. 1991. 'Canidia, Canicula, and the Decorum of Horace's *Epodes*'. *Arethusa* 24: 107–38.

Oliensis, Ellen. 1997. '*Ut arte emendaturus fortunam*: Horace, Nasidienus, and the Art of Satire'. In Habinek and Schiesaro 1997: 90–104.

Oliensis, Ellen. 1998. *Horace and the Rhetoric of Authority*. Cambridge: Cambridge University Press.

Osgood, Josiah. 2006. *Caesar's Legacy: Civil War and the Emergence of the Roman Empire*. Cambridge: Cambridge University Press.

Osgood, Josiah. 2014. *Turia: A Roman Woman's Civil War*. Oxford: Oxford University Press.

Östenberg, Ida. 1999. 'Demonstrating the Conquest of the World: The Procession of Peoples and Rivers on the Shield of Aeneas and the Triple Triumph of Octavian in 29 B.C. (*Aen.* 8.722–728)'. *ORom* 24: 155–62.

Östenberg, Ida. 2009. *Staging the World: Spoils, Captives, and Representations in the Roman Triumphal Procession*. Oxford: Oxford University Press.

Page, T. E. 1894. *The Aeneid of Virgil*. 2 vols. London.

Pandey, Nandini. 2018. *The Poetics of Power in Augustan Rome* Cambridge: Cambridge University Press.

Panoussi, Vassiliki. 2009. *Tragedy in Vergil's Aeneid: Ritual, Empire and Intertext*. Cambridge: Cambridge University Press.

Papanghelis, Theodore. 2006. 'Friends, Foes, Frames and Fragments: Textuality in Virgil's *Eclogues*'. In Fantuzzi and Papanghelis 2006: 369–402.

Parry, Adam. 1963. 'The Two Voices of Virgil's *Aeneid*'. *Arion* 2: 66–80.

Paschalis, Michael. 1986. 'Virgil and the Delphic Oracle'. *Philologus* 130: 44–68.

Pease, Arthur S. 1958. *M. Tulli Ciceronis de Natura Deorum. Libri Secundus et Tertius*. Cambridge, MA: Harvard University Press.

Pelling, Christopher. 1988. *Plutarch: Life of Antony*. Cambridge: Cambridge University Press.

Pelling, Christopher. 1996. 'The Triumviral Period'. *CAH* X: 1–69.

Perkell, Christine G. 1989. *The Poet's Truth. A Study of the Poet in Virgil's Georgics*. Berkeley: University of California Press.

Perkell, Christine G., ed. 1999. *Reading Vergil's Aeneid: An Interpretive Guide*. Norman: University of Oklahoma Press.

Perkell, Christine G. 2001. 'Vergil Reading His Twentieth-Century Readers: A Study of *Eclogue* 9'. *Vergilius* 47: 64–88.

Perutelli, Alessandro. 1995. 'Bucolics'. In Nicholas Horsfall, ed. 1995. *A Companion to the Study of Virgil*. Leiden: Brill, 27–62.

Petrovic, Ivana. 2008. 'Aitiologie des Triumphes: Die Hymnen von Kallimachos und Properz 4,6'. In Helmut Krasser, Dennis Pausch, and Ivana Petrovic, eds. 2008. *Triplici invectus triumpho: Der römische Triumph in augusteischer Zeit*. Stuttgart: Steiner, 191–208.

Pettit, Philip. 2012. *On the People's Terms: A Republican Theory and Model of Democracy*. Cambridge: Cambridge University Press.

REFERENCES   221

Pfeiffer, Stefan. 2016. 'The Ptolemies: Hellenistic Kingship in Egypt'. *Oxford Handbooks Online.* DOI: 10.1093/oxfordhb/9780199935390.001.0001/oxfordhb-9780199935390-e-23.

Pillinger, Hugh E. 1969. 'Some Callimachean Influences on Propertius, Book 4'. *HSPh* 73: 171–99.

Pina Polo, Francisco, ed. 2020. *The Triumviral Period: Civil War, Political Crisis and Socioeconomic Transformations.* Seville and Zaragoza: Editorial Universidad de Sevilla and Prensas de la Universidad de Zaragoza.

Pollini, John. 1990. 'Man or God: Divine Assimilation and Imitation in the Late Republic and Early Principate'. In Raaflaub and Toher 1990: 334–63.

Pollini, John. 1993. 'The Gemma Augustea: Ideology, Rhetorical Imagery and the Creation of a Dynastic Narrative'. In Peter J. Holliday, ed. 1993. *Narrative and Event in Ancient Art.* Cambridge: Cambridge University Press, 258–98.

Porter, David H. 1987. *Horace's Poetic Journey: A Reading of Odes 1–3.* Princeton: Princeton University Press.

Pöschl, Viktor. 1973. 'Die Dionysosode des Horaz (c. 2, 19)'. *Hermes* 101: 208–30.

Pöschl, Viktor. 1991. *Horazische Lyrik: Interpretationen.* Heidelberg: Winter.

Powell, Anton, ed. 1992. *Roman Poetry and Propaganda in the Age of Augustus.* London: Bristol Classical Press.

Powell, Anton. 2008. *Virgil the Partisan. A Study in the Re-integration of Classics.* Swansea: Classical Press of Wales.

Powell, Jonathan G. F. 2010. 'Horace, Scythia, and the East'. *Papers of the Langford Latin Seminar* 14: 137–90.

Price, Simon R. F. 1984a. *Rituals and Power: The Roman Imperial Cult in Asia Minor.* Cambridge: Cambridge University Press.

Price, Simon R. F. 1984b. 'Gods and Emperors: The Greek Language of the Roman Imperial Cult'. *JHS* 104: 79–95.

Putnam, Michael C. J. 1965. *The Poetry of the Aeneid.* Cambridge, MA: Harvard University Press.

Putnam, Michael C. J. 1980a. 'Propertius' Third Book: Patterns of Cohesion'. *Arethusa* 13: 97–113.

Putnam, Michael C. J. 1980b. 'Propertius and the New Gallus Fragment'. *ZPE* 39: 49–56.

Putnam, Michael C. J. 1986. *Artifices of Eternity: Horace's Fourth Book of Odes.* Ithaca: Cornell University Press.

Putnam, Michael C. J. 1995. 'From Lyric to Letter: Iccius in Horace *Odes* 1.29 and *Epistles* 1.12'. *Arethusa* 28: 193–207.

Putnam, Michael C. J. 1998. *Virgil's Epic Designs: Ekphrasis in the Aeneid.* New Haven and London: Yale University Press.

Putnam, Michael C. J. 2000. *Horace's Carmen Saeculare: Ritual Magic and the Poet's Art.* New Haven and London: Yale University Press.

Quint, David. 1993. *Epic and Empire: Politics and Generic Form from Virgil to Milton.* Princeton: Princeton University Press.

Raaflaub, Kurt A., and Mark Toher, eds. 1990. *Between Republic and Empire: Interpretations of Augustus and His Principate.* Berkeley: University of California Press.

Race, William H. 2010. 'Horace's Debt to Pindar'. In Davis 2010: 147–73.

Ramsey, John T., and A. Lewis Licht. 1997. *The Comet of 44 B.C. and Caesar's Funeral Games.* Atlanta: Scholars Press.

Reckford, Kenneth J. 1999. 'Only a Wet Dream? Hope and Skepticism in Horace, *Satire* 1.5'. *AJPh* 120: 525–54.

222   REFERENCES

Rehak, Paul. 2001. 'Aeneas or Numa? Rethinking the Meaning of the Ara Pacis Augustae'. *The Art Bulletin* 83: 190–208.

Reinhardt, Tobias, and Michael Winterbottom. 2006. *Quintilian: Institutio Oratoria Book 2*. Oxford: Oxford University Press.

Reitzenstein, Erich. 1969. 'Die Cornelia-Elegie des Properz (IV 11): eine Formuntersuchung und ihre Ergebnisse für die Textkritik'. *RhM* 112: 126–45.

Rich, John W. 1998. 'Augustus' Parthian Honors, the Temple of Mars Ultor, and the Arch in the Roman Forum'. *PBSR* 66: 71–128.

Rich, John W., and J. H. C. Williams. 1999. '*Leges et Iura P.R. Restituit*: A New Aureus of Octavian and the Settlement of 28–27 BC'. *NC* 159: 169–213.

Richter, W. 1966. 'Divus Julius, Octavianus und Kleopatra bei Aktion'. *WS* 79: 451–65.

Ricoeur, Paul. 1965. *De l'interprétation: Essai sur Freud*. Paris: Seuil.

Rimell, Victoria. 2015. *The Closure of Space in Roman Poetics*. Cambridge: Cambridge University Press.

Robinson, Matthew. 2011. *A Commentary on Ovid's Fasti, Book 2*. Oxford: Oxford University Press.

Roccos, Linda J. 1989. 'Apollo Palatinus: The Augustan Apollo on the Sorrento Base'. *AJA* 93: 571–88.

Rogerson, Anne. 2017. *Virgil's Ascanius: Imagining the Future in the Aeneid*. Cambridge: Cambridge University Press.

Roman, Luke. 2014. *Poetic Autonomy in Ancient Rome*. Oxford: Oxford University Press.

Rose, Charles B. 2005. 'The Parthians in Augustan Rome'. *AJA* 109: 21–75.

Rose, H. J. 1942. *The Eclogues of Virgil*. Berkeley: University of California Press.

Rosso, Emmanuelle. 2015. '*Genius Augusti*. Construire la divinité imperiale en images'. In Sylvia Estienne, Valérie Huet, François Lissarrague, and Francis Prost, eds. 2015. *Figures de dieux. Construire le divin en images*. Rennes: Presses universitaires de Rennes, 39–76.

Rowland, Robert J. 1968. 'Foreshadowing in Vergil, *Aeneid*, VIII, 714–28'. *Latomus* 27: 832–42.

Rudd, Niall. 1966. *The Satires of Horace*. Berkeley: University of California Press.

Rudd, Niall. 1989. *Horace. Epistles Book II and Epistle to the Pisones ('Ars Poetica')*. Cambridge: Cambridge University Press.

Rumpf, Lorenz. 2009. '*Caelum ipsum petimus stultitia*. Zur poetologischen Deutung von Horaz' c. 1.3'. *RhM* 152: 292–311.

Rundin, John. 2003. 'The Epicurean Morality of Vergil's *Bucolics*'. *CW* 96: 159–76.

Ryberg, Inez S. 1949. 'The Procession of the Ara Pacis'. *MAAR* 19: 77–102.

Ryberg, Inez S. 1958. 'Vergil's Golden Age'. *TAPhA* 89: 112–31.

Santirocco, Matthew S. 1986. *Unity and Design in Horace's Odes*. Chapel Hill: University of North Carolina Press.

Sartre, Maurice. 2005. *The Middle East under Rome*. Cambridge, MA: Belknap Press of Harvard University Press.

Schenker, David J. 1993. 'Poetic Voices in the Roman Odes'. *CJ* 88: 147–66.

Schiesaro, Alessandro. 2009. 'Horace's Bacchic Poetics'. In Luke B. T. Houghton and Maria Wyke, eds. 2009. *Perceptions of Horace: A Roman Poet and His Readers*. Cambridge: Cambridge University Press, 61–79.

Schmidt. Ernst A. 2002. *Form und Zeit: Dichtungen des Horaz*. Heidelberg: Winter.

Schmidt, P. L. (1984), 'Structure and Sources of Horace, *Ode* 1.12'. In Harold D. Evjen, ed. 1984. *Mnemai: Classical Studies in Memory of Karl K. Hulley*. Chico: Scholars Press, 139–49.

Schnegg-Köhler, Bärbel. 2002. *Die augusteischen Säkularspiele*. Munich: Saur.

REFERENCES   223

Scholl, Walther. 2014. *Der Daphnis-Mythos und seine Entwicklung. Von den Anfängen bis zu Vergils vierter Ekloge.* Hildesheim: Georg Olms.

Schwindt, Jürgen P. 2005. 'Zeiten und Räume in augusteischer Dichtung'. In Jürgen P. Schwindt, ed. 2005. *La représentation du temps dans la poésie augustéenne/Zur Poetik der Zeit in augusteischer Dichtung.* Heidelberg: Winter, 1–15.

Scott. K. 1928. 'Mercur-Augustus und Horaz C.I.2'. *Hermes* 63: 15–33.

Scott. K. 1933. 'The Political Propaganda of 44–30 BC'. *MAAR* 11: 7–49.

Seager, Robin. 1980. '*Neu sinas Medos equitare inultos*: Horace, the Parthians and Augustan Foreign Policy'. *Athenaeum* 58: 103–18.

Segal, Charles. 1981. 'Art and the Hero: Participation, Detachment, and Narrative Point of View in *Aeneid* 1'. *Arethusa* 14: 67–83.

Setaioli, Aldo. 1981. 'Gli "Epodi" di Orazio nella critica dal 1937 al 1972 (con un appendice fino al 1978)'. *ANRW* II 31.1, 1674–1788.

Shapiro, H. Alan. 1983. 'Hêrôs Theos: The Death and Apotheosis of Herakles'. *CW* 77: 7–18.

Sharrock, Alison. 1994. 'Ovid and the Politics of Reading'. *MD* 33: 169–82.

Sidebotham, Steven. 1986. 'Aelius Gallus and Arabia'. *Latomus* 45: 590–602.

Silk, Edmund T. 1969. 'Bacchus and the Horatian *recusatio*'. *YCIS* 21: 193–212.

Simpson, C. J. 2002. '*Exegi monumentum*: Building Imagery and Metaphor in Horace, *Odes* 1–3'. *Latomus* 61: 57–66.

Skinner, Quentin. 1998. *Liberty before Liberalism.* Cambridge: Cambridge University Press.

Skutsch, Otto. 1985. *The Annals of Q. Ennius.* Oxford: Oxford University Press.

Slater, W. J. 1976. 'Symposium at Sea'. *HSPh* 80: 161–70.

Smith, Joshua M. 2015. 'Horace *Odes* 2.7 and the Literary Tradition of *Rhipsaspia*'. *AJPh* 136: 243–80.

Smith, Martin S. 1975. *Petronius. Cena Trimalchionis.* Oxford: Clarendon Press.

Smith, R. Alden. 2005. *The Primacy of Vision in Virgil's Aeneid.* Austin: University of Texas Press.

Smith, R. R. R. 2021. '*Maiestas Serena*: Roman Court Cameos and Early Imperial Poetry and Panegyric'. *JRS* 111: 75–152.

Snijder, H. 2010. 'The Cosmology of Octavian's Divine Birth in Vergil's Fourth Eclogue'. In Carl Deroux, ed. 2010. *Studies in Latin Literature and Roman History XV.* Brussels: Latomus, 178–95.

Sonnabend, Holger. 1986. *Fremdenbild und Politik: Vorstellungen der Römer von Ägypten und dem Partherreich in der späten Republik und frühen Kaiserzeit.* Frankfurt: Peter Lang.

Spagnuolo Vigorita, Tullio. 2010. *Casta domus: un seminario sulla legislazione matrimoniale augustea.* Naples: Jovene.

Stahl, Hans-Peter. 1985. *Propertius: 'Love' and 'War': Individual and State under Augustus.* Berkeley: University of California Press.

Stahl, Hans-Peter, ed. 1998. *Vergil's Aeneid: Augustan Epic and Political Context.* Swansea: Classical Press of Wales.

Stahl, Hans-Peter. 2015. *Poetry Underpinning Power. Vergil's Aeneid: The Epic for Emperor Augustus. A Recovery Study.* Swansea: Classical Press of Wales.

Steel, Catherine E. W. 2001. *Cicero, Rhetoric, and Empire.* Oxford: Oxford University Press.

Stevens, John A. 1999. 'Seneca and Horace: Allegorical Technique in Two Odes to Bacchus (Hor. *Carm.* 2.19 and Sen. *Oed.* 403–508)'. *Phoenix* 53: 281–307.

Stewart, Peter C. N. 2003. *Statues in Roman Society: Representation and Response.* Oxford: Oxford University Press.

Stöckinger, Martin. 2016. *Vergils Gaben: Materialität, Reziprozität und Poetik in den Eklogen und der Aeneis.* Heidelberg: Winter.

224 REFERENCES

Stover, Tim. 2014. *Epic and Empire in Vespasianic Rome: A New Reading of Valarius Flaccus'* *Argonautica*. Oxford: Oxford University Press.

Sullivan, J. P. 1976. *Propertius. A Critical Introduction*. Cambridge: Cambridge University Press.

Sutherland, Elizabeth H. 2002. *Horace's Well-Trained Reader*. Frankfurt: Peter Lang.

Syed, Yasmin. 2005. *Vergil's Aeneid and the Roman Self: Subject and Nation in Literary Discourse*. Ann Arbor: University of Michigan Press.

Syme, Ronald. 1978. *History in Ovid*. Oxford: Clarendon Press.

Syme, Ronald. 1986. The *Augustan Aristocracy*. Oxford: Clarendon Press.

Syme, Ronald. 1987. 'Exotic Names, Notably in Seneca's Tragedies'. *AClass* 30: 49–64.

Syndikus, Hans P. 1972. *Die Lyrik des Horaz: eine Interpretation der Oden: Band I, Erstes und zweites Buch*. Darmstadt: Wissenschaftliche Buchgesellschaft.

Syndikus, Hans P. 1973. *Die Lyrik des Horaz: eine Interpretation der Oden: Band II, Drittes und viertes Buch*. Darmstadt: Wissenschaftliche Buchgesellschaft.

Tandy, David W. 1985. 'Vergil, *Georgics* 1.42: The Immanence of Octavian'. *Vergilius* 31: 54–7.

Tarpin, Michel. 2002. *Vici et pagi dans l'Occident romain*. Rome: École française de Rome.

Tarrant, Richard J. 1982. 'Aeneas and the Gates of Sleep'. *CPh* 80: 51–5.

Tatum, Jeffrey W. 1998. '*Ultra Legem*: Law and Literature in Horace, *Satires* II 1'. *Mnemosyne* 51: 688–99.

Tatum, Jeffrey W. 2020a. '"A Great and Arduous Struggle": Mark Antony and the Rhetoric of *Libertas* in 44–43 BC'. In Catalina Balmaceda, ed. 2020. *Libertas and Res Publica in the Roman Republic*. Leiden: Brill, 189–215.

Tatum, Jeffrey W. 2020b. 'Antonius and Athens'. In Pina Polo 2020: 451–73.

Taylor, Lily Ross. 1931. *The Divinity of the Roman Emperor*. Middletown, CT: American Philological Association.

Tempest, Kathryn. 2013. 'Hellenistic Oratory at Rome: Cicero's *Pro Marcello*'. In Christos Kremmydas and Kathryn Tempest, eds. *Hellenistic Oratory: Continuity and Change*. Oxford: Oxford University Press, 295–318.

Thomas, Richard F. 1982. *Lands and People in Roman Poetry: The Ethnographical Tradition*. Cambridge: Cambridge University Press.

Thomas, Richard F. 1983. 'Virgil's Ecphrastic Centerpieces'. *HSPh* 87: 175–84.

Thomas, Richard F. 1986. 'Virgil's *Georgics* and the Art of Reference'. *HSPh* 90: 171–98.

Thomas, Richard F. 1988. *Virgil. Georgics*. 2 vols. Cambridge: Cambridge University Press.

Thomas, Richard F. 2001. *Virgil and the Augustan Reception*. Cambridge: Cambridge University Press.

Thomas, Richard F. 2011. *Horace. Odes IV and Carmen Saeculare*. Cambridge: Cambridge University Press.

Vasaly, Ann. 2015. *Livy's Political Philosophy: Power and Personality in Early Rome*. Cambridge: Cambridge University Press.

Veyne, Paul. 1976. *Le pain et le cirque. Sociologie historique d'un pluralisme politique*. Paris: Seuil.

Volk, Katharina. 2002. *The Poetics of Latin Didactic: Lucretius, Vergil, Ovid, Manilius*. Oxford: Oxford University Press.

von Haehling, Raban. 1989. *Zeitbezüge des T. Livius in der ersten Dekade seines Geschichtswerkes: nec vitia nostra nec remedia pati possumus*. Stuttgart: Steiner.

von Hesberg, Henner. 1996. 'Mausoleum Augusti: Das Monument'. *Lexicon Topographicum Urbis Romae*. Rome: Edizioni Quasar, 234–7.

REFERENCES   225

von Wissmann, Hermann. 1976. 'Die Geschichte des Sabäerreichs und der Feldzug des Aelius Gallus'. *ANRW* II.9.1, 308–544.

Wagenvoort, Hendrik. 1956. *Studies in Roman Literature, Culture, and Religion*. Leiden: Brill.

Wallace-Hadrill, Andrew. 1982. 'Civilis Princeps: Between Citizen and King'. *JRS* 72: 32–48.

Wallace-Hadrill, Andrew. 1990. 'Roman Arches and Greek Honours: The Language of Power at Rome'. *PCPhS* 36: 143–81.

Wallis, Jonathan. 2018. *Introspection and Engagement in Propertius: A Study of Book 3*. Cambridge: Cambridge University Press.

Wardle, David. 2007. 'A Perfect Send-Off: Suetonius and the Dying Art of Augustus (Suet. *Aug*. 99)'. *Mnemosyne* 60: 443–63.

Wardle, David. 2009. 'Caesar and Religion'. In Miriam T. Griffin, ed. 2009. *A Companion to Julius Caesar*. Malden, MA and Oxford: Blackwell, 100–11.

Wardle, David. 2014. *Suetonius: Life of Augustus/Vita divi Augusti*. Oxford: Oxford University Press.

Watson, Lindsay. 2002. 'Horace and the Pirates'. In Anton Powell and Kathryn Welch, eds. 2002. *Sextus Pompeius*. Swansea: Classical Press of Wales, 213–28.

Watson, Lindsay. 2003. *A Commentary on Horace's Epodes*. Oxford: Oxford University Press.

Watson, Lindsay. 2007. 'The *Epodes*: Horace's Archilochus?'. In Harrison 2007d: 93–104.

Weinstock, Stefan. 1960. 'Pax and the "Ara Pacis"'. *JRS* 50: 44–58.

Weinstock, Stefan. 1971. *Divus Julius*. Oxford: Clarendon Press.

Welch, Kathryn. 2012. *Magnus Pius: Sextus Pompeius and the Transformation of the Roman Republic*. Swansea: Classical Press of Wales.

Welch, Kathryn. 2020. 'Marcus Antonius: Words and Images'. In Pina Polo 2020: 301–23.

Welch, Tara S. 2005. *The Elegiac Cityscape: Propertius and the Meaning of Roman Monuments*. Columbus: Ohio State University Press.

West, David. 1993. 'On Serial Narration and on the Julian Star'. *PVS* 21: 1–16.

West, David. 1995. *Horace Odes I: Carpe Diem*. Oxford: Oxford University Press.

West, David. 2002. *Horace Odes III: Dulce Periculum*. Oxford: Oxford University Press.

West, Martin L. 1990. *Studies in Aeschylus*. Stuttgart: Teubner.

Whitcomb, Katheryn. 2018. 'Vergil, Octavian and Erigone: Admiration and Admonition in the Proem to *Georgics* 1'. *CJ* 113: 411–26.

White, Peter. 1988. 'Julius Caesar in Augustan Rome'. *Phoenix* 42: 334–56.

White, Peter. 1991. 'Maecenas' Retirement'. *CPh* 86: 130–8.

White, Peter. 1993. *Promised Verse: Poets in the Society of Augustan Rome*. Cambridge, MA: Harvard University Press.

Whittaker, Hélène. 2000. 'Temples to Proconsuls? Some Remarks on Suetonius *Divus Augustus* LII'. *SO* 75: 99–106.

Wilkinson, L. P. 1951. *Horace and His Lyric Poetry*. 2nd edn. Cambridge: Cambridge University Press.

Wilkinson, L. P. 1960. 'Propertius III, 4'. In *Studi in onore di Luigi Castiglioni*. 2 vols. Florence: Sansoni 1091–1103.

Williams, Gordon W. 1968. *Tradition and Originality in Roman Poetry*. Oxford: Clarendon Press.

Williams, Gordon W. 1969. *The Third Book of Horace's Odes*. Oxford: Clarendon Press.

Williams, Gordon W. 1978. *Change and Decline. Roman Literature in the Early Empire*. Berkeley: University of California Press.

Williams, Gordon W. 1990. 'Did Maecenas "Fall from Favor"? Augustan Literary Patronage'. In Raaflaub and Toher 1990: 258–75.

226 REFERENCES

Williams, Gordon W. 1995. '*Libertino patre natus*: True or False?'. In Harrison 1995: 296–313.

Williams, Mary Frances. 2003. 'The *Sidus Iulium*, the Divinity of Men, and the Golden Age in Virgil's *Aeneid*'. *Leeds International Classical Studies* 2.1: 1–29.

Williams, R. D. 1972. *The Aeneid of Vergil: Books 1–6*. London: Bristol Classical Press.

Williams, R. D. 1981. 'The Shield of Aeneas'. *Vergilius* 27: 8–11.

Wimmel, Walter. 1998. 'Vergils Tityrus und der Perusinische Konflikt. Zum Verständnis der 1. *Ecloge*'. *RhM* 141: 348–61.

Winterbottom, Michael. 2002. 'Believing the *Pro Marcello*'. In John F. Miller, Cynthia Damon, and K. Sara Myers, eds. 2002. *Vertis in Usum: Studies in Honor of Edward Courtney*. Munich: Saur, 24–38.

Wirszubski, Chaim. 1950. *Libertas as a Political Idea at Rome during the Late Republic and the Early Empire*. Cambridge: Cambridge University Press.

Wissemann, Michael. 1982. *Die Parther in der augusteischen Dichtung*. Frankfurt: Peter Lang.

Wissowa, Georg. 1912. *Religion und Kultus der Römer*. 2nd edn. Munich: Beck.

Witke, Charles. 1983. *Horace's Roman Odes. A Critical Examination*. Leiden: Brill.

Woodman, Tony. 1974. '*Exegi monumentum*: Horace, *Odes* 3.30'. In Woodman and West 1974: 115–28.

Woodman, Tony. 1988. *Rhetoric in Classical Historiography: Four Studies*. London: Croom Helm.

Woodman, Tony, and Dennis C. Feeney, eds. 2002. *Traditions and Contexts in the Poetry of Horace*. Cambridge: Cambridge University Press.

Woodman, Tony, and David West, eds. 1974. *Quality and Pleasure in Latin Poetry*. Cambridge: Cambridge University Press.

Woodman, Tony, and David West, eds. 1984. *Poetry and Politics in the Age of Augustus*. Cambridge: Cambridge University Press.

Wright, David J. 2018. 'Giants, Titans, and Civil Strife in the Greek & Roman World down through the Age of Augustus'. PhD Dissertation. Rutgers, NJ.

Wright, James R. 1983. 'Virgil's Pastoral Programme: Theocritus, Callimachus and *Eclogue* 1'. *PCPhS* 29: 107–60.

Wyke, Maria. 2002. *The Roman Mistress*. Oxford: Oxford University Press.

Xinyue, Bobby. 2019. 'Divinization and Didactic Efficacy in Virgil's *Georgics*'. In Xinyue and Freer 2019: 93–103.

Xinyue, Bobby. 2021. '(Un)seeing Augustus: *Libertas*, Divinisation, and the *iuvenis* of Virgil's First *Eclogue*'. *JRS* 111: 31–48.

Xinyue, Bobby, and Nicholas Freer, eds. 2019. *Reflections and New Perspectives on Virgil's Georgics*. London: Bloomsbury.

Yavets, Zvi. 1983. *Julius Caesar and His Public Image*. London: Thames and Hudson.

Yona, Sergio. 2018. *Epicurean Ethics in Horace: The Psychology of Satire*. Oxford: Oxford University Press.

Zachos, Konstantinos L. 2003. 'The *tropaeum* of Augustus in Nikopolis'. *JRA* 16: 64–92.

Zachos, Konstantinos L. 2007. 'The Sculptures of the Altar on the Monument of Octavian Augustus at Nicopolis: A First Approach'. *Nicopolis B*: 411–34.

Zanker, Andreas T. 2010. 'Late Horatian Lyric and the Virgilian Golden Age'. *AJPh* 131: 495–516.

Zanker, Paul. 1970. *Forum Augustus: Das Bildprogramm*. Tübingen: E. Wasmuth.

Zanker, Paul. 1988. *The Power of Images in the Age of Augustus*. Ann Arbor: University of Michigan Press.

Zetzel, James E. G. 1989. 'Romane Memento: Justice and Judgment in Aeneid 6'. TAPhA 119: 263–84.

Ziogas, Ioannis. 2015. 'The Poet as Prince: Author and Authority under Augustus'. In Han Baltussen and Peter J. Davis, eds. 2015. *The Art of Veiled Speech: Self-Censorship from Aristophanes to Hobbes*. Philadelphia: University of Pennsylvania Press, 115–36.

Index Locorum

For the benefit of digital users, indexed terms that span two pages (e.g., 52–53) may, on occasion, appear on only one of those pages.

Alcaeus
fr. 428 Lobel-Page = fr. 201B
Voigt 133n.88
Anacreon
fr. 381b Campbell 133n.88
Apollodorus
Bibliotheca
2.7.7 149n.149
Appian
Bellum Civile
3.43.176 37n.8
3.51 37n.8
5.12–13 40n.21
5.100 77
5.132 37n.7
Aratus
Phaenomena
2 93n.88
10–13 93–4
Archilochus
fr. 5 West 133n.88
Athenaeus
537e 124–5
Augustus
Res Gestae
1 2–3, 35–6
3.3 89n.70
5.1 1n.1
10.2 55–6
13 113n.1, 114–16
15.3 89n.70
16 89n.70
20.4 113
24.2 1n.1
25 37n.10
34 2–4, 137–8
34.1 113
35 155–6

Bacchylides
5.155–8 110n.138

Callimachus
Aetia
fr. 1.20 Harder = 1.20 Pf. = 1.20
Mass. 100–1
fr. 1.21–24 Harder = 1.21–24
Pf. = 1.21–24 Mass. 46–8
fr. 110.64 Harder = 110.64 Pf. = 213.64
Mass. 92–3
Hymns
1.73–4 126n.63
4.165–70 183n.104
Cassius Dio
43.14 7n.29
43.14.6 16n.62
43.21.2 16n.62
45.7.1 3n.12
46.29.2 37n.8
46.30.1 37n.8
47.18.4 165n.39
48.31.5–6 77
48.48.5 77
48.6–12 40n.21
51.1.2–3 24n.94
51.19.7 55–8
51.20 113n.1
51.20.1 55–6
51.20.6–8 116
51.20.6–8 1n.1
51.3–4 89n.70
53.1.4 183n.102
53.2.6–22.5 113n.2
53.22.3 1n.1
53.25–8 149n.149
53.26.5 114–15
53.27.3 115–16

230 INDEX LOCORUM

Cassius Dio (*cont.*)
 53.29 116
 54.3.4–8 115n.10
 54.8.2 117
 54.18 155
Catullus
 64.384–5 93n.88
 66.63–4 93n.84
 68.70 20n.78
Cicero
 Ad Brut.
  1.15.7 37n.8
 Leg. Man.
  41 13–14
  41–42 11
  48 11–14
 Marcell.
  8 13–15
  18 13–14
  27–28 14–16
 Nat. D.
  2.62 8–9, 140
  3.39 140
 Off.
  3.80 47n.42
 Phil.
  2.87 7n.29
  3.3, 5 35n.2
  4.2, 4 35n.2
  5.42–43 44–6
  13.24 37n.8
 Rep.
  2.4 8–9, 82
  2.17 8–9
  2.17–20 82
  6.13 8–9, 82
  6.26 82
  fr. inc. 5–6 8–9
 Tusc.
  1.28 45n.34, 140
Consolatio ad Liviam
 495–6 108–9
Corpus Inscriptionum Latinarum (CIL)
 6.32323 181n.95

Diodorus Siculus
 1.11.1 175–6
Diogenes Laertius
 10.16–22 47n.41

Dionysius of Halicarnassus
 Ant. Rom.
  2.56.3 9–10
Donatus
 Vit. Verg.
  19 40n.21

Ennius
 Annales
  1.54–5 Sk. 9–10
  109 Sk. 195–6
  fr. 258 Sk. 24
 Opera Incerta
  V Sk. 86–7
 Varia
  3 86–7

Florus
 2.33.53 114–15

Gallus
 fr. 2.4 63n.97

Hesiod
 Theogony
  24–26 46–8
Homer
 Iliad
  1.514–27 91–2
  17.322–41 178n.88
  20.307–8 163n.29
 Odyssey
  6.229–35 167n.43
  23.156–62 167n.43
Horace
 Ars Poetica
  239 196n.18
  281–4 48n.46
 Carmen Saeculare 159, 180–2, 197
 Epistles
  2.1.4 18–19
  2.1.5–6 8–9
  2.1.15–16 199–201
  2.1.145–55 48n.46
  2.1.255 196n.18
  2.1.258–9 137–8
 Epodes
  1 79, 88–9
  1.1–10 79–80

INDEX LOCORUM 231

4 74–5, 77–8, 88–9
4.1–6 75–6
4.6 77
4.17–20 74–6
4.19 2–4, 77
7 52n.56, 85n.57
9 85n.58, 88–90
9.1–4 83
9.7–8 77
9.7–9 38n.15
9.7–14 84n.56
9.11–14 38n.15
9.23–4 82–3
9.29–38 83
9.37–8 133–4, 150
9.43–45 81–2
16 85nn.57, 58
Odes (*Carmina*)
1.1.35–6 118–19, 153–4
1.2 52n.56, 121–7, 131–4, 146
1.2.33–6 126–8
1.2.41 190–1
1.2.41–52 5–6, 57–8
1.2.45 91n.77
1.2.45–6 196–7
1.2.49–60 125–7
1.6.9–12 136–7
1.10.11–16 123–4
1.12 52n.56, 127–8, 131–3, 143–4
1.12.49 196n.18
1.12.49–60 20n.84
1.12.51–2 92n.79
1.21 128
1.28.29 196n.18
1.29 128–30
1.31 183n.102
1.35 128, 130–2
1.37 131–3, 147–8
2.7 133–5
2.7.21 151
2.17.30 196n.18
2.19 135–6, 141–2, 151
3.1–6 62, 137–8
3.1.1–4 149–50
3.1.5–8 143–4
3.3 139–42
3.3.9–12 5–6
3.3.9–16 8–9, 161n.25
3.4 22–3, 142–5

3.4.42–80 135–6
3.5 145–8
3.5.1–4 5–6
3.5.2–4 44n.30
3.6.1–3 113
3.14 80–1, 148–53
3.14.1 193–4
3.14.1–4 80–1
3.14.2 114–15
3.14.13 193–4
3.14.13–16 80–1
3.22.1 196n.18
3.24 114–15
3.25 136–8, 141–2, 151
3.25.19–20 153–4
3.27.73 86–7
3.30 152–4
3.30.1–2 115n.11
3.30.13–4 118–19
4 190
4.1 190
4.2 190, 192–4
4.3 190
4.4 190
4.4.24–28 190–1
4.5 195–201
4.5.1–8 195–6
4.5.9–16 196–7
4.5.17–28 197–8
4.5.29–40 5–6, 198–9
4.5.31–6 195
4.5.33–35 199–201
4.6.41–4 190
4.8 192
4.8.14–15 8–9
4.8.22–34 7
4.9 192
4.9.25–28 7
4.11.31–6 190
4.12 190
4.14 190
4.14.34–40 190–1
4.15.4 18–19, 191–2
4.5.31–36 55–6
Satires
1.3 88–9
1.3.4–6 71–2
1.4 48n.46
1.5 74, 88–9

232 INDEX LOCORUM

Horace (*cont.*)
    1.5.27–33 72–3
    1.5.28 89
    1.5.39–44 73n.23
    1.6 137–8
    1.10.72–7 67–8
    1.10.81–88 67–8
    2.1 86–90
    2.1.10–11 94–5
    2.1.11 68, 104
    2.1.13–15 97n.101
    2.1.18–20 88n.66
    2.1.82–6 68–9
    2.1.84 104, 108–9
    2.5.62 190–1
    2.6.15 196n.18
    2.6.51–8 89

Lactantius
  Divine Institutes 1.18.11 8–9
Livy
  Preface 9 58
  1.3.4 171n.60
  1.16.1–6 9–10
  1.19.3 58
  34.55.4 150n.152
  Epitomes 115 161n.22
Lucan
  Bellum Civile
    1.63 92n.82
Lucretius
  De Rerum Natura
    5.7–21 93–4
    5.8 80–1
    5.11 41n.25
    5.19 41n.25

Ovid
  Fasti
    2.635–8 55–6, 199–201
    4.521 109–10
  Heroides
    14.4–7 184–5
  Metamorphoses
    2.195–200 97n.98
    14.805–28 9–10
    15.746–61 184–5
  Tristia
    1.5.65–66 40n.22

    2.61–76 22–3
    2.533 159

Petronius
  60 55–6, 199–201
Phlegon of Tralles
  FGrH 257: F37 180n.92
Pindar
  Olympians 2.2 125
Plautus
  Mercator 138 48n.45
Pliny the Elder
  Natural History
    2.93–4 3n.12
    33.132 47n.42
    34.48 140n.124
    37.10 140n.124
Plutarch
  Life of Antony
    24.4–5 38n.14
    37.2 117
    40.4 117
  Life of Brutus
    24.4–7 164n.34
  Life of Caesar
    58.6 117
  Life of Marius
    27.9 47n.42
Posidippus
  39 Austin-Bastianini 24–5
Propertius
  2.1.17–42 22–3
  2.7.1–6 104–6
  2.7.5–6 109
  2.14.9–10 20n.78
  2.15.39–40 20n.78
  2.30.12–16 4
  2.31 183n.102
  2.31–32 60–1
  2.34 61n.86
  3 61–2
  3.1.1–4 183n.104
  3.2.17–26 20n.78
  3.2.18–22 115n.11
  3.3.1–4 24
  3.4 60–6
  3.4.1 5–6, 109
  3.4.1–2 130
  3.4.1–8 62

3.4.19–21 65n.103
3.5.1 62–4, 109
3.9.47–50 22–3
3.11 20–1
3.11.31–32 20–1
3.11.46–48 23
3.11.49–50 20–1
3.11.49–66 21
3.11.59–64 20–1
3.11.69 24n.94
3.11.69–72 24
3.11.71 25n.99
3.18.11–12 172n.62
3.18.31–4 171–2
3.20 184–5
4 183–6
4.6 159, 180
4.7.1 184–5
4.11 106–10
4.11.57–60 108–9
4.11.60 5–6

Quintilian
Institutio Oratoria
2.15.25 2–3
2.15.33 2–3
2.17.14 2–3

Sallust
Bellum Iugurthinum
5.1 82–3
Seneca
De Ira
3.18.1 47n.42
Servius
ad *Aen.* 5.34 44n.30
ad *Aen.* 6.612 81n.46
ad *Aen.* 12.139 44n.30
ad *Ecl.* 5.20 51n.53
Servius Danielis
ad Ecl. 9.46 3n.12
Sibylline Oracles
3 180–1
18–19 180n.92
Strabo
7.7.6 24n.94
16.4.22–4 116
Suetonius
Augustus
12 37n.8

13 40
16.1–2 77
17.3 89n.70
18.2 24n.94
31.5 155–6
51 2–3
52 1–2
70 36–7
85.1 114–15
99.1 1–2
100.3 191–2
Claudius
35.1 2n.7
Julius
37 161n.22
88 3n.12

Tacitus
Annals
1.4 189–90
1.9 58
Theocritus
Idylls
7.36, 92 47n.39
9.1 47n.39
14.52–55 43n.28
17.3–4 47n.40
17.13–22 53, 140
17.20–22 53n.58
17.73–4 126n.63
17.104–5 196n.18
17.124–30 46–8
Tibullus
1.1.50 18–19
1.7 29–30, 116
2.5.5–10 22–3

Valerius Maximus
1.5.7 164n.34
8.15.7 47n.42
Varro
De Lingua Latina.
fr. 2 Goetz-Schoell 44n.30
fr. 424 Funaioli 44n.30
Velleius Paterculus
2.61.3 37n.8
2.91.2 115n.10
Virgil
Aeneid
1.1 62

234 INDEX LOCORUM

Virgil (*cont.*)
1.228–9 109–10
1.259–96 160–2
1.279 170
1.284–5 163–4
1.291 170
1.450–93 158–9
1.588–93 166–8, 173, 175–6
1.613 167–8
2.681–4 174n.74
2.685–703 162–3
3.94–100 164
3.97–8 163–4
3.274–88 164–5
3.712–13 164
4.144 93n.88
5.47 164–5
6.69–74 165–6, 173
6.756–892 168–73
6.760–6 164
6.763–6 178
6.779–80 174n.74
6.789 169n.50
6.791–97 181
6.791–805 169–72
6.798–99 182
6.826–31 169n.50
6.832–34 178–9
6.851–53 180–1
6.853 178–9
6.872–81 171–2
6.873 115n.11
6.893–99 172–3
7.73–80 174n.74
8.200–04 149–50
8.273–4 149–50
8.285–6 149–50
8.671 174–5
8.671–713 22–3
8.675 98–9
8.675–713 128, 135–6
8.678–728 173–6
8.678–81 183–4
8.681 164–5
8.688 146
8.704–6 164–5
8.717 177–8
8.717–20 193–4
8.720 98–9

8.720–2 183–4
8.730–1 158–9
9.621–44 176–8
9.641–4 163–4
9.656 178
10.270–5 174n.74
10.464–5 109–10
Eclogues
1 35, 40–50, 54–5, 57–8, 65–6, 199
1.6 80–1
1.1–10 40–1, 43, 48–9, 102
1.18 170
1.18–35 42–3
1.40–45 43–8
1.41–42 80–1, 196–7
1.42 190–1
1.44 182n.98
1.63 45n.35
1.77 48–9
1.79–83 49–50
4 40, 52–5, 57–8, 191–2
4.12 46n.37
4.13–20 52–4
4.38–39 53–4
5.56–90 50–1
6 59n.76
6.7–12 46n.37
6.64 46n.37
9 40, 50–1
9.26–27 46n.37
9.47 46n.37
9.51–2 199
10 46n.37
Georgics
1.1–42 91–4
1.24 96–7
1.24–42 68–9, 100–1
1.24–5 5–6, 99–100
1.25–32 92–4
1.32–5 97n.98
1.40 97
1.40–42 91–2
1.51–2 52n.56
1.121–2 92n.79
1.466–514 95
1.498–501 196–7
1.498–503 56–8
1.498–514 95–7
1.500 190–1

1.501 121
1.509–10 101
1.512–4 99n.107
3.9–10 7
3.10–47 97–100
3.12–16 5–6
3.13 166
3.41 18–19
4.212 197–8
4.559–62 100–1
4.561–2 68–9, 104

4.561–6 58–60
4.563–64 80n.44
4.563–66 101–2
4.564 64–5

Xenophon
Oeconomicus
21.12 101n.112

Zosimus
2.6.1 180n.92

General Index

For the benefit of digital users, indexed terms that span two pages (e.g., 52–53) may, on occasion, appear on only one of those pages.

Actium 164–5
  battle of 20–1, 23–4, 55–6, 79–85,
    131–2, 183–6
Aemilia 108
Aeneas
  apotheosis of 160
  first meeting with Dido 166–8
  prefiguring Augustus 164–8
  shield of 158–9, 173–6
Aeschylus, *Edonians* 134–5
Agrippa 115–16, 155
Alba Longa 164, 169, 171n.60, 183–4
Alexander the Great 124–6, 140
Alexandria, Ptolemaic 25–6
Anchises 162–4, 168–73, 178–82
anonymity 51, 54–5
Antony 36–7, 44–5
  as Osiris 124–5
  failed expedition to Parthia 117
Antony and Cleopatra. *see* Actium, battle
    of; Cleopatra; Gigantomachy
Apollo 23–4, 27–8, 36–7, 157
  and Ascanius 176–9
  as patron god of Augustus 3–4, 55–6
  his oracle at Delphi 163–4
  painting of, in Augustus' house 4
  Palatine Temple of 4, 60–1, 98–9.
    see also temples
  statue of, on the Palatine 4
  traditional opponent of Dionysus 55–6
apotheosis
  in Roman political discourse 8–9
  of an unspecified Caesar, in *Aeneid* 1
    160–2, 168
  of Romulus 8–10
  of Scipio 8–10
Ara Maxima 9n.35
Ara Pacis 197
Arabia, Aelius Gallus' expedition to 116

Arsinoe 24–6, 46–8
Ascanius 162–3, 171–2, 176–8
Augusteum 115–16
Augustus
  as *Divi filius* 36–7, 44–6
  as legal authority 68–9, 86–7, 104–7
  as *pater patriae* 108–9
  as *praesens deus* 44n.30, 45–6, 145–7,
    193–4
  as reincarnation of Aeneas 180–1
  as restorer of Rome 4, 21, 46–8
  as *triumphator* 9n.35, 62–4, 81–2, 96–8,
    113, 140, 149–50, 175–6, 193–4
  death 1–2
  divine honours 1–5, 55–6, 91–2, 116,
    193–5, 199–201
  mortality 97, 109–10, 189–201
  Res Gestae 35–6
authoritarianism 49–50

Bacchus. *see also* Dionysus
  and Augustus 170–1
  as deified hero 139–40, 170–1, 192
  Bacchic poetics 82–3, 85, 133–7, 151
  in Euripides 170–1
bees 197–8
Berenice 46–8, 92–3
Brundisium
  Horace's journey to (*Sat.* 1.5) 72–3
  Treaty of 52
Brutus 37–8

Cacus 149–50, 170–1
Caesar, Julius. *see* Julius Caesar
Caesar, unspecified 160–2, 169n.50
Callicrates 24–5
Callimachus 46–9, 102, 183
Cantabrian campaign 114–16,
    144n.138, 148–50

GENERAL INDEX   237

Carrhae, battle of 63n.92, 114.
    see also Crassus
Cassius 37–8
Cato 125n.59, 127–8
Celaeno 164–5
Ceres 93–4
Cicero
    on apotheosis of statesmen 8–9
    on Octavian 44–6
    on the supposed divinity
        of Julius Caesar 10–11, 13–17
        of Pompey 10–13
    Pro lege Manilia 10–14, 17
    Pro Marcello 10–11, 13–17
civilitas 2–3
Claudia Quinta 108
clementia 13–14, 138n.113, 178–9
Cleopatra 20–1, 131–2, 147–8
Cocceius 72–3
coinage 3–4, 36–7, 55–6, 100n.109, 103–4,
    114n.8, 155–6, 191n.2, 194n.15
    Julian Star (*sidus Iulium*) on 3–4, 155
Consolatio ad Liviam 108–9
conspiracies against Augustus 115–16
Cornelia 106–10
Crassus 114, 116, 145–6. *see also* Carrhae,
    battle of
Cumae 162–6
Cybele 108–9

deified heroes, canon or catalogue of 8–9,
    124–5, 139–40, 149–50, 170–1,
    192, 198–9
Delphi, oracle at 163–4
Demetrius Poliorcetes 16–17
Diana 167n.42
dictatorships of Sulla and Julius
    Caesar 10–11
Dido 166–8, 175–6
Dionysus. *see also* Bacchus
    Antony as the 'New Dionysus'
    37–8, 117
Dioscuri 139–40, 192, 198–9
Divi filius 36–7, 44–6, 77, 193–4
divine self-imaging in the Late
    Republic 36–7
Drusus Caesar 108–9, 190–1, 193–4

ekphrastic 98n.102, 158–9, 167–8
Ennius 9–10, 24, 140–1

Epicureanism 39n.20, 46–8, 60n.78, 80–1,
    138n.112
Epicurus 41n.25, 47n.41, 93–4
Euphrates 58–9, 95–6, 100–1
Evander 149–50

Fabius Maximus, Paulus 190
Fates 160, 168
figured speech 6n.22
Fortuna 130–2
Forum Augustum 28–9, 155–6

Gaius and Lucius, Augustus'
    grandsons 155, 186
Gallus, Aelius 116, 130n.77
Gallus, Cornelius 39n.20, 46, 62–4
Gates of Sleep 172–3
Gemma Augustea 4–5
gens Iulia 3–4, 26–7, 26n.103, 155–8, 160,
    162–4, 168, 171–5, 177–8, 191–2
Geryon 149–50
Gigantomachy 22–3, 82–3, 137–8,
    142–5, 173–4
Golden Age 52–4, 181–2, 191–3
Gratidianus, Marius 46–8

Harvard School of reading the
    Aeneid 8n.32, 19
Heldenschau. see Parade of Heroes
Hellenistic encomia 6–9, 46–8
Hellenistic ruler cult 16–17, 24–5, 46–8,
    92–3, 124–5, 175–6
Hercules 8–9, 139–40, 148–50, 170–1, 192
hermeneutics of suspicion 39n.19

Iccius 128–30, 132
imperialism 118, 128–30, 141–2
Iullus Antonius 190, 192–3

Janus, the doors of the Temple of 113–15
Julia, the elder 155
Julius Caesar 10–11, 13–17, 37–8, 46, 95,
    117, 184–6
Juno 140–2
Jupiter 3–4, 20–1, 27–8, 86–9, 91–2, 100–1,
    104–5, 109, 127–8, 142–7, 160

land confiscations 40, 44–5, 50n.49
Lepidus 44–5
Leucas 164–5

238 GENERAL INDEX

libertas 35–48, 54–5, 60, 62–4, 196–7
Livy 27, 58
Lucina 54
ludi quinquennales 183

Maecenas 18–19, 22–3, 38, 72–3, 79–81, 83, 153–4
Manilius, Gaius 11
Marcellus, Augustus' heir 127n.68, 155, 171–2
Marcellus, Julius Caesar's enemy defended by Cicero 13–15
Marius, Gaius 46–8, 82–3
marriage legislation, Augustus' 104–7
Mars 9–10, 155–6
Marxist and Neo-Marxist cultural critique 19
Mausoleum of Augustus 99n.105, 115–16, 152–3
Mercury 57–8, 121–5, 133–4
Messalla, M. Valerius 18–19, 29–30, 116
mise en abyme 147n.144, 158–9, 175–6
Muses 46–9, 91–2, 142–3, 149–50

Naulochus, battle of 36–7, 38n.15, 44–5, 77, 84n.56, 93n.88, 191n.2
Neptune 3–4, 36–7, 77
Nicopolis 24, 103–4, 164–5
Numanus Remulus 176–8

Octavius Musa 67–8
Orientalism 20n.81, 197–8
Osiris 29–30, 124–5, 175–6
otium 36, 39, 41, 44, 46–8, 59–65, 80–1, 84n.56, 102, 151, 199

Palatine complex 4
  Temple of Apollo 60–1. *see also* temples
Pantheon, Augustus' monument 115–16
Parade of Heroes, in *Aeneid* 6 157, 168–73, 180–1
Parthenope (Naples) 59–60, 102
Parthia 57–8, 63n.92, 97–8, 114, 116–18, 121–3, 125–6, 128, 140–1, 146–7, 161–2, 181–2, 186, 197
Parthia, Crassus' expedition to 116–17
patronage 29–30
pax Augusta 114, 197
Pharsalus, battle of 14–15
Philippi, battle of 37–8, 40, 133–5, 151

Pindar 9n.35, 125–6, 131n.80, 133, 142n.131
Plancus, consulship of 151
poetry vs physical monuments 152–4, 192
Pollio, Gaius Asinius 39n.20, 46, 52, 67–8
Pompey
  Pompey the Great, Cn. Pompeius Magnus 10–13
  Sextus Pompey (son of Magnus) 36–7, 74–7, 84n.56
  the 'Pompeius' of *Ode* 2.7 133–5
Posidippus 24–5
Proculus, Julius 9–10
prophecy 140–1, 169–73, 176–9, 182, 191–2
  in the *Aeneid* generally 157–9, 162
  Jupiter's in *Aeneid* 1 160–2, 168
Ptolemy I Soter 24, 46–8, 140
Ptolemy II Philadelphus 24, 46–8, 183n.104
Ptolemy V 124–5
pudor 136–7

Regulus 146–7
remedium, in Livy and Tacitus 58
Remus 22–3
res publica restituta 151–2
Romulus 22–3, 140–2, 192, 195–6
  apotheosis of 8–10
Rosetta Stone 124–5

Sacred Way 64–5
saeculum Augustum 191–2
Sallust 27, 82–3
salus of the state 12, 14, 197–8
Scipio 82, 86–7
  apotheosis of 8–10
shield of Aeneas 158–9, 173–6
Sibylline books and prophecies 161, 166, 180–1
sidus Iulium (Julian Star) 4n.13, 28–9, 127, 155, 174–5
Silvius 164, 171–2, 178
slavery 42–3
Social War 150
Spartacus 150
statues
  in the Forum Augustum 155–6
  of Augustus

GENERAL INDEX   239

melted down to make tripods for
   Apollo 1–2
Prima Porta 117–18
quadrigate, in the Forum
   Augustum 155–6
of Julius Caesar
   in the Temple of Mars Ultor 155–6
   on the Capitoline 16–17
succession. see *gens Iulia*
Sulla 10–11
supplicatio 16–17, 150n.152
symposium 83–5, 186

Tacitus 27, 58, 189–90
temples
   Augustus' restoration of 113n.3, 137–8
   of Apollo
      at Cumae, promised by Aeneas 165–6
      at Leucas 164–5
      on the Palatine 60–1, 98–9,
         175–6, 183–4
   of Augustus and Roma 1–2
   of Augustus, promised by Virgil in
      Georgics 3 166

of Janus 113–15
of Mars Ultor 117, 122–3, 155–6
Thapsus, Battle of 16–17
Theocritus 42–3, 46–8, 53, 56
Tiberius Caesar 190–1, 193–4
Tibullus 5–6, 18–19, 29–30
Tigellius 71–2
timelessness 192–4, 199
Titanomachy 22–3
Tityrus 30–1, 35, 38–50, 54, 59–60, 80–1,
   102, 196–7
topos 6–7, 10
totalitarianism 69–70
translatio imperii et
   studiorum 25
Trebatius Testa 68, 86–8
tribunicia potestas 115–16
triumphus 28–9, 61–4, 193–4
   Augustus' triple triumph 9n.35, 113,
      149n.150, 175–6

Varus 39n.20, 46
Vesta 108–9
Virgin (Astraea, Justice) 54